TECH STOCK VALUATION

Investor Psychology and
Economic Analysis

TECH STOCK VALUATION

Investor Psychology and
Economic Analysis

Mark Hirschey, Ph.D.

School of Business
University of Kansas
Lawrence, Kansas

ACADEMIC PRESS

An imprint of Elsevier Science

Amsterdam   Boston   Heidelberg   London   New York   Oxford
Paris   San Diego   San Francisco   Singapore   Sydney   Tokyo

Academic Press
An imprint of Elsevier Science
525 B Street, Suite 1900, San Diego, California 92101-4495, USA
http://www.academicpress.com

Academic Press
84 Theobald's Road, London WC1X 8RR, UK
http://www.academicpress.com

Library of Congress Catalog Card Number: 2003105616

International Standard Book Number: 0-12-349704-3

PRINTED IN THE UNITED STATES OF AMERICA
03 04 05 06 07   7 6 5 4 3 2 1

To: Catherine and George
—for all the little things that make a big difference

CONTENTS

ACKNOWLEDGMENTS XIII
PREFACE XV

I The Tech Bubble

I. The Nifty 50   2
II. NASDAQ 100 as the New Nifty 50   5
III. As Technology Goes, So Goes the NASDAQ 100   15
IV. How High is Up?   21
V. Conclusion   25
VI. References   26

2 What Caused the Tech Bubble?

I. Efficient Market Hypothesis   30
II. The Time Series of Stock Prices   31

III. Daily Returns   32
IV. Random Walk Concept   35
V. Random Walk Research   37
VI. Stock Market Bubbles   38
VII. Stockholders and the Agency Problem   39
VIII. Risk Management Problems   40
IX. Investment Horizon Problems   41
X. Accounting Information Problems   43
XI. Stock Fraud   44
XII. Fraud on the Internet   46
XIII. Conclusion   48
XIV. References   49

3 Investment Advice on the Internet

I. Buy–Sell Recommendation Research   52
II. Investment Information on the Internet   54
III. The Motley Fool (TMF)   57
IV. TMF's Rule Breaker Portfolio   58
V. Other TMF Portfolios   61
VI. Methodology   65
VII. All Portfolio Returns   68
VIII. Individual Portfolio Returns   72
IX. Conclusion   78
X. References   79

4 A Dissertation on Tulips and America Online

I. How Much is a Tulip Worth?   82
II. The Tulip Mania   83
III. Estimating 17th Century Tulip Prices   84
IV. Psychology of Manias   87
V. The Late-1990s Internet Stock Mania   88
VI. AOL as a Growth Stock   90
VII. AOL Risk Assessment   94
VIII. AOL Growth Expectations   94
IX. AOL Valuation as a Growth Stock   95
X. AOL as a Value Stock   96
XI. AOL Customer Value   97
XII. Private–Market Value   98
XIII. Value of AOL–Time Warner   98
XIV. Conclusion   100
XV. References   101

5 The Crash of 2000–2002 and Imminent Rebound

I. Mean Reversion in Business Profits   104
II. Business Cycles vs. Market Cycles   105
III. Return Reversal in the S&P 500 and the NASDAQ   106
IV. Nonoverlapping Period Analysis   112
V. Return Reversal or Simply Regression to the Mean?   114
VI. Overreaction Hypothesis   116
VII. What About the Japanese Experience?   118
VIII. Conclusion   123
IX. References   124

6 Stock–Price Effects of Research and Development Expenditures

I. R&D as a Source of Intangible Capital   126
II. Corporate Governance, R&D, and R&D Effectiveness   128
III. R&D Spending by Industry Group   131
IV. Corporate leaders in R&D Spending   134
V. Measuring R&D Capital Using Tobin's q Ratio   139
VI. The Sample   141
VII. Effects of R&D on Tobin's q 147
VIII. Firm Size Effects   149
IX. Institutional Ownership and R&D Effectiveness   151
X. Conclusion   153
XI. References   155

7 Valuation Effects of Patent Quality

I. Usefulnesness of Nonfinancial Information   158
II. Questions about Long-Term Benefits of R&D   159
III. Patent Statistics   161
IV. Patent Citations   162
V. Scientific Merit of Patents   163
VI. Data   165
VII. Methodology   169
VIII. Stock–Price Effects of Patent Quality: U.S. Companies   170
IX. U.S. Companies: Effects of Size and Growth Opportunities   172
X. Patent Quality in Japan Versus the United States   176
XI. Valuation Effects of Patent Quality for Japanese Companies   178
XII. Conclusion   179
XIII. References   180

8 Goodwill Write-Off Decisions: Do They Matter?

I. Goodwill   184
II. New Goodwill Accounting Standards   185
III. Goodwill Write-Off Decisions   187
IV. Sample   189
V. Estimation Method   192
VI. Announcement Period Effects   194
VII. Announcement Effects and
Contemporaneous Announcements   196
VIII. Announcement Effects by Industry Group   197
IX. Preannouncement and Postannouncement Period Effects   198
X. Conclusion   201
XI. References   203

9 Shark Repellents and Research and Development: Does Management Have a Long-Run Perspective?

I. Shark Repellents   206
II. Data   208
III. Long-Term Performance and Financial Policies   209
IV. Measures of Long-Term Performance and
Financial Policies   210
V. Nonparametric Tests of Relative Performance   212
VI. Nonparametric Results for Industry-Adjusted
Performance   214
VII. Measures of Firm Financial Policy   218
VIII. Nonparametric Results for Industry-Adjusted
Financial Policy   220
IX. Regression Model Specification   223
X. Regression Results for Changes in Firm Performance   224
XI. Regression Results for Changes in Financial
Policy Decisions   224
XII. Conclusion   225
XIII. References   227

10 Corporate Governance and the Legal Environment

I. Role Played by Boards of Directors   230
II. Corporate Governance Mechanisms Inside the Firm   233
III. Franchise Agreements   235
IV. Strategic Alliances   236

V. Ownership Structure as a Corporate
Governance Mechanism   237

VI. Is Ownership Structure Endogenous?   241

VII. Federal Law Enforcement Actions as Tools for
Corporate Governance   242

VIII. Administration of Federal Laws and Regulations   244

IX. Valuation Effects of Enforcement Actions   245

X. Previous Studies   246

XI. Data   247

XII. Estimation Method   249

XIII. Announcement Effects by Type of Enforcement Activity   251

XIV. Announcement Effects by Violation Category   254

XV. Announcement Effects by Industrial Classification   257

XVI. Conclusion   261

XVII. References   263

INDEX   265

ACKNOWLEDGMENTS

A number of people have aided in the preparation of *Tech Stock Valuation*. I am especially grateful to the University of Kansas for the sabbatical leave support that helped make this research possible.

I am also indebted to the Elsevier staff and would like to thank Scott Bentley, Kirsten Funk, and Paul Gottehrer for their special efforts.

In particular, I owe an enormous debt to Christine Hauschel and Nick Hirschey who carefully read the entire manuscript and offered numerous helpful suggestions. A tremendous debt is also owed to my colleagues Vern Richardson and Sue Scholz. Vern and Sue worked with me on much of the material that forms the basis for my understanding of patent quality and the role it plays in firm valuation. We also worked together on the valuation effects of Internet stock advice. My debt to them is obvious, especially in Chapters 3 and 7. My colleague Pat Oslund provided expert research assistance and statistical advice concerning the analysis provided in Chapter 6. Vern and I collaborated on the underlying analysis of the stock market effects of recent changes in goodwill accounting, the subject of Chapter 8. And finally, I worked closely with Elaine Jones in putting together the primary work on corporate governance and R&D investments that underlies Chapters 9 and 10. It would be tough to overestimate the value I have gained working with these fine colleagues.

PREFACE

During the mid- to late-1990s, the investment attention and economic resources of growth stock investors became riveted on giant tech stock favorites. Not since the early-1970s, and the days of the Nifty 50, had U.S. investor interest been so narrowly focused on a relative handful of growth stocks. In fact, there had never been a group of U.S. stocks accorded the P/E multiple and extreme market capitalizations accorded to such companies. In a U.S. investment environment where conventional P/E ratios for the most successful corporations fall in a broad range from 10–20, P/E ratios for the tech stock favorites that commonly exceeded 100 can only be described as extraordinary. In light of recent investment experience culminating in the crash of 2000–2002, the extreme valuations accorded to giant tech stock favorites at the March, 2000 market peak reflected optimistic tech investor overreaction giving rise to a stock-market bubble.

Today, a similar mistake stemming from pessimistic tech stock investor overreaction may be in the works. Tech stock investors, rattled by devastating terrorist attacks and armed conflict in the Mideast during the first severe bear market in a decade, continue to dump tech stocks and hunker down for ongoing dismal performance. However, by giving extreme weight to recently negative returns, such investors run the risk of failing to benefit from the typically positive risk premium enjoyed by equity holders. Evidence suggests that the "irrational exuberance" displayed by tech stocks in early-2000 is now fully discounted in the market. A careful reading of stock market history suggests that present investors can expect annual rates of return of roughly 8–10% per year from present levels. Going forward, the overreaction hypothesis predicts a reversal of recent sharp losses in the overall market, and in the tech sector. Long-term returns for tech stock investors are apt to once again reflect the inherently attractive economic fundamentals of companies in the technology sector.

To appreciate the attractive economic underpinnings of companies in the technology sector, it is necessary to consider important intangible sources of stock market valuation. For example, stock-price effects of corporate research and development (R&D) expenditures have been used to provide helpful, albeit indirect, evidence on the economic consequences of the firm's inventive and innovative activity. Recent research in financial economics documents that corporate R&D spending announcements have predictably positive effects on the market value of the firm. At the same time, studies in financial economics document that other types of corporate expenditures, like advertising, have similar intangible capital-like influences. Goodwill accounting numbers on corporate balance sheets also appear to capture elements of the intangible nature of corporate assets. Like information on current cash flows, data on R&D, advertising, and accounting goodwill appears to help investors form appropriate expectations concerning the size and variability of future cash flows. Such findings imply that corporate spending on R&D can be viewed as a type of investment in intangible assets with predictably positive effects on the value of the firm. Such findings also suggest the potential for synergy between the market value effects of R&D and advertising.

Consistent with the fact that only a handful of firms is responsible for the bulk of private-sector financed R&D spending, positive stock-price effects of R&D are most evident in the case of large firms. Nevertheless, smaller firms are not precluded from making profitable investments in R&D. The well-targeted R&D efforts of the smallest high tech firms can be highly profitable. Studies show that R&D expenditures have consistently large and positive influences on market values for firms from all size classes, but the strength of the R&D influence on market value is inversely related to firm size. While prior research strongly suggests that data on R&D spending helps investors form appropriate expectations concerning the magnitude and variability of future cash flows, these results give only indirect evidence on the stock-price effects of inventive output. This stems from the fact that R&D expenditures are a useful indicator of R&D *input*, whereas patents are a effective indicator of R&D *output*.

This book extends the R&D literature by providing detailed direct evidence on the market value implications of inventive and innovative output. Specifically, the book documents that the stock-price effects of patent output are most pronounced in the case of high-quality patents, where patent quality is measured by scientific merit. Scientific measures of patent quality give tech stock investors and R&D managers a valuable new tool that can be used to measure R&D program effectiveness. This research is also of direct interest to professional investors and academics in financial economics because it adds precision to prior work on patent activity, the value of the firm, and the value of R&D output. Scientific measures of patent quality give investors a new tool to help them assess the value of hard-to-measure intangible assets. Further implications of this research are obvious for the theory and practice of financial accounting. This research suggests that the value of accounting information in the high-tech sector could be enhanced with added disclosure about third-party assessments of R&D effectiveness. Of course, the public policy literature is not just concerned with the quality and reliability of accounting information. It is also concerned with a host of issues related to R&D effectiveness, business activity and economic betterment.

Mark Hirschey
Lawrence Kansas
March 2003

I

THE TECH BUBBLE

In the early-1970s, a group of institutional investor favorites known as the Nifty 50 were widely touted as "one-decision" buy-and-hold stocks.[1] No matter how high the current price, investors came to believe that the easy-to-predict rapid earnings growth of these stock market favorites would be sufficient to provide them with market-beating results. At the time, investor excitement for Nifty 50 stocks pushed valuations to unheard of peaks. At the time, Nifty 50 stocks sold at an average price–earnings (P/E) of 37.3 versus a market multiple of 18.2. The severe market downturn of 1972–74 brought devastation to Nifty 50 stock valuations, teaching a generation of investors that price does indeed matter and that investors can sometimes overpay for even the best of companies.

Unfortunately, the lessons of the Nifty 50 appear to have been lost on a subsequent generation of investors. In the late-1990s, the Nifty 50 phenomenon was reborn. The Nasdaq 100 Index was the late 1990s reincarnation of the Nifty 50 phenomenon. Unlike the Nifty 50 of the early 1970s, however, many of these recent institutional favorites were relative newcomers with short operating histories, modest revenues, and sparse profits. Another difference is the extraordinary valuation of the Nasdaq 100 favorites. In February 2000, the Nasdaq 100 P/E reached

---

[1]For early analyses of the recent bubble in tech stocks, see Hirschey (1998, 2001).

1

134.7, or roughly 4–6 times higher than P/E ratios typical of the Dow Jones Industrial Average (DJIA) and Standard & Poor's 500 (S&P 500) companies. At the same time, the P/E ratio for the Nasdaq Composite reached an average P/E of 245.7, or roughly 6–8 times higher than market-wide averages. In retrospect, it is now clear that Nifty 50 valuations in the early-1970s and Nasdaq 100 valuations during the late-1990s were indicative of extraordinary stock market bubbles.

I. THE NIFTY 50

The Nifty 50 was a group of 50 premier growth stocks identified by Morgan Guaranty Trust as stockmarket darlings during the early-1970s. At the stock market peak in 1972, the group of Nifty 50 stocks sold at an average P/E multiple of 37.3, more than double the market average P/E of 18.2. Each of these stocks had proven growth in revenues, earnings, and dividends. Virtually none had experienced a dividend cut during the post-World War II period. All had sufficiently large market capitalizations to allow large institutional investors to buy as much of them as their portfolios could hold. They represented the ultimate in one-decision stock investing. An investor simply had to buy and hold. No matter how high Nifty 50 stock prices seemed relative to current revenue, earnings, or any other fundamental factors, any perception of being overvalued was sure to be temporary. Investors believed that superior rates of growth would bail out any buyer, no matter how high the price seemed at the time of purchase. In January 1972, top investor favorites among the Nifty 50 included Polaroid Corp. (P/E = 93.5), McDonald's Corp. (P/E = 59.8), Baxter International, Inc. (P/E = 59.5), International Flavors & Fragrances (P/E = 57.9), and Johnson & Johnson (P/E = 55.5).

Nifty 50 investors could not lose, or so the story went, until the vicious bear market of 1972–74. From a bull market peak of 1036.27 on December 11, 1972, the Dow Jones Industrial Average crashed to 577.60 on December 6, 1974. This bone-chilling drop of 44.3% for the overall market was relatively mild when compared with the devastation suffered by many Nifty 50 darlings. Coca-Cola dove 66.9% from 149-3/4 to 49-5/8, Disney cascaded down 91.3% from 236-3/4 to 20-1/2, Eastman Kodak tumbled 58.9% from 149-1/4 to 61-1/4, McDonald's plunged 63.2% from 77-3/8 to 28-1/2, and Phillip Morris plummeted 59.4% from 118-1/4 to 45.

The plunge in prices for Nifty 50 stocks during the severe bear market correction of 1972–74 has long been viewed as just punishment for absurdly valued stocks and the naive investors willing to buy them. Until recently, no one rose to defend such excesses. No one, that is, until Jeremy Siegel, professor of finance at the University of Pennsylvania's Wharton School, became part of the Nifty 50 story in 1994 when he published an eminently readable book titled *Stocks for the Long Run*. In his book and in a subsequent article, Siegel (1994, 1995) laid down the bullish argument for Nifty 50 investing. Siegel calculated that an investor paying top dollar for the Nifty 50 in late-1972 would have earned nearly the same returns over the next 20 years as someone holding the S&P 500 (see Table 1.1).

TABLE 1.1   Nifty 50 Returns from 1/1/72 to 5/31/93

Company	Symbol	Annualized return (%)	1972 P/E ratio	Warranted P/E ratio Before tax	After tax
American Express Co.	AXP	8.77	28.4	16.1	18.9
American Home Products Corp.	AHP	11.69	32.9	32.9	33.7
American Hospital Supply Corp.	AHS	10.34	47.9	37.0	46.7
AMP Inc.	AMP	11.77	36.4	37.1	48.0
Anheuser-Busch, Inc.	BUD	11.02	36.7	32.3	38.5
Avon Products, Inc.	AVP	2.85	55.4	9.5	12.5
Baxter International, Inc.	BAX	7.89	59.5	28.4	39.9
Black & Decker Mfg.	BDK	1.69	40.9	5.5	8.9
Bristol-Myers Co.	BMY	13.95	24.4	37.5	40.7
Burroughs Inc.	BGH	−0.82	41.0	3.2	6.5
Chesebrough-Ponds, Inc.	CBM	12.13	31.0	37.1	39.2
Digital Equipment Corp.	DEC	5.87	53.2	16.9	27.7
Dow Chemical Co.	DOW	11.52	22.3	21.6	22.2
Eastman Kodak Co.	EK	4.89	37.7	9.8	12.5
Eli Lily & Co.	LLY	4.38	37.7	23.4	27.4
Emery Air Freight Corp.	EAF	−4.41	49.6	1.8	5.3
First National City (Citicorp)	CCI	8.94	17.5	10.3	10.8
General Electric Co.	GE	12.77	22.6	27.8	28.7
Gillette Co.	GS	16.23	19.7	46.3	43.0
Haliburton Co.	HAL	8.77	27.7	15.7	19.3
Heublein Inc.	HBL	14.81	26.7	48.3	47.5
IBM	IBM	2.86	35.5	6.1	8.7
International Flavors & Fragrances	IFF	10.40	57.9	45.3	53.4
ITT	ITT	7.01	14.8	5.9	6.0
J.C. Penney Co., Inc.	JCP	8.93	28.7	16.8	18.3
Johnson & Johnson	JNJ	10.18	55.5	41.5	52.9
Jos. Schlitz Brewing Co.	SLZ	6.08	32.2	10.7	13.9
Kresge (Kmart Corp.)	KM	6.66	42.5	15.9	20.2
Louisana Land & Expl. Co.	LLX	9.21	27.0	6.3	8.2
Lubrizol Corp.	LZ	7.66	34.9	15.9	19.0
McDonald's Corp.	MCD	13.96	59.8	92.2	126.3
Merck	MRK	14.47	25.9	43.9	50.8
MGIC Investment Corp.	MGI	−8.72	53.0	0.7	4.1
Minnesota Mining & Mfg. (3M)	MMM	9.65	35.7	24.1	27.0
PepsiCo Inc.	PEP	16.20	27.0	63.1	68.9
Pfizer Inc.	PFE	12.60	27.9	33.2	37.1
Philip Morris Cos.	MO	19.48	21.0	89.1	94.2
Polaroid Corp.	PRD	1.24	93.5	11.4	19.5
Procter & Gamble	PG	11.32	24.0	22.4	24.5
Revlon Inc.	REV	11.62	25.5	25.2	28.4
Schering-Plough Corp.	SGP	11.94	39.3	41.3	46.5
Schlumberger Ltd.	SLB	13.40	35.7	49.5	62.5
Sears Roebuck & Co.	S	4.97	28.6	7.6	9.1
Simplicity Pattern	SYP	0.20	45.0	4.4	7.9

(continues)

TABLE I.I (*continued*)

Company	Symbol	Annualized return (%)	1972 P/E ratio	Warranted P/E ratio Before tax	After tax
Squibb Corp.	SQB	12.54	30.2	41.4	46.4
Texas Instruments Inc.	TXN	7.43	36.8	16.0	22.1
The Coca-Cola Co.	KO	14.25	42.3	68.8	70.1
Upjohn Co.	UPJ	10.87	32.8	28.1	32.2
Walt Disney Co.	DIS	13.10	55.3	72.5	99.0
Xerox Corp.	XRX	2.06	46.9	6.8	10.3
Nifty 50 with annual rebalancing		**12.02**	**37.3**	**28.1**	**33.3**
S&P 500		**11.68**	**18.2**		
Nifty 50 buy and hold		**8.73**			

Source: Siegel J. J. (1994). *Stocks for the Long Run*. New York: Irwin Professional Publishing, pp. 98–99.

Over the 1972–93 period, Siegel calculated that the original Nifty 50 produced a 12.02% annualized return before taxes, an amount roughly in line with the 11.68% compound rate of return earned by the overall market (S&P 500) during the same period. In this calculation, Siegel assumes that investors would rebalance their holdings on an annual basis so that each Nifty 50 stock would represent 2% of the investor's portfolio at the start of each year. Using this assumption, Siegel calculates that after-tax returns on the Nifty 50 would have exceeded those for the overall market. On a risk-adjusted basis, Siegel's findings suggest that the Nifty 50 were only slightly overvalued relative to the market at their 1972 price peak. As a group, premiere growth stocks are expensive, but some, according to Siegel, can be worth the price. Interestingly, 10 of the original Nifty 50 remain among the top 50 companies according to total market capitalization as of August 31, 2000. Three of them, General Electric, Pfizer, and Citigroup, are today among the top 10 corporations in terms of total market capitalization.

Nifty 50 long-term winners include Pfizer and Merck. Both have efficiently managed the difficult process of keeping a valuable drug pipeline filled with important new therapies. Consumer multinationals, such as Coca-Cola and Gillette, have also done well. Both have survived and prospered on the basis of extremely effective advertising that builds durable brand name reputations. While some original members of the Nifty 50 are no longer considered great growth stocks, many continue as successful pillars of corporate America. Nevertheless, focusing on subsequent market returns for the overall group tends to obscure suggestions of overvaluation for important subcomponents of the Nifty 50. Dismal long-run returns were commonly earned by the highest P/E stocks found within the Nifty 50. Over the 20-year and 5-month period from January 1, 1972 to May 31, 1993, Siegel found that investors earned compound annual returns in Polaroid Corp. of only 1.24%, in McDonald's Corp. of 13.96%, in Baxter

International, Inc. of 7.89%, in International Flavors & Fragrances of 10.40%, and in Johnson & Johnson 10.18%. Among these top picks, only McDonald's subsequent performance justified its superior 1972 P/E ratio. Within the Nifty 50, long-term performance by drug and consumer products giants tended to vastly exceed market returns for technology companies, which lagged badly. Over the 1972–93 period, highly touted technology giants like Burroughs, Polaroid, Xerox, IBM, Eastman Kodak, Digital Equipment, and Texas Instruments notably underperformed Nifty 50 contemporaries and the overall market. According to Siegel, given 20/20 hindsight, only 16 (32%) of the original Nifty 50 were worth their 1972 peak P/E ratios. The devastation experienced by stockholders of various Nifty 50 survivors does not represent the worst part of the story. Some other former Nifty 50 companies and their shareholders did not fare nearly as well. Former Nifty 50 companies such as Burroughs, Digital Equipment, Joseph Schlitz Brewing, and MGIC Investment are gone forever. Their status as "bullet proof" growth stocks failed to protect them from disturbing volatility in a full-fledged bear market.

It is also worth noting that Siegel's long-term 12.02% annual rate of return calculation for Nifty 50 investors will be confusing to readers who note that the average annual rate of return for Nifty 50 stocks studied by Siegel was, in fact, only 8.73% per year over this period. It must be emphasized that Siegel calculated the equally weighted Nifty 50 portfolio returns as 12.02% when this "portfolio" was rebalanced every year so that each stock maintained a 2% allocation at the start of each year. Given that Nifty 50 stocks were ballyhooed as one-decision stocks, it may be much more reasonable to assume that Nifty 50 investors would adopt a simple buy-and-hold strategy. Using the assumption of a simple buy-and-hold strategy, the equally weighted average annual return for Nifty 50 stocks was only 8.73% and below the market average of 11.68% over the 1972–93 period. Therefore, the modest outperformance alleged by Siegel is wholly a result of his assumption of annual rebalancing so that each stock maintained a 2% allocation at the start of each year. Assuming a much more reasonable buy-and-hold strategy, the Nifty 50 returned a worse-than-market average return.

Siegel's Nifty 50 research was commonly cited during the late-1990s as justification for the extraordinary valuations accorded to large-capitalization technology stock favorites in the period leading up to the March 2000 market peak. Like investors in the Nifty 50 era, recent tech stock investors came to believe that "premiere growth stocks" were worth any price. Like investors in the Nifty 50 era, recent tech stock investors have learned that the risk of loss is great when buying stocks with extraordinary valuation metrics.

II. NASDAQ 100 AS THE NEW NIFTY 50

For both institutional and individual investors, the late-1990s bullet proof growth stocks were found among the largest market capitalization stocks on the Nasdaq Stock Market, particularly among the companies included within the Nasdaq 100

Index. Launched on January 31, 1985, with a (split-adjusted) base value of 125, the Nasdaq 100 Index represents the largest and most active nonfinancial domestic and international issues listed on the Nasdaq Stock Market based on market capitalization. On December 21, 1998, the Nasdaq100 was rebalanced to a modified market capitalization weighted index. Such rebalancing is expected to retain the economic attributes of capitalization weighting while providing enhanced diversification. To accomplish this, Nasdaq reviews the composition of the Nasdaq 100 on a quarterly basis and adjusts the weight of index components using a proprietary algorithm if certain preestablished weight distribution requirements are not met.

The Nasdaq 100 reflects Nasdaq's largest companies across major industry groups, including computer hardware and software, telecommunications, retail/wholesale trade, and biotechnology. Broadly speaking, the Nasdaq 100 includes 100 of the largest nonfinancial domestic and international companies listed on the National Market tier of the Nasdaq Stock Market. Eligibility criteria for the Nasdaq 100 include a minimum average trading volume of 100,000 shares per day. In general, companies also must have been seasoned on the Nasdaq or another major exchange, which means they have been listed for a minimum of two years. If a security would otherwise qualify to be in the top 25% of the issuers included in the index by market capitalization, then a one-year seasoning criteria would apply. If the issue represents ownership in a foreign security, the company must have a worldwide market value of at least $10 billion, a U.S. market value of at least $4 billion, and an average trading volume of at least 200,000 shares per day. In addition, foreign securities must be eligible for listed-options trading. The large number of securities in the Nasdaq 100 Index makes it an effective vehicle for arbitragers and securities traders. Other innovations have made the Nasdaq 100 Index an attractive investment vehicle for small investors.

In October 1993, financial derivatives tied to the Nasdaq 100 Index began trading on the Chicago Board Options Exchange. On March 10, 1999, the Nasdaq 100 Trust Series, a pooled investment designed to provide investment results that generally correspond to the price and yield performance of the Nasdaq 100, was introduced. At the market peak during early 2000, roughly $12 billion was invested in the Nasdaq 100 Trust Series, affectionately referred to by investors as the QQQs. Despite the devastating recent decline on the Nasdaq, the popularity of the QQQs has continued to rise. In late-2002, for example, more than $17.5 billion was invested in QQQs.[2] The popularity of the Nasdaq 100 Trust Series stems from the fact that it gives individual and institutional investors a low-cost investment vehicle to facilitate their direct participation in the investment performance of the Nasdaq 100.[3]

---

[2]For up-to-date information on the Nasdaq 100 Trust Series, see http://www.nasdaq.com/indexshares/nasdaq100_intro.stm.

[3]The annual expense ratio for the QQQs is a mere 0.2% per year. It is important to note that on January 1, 1994, the Nasdaq 100 base was reset by division of a factor of 2.

As shown in Fig. 1.1, the compound return on the Nasdaq 100 broadly outperformed the overall market as captured by the DJIA during the 1990s. This represented a big turnaround from the Nasdaq 100's under-performance during the late-1980s. During the first five years of the Nasdaq 100 Index's existence, the DJIA handily outperformed the Nasdaq 100. From a base of 1286.80 in January 1985, the DJIA rose to 2590.50 by January 1990, or by 15.02% per year. During this same time period, the Nasdaq 100 rose from 125 to 201.94, or by 6.84% per year. During the 1990s, the DJIA rose by a record setting 15.503% per year, while the Nasdaq 100 soared by an almost unbelievable 33.27% per year. During this time frame, the Nasdaq 100 far outpaced any other domestic market index. Indeed, the performance of the Nasdaq 100, culminating with the market peak of 2000, is unprecedented for any broadly based stock market index in the world.

By definition, the Nasdaq 100 involves fewer companies and is more narrowly focused than the Nasdaq Composite Index. The Nasdaq Composite Index measures all Nasdaq domestic and non-U.S. based common stocks listed on the Nasdaq Stock Market. Today, the Nasdaq Composite includes over 4000 companies. Because it is so broadly based, the Nasdaq Composite is one of the most widely followed and quoted major market indices. Every security assigned to the Nasdaq Composite Index is also assigned to one of the eight Nasdaq sub-indices (Bank, Biotechnology, Computer, Industrial, Insurance, Other Finance, Telecommunication, Transportation). The determination for assignment to an appropriate sub-index is generally based upon Standard Industrial Classification (SIC) codes relative to a company's major source of revenues. The large relative size of Nasdaq 100 companies causes the Nasdaq 100 Index to closely track the broader Nasdaq Composite Index, especially during recent years. Therefore, the data depicted in Fig. 1.1 pertain not only to the Nasdaq 100, but to the Nasdaq market overall as well.

Table 1.2 depicts the Nasdaq 100 Index as a recent incarnation of the Nifty 50 phenomenon of the early-1970s. Like then, investors recently accorded superior market capitalizations to a relative handful of companies thought to possess exceptional long-term growth characteristics. While the Nasdaq 100 Index includes 100 large Nasdaq stocks, a relative handful typically dominate that index and the overall Nasdaq Stock Market. Notice that the top five Nasdaq 100 stocks accounted for more than one-quarter (29.24%) of the value of this market value-adjusted index during the market peak of 2000. Only 16 Nasdaq stocks accounted for more than one-half (51.36%) of the Nasdaq 100; and 33 Nasdaq stocks accounted for roughly three-quarters (75.18%) of the Nasdaq 100. The top 50 Nasdaq 100 stocks accounted for 86.85% of the overall index.

Among the most favored Nasdaq 100 stocks, valuation ratios greatly exceed the P/E ratios observed for similar stock market favorites during the Nifty 50 era. At the market peak, investors commonly accorded Nasdaq 100 growth stock favorites P/E ratios that greatly exceeded norms established for the Nifty 50. Remember, Polaroid set the high-water mark for Nifty 50 companies with a P/E ratio of 93.5. Among 79 Nasdaq 100 companies reporting positive earnings per

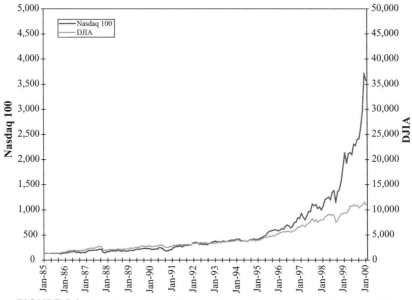

FIGURE 1.1   The Nasdaq 100 vastly outperformed the overall market during the 1990s.

share during the trailing 12-month (ttm) period, fully 24 sported P/E ratios greater than the 93.5 standard borne by Polaroid in 1972. Another 21 reported losses for the most recent period. When compared with recent tech stock favorites, Polaroid's P/E of 93.5 in 1972 would appear modest. Near the market peak in 2000, 45% of the Nasdaq 100 stocks had P/E ratios that exceeded the P/E high-water mark set for the Nifty 50 by Polaroid.

When compared using P/E ratios at their market peaks, Nasdaq 100 stocks were much more expensive than the Nifty 50. As shown in Table 1.2, the average P/E ratio for 79 Nasdaq 100 stocks reporting positive earnings during the ttm period is a whopping 131.2, or more than three and one-half times greater than the Nifty 50 average P/E of 37.3 (see Table 1.1). Of course, such averages can be skewed upward by a few very high P/Es for a handful of very low profit Nasdaq 100 companies. However, according to monthly market statistics and information provided by the National Association of Stock Dealers (NASD), the Nasdaq 100 sports a P/E ratio of 93.5 when market values and earnings are considered for both profitable and unprofitable component companies.[4] Therefore, as a group, recent P/E valuation ratios for the Nasdaq 100 exceeded the highest P/E ratio accorded to Polaroid or any other member of the Nifty 50.

When considering the investment implications of current P/E ratios for Nasdaq 100 companies, it is worth emphasizing that many Nasdaq 100 stocks can

---

[4]See http://www.nasd.com/mrktstat/default.html for details.

TABLE 1.2 The Nasdaq 100: Investor Favorites among the New Nifty 50

	Company	Symbol	Market capitalization ($ billions)	P/E (ttm)	Historical EPS growth (5 years)	Consensus security analyst EPS growth (%)	Projected P/E (5 years)	Average recommendation (strong buy = 1, strong sell = 5)	% of index (adj.)	Total % of index (adj.)
1	Intel Corporation	INTC	502.700	63.6	16.5%	21.1	45.0	1.50	7.70	7.70
2	Cisco Systems, Inc.	CSCO	482.000	125.6	39.2%	32.5	56.7	1.32	7.36	15.06
3	Microsoft Corporation	MSFT	367.400	41.2	34.3%	21.5	28.7	1.70	5.69	20.75
4	Oracle Corporation	ORCL	256.000	42.0	48.8%	25.4	25.0	1.67	4.60	25.35
5	Sun Microsystems, Inc.	SUNW	201.800	115.6	31.6%	23.1	75.3	1.43	3.89	29.24
6	LM Ericsson Telephone Company	ERICY	160.500	50.5		25.9	29.4	1.54	1.02	30.26
7	Dell Computer Corporation	DELL	112.900	58.7	68.0%	31.1	27.9	1.59	1.71	31.97
8	WorldCom, Inc.	WCOM	104.900	21.5	37.1%	28.5	11.3	1.28	1.67	33.64
9	JDS Uniphase Corporation	JDSU	97.353		67.8%	48.4		1.45	4.78	38.42
10	Amgen Inc.	AMGN	77.955	68.9	20.1%	17.9	55.7	1.73	1.53	39.95
11	Applied Materials, Inc.	AMAT	69.702	42.4	20.0%	25.3	25.3	1.47	1.57	41.52
12	Yahoo! Inc.	YHOO	66.744	324.3		46.5	88.6	1.56	1.40	42.92
13	VERITAS Software Corporation	VRTS	48.465			45.5		1.52	2.14	45.06
14	QUALCOMM Incorporated	QCOM	44.610	67.0	53.1%	35.8	26.7	1.71	2.38	47.44
15	Nextel Communications, Inc.	NXTL	42.208		−258.0%	30.3		1.60	1.99	49.43
16	Siebel Systems, Inc.	SEBL	41.206	412.1		43.6	124.3	1.18	1.93	51.36
17	VeriSign, Inc.	VRSN	38.672	1383.9		54.6	288.7	1.44	1.51	52.87
18	Gemstar-TV Guide International Inc	GMST	36.929	210.7		38.2	77.0	1.31	1.49	54.36
19	Network Appliance, Inc.	NTAP	36.553	619.1		50.1	149.7	1.14	1.54	55.90

(continues)

TABLE 1.2 (*continued*)

	Company	Symbol	Market capitalization ($ billions)	P/E (ttm)	Historical EPS growth (5 years)	Consensus security analyst EPS growth (%)	Projected P/E (5 years)	Average recommendation (strong buy = 1, strong sell = 5)	% of index (adj.)	Total % of index (adj.)
20	PMC-Sierra, Inc.	PMCS	34.850	278.8	34.8%	44.6	81.3	1.42	1.87	57.77
21	SDL, Inc.	SDLI	34.386	510.7		44.1	151.4	1.30	1.51	59.28
22	Comcast Corporation	CMCSK	33.702	36.2		15.3	32.7	1.24	0.69	59.97
23	i2 Technologies, Inc.	ITWO	33.520			43.0		1.61	1.45	61.42
24	Level 3 Communications, Inc.	LVLT	31.979			9.4		1.50	0.91	62.33
25	CIENA Corporation	CIEN	31.485	525.3		34.3	221.5	1.70	1.57	63.90
26	Xilinx, Inc.	XLNX	29.204	43.3	24.5%	28.1	23.1	1.56	1.68	65.58
27	ADC Telecommunications, Inc.	ADCT	29.026	80.4	27.3%	29.3	41.0	1.26	1.55	67.13
28	Global Crossing Ltd	GBLX	26.471		35.7		1.79	1.24	68.37
29	Altera Corporation	ALTR	25.858	84.4	31.1%	26.8	47.5	1.57	1.54	69.91
30	Applied Micro Circuits Corporation	AMCC	25.463	353.0		41.4	115.1	1.21	1.22	71.13
31	Immunex Corporation	IMNX	25.271	231.6		50.7	54.9	2.19	1.45	72.58
32	Maxim Integrated Products, Inc.	MXIM	24.785	94.7	30.5%	27.7	51.4	1.50	1.44	74.02
33	VoiceStream Wireless Corporation	VSTR	24.158			27.7		1.72	1.16	75.18
34	EchoStar Communications Corporation	DISH	23.049			31.0		1.34	0.46	75.64
35	Tellabs, Inc.	TLAB	23.043	36.7	39.2%	28.9	19.0	1.52	0.59	76.23
36	Linear Technology Corporation	LLTC	22.523	79.0	23.8%	26.7	44.6	1.63	1.27	77.50

	Company	Ticker								
37	Metromedia Fiber Network, Inc.	MFNX	21.943					1.29	0.81	78.31
38	Apple Computer, Inc.	AAPL	19.803	29.3	30.0%	17.3	24.3	1.53	1.19	79.50
39	Sanmina Corporation	SANM	17.864	115.8	40.2%	33.0	51.3	1.43	0.75	80.25
40	MedImmune, Inc.	MEDI	17.651	205.0		40.0	70.2	1.28	0.76	81.01
41	eBay Inc.	EBAY	16.642	1017.7		54.2	215.1	1.62	0.53	81.54
42	Paychex, Inc.	PAYX	16.610	86.2	33.6%	28.5	45.3	2.04	0.64	82.18
43	Vitesse Semiconductor Corporation	VTSS	15.952	145.2		38.9	51.7	1.39	0.79	82.97
44	Adobe Systems Incorporated	ADBE	15.623	58.6	15.6%	25.8	34.3	1.73	0.68	83.65
45	Costco Wholesale Corporation	COST	15.393	28.5	19.5%	14.5	26.7	2.33	0.36	84.01
46	Amazon.com, Inc.	AMZN	14.768			55.0		2.13	0.41	84.42
47	Comverse Technology, Inc.	CMVT	14.619	73.0		28.2	38.8	1.21	0.64	85.06
48	CMGI, Inc.	CMGI	13.212			42.5		1.62	0.55	85.61
49	KLA-Tencor Corporation	KLAC	12.205	49.4	23.0%	25.1	29.7	1.46	0.62	86.23
50	Intuit Inc.	INTU	12.181	90.4	19.6%	21.4	63.2	1.56	0.62	86.85
51	NTL Incorporated	NTLI	11.864		-265.0%			1.50	0.49	87.34
52	Molex Incorporated	MOLX	10.360	44.7	12.5%	15.4	40.2	2.00	0.21	87.55
53	Biogen, Inc.	BGEN	10.229	33.2	57.9%	21.4	23.2	1.96	0.58	88.13
54	Chiron Corporation	CHIR	9.881	59.0	87.8%	23.3	38.1	2.30	0.56	88.69
55	NEXTLINK Communications, Inc.	NXLK	9.607			40.0		1.24	0.42	89.11
56	Atmel Corporation	ATML	9.220	44.9	1.6%	21.9	30.7	1.50	0.28	89.39
57	BroadVision, Inc.	BVSN	9.217	287.5		48.4	73.6	1.57	0.40	89.79
58	McLeodUSA Incorporated	MCLD	9.212			12.0		1.13	0.34	90.13
59	PeopleSoft, Inc.	PSFT	9.019	263.1	-0.2%	24.1	164.7	2.53	0.50	90.63
60	USA Networks, Inc.	USAI	8.857			19.8		1.11	0.36	90.99
61	QLogic Corporation	QLGC	8.486	128.5		31.3	60.7	1.33	0.41	91.40
62	Conexant Systems, Inc.	CNXT	8.472			29.0		1.53	0.39	91.79
63	Lycos, Inc.	LCOS	7.839	350.6		49.3	87.1	1.93	0.41	92.20

(continues)

TABLE 1.2 (*continued*)

	Company	Symbol	Market capitalization ($ billions)	P/E (ttm)	Historical EPS growth (5 years)	Consensus security analyst EPS growth (%)	Projected P/E (5 years)	Average recommendation (strong buy = 1, strong sell = 5)	% of index (adj.)	Total % of index (adj.)
64	Electronic Arts Inc.	ERTS	7.659	100.2	16.2%	23.1	65.3	1.50	0.30	92.50
65	RealNetworks, Inc.	RNWK	7.610			53.0		1.60	0.29	92.79
66	RF Micro Devices, Inc.	RFMD	7.191	143.3		44.6	41.8	1.25	0.35	93.14
67	Staples, Inc.	SPLS	7.189	24.7	38.2%	27.0	13.8	1.59	0.22	93.36
68	Cintas Corporation	CTAS	7.004	36.5	20.0%	20.1	26.9	2.00	0.36	93.72
69	Starbucks Corporation	SBUX	6.852	56.4	26.7%	25.8	33.0	1.66	0.40	94.12
70	Concord EFS, Inc.	CEFT	6.832	42.1	41.0%	32.9	18.7	1.00	0.33	94.45
71	Fiserv, Inc.	FISV	6.677	43.0	16.6%	19.4	32.7	1.40	0.35	94.80
72	BMC Software, Inc.	BMCS	6.664	26.8	27.7%	23.8	17.0	2.43	0.21	95.01
73	Genzyme General	GENZ	6.480	31.2	18.7%	18.0	25.1	1.77	0.33	95.34
74	Biomet, Inc.	BMET	6.015	52.7	16.2%	14.6	49.1	1.58	0.36	95.70
75	At Home Corporation	ATHM	5.858			56.4		1.97	0.18	95.88
76	3Com Corporation	COMS	5.802	8.8	−10.9%	21.2	6.2	2.35	0.13	96.01
77	Microchip Technology Incorporated	MCHP	5.388	47.9	21.7%	25.9	27.9	1.55	0.20	96.21
78	Bed Bath & Beyond Inc.	BBBY	4.964	36.7	32.5%	25.6	21.6	1.26	0.30	96.51
79	PanAmSat Corporation	SPOT	4.853	27.2		23.5	17.4	1.83	0.28	96.79
80	Adelphia Communications Corporation	ADLAC	4.717			16.0		1.38	0.18	96.97
81	American Power Conversion Corporation	APCC	4.633	22.1	24.9%	23.5	14.1	2.00	0.27	97.24

#	Company	Ticker								
82	Dollar Tree Stores, Inc.	DLTR	4.356	43.3		24.8	26.4	1.67	0.18	97.42
83	Citrix Systems, Inc.	CTXS	4.086	37.5		35.0	15.4	2.44	0.21	97.63
84	Novell, Inc.	NOVL	3.979	24.3	-11.1%	19.7	18.2	2.45	0.19	97.82
85	Compuware Corporation	CPWR	3.854	13.0	37.0%	23.8	8.2	2.90	0.09	97.91
86	Parametric Technology Corporation	PMTC	3.642	123.3	19.6%	20.7	88.7	2.21	0.22	98.13
87	Network Associates, Inc.	NETA	3.565	75.0	-215.6%	23.9	47.3	2.13	0.15	98.28
88	PACCAR Inc	PCAR	3.248	5.4	22.6%	9.4	6.3	2.44	0.16	98.44
89	Smurfit-Stone Container Corporation	SSCC	3.196	9.4		8.0	11.7	1.61	0.13	98.57
90	Apollo Group, Inc.	APOL	3.069	48.3		24.1	30.3	1.75	0.12	98.69
91	CNET Networks, Inc.	CNET	2.914			40.9		1.39	0.14	98.83
92	Northwest Airlines Corporation	NWAC	2.654	7.8		11.7	8.2	2.05	0.09	98.92
93	Synopsys, Inc.	SNPS	2.650	15.6	31.2%	21.0	11.1	2.00	0.13	99.05
94	Herman Miller, Inc.	MLHR	2.469	18.1	15.5%	15.0	16.6	1.88	0.08	99.13
95	Adaptec, Inc.	ADPT	2.430	24.5	6.8%	19.5	18.5	2.60	0.09	99.22
96	Sigma-Aldrich Corporation	SIAL	2.342	18.4		11.2	19.9	2.54	0.11	99.33
97	PacifiCare Health Systems, Inc.	PHSY	1.883	7.1	14.8%	13.7	6.9	2.75	0.07	99.40
98	VISX, Incorporated	VISX	1.668	22.7		24.0	14.3	2.34	0.08	99.48
99	Quintiles Transnational Corp.	QTRN	1.611	57.3		21.7	39.5	2.34	0.10	99.58
100	Legato Systems, Inc.	LGTO	1.054			34.5		2.68	0.05	**99.63**
	Average		**37.812**	**131.2**	**12.5%**	**29.1**	**50.5**	**1.71**	**1.00**	

Data source: All data obtained from yahoo.com as of August 31, 2000.

only be regarded as new and untested. Nifty 50 stocks had proven growth in revenues, earnings, and dividends. Virtually none had experienced a dividend cut during the post-World War II period. By way of contrast, the Nasdaq 100 includes just 79 companies that report profits in the ttm period, 54 that have an operating history of positive profitability that runs at least 5 years, and only 12 companies that pay even modest dividend income.

None of this seemed to bother the security analyst community. Table 1.2 shows 5-year consensus earnings per share (EPS) growth estimates provided by security analysts and reported by Zacks Investment Research in the period surrounding the 2000 market peak. The average consensus 5-year EPS growth forecast for 98 Nasdaq 100 firms was 29.1% per year, or more than twice the 12.5% per year EPS growth rate enjoyed by 54 profitable Nasdaq 100 firms over the past 5 years. This implies that security analysts were confident that new and unprofitable components of the Nasdaq 100 would be able to dramatically improve upon the earnings success achieved by the slim majority of Nasdaq 100 firms that had already compiled a five-year record of EPS growth. It is also interesting to consider long-term implications of these market valuations.

Table 1.2 shows a projected P/E ratio for members of the Nasdaq 100 assuming that the consensus five-year EPS growth forecast was achieved and that a market-like annual return of 13% per year was earned by investors. After such a period of unprecedented EPS growth by Nasdaq 100 companies, the average P/E ratio for the 79 presently profitable Nasdaq 100 companies would be 50.5. When both money-making and unprofitable Nasdaq 100 firms are considered, and assuming market returns of 13% and EPS growth of 29.1% per year, the 5-year forward-looking P/E ratio for the Nasdaq 100 would only shrink from the peak level of 98.0 to 50.3. Thus, after assuming unprecedented EPS growth in the coming 5-year period, the P/E ratio for the Nasdaq 100 would remain measurably above the 2000 market P/E for the DJIA of 19.0 and the S&P 500 of 26.5, which were then among the highest on record for those indexes. Similarly, even after assuming unprecedented EPS growth in the coming 5-year period, the P/E ratio for the Nasdaq 100 would remain measurably above the 1972 standard set for the Nifty 50 of 37.3.

At the 2000 market peak, it is obvious that P/E ratios accorded Nasdaq 100 companies far exceeded the valuation ratios conferred by investors on the Nifty 50 during the early-1970s. The clearest similarity between the Nifty 50 and the Nasdaq 100 of today is that both groups of stocks have sufficiently large market capitalizations to allow large institutional investors to buy as much of them as their portfolios can hold. However, there remain important differences.

As shown in Table 1.2, not only were Nasdaq 100 companies accorded P/E ratios that far exceeded established norms for the Nifty 50, the valuation numbers themselves were enormous. A big difference between the Nifty 50 and the Nasdaq 100 phenomenon of today is size. Back in 1972, the market was dominated by non-Nifty industrials such as General Motors and Ford, utilities such as AT&T, and the major oils. At the 2000 market peak, tech stock favorites not only dominated over the Nasdaq 100, they also overshadowed other major stock market indices such as the S&P 500 and the DJIA.

As shown in Table 1.2, with a peak average market capitalization of $38.7 billion, the Nasdaq 100 could only be described as the home of large-cap stocks. Led by Intel ($502.7 billion), Cisco ($482 billion), and Microsoft ($367.4), the Nasdaq 100 included many of the largest market capitalization companies in the world. Nasdaq 100 behemoths Intel, Cisco, Microsoft, and Oracle ($256 billion) were then among the 10 largest S&P 500 stocks. Intel and Microsoft were among the three largest DJIA stocks. It is one thing to accord a P/E ratio of 100 to small-cap stocks with enormous but risky growth opportunities; however, it is quite another thing to accord a P/E ratio of 125.6 to a large-cap stock worth $482 billion (such as Cisco). Taken as a group, the market capitalization of the Nasdaq 100 was *$3.9 trillion* near the 2000 market peak.

Size is important. Historically, very few large companies prove to be worth above-average P/E ratios. To be sure, the notion that a few widely recognized growth companies can be worth more than 50 times earnings has been proven by the facts. In Table 1.1, Siegel shows the "warranted" P/E of the original Nifty 50 using a stock price that would result in a return equal to the S&P 500 over the ensuing 20+ years. Coca-Cola, for example, traded for a P/E of 42.3 in January 1972, but was actually worth a P/E of 68.8 given its market-beating results since then. That being said, it is clear that some of the best performances turned in by former Nifty 50 stocks have been generated by lower multiple consumer products companies such as Philip Morris, Gillette, and PepsiCo. Nearly all of the super high P/E stocks lagged behind, including Avon, International Flavor & Fragrances, and Polaroid.

At a certain point it becomes mathematically impossible for big companies to grow rapidly enough to justify their multiples. At the 2000 market peak, the tech sector was discounting 20%+ annual profit growth over the next decade. This was an extremely optimistic expectation in light of market history where double-digit sector-wide earnings growth is rarely achieved. An annual growth rate of 20% implies more than a sixfold increase in EPS during the next decade. Internet stocks appeared to discount 35–50% annual profit growth over a 10-year span. At that rate of growth, future earnings would equal a phenomenal 20–60 times current earnings. We now know how silly this expectation was, but even under the best of circumstances, such growth is far from certain.

III. AS TECHNOLOGY GOES, SO GOES THE NASDAQ 100

Growth stock investors always display asset category preferences reflecting strong underlying beliefs about where the best growth opportunities can be found. However, recent investors in the Nasdaq 100 seem to have forgotten the below-market returns earned by investors in Nifty 50 tech stocks.

Figure 1.2 shows the enormous EPS growth expectations imbedded in stock prices for Nasdaq companies, in general (panels 2a and 2b), and Nasdaq tech

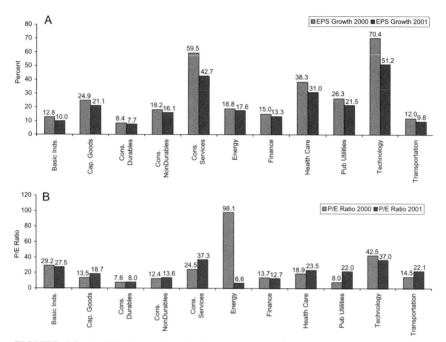

FIGURE 1.2   Peak Nasdaq stock valuations incorporated enormous EPS growth expectations. (A) Nasdaq projected EPS growths; (B) Nasdaq P/E ratios.

stock favorites, in particular (panels 2c and 2d), near the 2000 market peak. For the Nasdaq as a whole, projected EPS growth and P/E ratios were highest for companies in technology, consumer services, and health care. Within technology, electronics, office equipment, and semiconductors were stand-out industries in terms of EPS growth expectations. In consumer services, rapid EPS growth was expected for firms in leisure, retail, and industrial services. Rapid EPS growth was also expected for health care companies in home care (assisted living), medical services, and medical supplies. Note how high P/E ratios suggested a high level of confidence on the part of stock market analysts and investors that truly stunning rates of EPS growth would be achieved.

During the late-1990s, Nasdaq 100 investors have displayed an especially strong preference for technology stocks at the vanguard of important new innovations in computer software, components, and networks; telecommunications equipment; biotechnology; wireless communication devices; and the Internet.

As shown in Table 1.3, 86.90% of the Nasdaq 100 Index was composed of only 10 industry groups within the technology sector during the bubble period. Seventeen large computer software companies, led by Microsoft, Oracle Corp., and Veritas Software Corp., accounted for more than one-quarter (25.26%) of the Nasdaq 100 Index. Fifteen semiconductor manufacturers, led by Intel, Maxim

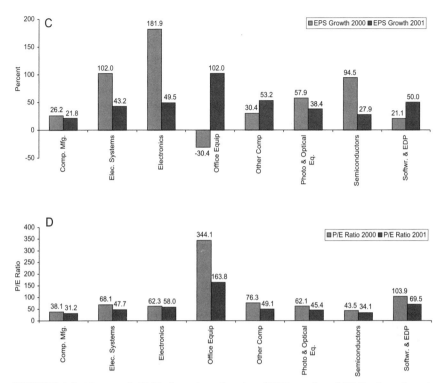

FIGURE 1.2 (*Continued*) (C) Nasdaq tech stock projected EPS growth; and (D) Nasdaq tech stock P/E ratios. (Data from nasdaq.com, August 31, 2000.

Integrated Products, and Xilinx, accounted for another 16.46%. Six large telecom equipment companies, the third largest industry group within the Nasdaq 100, accounted for 9.92% of the index. Nasdaq 100 telecom equipment companies were led by Qualcomm, JDS Uniphase, and Comverse Technology. Together, these three high-tech industry groups accounted for more than one-half (51.64%) of the Nasdaq 100 Index. It is fair to say that the Nasdaq 100 is a technology stock index. Three retailers (Costco, Staples, and Bed, Bath & Beyond), two media companies (TMP Worldwide and USA Networks), one restaurant (Starbucks), and one linen supply company (Cintas) were among the few Nasdaq 100 Index components that had little or no tie to technology.

The historical allure of tech stock investing is obvious. Tech stocks tend to do well as capital spending rises during economic expansions, and the U.S. economy was on an uninterrupted boom throughout the 1990s. Fundamentally important new innovations during the 1990s also contributed to the explosion of interest in tech stocks. First, the advent of amazingly powerful microprocessors transformed the PC into a mighty tool for business calculations. Then, even more

TABLE 1.3   Tech Stocks Dominate the Nasdaq 100

Top 10 holdings	Nasdaq 100 Index weight (%)	Top 10 industries	Nasdaq 100 Index weight (%)
Microsoft Corp.	9.42	Computer Software	25.26
Intel Corp.	5.77	Semiconductors	16.46
Qualcomm Inc.	4.54	Telecom Equip.	9.92
Cisco Systems Inc.	3.66	Biomedical	8.51
Oracle Corp.	3.56	Electronic Prod. (misc.)	6.08
J D S Uniphase Corp.	2.62	Computer	5.63
Amgen Inc.	2.23	Computer Networks	5.43
Sun Microsystems Inc.	2.21	Telecom (wireless)	3.94
Voicestream Wireless Corp.	2.19	Computer Services	3.23
Dell Computer Corp.	2.18	Cable TV	2.44
Total	**38.38**		**86.90**

Note: Nasdaq 100 Index weights as of 3/30/01.

powerful microprocessors and the arrival of the Internet made PCs the focus of a communications industry revolution. Cameras, cellular phones, computers, copy machines, Fax machines, printers, telephones, and televisions are quickly converging toward multicapability communications devices.

Huge potential rewards await those tech companies able to successfully navigate in such a rapidly changing environment. Somewhat less understood are the equally enormous risks facing companies unable to successfully anticipate and adapt to such challenges. To illustrate, Table 1.4 shows the rapidly changing competitive landscape for high-tech companies in the computer networking equipment and computer software industries. Notice how few industry giants have been able to stay atop their competitors over the 1980–2000 time frame. While IBM has been able to remain a force in the production of computers and peripheral equipment, no other company has been able to maintain a top 10 position in the industry for even 20 years.

Present-day giants, such as Microsoft Corp. (founded in 1975) and Cisco Systems, Inc. (founded in 1984) have literally come out of nowhere. Rather than assume that Cisco and Microsoft will naturally dominate such a quickly changing landscape for the next 20 years, long-term investors may want to consider what will happen to their stock prices if (or when) they stumble. Among current favorites, Microsoft could well live up to its lofty P/E. Still, it is worth remembering that before Microsoft was born IBM was thought to be invincible. Siegel's research on the Nifty 50 shows that technology companies have a tough time maintaining their edge over the long run. Technology changes in ways that are not easy to predict. Developing a cost-efficient way of building and delivering made-to-order desktop computers has greatly favored the growth of Dell Computer. Meanwhile, Burroughs and Digital Equipment got buried when they failed to keep up.

TABLE 1.4 High-Tech Market Capitalization Rankings Change Dramatically over Long Time Periods

1980	$ millions	1990	$ millions	2000	$ millions
A. Computers and peripheral equipment					
1 IBM	39,625.9	IBM	64,567.2	Cisco Systems	347,897.3
2 Computer Sciences Corp.	240.4	Computer Sciences Corp.	1,071.4	IBM	209,148.0
3 American Management Systems	53.9	American Management Systems	175.4	Dell Computer	127,437.4
4 CGA Computers Inc.	34.3	Computer Task Group Inc.	62.8	Sun Microsystems	111,242.8
5 Hadron Inc.	32.6	BRC Holdings Inc.	55.2	Hewlett-Packard	109,277.4
6 Computer Task Group Inc.	20.5	Data Transmission Network	39.1	EMC Corp.	104,803.0
7 Dyatron Corp.	17.1	Medstat Group Inc.	33.0	Compaq Computer	47,600.0
8 BRC Holdings Inc.	12.7	National Information Group	30.9	Gateway Inc.	18,042.5
9 Cerplex Group Inc.	6.3	Cerplex Group Inc.	21.0	Apple Computer	16,731.5
10 Auxton Computer Enterprises	5.7	Mpsi Systems Inc.	19.0	3Com Corp.	15,203.0
B. Computer software and services					
1 Computervision Corp.	1,206.2	Microsoft Corp.	8,641.1	Microsoft Corp.	588,884.1
2 Wang Labs Inc.	875.0	Novell Inc.	1,742.7	Oracle Corp.	145,214.6
3 Cullinet Software Inc.	196.5	Computer Associates Intl Inc.	1,615.4	Computer Associates	33,864.2
4 UCCEL Corp.	190.9	Autodesk Inc.	1,110.7	VERITAS Software	32,736.7
5 Tyler Technologies Inc.	150.3	BMC Software Inc.	1,030.1	Automatic Data Proc.	32,193.1
6 Banctec Inc.	78.8	Oracle Corp.	1,022.2	Electronic Data Sys.	28,070.4
7 Intelligent System Corp.	51.3	Lotus Development Corp.	844.4	First Data Corp.	20,567.2
8 Informatics General Corp.	51.0	Inprise Corp.	807.9	Intuit Inc.	14,646.2
9 Comshare Inc.	45.7	Policy Management Systems Corp.	801.1	Siebel Systems	13,810.7
10 Continuum Inc.	37.7	Cadence Design Sys Inc.	713.0	Computer Sciences	13,778.9

Data sources: 1980, 1990 data from *Compustat PC+*; 2000 data from *Value Line Investment Survey for Windows* January 2000.

Time will tell if tech stock favorites in the Nasdaq 100 are more effective than IBM and other Nifty 50 ancestors in maintaining an edge in the rapidly changing high-tech world. It is easy to predict that Coca-Cola will be an important soft drink company in 10 years. In 10 years, Wrigley will be big in chewing gum, Kellogg's will be an important cereals food company, and Mars will be a leader in candy. Does anyone have similar confidence in their prediction of who will be the largest Internet service provider (ISP) equipment provider in a decade?

Finally, it is interesting to note that the extraordinary recent performance of the Nasdaq 100 cannot be attributed to the "irrational exuberance" of inexperienced individual investors. The growing importance of institutional investors on the Nasdaq suggests that institutional buyers, not suddenly affluent baby boomers, were behind the surge on the Nasdaq. As shown in Fig. 1.3, the recent surges in the Nasdaq 100 and the Nasdaq Composite have coincided with a burst of institutional net buying activity. In 1985, the percentage of Nasdaq market capitalization held by institutional buyers stood at 28.3%. At that time, it was fair to characterize the Nasdaq Stock Market as a retail market with primary appeal to individual investors. At the market peak, the percentage of Nasdaq market capitalization held by institutions had nearly doubled to 53.3%. During the period leading up to the market peak, the simple correlation between the year-end

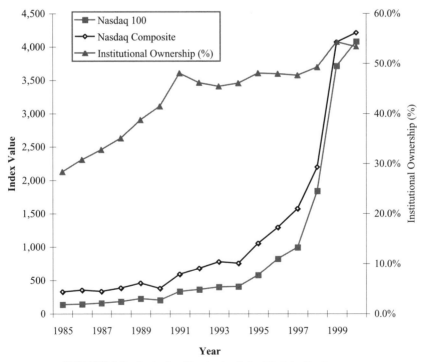

FIGURE 1.3 Institutional buying has helped fuel the Nasdaq surge.

Nasdaq 100 Index value and the percentage of institutional ownership was a statistically significant 67.0%. The simple correlation between the year-end Nasdaq Composite Index value and the percentage of institutional ownership was a statistically significant 71.6%.

At the 2000 peak, the Nasdaq Stock Market could clearly be characterized as a market with significant appeal to institutional stock buyers. The Nasdaq was no longer a retail market with primary appeal to individual investors. The Nasdaq is largely an institutional market, and institutional owners control an important portion of the total market capitalization on the Nasdaq. The Nasdaq 100 is not only a collection of investor favorites, but like the Nifty 50 of years ago, the Nasdaq 100 is a collection of *institutional* investor favorites.

IV. HOW HIGH IS UP?

Perhaps the most popular measure of investor expectations and market valuation risk is given by P/E ratios. High P/E ratios usually signify high risk, and low P/E ratios typically signal low valuation risk. However, P/E ratios for the market as reflected by the DJIA, as shown in Fig. 1.4, can be distorted during recessions when massive write-offs can cause index earnings to collapse and the DJIA P/E ratio to soar. In 1981, for example, the DJIA P/E ratio soared to 114.4 because of a collapse in earnings caused by massive write-offs following a deep recession. Similar peaks of 64.3 times earnings in 1991 and 47.3 times earnings in 1933 were caused by significant earnings shortfalls at a few DJIA companies. To get a clear picture of conventional P/E ratios for the overall market during typical operating conditions, it is necessary to control for periods of dramatic earnings shortfalls. Figure 1.4 illustrates the actual DJIA P/E ratio data after index earnings have been normalized for three brief periods (1931–35, 1982–83, 1991–92) when index earnings plummeted by 50% or more in a single year. In those three instances, actual prior-year earnings were used instead of depressed current-year earnings.

After adjustment, it is easy to see in Fig. 1.4, panel A, that P/E ratios for the DJIA almost always fall within a band from 10–20. Near the market peak, the P/E ratio of 19.0 for the DJIA greatly exceeded the long-term median of 13.6 and was among the highest on record. What made this elevated P/E ratio for the DJIA worrisome was that further rapid surges in earnings were then extremely unlikely. Coming out of a recession, a sharp rebound in earnings is typical. Coming on top of an already robust economic expansion, further earnings gains would have been tough to come by.

Another popular measure of investor expectations and market valuation risk is given by price-book (P/B) ratios. High P/B ratios usually signify high risk, and low P/B ratios typically signal low valuation risk. Unlike P/E ratios, P/B ratios do not tend to be distorted by economic recessions. Until recently, P/B ratios for the DJIA almost always fell within a band from 1 to 2 (see Fig. 1.4, panel B). However, the

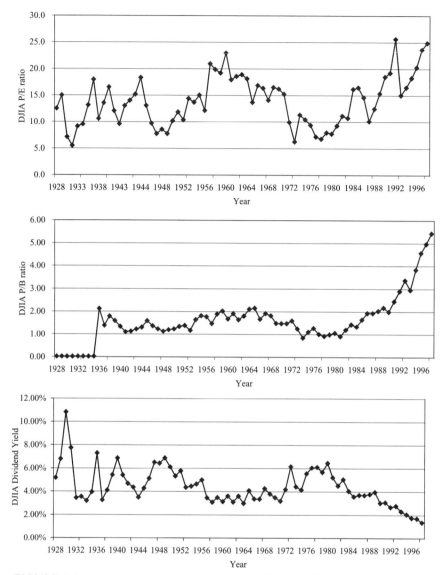

FIGURE 1.4   At the start of the new millenium, the DJIA was at all-time highs. (A) P/E ratios were never higher; (B) P/B ratios were never higher; (C) dividend yields were at all-time lows. Note that P/E ratios in 1931–35, 1982–83, and 1991–92 have been adjusted for massive losses at component firms. (Data source: Dow Jones & Comapny.)

market peak P/B ratio for the DJIA was 6.22, or roughly four times the long-term median of 1.5:1, and among the highest on record.[5] As in the case of elevated P/E ratios, an elevated P/B ratio for the DJIA at the start of the new millennium was worrisome in that further rapid surges in earnings seemed unlikely.

A similar picture of high investor expectations and high valuation risk in the market is given when one considers dividend yield information, as shown in Fig. 1.4, panel C. High dividend yields reflect investor caution and concern about future business prospects. Low dividend yields reflect investor optimism and enthusiasm for future business prospects. Investment returns have been best when investors have bought stocks during periods of high dividend yields and sold stocks during periods of low dividend yields. Hence, the time-tested admonition to "buy fear, sell greed." Near the 2000 market peak, the dividend yield on the DJIA of 1.73% was far below the long-term median of 4.37% and among the lowest on record.[6]

Although some contend that dividends are unimportant for growth stock investors, it is worth remembering that roughly 40% of the total return earned by common stock investors comes in the form of dividend income. Over the long run, dividends matter.[7] Some may explain away the importance of the recent decline in dividend income by contending that because dividends are taxed as regular income, tax-savvy companies tend to announce share repurchases in lieu of dividend increases. To be sure, shareholder-friendly corporations are making increased use of share repurchases as an efficient means for returning excess cash flow to shareholders. At the same time, many companies are issuing a record number of shares tied to executive and employee stock-option incentive plans. Because the scope of share repurchases is roughly offset by the pace of new share issuance, the recent decline in dividend income represents a real decline in the amount of cash payments received by shareholders.

Against the backdrop of typical values for the overall market's traditional valuation benchmarks, it is interesting to consider valuation indicators for Nasdaq and Nasdaq 100 companies near the 2000 market peak. As shown in Table 1.5, Nasdaq valuation data diverged starkly from broader market norms.[8] According to NASD data, P/E ratios averaged well over 100 on the Nasdaq following the late-1990s surge in equity prices. In the period surrounding the early-March 2000 peak on the Nasdaq, P/E ratios approached the heretofore unheard of level of 200 for a major domestic market index. Considering domestic common stocks only, the P/E for the Nasdaq Composite reached an incredible average of 245.7 at the end of February 2000. These valuation levels were for companies that can only

---

[5]Near the market peak, the P/B ratio for the S&P 500 was 6.56 and was among the highest on record. [6]Near the market peak, the dividend yield on the S&P 500 was also near a historic low of only 1.15%.

[7]Benartzi, Michaely, and Thaler (1997) give a recent analysis of the economic implications of dividend policy.

[8]While valuation metrics for the DJIA, the S&P 500, and other broad measures of the market are widely quoted and commented upon in the business press, no such similar coverage is accorded to traditional valuation indicators for the Nasdaq and the Nasdaq 100. Recently, this information void has started to fill with data reported on the NASD Web site (http://www.nasd.com). Since January 1999, the NASD has reported monthly statistics on total assets, revenues, shareholders' equity, net income, and market capitalization for the Nasdaq Composite and Nasdaq 100 indices.

TABLE 1.5 Average Valuation Ratios for Nasdaq and Nasdaq 100 Companies

	Nasdaq									Nasdaq 100							
Month-year	Assets ($)	Revenues ($)	Equity ($)	Net income ($)	Market cap ($)	ROE	P/B ratio	P/E ratio	P/E Ratio[a]	Assets ($)	Revenues ($)	Equity ($)	Net income ($)	Market cap ($)	ROE	P/B ratio	P/E ratio
Jan-99	587.1	289.5	168.0	8.9	592.3	5.3%	3.5	66.6	105.6	4,230.7	2,927.6	1,981.4	237.1	18,267.1	12.0%	9.2	77.0
Feb-99	589.2	291.8	164.0	9.2	548.1	5.6%	3.3	59.6	93.3	4,304.2	2,946.0	2,045.3	249.9	16,491.4	12.2%	8.1	66.0
Mar-99	596.9	302.4	162.9	9.4	626.2	5.8%	3.8	66.6	104.4	4,061.9	2,962.8	2,043.8	250.3	17,838.6	12.2%	8.7	71.3
Apr-99	601.3	317.4	162.9	8.6	615.6	5.3%	3.8	71.6	120.1	4,273.6	3,219.4	2,107.7	234.8	17,781.5	11.1%	8.4	75.7
May-99	613.3	317.0	167.1	8.3	609.2	5.0%	3.6	73.4	125.5	4,398.0	3,194.8	2,222.4	232.4	17,295.8	10.5%	7.8	74.4
Jun-99	610.0	317.8	167.6	7.3	661.2	4.4%	3.9	90.6	153.8	4,405.6	3,128.5	2,226.4	222.3	19,050.3	10.0%	8.6	85.7
Jul-99	600.0	310.9	165.9	6.9	606.9	4.2%	3.7	88.0	145.3	4,351.4	3,131.5	2,201.4	218.9	18,965.5	9.9%	8.6	86.6
Aug-99	619.4	311.4	173.7	6.9	689.2	4.0%	4.0	99.9	158.8	4,576.5	3,118.2	2,377.6	226.9	20,326.3	9.5%	8.5	89.6
Sep-99	603.7	294.6	166.5	6.8	703.3	4.1%	4.2	103.4	136.4	4,660.1	3,123.3	2,428.7	266.5	20,475.7	11.0%	8.4	76.8
Oct-99	599.7	292.0	167.0	6.8	769.0	4.1%	4.6	113.1	147.0	4,655.4	3,088.0	2,435.2	270.5	22,175.7	11.1%	9.1	82.0
Nov-99	618.0	291.3	175.0	6.7	888.7	3.8%	5.1	132.6	170.9	5,026.0	3,120.5	2,683.9	269.3	24,674.8	10.0%	9.2	91.6
Dec-99	616.6	291.1	176.2	6.9	1097.5	3.9%	6.2	159.1	205.5	5,015.2	2,863.9	2,658.6	265.1	31,481.2	10.0%	11.8	118.8
Jan-00	615.5	291.9	176.1	7.2	1062.3	4.1%	6.0	147.5	187.2	5,059.4	2,873.9	2,689.8	271.2	30,153.1	10.1%	11.2	111.2
Feb-00	617.6	289.5	178.7	6.8	1287.7	3.8%	7.2	189.4	245.7	5,215.3	2,894.8	2,776.5	259.7	34,981.6	9.4%	12.6	134.7
Mar-00	631.7	303.8	185.8	8.6	1291.6	4.6%	7.0	150.2	176.3	5,552.1	3,305.9	2,948.1	348.1	37,755.3	11.8%	12.8	108.5
Apr-00	642.0	307.1	190.5	7.1	1098.1	3.7%	5.8	154.7	199.6	5,739.4	3,403.4	3,021.1	327.2	32,826.0	10.8%	10.9	100.3
May-00	687.9	309.3	213.6	7.4	979.7	3.5%	4.6	132.4	178.1	6,384.3	3,413.7	3,373.1	326.0	29,200.0	9.7%	8.7	89.6
Jun-00	701.6	319.8	224.2	8.3	1168.7	3.7%	5.2	140.8	181.1	6,523.8	3,461.9	3,463.7	332.0	33,773.7	9.6%	9.8	101.7
Jul-00	698.9	316.1	225.8	8.6	1119.8	3.8%	5.0	130.2	170.4	6,525.9	3,464.8	3,465.8	332.4	32,584.0	9.6%	9.4	98.0
Aug-00	720.3	308.3	237.4	8.7	1247.2	3.7%	5.3	143.4	182.1	7,126.6	3,464.9	3,916.1	386.6	36,140.7	9.9%	9.2	93.5
Averages	**628.5**	**303.7**	**182.4**	**7.8**	**883.1**	**4.3%**	**4.8**	**115.6**	**159.4**	**5,104.3**	**3,155.4**	**2,653.3**	**276.4**	**25,611.9**	**10.5%**	**9.6**	**91.7**

[a]Domestic common stocks and shares of beneficial interest only. Total market value divided by earnings ($ millions).
Data source: http://www.nasd.com.

be described as having fairly modest levels of profitability. During recent years, the rate of return on stockholders' equity (ROE) for Nasdaq companies has averaged in the low single digits, or less than 5% per year. Contrary to popular perceptions that profits were growing rapidly for Nasdaq companies, NASD data suggested stagnant profits. Little or no profit growth during the 1999–2000 period was common. In contrast, during this same period, the ROE averaged 20%+ for components of the DJIA and the S&P 500, and double-digit earnings per share growth was common. Valuation data for the Nasdaq 100 were only slightly more typical of conventional market norms. According to NASD information, P/E ratios have recently averaged nearly 100 for Nasdaq 100 companies. In the period surrounding the early-March 2000 peak on the Nasdaq, P/E ratios for Nasdaq 100 companies averaged 134.7. Again, this is a heretofore unheard of level for a major market index. During recent years, the ROE for Nasdaq 100 companies has averaged in the low double digits, or roughly 10.5% per year. In contrast with stagnant profits for the overall Nasdaq, profits seem to be growing, but in an irregular fashion, for Nasdaq 100 companies.

When considering the highly unusual valuation levels now accorded to Nasdaq and Nasdaq 100 companies, it is important to keep in mind that these are broad market indexes that cover a significant portion of the U.S. equities market. At the 2000 market peak, Nasdaq was then a $6.1 trillion market covering 4896 companies. The Nasdaq 100 represented $3.9 trillion of market capitalization. When compared with the DJIA, the S&P 500, and the Nifty 50 of the early-1970s, nothing compares with the present valuation ratios accorded to Nasdaq and Nasdaq 100 companies. Traditional broad market valuation metrics have been thrown out the window (see Campbell and Shiller, 1998; Chan, Karceski, and Lakonishok, 2000). After the most rampant bull stampede in stock market history, the average P/E on the Nasdaq was now 6–8 times higher than the P/E of the DJIA. The average P/E on the Nasdaq was more than 4–6 times higher than the P/E of the S&P 500. At peak valuation levels, Nasdaq valuation was greater than the Japanese market, the world's second largest stock market, and no modern financial market was ever accorded such an optimistic valuation.

V. CONCLUSION

During the late-1990s, the investment attention and economic resources of growth stock investors became riveted on the Nasdaq 100. Not since the early-1970s, and the days of the Nifty 50, had U.S. investor interest been so narrowly focused on a relative handful of growth stock favorites. Never before had a group of U.S. stocks been accorded the P/E multiple and extreme market capitalizations accorded to the Nasdaq 100 during the period leading up to the 2000 market peak. In a U.S. investment environment where conventional P/E ratios for the most successful corporations tend to fall in a broad range from 10 to 20, P/E ratios of roughly 100 for the Nasdaq 100 can only be described as extraordinary. Similarly, in an investment environment where decade-long, double-digit EPS growth is rarely achieved, conventional expectations of 20–50% long-term EPS growth for tech stock favorites can only be described as unreasonable. The extreme valuations accorded to the Nasdaq 100 stocks in early-2000 should have caused seasoned investors to ask if the extreme market capitalizations were indicative of a stock market bubble.

Many financial economists and market observers argue that stock market prices sometimes reflect a bubble component. These critics of efficient markets theory point out that conventional theory cannot account for unusual periods of volatility in security prices. Similarly, conventional economic analysis of stock market fundamentals sometimes fails to explain extreme valuations for individual equities and market sectors. This is the situation with respect to the Nasdaq 100 during the period leading up to the 2000 market peak. Extreme valuation levels accorded to these tech stock favorites were simply way too high to be consistent with a century of stock market evidence. Two possible explanations are obvious.

On the one hand, perhaps a comparison of recent Nasdaq 100 valuation to the Nifty 50 of the early-1970s and to conventional U.S. investment experience is inappropriate. In the late-1990s, some market observers argued that we had entered into a "new era" where extraordinary stock market expectations were reasonable and warranted. Advocates of the efficient market hypothesis argue that the gap between Nasdaq 100 valuations and conventional economic reasoning can be explained by gaps in understanding. According to efficient market hypothesis theory, stock market prices are always right. When stock market analysts fail to grasp the underpinnings of current stock prices, it is their ignorance that needs to be rectified rather than stock prices that need correcting.

On the other hand, it is possible that present-day investors embraced a select handful of high-tech favorites and pushed them to valuations that will later be judged to be "too high" or "crazy." This has happened before with commodities so prosaic as 17th century tulips in Holland (see Hirschey, 1998) and in broader markets such as the Japanese stock market of the late 1980s. This line of reasoning suggests it is possible that the efficient market hypothesis gives useful but not complete guidance regarding asset pricing. In that case, most stocks can be expected to be properly priced most of the time. No one should be surprised if a few hard-to-value equities display unusual prices all the time (e.g., short squeeze candidates). In rare instances, a typically efficient market might well display anomalous pricing of certain investor favorites, such as Nasdaq 100 stocks, the new Nifty 50.

VI. REFERENCES

Benartzi, S., Michaely, R., and R. T. (1997). Do Changes in Dividends Signal the Future or the Past? *Journal of Finance* 52, 1007–1034.

Campbell, J. Y. and Shiller, R. J. (1998). Valuation Ratios and the Long-Run Stock Market Outlook. *Journal of Portfolio Management* 24, 11–26.

Chan, L. K. C., Karceski, J., and Lakonishok, J. (2000). New Paradigm or Same Old Hype in Equity Investing? *Financial Analysts Journal* 56, 23–36.

Hirschey, M. (1998). How Much Is a Tulip Worth? *Financial Analysts Journal* 54, 11–17.

Hirschey, M. (2001). Cisco and the Kids. *Financial Analysts Journal* 57, 48–59.

Siegel, J. J. (1994). *Stocks for the Long Run*. New York: Irwin Professional Publishing.

Siegel, J. J. (1995). The Nifty-fifty Revisited: Do Growth Stocks Ultimately Justify Their Price? *Journal of Portfolio Management* 21, 8–20.

2

WHAT CAUSED
THE TECH BUBBLE?

In the period leading up to the 2000 market peak, a spirited debate raged among market professionals and academics as to whether stock prices always correspond to fundamental values, where fundamental value is defined as the present value of the expected payoff from future dividends, share repurchases, and so on. According to the efficient market hypothesis, stock prices fluctuate only when investors respond to new information concerning changes in market fundamentals (e.g., see Malkiel and Yexiao, 1997). The efficient market hypothesis implies that whatever change occurs in stock prices is inherently unpredictable and can be completely accounted for by new fundamental information. An important implication is that the best forecast for tomorrow's stock price is today's price. For every security at every point in time, prices fairly reflect all that can be known about future prospects. In a perfectly efficient market, stocks cannot be undervalued or overvalued. Neither are there good or bad times to purchase stocks. From an efficient markets perspective, the dominant investment strategy is to simply buy and hold a diversified portfolio.

In the aftermath of the 2000–02 crash, most market professionals and many academics now concede that the stock market, in general, and the prices of tech stocks, in particular, were simply too high at the 2000 market peak.[1] This chapter

---

[1]For early analyses of the recent bubble in high-tech stock prices, see Hirschey (1998, 2001a).

asks how such a divergence between stock prices and underlying economic fundamentals could result. Clues are provided by recent discoveries of accounting fraud and other corporate malfeasance at leading high-tech companies. In the late-1990s, at least some leading corporations failed to provide investors with accurate operating information. In other instances, unscrupulous stock promoters and basic gaps in understanding about the risks and potential rewards of tech stock investing led investors to pay exorbitant prices.

I. EFFICIENT MARKET HYPOTHESIS

The efficient market hypothesis states that security prices fully reflect all available information. The implications of this simple premise are truly profound. Individual and professional investors buy and sell stocks under the assumption that they have discovered a divergence between intrinsic value and market price. When market price is below perceived intrinsic value, buyers aggressively acquire and bid up the price of such securities. When market price is above perceived intrinsic value, sellers aggressively abandon such securities and prices fall.

However, it is worth remembering that every transaction includes both buyers and sellers. Through their market activity, each buyer and each seller is behaving in such a way as to imply that they somehow know more than the person acting on the other side of each transaction. If the stock and bond markets are perfectly efficient and current prices fully reflect all available information, then neither buyers nor sellers have an informational advantage. In an efficient market, both buyers and sellers have the same exact set of information.

In such circumstances, buying and selling securities in an attempt to outperform the market is a game of chance rather than skill. In other words, in an efficient market there is a 50/50 chance that the buyer will profit at the expense of the seller. Similarly, there is a 50/50 chance that the seller will profit at the expense of the buyer.

Within the context of the efficient market hypothesis, important characteristics of a perfectly competitive securities market include the following:

- New information arrives at the marketplace in an independent and random fashion.
- Investors rapidly adjust stock prices to reflect new information.
- Current stock prices reflect all relevant risk and return information.

The efficient market hypothesis can be viewed as a simple statement of the effectiveness with which financial securities such as stocks and bonds are priced. It implies that with the near-perfect distribution of financial information that is typical of our electronic society, stock prices accurately reflect everything that is known. As a result, stock prices only change when new information comes to the market. However, because new information cannot be anticipated, there is no way for the average investor to gain an edge.

II. THE TIME SERIES OF STOCK PRICES

Most investors are well aware of the fact that stock market indexes move together over extended time frames. For example, as shown in Fig. 2.1, during the 5-year period from April 1, 1995, to March 31, 2000, the Dow Jones Industrial Average (DJIA) went on an unprecedented run from 4168.4 to 10,921.9. This stunning advance of 162.0% represented a compound annual rate of growth before dividends of 21.2% per year. During this same time frame, the Standard & Poor's (S&P) 500 Index jumped from 501.9 to 1498.6 or 198.6 and 24.5% per year, while the Nasdaq leapt from 818.1 to 4572.8, an astonishing run of 459.0%, or 41.1% per year.

As shown in Fig. 2.1, the DJIA, S&P 500, and Nasdaq indexes move together over this time frame. Market indexes typically move up or down together. In statistical terms, these measures of overall market performance are correlated over time. Whenever the movement of stock prices over time is being analyzed, these data are described as a time series of market data. Correlation is said to be high and positive when large values of one index set are associated with large values of another index. A correlation coefficient of +100% indicates perfect positive correlation. Correlation is said to be high and negative when large values of one index set are associated with small values of another index. A correlation coefficient of −100% indicates perfect negative or inverse correlation. When the values of market indexes are unrelated to each other, their correlation is near zero. A correlation coefficient of 0% indicates that two sets of data have no relation.

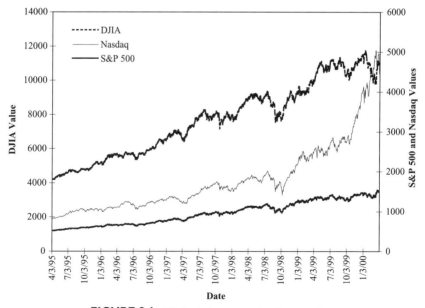

FIGURE 2.1   Market indexes move together over time.

TABLE 2.1   **The Degree of Correlation Shows How Stock Market Indexes Move Together**

	DJIA	S&P 500	Nasdaq
DJIA	100.00%		
S&P 500	93.72%	100.00%	
Nasdaq	66.12%	80.97%	100.00%

Note: Data are for the 5-year period from 4/1/95 to 3/31/00.
Data source: http://finance.yahoo.com.

Over this time frame, the correlation coefficient between daily returns for the DJIA and the S&P 500 is 93.72% (Table 2.1). These two indexes closely capture movement among large-cap stocks and are similarly influenced by changes in interest rates and economic conditions. The correlation coefficient between daily returns for the DJIA and the Nasdaq is only 66.12%. This is consistent with the observation that over this period the DJIA and the Nasdaq indexes captured somewhat different aspects of the long-term advance in stock prices. The DJIA is dominated by established and diversified firms that represent a broad cross-section of U.S. industry. By way of contrast, during this period, the Nasdaq Index was dominated by large high-tech stocks such as Microsoft Corp., Intel Corp., Cisco Systems, Inc., MCI WORLDCOM, Inc., and Dell Computer Corp. Although none of these companies was included in the DJIA during this period, all were important components of the S&P 500. Thus, it comes as no surprise that the correlation of 80.97% between the S&P 500 and the Nasdaq tends to be somewhat greater than the correlation between the DJIA and the Nasdaq.

III. DAILY RETURNS

In any given year during the post-World War II period, the expected rate of return on a diversified portfolio of common stocks is roughly 12–14%, the long-term average rate of return. This means that market indexes, such as the DJIA and the S&P 500, typically advance at low double-digit rates. There are good economic reasons why stocks typically go up in price. Because stocks represent part ownership in real businesses, they benefit from economic growth made possible by technical progress and a growing population.

Although stocks can be counted on to advance over long periods of time, it is important to recognize that day-to-day changes in stock prices occur in an irregular and unpredictable pattern. Figure 2.2 shows the pattern of daily returns for the DJIA, S&P 500, and Nasdaq Indexes over the 5-year period from 4/1/95 to 3/31/00. Notice how closely centered these daily returns are around zero. In fact, the average daily return on the DJIA over this period was a scant 0.08%. During this same period, the average daily return on the S&P 500 was 0.09% and

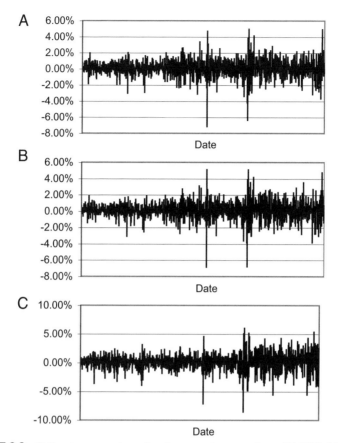

FIGURE 2.2 Daily returns are noisy and random around a mean of zero. (A) DJIA daily returns; (B) S&P 500 daily returns; and (C) Nasdaq daily returns.

on the Nasdaq Index it was 0.15%. As shown in Fig. 2.2, this was a period of unusually robust growth in the market, so the daily returns shown in Fig. 2.2 are well above historical norms, on average. In fact, these average daily returns were roughly double the long-term averages.

Even during a period of historical market returns, it is interesting to note how commonly negative-return days occur. With respect to the DJIA, for example, Table 2.2 shows that 679 of 1261 trading days were positive-return days and 579 return days were negative. During one of the most robust five-year periods in stock market history, the DJIA experienced a downtick on 45.9% of all trading days! Significant volatility in the daily returns of the S&P 500 and the Nasdaq Index are also evident over this period. On 566, or 44.9%, of all trading days, the S&P 500 experienced negative returns, whereas the Nasdaq Index went down on 530, or 42.0%, of all trading days.

TABLE 2.2 Daily Market Returns Fluctuate Around a Mean of Roughly 0%

Bin	DJIA frequency	S&P 500 frequency	Nasdaq frequency
−10.00%	0	0	0
−7.50%	0	0	1
−5.00%	2	2	3
−4.00%	1	0	5
−3.00%	6	7	22
−2.75%	4	3	9
−2.50%	4	8	14
−2.25%	10	2	15
−2.00%	12	15	11
−1.75%	13	20	22
−1.50%	23	20	34
−1.25%	26	31	35
−1.00%	36	30	36
−0.75%	78	63	53
−0.50%	78	90	87
−0.25%	126	117	92
0.00%	163	159	91
0.25%	157	158	117
0.50%	123	138	112
0.75%	99	114	112
1.00%	107	92	98
1.25%	71	65	76
1.50%	41	39	46
1.75%	23	29	43
2.00%	24	19	32
2.25%	12	13	22
2.50%	8	7	18
2.75%	4	9	17
3.00%	1	3	9
4.00%	5	4	19
5.00%	4	2	6
7.50%	0	2	4
10.00%	0	0	0
More	0	0	0
Average	0.08%	0.09%	0.15%
Standard deviation	1.04%	1.05%	1.43%
Positive	679	694	731
Negative	579	566	530
Unchanged	3	1	0
Total days	1261	1261	1261

Note: Data are for the five-year period from 4/1/95 to 3/31/00.
Data source: http://finance.yahoo.com.

As depicted in Fig. 2.2 and Table 2.2, there is significant day-to-day volatility in stock market returns. This means that there is a significant amount of dispersion around the average daily return. During this five-year time frame, the standard deviation of daily returns averaged more than 1%, or more than 10 times the average daily return. This means that the typical daily deviation in stock market returns tends to be far greater than the average daily return. No wonder day traders and other short-term speculators have a difficult time in deciphering the short-term direction of the market! Up-days seem to be closely followed by down-days in a day-to-day pattern that appears essentially chaotic.

As shown in Table 2.2, daily returns are clearly centered in the region around zero, with small positive daily returns on the order of 0.00–0.25% most common. Notice how the frequency of large up-days tends to diminish as the magnitude of the advance grows. Notice too how the frequency of declining markets tends to diminish with the size of the daily downtick. From a statistical perspective, the distribution of daily returns closely resembles a normal distribution, or bell-shaped curve, with an average daily return around zero.

IV. RANDOM WALK CONCEPT

Closely tied to the idea of the efficient markets is the concept of a random walk. A random walk is an irregular pattern of numbers that defy prediction. With respect to the stock market, random walk theory asserts that stock-price movements do not follow any pattern or trend. As a result, past price action cannot be used to predict future price movements. All subsequent price changes represent arbitrary departures from previous prices.

Random walk theory goes back a long way. Much of the random walk theory can be traced to a French mathematician named Louis Bachelier who wrote a famous Ph.D. dissertation titled *The Theory of Speculation* in 1900. Bachelier's work includes insights and commentary that are still remarkable today. A century ago, Bachelier came to the conclusion that the mathematical expectation of the speculator's profit is zero when stock prices follow a random walk. He described this market situation as a fair game in which the professional and the novice alike face the exact same chance for success. Unfortunately, Bachelier's insights were so far ahead of the times that they went largely unnoticed for more than 50 years, until his work was rediscovered and eventually translated into English.

The reasoning behind the random walk concept as it applies to the stock market is disarmingly simple. Securities markets are flooded with tens of thousands of intelligent, well-paid, and well-educated professional investors and security analysts. Millions of similarly capable individual investors are also standing by. All such market participants are constantly seeking undervalued securities to buy and overvalued securities to sell. The more contestants in the market, the faster the dissemination of relevant information, and the more efficient the market becomes.

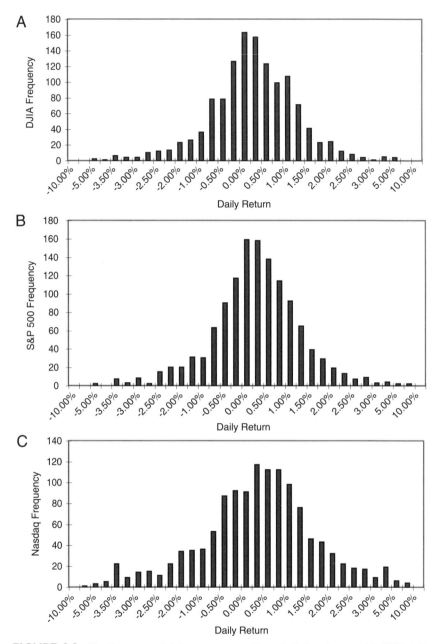

FIGURE 2.3 The frequency of daily returns resembles a bell-shaped curve. (A) DJIA daily returns; (B) S&P 500 daily returns; and (C) Nasdaq daily returns. Note that data are for the five-year period from 4/1/95 to 3/31/00. (Data source: http://finance.yahoo.com.)

When new information arises about a stock or the market as a whole, the news spreads very quickly and tends to be quickly reflected in security prices. The logic of the random walk idea is not that market prices are erratic. It is simply that when the flow of information is unimpeded, all of today's news is reflected in today's stock prices. Tomorrow's price changes reflect only tomorrow's news. By definition, news is unpredictable and random. Thus, price changes that result when news is released must also be unpredictable and random.

Although stocks can be expected to advance over long periods of time, day-to-day rates of return in the stock market can be expected to exhibit what might be called a random walk with drift. Daily rates of return on commons stocks have a slight upward bias, or upward drift, given the long-term positive expectation for investor rates of return. Still, random walk theory asserts that the overwhelming characteristic of short-term rates of return in the stock market is their unpredictability.

As shown in Fig. 2.3, the distribution of daily returns on major stock market indexes closely resembles a normal distribution, or bell-shaped curve, with an average daily return around zero. This is the essential characteristic of a daily return pattern that resembles the conceptual prediction of random walk theory.

V. RANDOM WALK RESEARCH

The efficient market debate has resulted in literally thousands of empirical studies attempting to determine the extent to which specific markets can be judged efficient. Many amateur investors are surprised to learn that a tremendous amount of stock market evidence has accumulated to support the notion that short-term stock prices follow a random walk.

Early tests of the efficient market hypothesis focused on technical analysis, or the use of patterns in historical stock prices and trading volume activity to predict future stock prices. Common techniques include strategies based on relative strength, moving averages, and support and resistance. Practitioners of technical analysis, called chartists, are especially threatened by theory and empirical evidence that supports the efficient market hypothesis. If stock prices do indeed follow a random walk, then there are no predictable patterns or trends in stock prices and technical analysis is worthless. That is just what empirical evidence on technical analysis tends to suggest.

Almost all studies on technical analysis have found that trading strategies based on past trends in prices and trading activity are completely useless. Even in those instances in which traders or stock analysts have detected inexplicable regularities in the pattern of historical stock market returns, transaction costs and/or tax penalties tend to reduce, if not eliminate, such advantages. The overwhelming majority of researchers that have tested technical trading systems conclude that prices adjust rapidly to stock market information and that technical analysis provides no advantage to investors. As a result, it is generally accepted today that the central proposition of charting is absolutely false. Investors who follow technical trading rules to guide their buying and selling will accomplish nothing but to increase substantially the brokerage charges that they pay. Indeed, there has been remarkable uniformity in the conclusions of studies done on all forms of technical analysis. None has consistently outperformed a simple buy-and-hold strategy.

The findings from random walk research seem to eliminate the possibility of bubbles in the stock market. The bubble phenomenon is popularly understood to mean an extraordinary and unsustainable rise in stock prices followed by a sharp crash. However, random walk research clearly documents that short-term changes in stock prices are uncorrelated. In the short run, there is no reason to fear a downtick following an uptick; short-run upticks and downticks in the stock market are uncorrelated. The very existence of stock market bubbles rests on the conflicting hypothesis that long-run rates of return are negatively correlated in the stock market, especially in the case of extreme outliers.

VI. STOCK MARKET BUBBLES

Critics of the efficient market hypothesis argue that the volatility of security prices is sometimes too high to be justified by changes in market fundamentals (e.g., see Shiller, 1989; Statman, 1999; and Thaler, 1999). In addition, some traders and financial analysts claim that new information about market fundamentals provides only a partial explanation of observed price fluctuations. These critics acknowledge that long-term movements in securities prices correspond to changes in market fundamentals, but they argue that short-term fluctuations can be caused by shifts in market psychology or events that have no direct bearing on business prospects or economic conditions (see Fisher and Statman, 2000). Within this context, current stock prices can sometimes be driven "too low" by investor fear or "too high" by investor greed. In such circumstances, stock market bubbles can be created.

A stock market bubble is defined as any stark deviation of stock prices from fundamental values. A number of historical episodes of extreme price movements have been interpreted as bubbles, panics, and crashes (see Kindleberger, 1978). Perhaps the most famous such episode occurred in 17th century Holland. A fascinating early account of Holland's tulipomania and a handful of other such asset pricing bubbles can be found in Mackay's (1841) classic *Memoirs of Extraordinary Popular Delusions and the Madness of Crowds*. More recently, extreme bubble-like prices appear to have been paid at various times for "go-go" computer ("tronics") stocks, "nifty fifty" companies, oil stocks, gold, silver, various agricultural commodities, Japanese stocks, and biotech companies.

Bubble theory suggests that securities go through periods of undervaluation and overvaluation relative to fair-market values. One reason for this may be that investors are sometimes overly optimistic in evaluating the potential for further increases in firm profits. Momentum investors may also display a tendency to buy stocks on the premise that the anticipation of rising prices will become a self-fulfilling prophecy, even when companies do not enjoy favorable business prospects (see Shefrin and Statman, 2000). Certain types of stock market bubbles can be difficult to explain in a sensible way (see Siegel, 1999). They are similar to Ponzi schemes that unravel when it becomes difficult or impossible to find other willing participants. Stock market bubbles simply burst in an unpredictable way when investors as a whole realize that prices are unsustainable.

Whereas stock market bubbles are often described as inconsistent with rational behavior, there is a class of bubbles called rational bubbles. A rational bubble reflects a self-fulfilling belief among rational investors that stock prices sometimes depend on variables unrelated to market fundamentals. In this context, a rational investor is an individual who efficiently uses relevant information that may or may not be fundamental in nature. Within the bubbles framework, the fact that investors are rational means that bubbles can exist, but obvious profit opportunities do not exist. If easy profit opportunities were available, rational investors would exploit them and they would be quickly eliminated. In an efficient and rational market, perfectly anticipated prices fluctuate randomly based upon their fundamental value. In a rational bubble market, stock prices fluctuate randomly based upon both economic (fundamental) and noneconomic (nonfundamental) factors.[2]

A basic requirement that must be met in perfectly competitive markets is the widespread availability of accurate investment information. Not only must accurate investment information be available, but investors must be sufficiently knowledgeable to properly interpret and act on such information. The disturbing recent prevalence of accounting fraud at major U.S. high-tech corporations and Internet stock fraud in general gives one pause in asserting that the entire stock market is perfectly efficient for all companies at all times. Around the edges of the public marketplace, evidence of market imperfections is common.

VII. STOCKHOLDERS AND THE AGENCY PROBLEM

Given their ownership position, stockholders are the principals of any publicly traded corporation. Managers and other employees without any ownership interest can be thought of as hired hands or agents of the stockholders. An agency problem is present to the extent that unresolved material conflicts exist between the self-seeking goals of (agent) managers and the value maximization goal of (principal) stockholders. Agency costs are the explicit and implicit transaction costs necessary to overcome the natural divergence of interest between agent managers and principal stockholders. Agency costs incurred by stockholders are reflected in expenses for managerial monitoring, the overconsumption of perquisites by managers, and lost opportunities due to excessive risk avoidance. This characterization of the conflict problem within firms has a long history in managerial economics. Modern concern with the topic began in the 1930s when Adolf Berle and Gardiner

Means predicted that managers with little direct ownership interest, and thus having their "own" rather than stockholder interests in mind, would come to run the bulk of business enterprise by the latter part of the 20th century. Before them, economists' concern with the "other people's money" problem dates from 1776 and Adam Smith, who noted that people tend to look after their own affairs with more care than they use in looking after the affairs of others.

Agency problems exist because of conflicts between the incentives and rewards that face owners and managers. Such conflicts commonly arise given owner-manager differences in

- Risk exposure
- Investment horizons
- Familiarity with investment opportunities

Problems mount because differing economic incentives between owners and managers can cause predictable, but hard to correct, hurdles that must be overcome if the shareholder's value maximization objective is to be achieved (see Hirschey, 2003).

VIII. RISK MANAGEMENT PROBLEMS

Significant differences in the risk exposure of managers and stockholders often lead to an excessive risk-taking problem. In 1995, for example, London's famous Barings Bank, a bank founded in 1762 that had helped fund Britain's war effort against Napoleon, was brought to its knees given excessive risk taking by a single individual. A trader by the name of Nick Leeson in Baring's Singapore branch had been charged with the responsibility of overseeing the branch's risk-free arbitrage business. In risk-free arbitrage, banks and other financial institutions seek to profit by taking advantage of price discrepancies in different markets. By instantaneously buying and selling the same security in different markets, arbitrage by banks and other financial institutions can result in small but risk-free profits. Unfortunately, when imperfect hedging led to losses rather than profits, Leeson began to engage in the far riskier business of foreign currency market speculation. Leeson guessed wrong and lost $1.4 billion of the bank's money. Although Leeson ended up in jail, Barings Bank was sold to ING, the large Dutch financial institution, for a mere £1.

This Barings Bank episode is an obvious manifestation of the other people's money problem. It stemmed from the fact that Leeson was not speculating with his own resources; he was gambling with Barings Bank funds. Other related agency problems tied to differences between the investment horizons of stockholders and management can also emerge. Salary and bonus payments tied to short-term performance often constitute a large part of the annual total compensation package earned by management. Thus, managers typically have huge personal incentives to turn in favorable year-to-year growth in revenues, profits, and earnings per share. This can sometimes have the unfortunate effect of focusing managerial attention on near-term accounting performance to the detriment of long-term value maximization. To combat such myopic behavior, more and more companies are insisting that managerial compensation be directly tied to long-term performance. An efficient means for establishing this link is to demand that top management hold a significant stock position that cannot be sold until some time *after* retirement. When it was an independent entity, investment bank Salomon, Inc. established a compensation plan whereby managers were required to take a significant portion of total compensation in the form of common stock that could not be sold until 5 years after the employee left the bank. Over time, traders managing directors, top management, and other employees at Salomon came to own roughly 35% of the company. Most impressively, this significant employee ownership was achieved through direct stock purchases in the open market; no outright grants of employee or executive stock options were involved. At Salomon, a giant boost to employee stock ownership was being accomplished in such a way as to preserve the ownership position of other stockholders. This contrasts with the much more common situation where generous grants of stock options to top management realizes the desired end of aligning managerial and shareholder interests, but only at the significant cost of a material dilution in the ownership interest of outside shareholders.

Many credit the resurgence in Salomon's performance during the mid-1990s to its enlightened management compensation and stock ownership practices. Traveler's Group, Inc. chairman and chief executive officer (CEO) Sandy Weill was sufficiently impressed to buy Salomon, Inc. during late 1997 and later merged the entire firm into what is now called Citigroup, Inc. Interestingly, other investment banks, such as Lehman Brothers Holdings, Inc., have also come to appreciate the advantages of encouraging top executives to make open market purchases of the firm's common stock. Managers and stockholders of high-tech companies could benefit enormously if a similar trend spread to the high-tech sector.

IX. INVESTMENT HORIZON PROBLEMS

The typical CEO of a giant U.S. corporation is 55–60 years old, has been with the company 20–25 years, and looks forward to a term in office of 8–10 years. With this demographic background, most top executives can only expect to see the fruits of their actions at the top of the organization if such benefits accrue quickly as opposed to slowly. Similarly, many managers pin their hopes for promotion on the basis of results achieved during fairly short time frames. As a result, top executives and many other managers tend to have fairly short time horizons within which they and others within the corporation evaluate investment and operating decisions. This tendency toward focusing on short-term versus long-term results is both reflected in and reinforced by compensation plans that rely on near-term corporate performance.

During 2000, *Business Week* reported that the average CEO at a giant U.S. corporation pulled in a stupendous $13.1 million in total compensation. On average, more than 75% of this total is tied to near-term company and stock-price performance in the form of salary, bonus pay, and other compensation. Salary and other compensation (such as health and retirement benefits) are often tied to longevity; bonus pay is typically tied to accounting performance as measured by the annual growth in earnings per share, profitability as captured by the annual rate of return on stockholders' equity, or other such annual measures of firm performance. Despite the obvious benefits of bonus plans and the incentive-based pay, short-term compensation plans can narrow the focus of top executives to near-term versus long-term corporate performance.

To combat the potential for shortsighted operating and investment decisions, sometimes referred to as the managerial myopia problem, most corporations now tie a significant portion of total compensation for top executives and other managers to the company's long-term stock-price performance. Stock options and other payments tied to stock-price appreciation now account for a significant portion of top executive pay. Similarly, a wide variety of employee stock ownership plans give managers and other employees strong incentives to consider the long-term implications of present-day decisions. Such plans work best if they consider stock-price gains over extended periods, say 10 years. To reflect the *marginal* contribution of a given top executive or managerial team, managers must only be rewarded for *above-average* stock-price appreciation.

For example, most would agree that Roberto Goizueta did a superb job as head of soft drink juggernaut Coca-Cola. During the 1980s and 1990s, Goizueta set an enviable standard for CEO performance in terms of global brand development, market share expansion, profitable asset deployment, and market value creation. From when Goizueta took charge in 1981 until his death in 1998, Coca-Cola revenues grew at roughly 8% per year, earnings per share soared more than 16% per year, and its stock price skyrocketed a whopping 27% per year. In light of the company's outstanding performance, one can understand why the Coca-Cola board of directors awarded Goizueta a generous salary, bonus, and stock awards totaling over $1 billion dollars during his tenure.

However, such executive rewards can only be justified if they reflect truly extraordinary performance. Because the average rate of appreciation for all common stocks is roughly 12–14% per year, it is difficult to credit Goizueta with the first 12–14% of Coca-Cola's annual stock-price appreciation. However, Goizueta's superior performance can be cited as an important contributor to Coca-Cola's above-market performance during his tenure. As such, his total compensation, like that of any top executive, should have reflected a share of above-market returns, not including the easy-to-achieve typical return of 12–14% per year.

Finally, given the advanced age of most top executives and many senior managers, firms must be on guard against what is sometimes referred to as the end-of-game problem. The end-of-game problem is the most serious manifestation of myopic decision making, or inefficient risk avoidance, and reflects the fact that it becomes difficult to discipline poorly performing managers at the end of their career. Young managers have lucrative future job opportunities both inside and outside the firm as an incentive for hard work and honest dealings with their current employer. Older managers enjoy no such future opportunities and face correspondingly weaker incentives for hard work and honest dealing. Like any such problem involving managerial myopia, most firms deal with the end-of-game problem by insisting that senior managers take a significant portion of total compensation in the form of pay tied to long-term stock-price appreciation.

X. ACCOUNTING INFORMATION PROBLEMS

Yet another potential source of agency problems is tied to management's inherently superior access to accounting information inside the firm, or the information asymmetry problem. When compared with outside shareholders, management inside the firm has access to more and better information concerning the firm's relative performance and investment opportunities. By definition, "insiders" know more than "outsiders" about the firm's performance, prospects, and opportunities. The problem is made more serious by the fact that, despite the conspicuous limitations of accounting earnings information, most indicators of firm and top executive performance typically rely upon accounting measures that are collected and reported by management. Because managers are themselves responsible for the collection and processing of accounting information, they control the reporting mechanism designed to monitor managerial and firm performance. Incentive pay plans linked to accounting performance offer more than just incentives for efficient operating and financial decisions. Such plans also give inducements for accounting earnings manipulation and bias.

Earnings manipulation and bias can occur when managers choose accounting methods that lead to income inflation, income smoothing, or both. Managers have incentives for income inflation when higher reported earnings boost managerial compensation, provide greater job security, or both. Incentives exist for income smoothing to the extent that spectacular short-run performance creates expectations that are difficult or impossible to satisfy and, therefore, leads to stockholder disappointment and sanctions. Incentives for income smoothing are also present if stockholder risk aversion leads to an asymmetry of managerial rewards and penalties following short-term earnings "success" versus "failure." Recent studies in managerial economics document the effects of executive incentive pay plans on the reporting strategy of top managers. Their results confirm that the compensation schemes chosen by shareholders and/or boards of directors have a direct influence on the degree of earnings manipulation and bias.

In the modern corporate environment, it is shortsighted to focus concern about poor firm performance on the tendency of inefficient managers to waste money on fancy offices, corporate aircraft, and other such perquisites.

Knowledgeable critics of managerial inefficiency are much more troubled about the inherent difficulty of gauging excess compensation, unprofitable empire building, and other elements of managerial malfeasance when managers control the flow of information about firm and managerial performance.

XI. STOCK FRAUD

Information problems faced by high-tech investors are not limited to difficulties tied to management's propensity to show accounting information about the firm in its most favorable light. The biggest difference between high-tech stocks and the stocks of more prosaic industrial and service companies is the amount of reliable public information about the company. Larger public companies file reports with the Securities and Exchange Commission (SEC) that any investor can download for free from the SEC's Web site. Professional securities analysts also regularly provide research reports about larger public companies, and it is easy to find timely stock quotes on the Internet or in leading financial newspapers.

Unfortunately, high-tech investors often face a steep knowledge gap when it comes to making sense of the information provided by high-tech companies. Whereas established companies with stock listed on major exchanges or the Nasdaq Stock Market must meet minimum financial standards, emerging high-tech companies often come up short when measured using traditional financial criteria tied to revenues, cash flow, and profits. Many emerging high-tech companies are new and have no proven performance record. Some have products and services that are still in development or are untested in the marketplace; others have virtually no assets.

In general, a company must file reports with the SEC if it has 500 or more investors and $10 million or more in assets or if it lists its securities on a major stock exchange or the Nasdaq. To prevent securities fraud, federal securities laws require all but the smallest of public companies to file regular comprehensive reports with the SEC. With few exceptions, companies that file reports with the SEC must do so electronically by using the SEC's EDGAR system. EDGAR stands for electronic data gathering and retrieval. The EDGAR database is available on the SEC's Web site at http:<//www.sec.gov>. Corporate filings in the EDGAR database include annual and quarterly reports and registration statements. Any investor can access and download this information for free from the SEC's Web site. By law, company reports filed with the SEC must be truthful and complete. However, the SEC does not guarantee the accuracy of filed company reports. Dishonest companies occasionally break the law and file false reports, thus triggering an SEC enforcement action.

Almost all publicly traded companies are legitimate businesses with real products or services. However, the lack of reliable available information about some emerging high-tech companies opens the door to fraud. It is simply far easier for stock promoters and con artists to manipulate a stock when there is little or no reliable public information about the company. Stock fraud depends on spreading false information. Con artists have been known to issue press releases that contain exaggerations or outright lies about high-tech company sales, acquisitions, revenue projections, and new products or services. Some high-tech companies also pay brokers and other stock promoters to recommend or "tout" its stock in supposedly independent and unbiased investment newsletters, research reports, or radio and television shows. Federal securities laws require that newsletters disclose who paid them and the amount and type of payment. Many illegal stock promoters mislead investors into believing that they are receiving independent advice.

Dishonest brokers and stock promoters also assemble small armies of high-pressure salespeople to make literally hundreds of telephone cold calls to potential investors. For many businesses, including securities firms, random telephone solicitations serve as a legitimate way to reach potential customers. In the securities business, however, unwitting investors sometimes suffer serious financial losses when dishonest brokers pressure them to make unsuitable investments.

A classic example of cold calling abuse in the securities business is the three-call technique. In the first call, the "warm-up," the broker tries to build investor trust and confidence by describing the broker's past successes and high-quality research. No solicitation for business is made at this time, the caller simply asks permission to call again if an "exciting" deal comes along. In their second call, the "set-up," dishonest brokers whet the investor's appetite by telling them about fabulous deals that they "think" they can get them into. In the third call, the "closer," dishonest brokers often frantically urge the investor to buy now or miss the opportunity of a lifetime.

What makes the cold calling efforts of dishonest brokers especially objectionable and illegal is their propensity for bait-and-switch tactics. Dishonest brokers often lure new customers by encouraging them to purchase well-known and widely traded "blue-chip" stocks, but ultimately pressure them to invest in small or unknown companies with little or no earnings. Not only do such stocks tend to be very risky and thinly traded, dishonest brokers often work for firms that themselves own large amounts of the stock. The broker's employer may have been involved in the company's initial public offering (IPO) or simply make a market in it. If only one dealer or a small group of dealers makes a market in a thinly traded stock, its price can often be easily manipulated. Some dishonest brokers overcharge their customers by adding an undisclosed mark-up to the price the broker's employer paid for the stock. Although it is illegal for brokers to charge excessive mark-ups, some dishonest brokers mark up the prices of the stocks that they sell by 100% or more. Many investors find that once they buy a house stock, they cannot get what they paid for it, even if they decide to sell immediately. Some dishonest firms follow "no net sales" policies in which brokers cannot execute orders to sell house stocks unless they find a customer to buy an equal number of shares. Other dishonest firms discourage brokers from selling house stocks for customers by offering little or no commissions on such sales.

The best way for an individual investor to fight stock fraud is to become better armed with reliable information. Even when working with a broker or an investment adviser, investors should always obtain detailed written information about the company that they are investing in, its business plan, finances, and management. Company annual reports to shareholders often give a good overview of the company's historical performance and future prospects. Although the always colorful annual report is a promotional document that places the firm's performance in the most favorable light possible, the plain, black-and-white annual 10K report to the SEC gives a much more guarded view of the company's operating strengths and weaknesses. The annual Proxy Statement (Def. 14A) also gives valuable insight concerning inside ownership and managerial compensation. Like virtually all SEC reports, most 10K and Proxy Statement information can be downloaded for free at the EDGAR Web site. State regulators can also be a productive source of information, as are libraries and investments research Web sites on the Internet.

The SEC has recently increased its focus on fraud in the division of enforcement in Washington, DC, and in the regional and district offices around the country to bring actions against fraudulent companies, promoters, and brokers. In such cases, the SEC seeks immediate relief such as temporary restraining orders and asset freezes, as well as strong remedies such as permanent industry bars, registration revocations, and fines. In addition, the SEC has increased its use of trading suspensions to minimize investor harm by intervening early in ongoing market manipulations when there is misinformation about the issuer in the market.

XII. FRAUD ON THE INTERNET

The Internet is a marvelous tool that allows investors to easily and inexpensively research investment opportunities. Unfortunately, the Internet is also an excellent tool for stock promoters and con artists. Increasingly, the Internet is a wild and wooly frontier for stock fraud and manipulation. The Internet allows individuals or companies to communicate with a large audience without spending a lot of time, effort, or money. Anyone can reach tens of thousands of people by building an Internet Web site, posting a message on an online bulletin board, entering a discussion in a live "chat" room, or sending mass e-mails. It is easy for con artists to make their messages look credible. At the same time, it is extremely difficult for investors to tell the difference between fact and fiction.

Online bulletin boards on the Internet and proprietary networks, such as America Online, have become an increasingly popular forum for investors to share information. These bulletin boards typically feature "threads" of information focused on individual stocks or investment strategies. Although many messages reflect the sincere questions and opinions of individual investors, many are bogus and reflect the efforts of stock promoters and con artists who seek to use the Internet medium to widely spread false information. Fraudulent promoters sometimes pump up a company by pretending to reveal inside information about company management, new product announcements, mergers, acquisitions, or lucrative contracts. Determining the veracity of bulletin board information is made difficult by the fact that readers never know for certain with whom they are dealing. On bulletin boards it is easy for those posting messages to hide behind multiple aliases. Persons claiming to be unbiased investors who have carefully researched a company may actually be insiders, disgruntled employees, large shareholders, or paid promoters. A single individual can easily create the illusion of widespread interest in small, thinly traded stocks by posting a series of messages under various aliases. Alternatively, a single individual can wrongly create a sense of widespread panic among shareholders by suggesting fraudulent behavior on the part of management, order cancellations, cost overruns, and so on.

Stock fraud on the Internet is a big problem. For example, on February 25, 1999, the SEC announced 4 enforcement actions against 13 individuals and companies, including 1 current and 2 former stock brokers, for committing fraud over the Internet. The filing of these cases followed the SEC's October 1998 Internet Sweep, the first orchestrated nationwide operation by the SEC to combat Internet fraud. These first Internet fraud cases involved a range of illicit Internet conduct including fraudulent spam (Internet junk mail), online newsletters, message board postings, and Web sites. The SEC's allegations include violations of the antifraud provisions and the antitouting provisions of federal securities laws. Suspected violations included making misrepresentations about company operations or failing to disclose adequately the nature, source, and amount of compensation paid by the touted company. Alleged creators of the fraudulent Internet touts purported to provide unbiased investment opinions, while at the same time receiving more than $450,000 in cash and approximately 2.7 million stock shares and options for their services.

In a typical case, con artists sold their stock or exercised their options immediately following their buy recommendations. A classic pump-and-dump market manipulation scheme involved the securities of software developer Interactive MultiMedia Publishers, Inc. (IMP) of Akron, Ohio. The SEC alleged that corporate insider P. Joseph Vertucci and stockbroker Bruce Straughn sold to the public essentially worthless securities that were not registered with the SEC as required by federal securities laws. They also paid touters undisclosed compensation in the form of cheap or free stock to publicize IMP on the Internet and elsewhere. When the IMP's price rose in the wake of these touts, Vertucci, Straughn, and the touters all sold their shares at a profit, a deceptive practice also known as scalping. Subsequently, IMP's stock price collapsed and the company ceased operations. The SEC sued the various participants involved for violations ranging from the fraudulent sale of securities to the fraudulent touting of securities. Enforcement remedies sought by the SEC included federal injunctions against further violations of federal securities laws, civil penalties, and disgorgement of ill-gotten gains.

One of the most compelling advantages of the Internet is that it allows the widespread dissemination of information on an almost cost-free basis. E- mail is one of the Internet's most popular uses. However, like any inherently useful tool, the use of e-mail can be corrupted to serve illegal purposes. So-called e-mail spam is a favorite tool of con artists who seek to promote bogus investment schemes or to spread false information about a company over the Internet. Using low-cost but sophisticated software, spam artists can send literally thousands of e-mail messages to potential investors with a simple mouse click. E-mail spam allows the unscrupulous to target many more potential investors than ever could be reached by traditional cold calling or mass-mailing techniques. In this way, the Internet has become a powerful new medium for illegal stock promotion and fraud.

To gain full advantage of the information-gathering potential of the Internet, investors must learn how to use this powerful new medium to invest wisely. To invest wisely and steer clear of Internet fraud, investors must rely on information reported by reputable individuals and institutions that can be independently verified. Investors should never make an investment decision based solely on what can be read in an online newsletter or bulletin board posting. This is especially true for investments in small, thinly traded companies that are not well known. No investor should contemplate investing in high-tech stocks that do not file regular reports with the SEC unless such an investor is capable of independently investigating and verifying all pertinent financial and nonfinancial information.

XIII. CONCLUSION

According to the efficient market hypothesis, current stock prices precisely reflect all relevant risk and return information. This implies that near-term stock-price changes are random and independent. In a rational pricing environment, investing in the stock market is a "fair game" in which the expected excess return for each security is zero. Taken literally, this means that every stock at every point in time is an equally good buy or sell.

In the present stock market environment, accounting misrepresentation and outright fraud at major corporations, the difficulty of assessing future growth prospects for emerging high-tech companies with scant historical experience, and stock market manipulation have all helped undermine the idea of perfect and free information in the stock market. As such, the basis for assuming that the stock market is always perfectly efficient has also been undermined. In such an imperfect environment, bubbles in the stock market can and do occur. Billionaire investor George Soros, among others, disputes the notion that markets are perfectly efficient. Soros (1995) suggests that subtle psychological influences can help explain certain anomalous pricing situations. In the words of Soros, "Classical economic theory assumes that market participants act on the basis of perfect knowledge. That assumption is false. The participants' perceptions influence the market in which they participate, but the market action also influences the participants' perceptions. They cannot obtain perfect knowledge of the market because their thinking is always affecting the market and the market is affecting their thinking."

Within this context, it becomes reasonable to regard the efficient market hypothesis as a working hypothesis regarding *primarily* rational investors that *typically* price securities in a rational fashion. Nevertheless, history seems to suggest that outbreaks of crowd behavior, typified by bouts of extraordinary optimism and extraordinary pessimism, can and do affect stock market prices. The age-old Wall Street adage to "buy fear and sell greed" reflects recognition that asset prices sometimes get out of whack with underlying economic fundamentals. Although most stocks appear to be fairly priced almost all the time, some stocks with hard-to-decipher economic characteristics will undoubtedly be mispriced from time to time. Similarly, manias and crashes sometimes occur when overall markets take leave of the underlying economics.

XIV. REFERENCES

Fisher, K. L. and Statman, M. (2000). Investor Sentiment and Stock Returns. *Financial Analysts Journal* 56, 16–23.

Hirschey, M. (1998). How Much Is a Tulip Worth? *Financial Analysts Journal* 54, 11–17.

Hirschey, M. (2001a). Cisco and the Kids. *Financial Analysts Journal* 57, 48–59.

Hirschey, M. (2001b). *Investments: Theory & Applications.* Mason, OH: South-Western Thompson Learning, Inc.

Hirschey, M. (2003). *Managerial Economics (Tenth Edition).* Mason, OH: South-Western Thompson Learning, Inc.

Kindleberger, C. P. (1978). *Manias, Panics, and Crashes: A History of Financial Crises.* New York: Basic Books, Inc.

Mackay, C. (1841). *Memoirs of Extraordinary Popular Delusions and the Madness of Crowds.* London: Bentley.

Malkiel, B. G. and Yexiao, X. (1997). Risk and Return Revisited. *Journal of Portfolio Management* 23, 9–14.

Shefrin, H. and Statman, M. (2000). Behavioral Portfolio Theory. *Journal of Financial & Quantitative Analysis* 35, 127–151.

Shiller, R. J. (1989). *Market Volatility.* Cambridge, MA: MIT Press.

Siegel, J. J. (1999). The Shrinking Equity Premium. *Journal of Portfolio Management* 26, 10–17.

Soros, G. (1995). *Soros on Soros: Staying Ahead of the Curve.* New York: John Wiley & Sons.

Statman, M. (1999). Behavior Finance: Past Battles and Future Engagements. *Financial Analysts Journal* 55, 18–27.

Thaler, R. H. (1999). The End of Behavioral Finance. *Financial Analysts Journal* 55, 12–17.

3

INVESTMENT ADVICE ON
THE INTERNET

Nowhere is the exploding interest in Internet investing more evident than on the Internet itself. "Dot.com daffiness" or "Tilt-a-whirl Technology" is how *Barron's* describes it.[1] When it comes to Internet investing, poring over earnings reports and balance sheets often seems to do little good. During the late-1990s, big winners among the Internet stocks seldom had any earnings, book values, meaningful revenues, or fundamental value of any kind—at least when measured using conventional criteria (see Hirschey, 1998). In the seemingly upside-down world of Internet investing, Internet stock analysts sometimes describe a lack of earnings as an *advantage* because it made most Internet stocks fairly *immune* from earnings disappointments. "How can Internet stocks have disappointing earnings growth when they have no earnings?" What appeared to matter most when it came to Internet investing was the endorsement provided by so-called Internet stock gurus and the resulting "buzz" in Internet "chat rooms."

This chapter investigates the effects of recommendations given by The Motley Fool (TMF), an investment Web site that has attracted significant notoriety for stock market buy–sell advice on the Internet. Across five different

[1]See Randall W. Forsyth, "The Best Place to Look for Info on Net Stocks is the Net," *Barron's,* January 4, 1999, 49.

investment portfolios, TMF buy recommendations appear to generate an average 1.62% rise in stock prices on the announcement day (0) and 2.40% returns over the announcement period $(-1, +1)$. Sell recommendations seem to cause a -1.49% announcement day return and -3.33% announcement period returns. Small-cap tech stock buy recommendations for TMF's flagship Rule Breaker Portfolio are associated with returns of 3.66% on the announcement day and 6.15% over the announcement period. These findings suggest herd-like behavior among Internet investors and that such announcements are more newsworthy than second-hand buy–sell recommendations published in traditional print and electronic media.

I. BUY–SELL RECOMMENDATION RESEARCH

The most popular Internet stock chat Web site is TMF, run by brothers David and Tom Gardner. On the launch date of August 4, 1994, the Gardner's had no marketing budget and claimed only 60 original "Fools" (customers) for their America Online chat site. Since then, the popularity of TMF has skyrocketed. Without the benefit of major advertising campaigns, at least as defined in the traditional sense, the Gardners now claim that *1.5 million* Fools regularly visit with them online, another *4 million* Fools listen in on their syndicated radio program, and "countless" others read their newspaper columns and books.[2] The popularity and high visibility of TMF make it an attractive basis upon which to analyze the ability of broadly published Internet stock advice to move share prices. To measure the impact of Internet stock advice and online chat, this study considers the magnitude of stock-price reactions surrounding buy/sell recommendations published on TMF's Web site.

Few studies have appeared that consider the stock-price implications of investment advice provided over the Internet, but a continuing stream of financial research considers the success of investment newsletters in the print media.[3] For example, Graham and Harvey (1996) analyze the market-timing advice contained in a sample of 237 investment newsletter strategies over the 1980–92 period. Each newsletter strategy recommends a mix of equity and cash. Graham and Harvey (1996) find no evidence that letters systematically increase equity weights before market rises or decrease weights before market declines. Thus, there is no proof of superior market-timing ability on the part of popular newsletter writers. Interestingly, disagreement among newsletters appears to be correlated with future market volatility.

Jaffe and Mahoney (1999) analyze the common stock recommendations of investment newsletters followed by the *Hulbert Financial Digest*. Taken as a whole, securities that newsletters recommend do not outperform appropriate benchmarks. Modest evidence exists that the future performance of a newsletter

---

[2]See David Gardner, "Past, Present, & Future: All We Care About Now Is The Future," August 4, 1999, http://www.fool.com/portfolios/rulebreaker/1999/rulebreaker990804.htm.

[3]This chapter summarizes two of the earliest studies of the stock market implications of investment advice provided over the Internet, by Hirschey, Richardson, and Scholz (2000a, 2000b).

is related to past performance when performance is measured by raw returns. Evidence of persistence vanishes, however, when performance is measured by abnormal returns. There is also evidence that newsletters tend to recommend securities that have performed well in the recent past.

Metrick (1999) also studies the investment performance and transactions cost experience of investment newsletters followed by the *Hulbert Financial Digest*. On an overall basis, investment newsletters do not appear to demonstrate significant stock-picking ability. Average abnormal returns are close to zero. The number and performance of the best performing newsletters are usually given the sample size. Weak suggestions of superior stock-picking ability disappear when return dependencies across newsletters are explicitly considered. While an investment strategy of buying the best past performers and selling the worst past performers would have earned positive raw returns over the sample period, abnormal returns would have been negative and statistically insignificant. Thus, there is no evidence of superior skill by newsletters over short-term or long-term investment horizons.

Graham (1999) develops an interesting model to study the importance of "herding" among the recommendations of investment newsletters. Herd behavior is said to occur when investors mimic each other by taking the same action. In the field of finance, herd behavior has been linked to investment recommendations (Scharfstein and Stein, 1990), initial public offering (IPO) pricing (Welch, 1992), and earnings forecasts (Trueman, 1994). Graham (1999) shows that followers tend to act the same as leaders when followers have little ability, private information signals are highly correlated, prior information is strong and consistent with the leader's announcement, and the initial reputation of followers is high. Consistent with the herding hypothesis, Graham finds that the investment recommendations of investment newsletters with established reputations tend to mimic the highly respected *Value Line Investment Survey*.

This chapter considers the stock-price moving ability of buy–sell recommendations published over the Internet. In doing so, this chapter also builds upon an interesting line of research that documents stock-price effects of buy–sell recommendations made in the print media. For example, Mathur and Waheed (1995) report abnormal stock returns of 2.35% and abnormal trading volume in the period surrounding so-called "second-hand" stock recommendations in *Business Week* magazine's "Inside Wall Street" column. These recommendations represent second-hand information because they merely represent the broad dissemination of buy–sell advice that had already been disclosed to the customers of buy–sell analysts. Mathur and Waheed's (1995) finding is on the same order of magnitude of Barber and Loeffler's (1993) finding of average positive abnormal returns of 4.06% and abnormal trading volume in the period surrounding second-hand publication of analyst recommendations in the *Wall Street Journal's* "dartboard" column. This study also adds perspective to Griffin, Jones, and Zmijewski's (1995) finding of an average stock-price increase of 1.1% on the first trading day after a stock purchase is recommended on PBS's *Wall $treet Week* television program. Similarly, results reported here compare with Desai and Jain's (1995) conclusions regarding common stock recommendations made by prominent money managers at *Barron's* Annual Roundtable from 1968–1991. Such buy recommendations earn significant abnormal returns of 1.91% from the recommendation day to the publication day, a period of about 14 days. However, abnormal returns are essentially zero for one- to 3-year postpublication day holding periods. Thus, individual investors would not benefit by investing according to Roundtable recommendations published in *Barron's*.

II. INVESTMENT INFORMATION ON THE INTERNET

Some analysts contend the Internet has the potential to become more important than the printing press, arguably the most important invention in communications technology prior to the Internet. While the printing press made widespread dissemination of information easy and inexpensive, it was a one-way method of communicating from the printer to the general public. The Internet is a two-way method of communication that is even cheaper than the printed form. It is the potential for feedback from one investor to another, or from one consumer to another, that makes the Internet a unique communications tool. While Internet hyperbole is commonplace, the potential of the Internet as an information resource and method of communication is undeniable.

For the first time, the Internet gives investors and consumers in New York City; in Jackson, WY; and in the wilds of Africa, the same timely access to widely publicized company financial news and information. With the Internet, up-to-the-minute global news and analysis are just mouse clicks away from large and small investors on a worldwide basis. The Internet also gives global consumers and investors the opportunity to communicate with one another and thereby *create* fresh news and information. Over the Internet, customers can communicate with investors about pricing or product quality concerns. Similarly, investors can communicate with customers about the threat posed by potential competitors. In a sense, the Internet makes the production of financial news and information somewhat more democratic by reducing the information gathering advantages of traditional print and broadcast media.

With the Internet, large and small investors are also able to give and receive up-to-the-minute commentary and analysis concerning the investment implications of company news and information. Message boards and chat rooms give investors the opportunity to trade anonymous tips and information about specific companies. Unfortunately, many tech-savvy investors appear to have little experience with calculating expected rates of return or determining economic factors that shape a firm's ability to generate sustainable profits and attractive long-term rates of return.

Table 3.1 shows a number of leading Web sites for investor information. cbsmarketwatch.com, for example, is among the best at focused financial news and information. This Web site has excellent stock-price and volume information

TABLE 3.1 Popular Investing Supersites on the Internet

Web site	Delayed quotes and charts	Investment ideas	Stock research	News and commentary	IPOs	Mutual funds	Options	Bonds	Cost
CBS MarketWatch	✓	Stock screening	Stock splits, up/down grades	Columns, earn.surprises	IPO Center	Fund section	OptionsWatch; option quotes	Bond report Bazdarich on Bonds	Free
CNBC.com	✓	Stock to watch Stocks in news Searches/screens	Std. research, insider trading	Intraday updates, columns					Free
Individual Investor Online	✓	Stock of day, magic 25 portfolio	Std. research, industry analysis	INDI Small Cap 500		Fund section			Free
INVESTools	✓	Stock screening	Std. research, insider reports	More than 30 investment newsletters		Fund screening		Bond funds	$ for newsletters
Morningstar.net	✓	Stock screening	QuickTakes (std. research)	Mutual fund columns and news		Fund section		Bond funds	Free
The Motley Fool	✓	Screens, picks, portfolios	Std. research, conf. calls, StockTalk, interviews	3× day updates					Free
MSN Investor	✓	Screens, searches, strategy labs	Std. research, up/downgrades, splits, insider reports	Advisor FYI	IPO section	Fund section			Free + mo. subsc. $9.95
PersonalWealth.com	✓	Screens, picks, strategies	S&P reports, splits, takeovers	Word on street, S&P indexes, economy	IPO section	Fund section		Bond section	Free + mo. subsc. $9.95

(continues)

TABLE 3.1 (*continued*)

Web site	Delayed quotes and charts	Investment ideas	Stock research	News and commentary	IPOs	Mutual funds	Options	Bonds	Cost
Quicken.com	✓	Screens, searches, picks, stock evaluator	Std. research, up/downgrades, earn.releases, insider trading	Columns, news from Briefing.com, S&P	IPO section	Fund section, columns		Bond section	Free
Quote.com	Streaming real-time quotes/ charts		Std. research, up/downgrades, earn.surprises, insider trading	CityWatch, Industry Watch	IPO section	Fund section	Quotes, analytics, option chains	Quotes	Free + mo. subsc. $9.95
SmartMoney.com	Comparative charts, some tech analysis	Daily screens, picks, model portfolios	Std. research (Stock Snapshot)	Map of the market, sector tracker, Dow tracker		Fund section		Bond section	Free
Silicon Investor	✓	Stock picks, most actives	Std. research, stock splits, up/downgrades, earns.calendar	StockTalk	Yes				Free + $
Thomson Investors Network	Interactive charting, real-time quotes	Stock of day, insider tip of day, screening	Std. research, insider trading	Live monitor CNBC/ DowJones		Fund center		Municipal bonds	Some free; annual subsc. $34.95
Wall Street City	Interactive charting, tech. analysis, real-time quotes	Stock of the hour, screens, searches	Std. research, insider trading, S&P, MarketScope	3× daily updates, columns, global markets		Fund center	Quotes, chains, search		Some free; mo. subsc. $9.95 up
Yahoo!Finance	✓	Screening, most actives	Std. research, up/downgrades, earn.surprises	News by industry, world markets		Fund message boards	Links	Links	Free

Data source: http://www.cyberinvest.com.

and also pertinent financial data on individual companies, industries, and the overall economy. Late-breaking news tied to individual companies is also offered on a real-time basis. This gives today's individual investors more detailed and more timely information than even Wall Street professionals enjoyed until recently. Stock screening ability is also featured on cbsmarketwatch.com and other sites such as morningstar.net. This allows investors to select investment opportunities from among lists of companies that share certain user-specific financial criteria, such as low price–earnings (P/E) ratios or high expected earnings per share (EPS) growth.

Other investment Web sites are primarily known as venues for user message boards and chat rooms. Silicon Investor (www.siliconinvestor.com) is among the most popular Web sites for investors seeking to share their investment opinions in a chat room format. While Silicon Investor does not employ analysts to dispense investment advice, many high-tech investors monitor the messages generated by popular individuals (posters) with reputations for market-moving commentary. However, the lack of a systematic method for compiling an accurate list of historical recommendations and assessing the degree of investment notoriety makes it difficult to measure the historical success of such Internet stock gurus. Similarly, many Internet investors go to Yahoo!Finance (yahoo.com) to learn the stock market opinions of anonymous posters on the company's hyperactive message boards. Like other investor Web sites, Yahoo! offers an array of conventional quotes, charts, news, Securities and Exchange Commission (SEC) filings, stock research reports, earnings estimates, magazine articles, and fundamentals. However, it is Yahoo!'s message boards that attract the most attention. Unfortunately, because users can adopt numerous anonymous screen names, it is impossible to accurately establish responsibility or measure the importance of individual messages.

III. THE MOTLEY FOOL (TMF)

In July 1993, David Gardner, Tom Gardner, and Erik Rydholm launched TMF as an offline investment newsletter designed to "educate, enlighten and entertain investors." TMF's name comes from Shakespeare's "As You Like It." According to David Gardner, Fools (with a capital letter efe) were the happy fellows paid to entertain the king and queen with self-effacing humor that instructed as it amused. In fact, Fools were really the only members of their societies who could tell the truth to the king or queen without having their heads lopped off. After all, as David and Tom Gardner (1996, p. 14) write, "The Wise [with a capital letter doubleu] have you believe that 'A Fool and his money are soon parted.' But in a world where three quarters of all *professional* money managers lose to the market averages, year in and year out, how Wise should one aspire to be?" In the letter case-specific world of TMF, the serious Wall Street advice provided by traditionally Wise analysts is indeed "foolish." It is only the fun-loving, or Foolish, advice provided by TMF that is truly "wise" and useful to investors.

Unfortunately for the Gardners, the offline newsletter version of TMF was a commercial failure. After attracting only 38 subscribers during its first month of operation, the Gardners made the momentous decision to take their "conversation" about stocks to cyberspace. TMF originally appeared on America Online on August 4, 1994.[4] The rest, as they say, is cyberhistory. Today, America Online is the most popular online service. America Online advertises a worldwide membership in excess of 30 million members, and TMF is its most popular feature. TMF also attracts a large and growing audience on the Internet.[5] TMF features a daily portfolio update which provides market commentary and tracks the day-to-day performance of 10–12 stocks held in the Rule Breaker Portfolio, plus a host of linked Web sites such as the "Lunchtime News," "Nightly News," "The Fool School," and so on. TMF's most popular feature is a nightly performance recap for the Rule Breaker Portfolio, often edited by David and Tom Gardner. Also immensely popular is a series of message boards where TMF employees and individual investors "chat" about investment prospects, hard news, and rumors surrounding individual companies.

IV. TMF'S RULE BREAKER PORTFOLIO

The Rule Breaker Portfolio is the first and by far the most famous TMF portfolio strategy. The Rule Breaker Portfolio was launched on August 5, 1994, with $50,000. Additional cash is never added, all transactions are announced and explained publicly before being made. Returns are compared daily to the Standard & Poor's (S&P) 500, including dividends in the yearly, historic, and annualized returns.

In the Rule Breaker Portfolio, TMF consciously seeks high risk using two distinct sub-strategies, believing that for Foolish investors high risk will lead to high reward. The dominant investment strategy of the Rule Breaker Portfolio is to seek companies that enjoy "first mover" benefits by being the "top dog" in an important, emerging industry. A second and less important substrategy is to devote a modest percentage (less that 10%) of the Rule Breaker Portfolio to a handful of high-yield stocks selected from the Dow Jones Industrial Average (DJIA). These stocks are called the "Foolish Four."

During the height of the tech stock bubble period, TMF's model portfolio, called the Rule Breaker Portfolio, was composed of a mix of high-flying Internet stocks (such as America Online, amazon.com, and @Home), small-cap high-tech stocks (such as Iomega Corp., and 3Dfx), larger cap high-tech companies (such as Amgen and Lucent Technologies), and beaten-down Dow stocks (such as DuPont and Exxon).

---

[4]See David Gardner, "Welcome to the Motley Fool Online!" http://www.fool.com/School/StepOne.htm; and Gardner and Gardner (1996).

[5]*The Motley Fool* is on the Internet at http://www.fool.com; and *The Daily Dow*, a Web site devoted exclusively to promoting the Dogs of the Dow and various other investment strategies tied to the Dow Jones Industrial Average, is featured at http://www.fool.com/DDow/DD.

The Rule Breaker Portfolio is advertised as a real-money portfolio. The dollar amounts described for each position are derived from an initial investment of $50,000 made on August 5, 1994.

As *The Motley Fool* describes it:
Your portfolio is a real portfolio with real money. We've made ours one, too. You make real trades, WE make real trades. You pay commissions, WE pay commissions. You have to accept the bid/ask spread on every trade, WE have to pay the piping market maker too. Your returns come right off the data on your brokerage statement, so do ours. … all real money, and adjusted for interest and dividends. There's nothing "virtual" about any of this; we all sink or swim—in the best, most Foolish tradition—with our own decisions and our own money…. We're not one of those services that buys a stock and then tells you about it a day (or a week) later. We've Foolishly designed the portfolios in our Hall of Portfolios so that they could be duplicated, if anyone were inclined to do so. *We don't actually want you to do this, and don't derive any financial benefit from you doing so* [emphasis added].[6]

Interestingly, TMF says the "the whole point of Foolishness is to make your own decisions, sink or swim based on your own beliefs. You'll never actually learn anything, or feel real satisfaction, if you're copying others."[7] Still, to help the novice investor make up his or her own mind, TMF provides up-to-the-minute coverage of stock-price changes for Rule Breaker Portfolio stocks, twice daily updates on portfolio news and information, detailed analysis of company announcements, ongoing detailed opinions on each holding, and an opportunity to discuss these and other stocks with thousands of like-minded investors from across the nation and around the world.

What is interesting, and not generally known during the late-1990s, is that America Online owned a 20% interest in *The Motley Fool*.[8] While many would regard it as inappropriate if *The Wall Street Journal* routinely published favorable investment commentary on parent company Dow Jones, Inc., such qualms were not part of TMF's online culture. Similarly, TMF was eager to extol the investment virtues of amazon.com, an important online commerce partner of America Online, while amazon.com aggressively promotes stock-advice books published by TMF.

Of all TMF portfolios, the Rule Breaker Portfolio is the most aggressive. TMF downgrades the importance of valuation metrics, such as P/E ratios, for Rule Breaker stocks because they tend to be so unpredictable. Instead, TMF urges investors to simply try and figure out whether a business will succeed in the long term. It makes no attempt to learn whether or not the market has priced them accurately. Such companies are apt to have a sustainable advantage gained through business momentum, patents, visionary leadership, and/or inept competition; to display excellent past share appreciation; to benefit from good management

---

[6]See "Introduction to the Rule Breaker Portfolio" at http://fool.com/portfolios/RuleBreaker/Introduction.htm.

[7]See "Introduction to the Rule Breaker Portfolio" at http://fool.com/portfolios/RuleBreaker/Introduction.htm.

[8]See Jean Macaulay (*The Motley Fool* Jeanie) "For Prof. Hirschey," #687 in America Online, March 6, 1998. http://boards.fool.com/Registered/Message.Asp?id=1060151000398004&sort=postdate.

and smart backing; to deploy great consumer brands; and finally, to have a share price that is depressed by a significant constituent of the financial media going on record for calling it overvalued.

TMF employs no explicit measures to assess portfolio risk. They have little interest in traditional measures of risk, such as beta or P/E ratios, that purport to measure risk based on the volatility of a stock or a portfolio. In TMF's opinion, a better measure of risk might be market cap. The higher the cap, the lower the risk. TMF often buys small-to-mid-cap stocks in the Rule Breaker Portfolio in the hope that "the smaller the acorn, the larger the oak."[9]

For example, after the market close on Thursday, December 16, 1999, TMF announced that at some point during the next five market days, the Rule Breaker Portfolio would buy approximately $50,000 (or about 5.7% of the Rule Breaker Portfolio's market value) of Norwalk, CT-based PE Celera Genomics Corp. [New York Stock Exchange (NYSE): CRA]. On that day, the closing price for CRA was $76-3/16 against an average daily volume of 276,000 shares. With a market cap of $1.98 billion and 12-month revenues of $16.9 million, CRA was then selling at a lofty 117 times annual sales. CRA had closed at 21-1/4 on May 6, 1999, its first day of public trading on the NYSE, and had traded below that opening price as late as August 17, 1999. In buying CRA, TMF once again displayed its preference for stocks with high price momentum.

In a grandiloquent 7081 word buy announcement, TMF pronounced, "We are Rule Breaker investors, and we love biotechnology. We are amazed by our species' increasing ability to understand, and in some critical and exciting ways, re-engineer the world in which we live."[10] Short on financial analysis, this buy announcement was nothing if not bold. In closing, TMF chortled "We are calling this stock grossly overvalued ourselves. We are part of the financial media and we are officially calling this stock, Celera, GROSSLY OVERVALUED. We mean, come on! This thing has no profits, no real revenue, and it has no clear business model, just a bunch of promises. At a market capitalization of more than $1.8 billion, this stock is grossly overvalued! There. That feels better. We're ready to buy it now."[11]

Apparently, so were TMF readers. On Friday, December 17, 1999, TMF did, in fact, buy 630 shares of CRA for $50,093, or roughly 79-1/2. On the first trading day following the TMF buy announcement, and on the TMF buy day, CRA traded between $79 and $94, before ending at an all time high of $88, up +11 13/16 (or +15.50%) on the day. Without any company-specific or industry news, trading volume in CRA was a record 1,695,500 shares, or more than 6-1/2 times normal trading volume of 258,090 shares per day. On the next trading day, CRA traded between 100 and 115-1/2 and closed at 102, up 14 (or 15.91%) on trading volume of 1,102,300 shares, again without any company-specific or industry news. On the second trading day following the TMF buy announcement, CRA

---

[9]See http://www.fool.com/portfolios/RuleBreaker/RuleBreaker1.htm.
[10]See http://www.fool.com/portfolios/rulebreaker/trades/rulebreakertrade_cra2991216.htm.
[11]See http://www.fool.com/portfolios/rulebreaker/trades/rulebreakertrade_cra2991216.htm.

traded between 105 and 135 and closed at 125, up 23 (or 22.55%) on trading volume of 1,065,300 shares, again without any company-specific or industry news. The sole bit of favorable news coverage on both days pertained to the TMF buy announcement. Evidently, TMF followers are eager to embrace risk by buying a stock that TMF itself described as grossly overvalued.

TMF also takes risk in the Rule Breaker Portfolio allocations. At various points in this portfolio's history, one or two stocks have represented huge slices of the overall pie. In late-1999, for example, America Online (AOL) and amazon.com represented roughly 70% of the Rule Breaker Portfolio. This has been used as a criticism of the portfolio, the idea being that (1) TMF got lucky with a couple of good picks and (2) TMF is being irresponsible by allowing these stocks to occupy as much of their holdings as they do. In answering these criticisms, TMF points out that it has never put more than 10% of its portfolio into any single holding. The only way a given stock begins to look overweighted is because it appreciates at a much faster rate than the rest of the portfolio. Having found profit-making investments such as AOL and amazon.com, TMF is loath to start selling off portions in order to fund what will most likely be less satisfactory investments. From time to time, TMF has balanced the portfolio by selling off a portion of a big winner, such as AOL, but they generally do that much later than most people expect and only when TMF believes that the money will be equally or better invested in some new selection.

Holdings for the Rule Breaker Portfolio and other TMF portfolios, as of year-end 1999, are shown in Table 3.2.

V. OTHER TMF PORTFOLIOS

In addition to the Rule Breaker Portfolio, TMF has also articulated strategies for the Rule Maker, Foolish Four, DRIP, and Boring portfolios.[12]

The Rule Maker Portfolio began with $20,000 on February 2, 1998. It added $2000 in August 1998 and February 1999. Beginning in July 1999, $500 in cash is added every month and quickly invested in stocks. A buy-and-hold strategy is employed to limit transaction costs. Rule Maker criteria are both qualitative and quantitative in nature. To be included, stocks must entail most, if not all, of the following ten "Rule Maker Essentials": dominant brand, repeat-purchase business, convenience, expanding possibilities, personal familiarity and interest, sales growth of at least 10% per year, gross margins of at least 50% of sales, net profit margins of at least 7% of sales, cash no less than 1.5 times total debt, and efficient use of cash flow.

According to TMF, companies that are Rule Makers are looking to establish a direct connection with billions of consumers, day in and day out. They like to consistently draw a clear distinction between their product and the generic,

---

[12]In late-1999, TMF also launched a new series of "retirement portfoloios." See http://www.fool.com/retirement/retireport/retireeportarchive.htm.

TABLE 3.2   The Motley Fool Portfolio Holdings (12/31/99)

Buy date	Shares	Company	Cost ($)	Market value ($)	Change ($)
A. Rule Breaker Portfolio					
8/5/94	4020	AMERICA ONLINE	1,847.65	305,017.50	303,169.85
9/9/97	2640	AMAZON.COM	8,415.03	200,970.00	192,554.97
12/17/99	630	PE CORP-CELERA GENOMICS GRP	50,093.00	93,870.00	43,777.00
12/16/98	1160	AMGEN INC	24,875.50	69,672.50	44,797.00
12/4/98	900	AT HOME CORP CL A	25,236.13	38,587.50	13,351.37
2/26/99	300	EBAY	30,158.00	37,556.25	7,398.25
2/20/98	260	DU PONT (EI) DE NEMOURS	15,299.44	17,127.50	1,828.06
2/23/99	180	CHEVRON CORP	14,250.50	15,592.50	1,342.00
2/23/99	300	CATERPILLAR INC	14,089.25	14,118.75	29.50
7/2/98	470	STARBUCKS CORP	13,138.63	11,397.50	(1,741.13)
2/23/99	290	GOODYEAR TIRE & RUBBER CO	14,127.38	8,138.13	(5,989.25)
			Cash	359.36	
			Total	812,407.49	
B. Rule Maker Portfolio					
6/23/98	75	CISCO SYSTEMS	2,464.86	8,034.38	5,569.52
2/17/99	16	YAHOO INC	2,020.95	6,923.00	4,902.05
2/3/98	59	MICROSOFT CORP	2,911.79	6,888.25	3,976.46
2/13/98	59	INTEL CORP	2,986.79	5,350.31	2,363.52
5/1/98	82	GAP INC	1,862.06	3,772.00	1,909.94
5/26/98	18	AMERICAN EXPRESS	1,873.20	2,992.50	1,119.30
2/3/98	66	PFIZER, INC	1,810.58	2,140.88	330.30
2/3/98	56	T.ROWE PRICE ASSOC	1,885.70	2,068.50	182.80
8/21/98	44	SCHERING-PLOUGH	2,111.70	1,864.50	(247.20)
3/12/98	20	EXXON MOBILE CORP	1,286.70	1,611.25	324.55
2/27/98	27	COCA COLA CO	1,865.89	1,572.75	(293.14)
3/12/98	20	EASTMAN KODAK	1,262.95	1,325.00	62.05
2/12/98	15	CHEVRON CORP	1,250.14	1,299.38	49.24
3/12/98	17	GENERAL MOTORS	1,026.79	1,235.69	208.90
3/12/98	11	DELPHI AUTOMOTIVE SYSTEMS	189.22	173.25	(15.97)
			Cash	146.00	
			Total	47,397.64	
C. Foolish Four Portfolio					
12/27/99	20	EASTMAN KODAK	1,301.75	1,325.00	23.25
12/27/99	18	GENERAL MOTORS	1,318.63	1,308.38	(10.25)
12/24/98	9	MORGAN (JP)	949.63	1,139.63	190.00
12/24/98	24	CATERPILLAR INC	1,034.00	1,129.50	95.50
			Cash	19.52	
			Total	3,597.03	

(continues)

TABLE 3.2 (*continued*)

Buy date	Shares	Company	Cost ($)	Market value ($)	Change ($)
D. DRIP Portfolio					
9/8/97	22.3909	INTEL CORP	998.70	1,843.05	844.35
11/14/97	11.2920	JOHNSON & JOHNSON	903.44	1,052.98	149.54
11/5/98	28.3741	MELLON FINANCIAL CORP	976.51	966.49	(10.02)
4/13/98	8.1740	CAMPBELL SOUP	446.18	316.23	(129.95)
		Cash		24.32	
		Total		4,203.07	
E. Boring Portfolio					
12/31/98	12	BERKSHIRE HATHAWAY 'B'	27,340.00	21,960.00	(5,380.00)
2/9/99	200	GATEWAY INC	7,255.50	14,412.50	7,157.00
4/20/99	460	AMER POWER CONVERSION	6,659.25	12,132.50	5,473.25
9/13/99	110	COSTCO WHOLESALE CORP	7,601.13	10,037.50	2,436.37
8/13/96	200	CARLISLE COS	5,264.99	7,200.00	1,935.01
		Cash		10,490.52	
		Total		76,233.02	

competing brand. TMF also likes repeat-purchase businesses because every time a sale is made, the customer is reminded of the value of the company's product. The more often such free advertising occurs, the better. To become established as a Rule Maker, a business must position its products as the most accessible and convenient in its industry. Rule Makers also enjoy expanding possibilities where future markets look to be larger and more profitable than those enjoyed at present. TMF also argues that investors will dramatically improve their chances for above-average investment returns if they weed out the unfamiliar and concentrate on companies whose products, marketing approach, management, and reputation with customers they understand and will enjoy following.

In terms of quantitative criteria, Rule Makers must enjoy annual sales growth of at least 10% per year. TMF regards sales growth as the most fundamental indication of an expanding business. While net profit growth is important also, it can be the result of cost-cutting measures rather than pure business growth. Cost-cutting is fine and good, but TMF wants tech stocks. TMF also likes to see gross margins above 50%. In the Rule Maker Portfolio, TMF also looks for net profit margins of at least 7% and financial statements that show little or no debt. They require that a company's cash be at least 1.5 times greater than total debt. And finally, TMF likes companies that have relatively low levels of noncash current assets relative to the amount of current liabilities.

Like the Rule Breaker Portfolio, buy–sell decisions are articulated before the fact for the Rule Maker Portfolio. However, this strategy involves far fewer transactions than the Rule Breaker Portfolio and engenders much less comment on the Internet and in the traditional print and broadcast media. Furthermore, the Rule Maker Portfolio's buy-and-hold strategy has resulted in no sale decisions through the period covered by this study.

When measured by relative notoriety, the Foolish Four Portfolio may be the second best known TMF portfolio strategy, after the Rule Breaker Portfolio. TMF's Foolish Four strategy is a simple mechanical variation of the well-known Dogs of the Dow high-yield strategy. The Dogs of the Dow strategy is to simply buy equal dollar amounts of the ten stocks in the DJIA with the highest yield on the first trading day of the year and hold them for one year. After the year is up, an investor simply finds the 10 DJIA stocks with the highest current yield, sells any previously purchased stocks not still on the top 10 list, and replaces them with the new highest yielding DJIA stocks. In the Foolish Four Portfolio, TMF divides dividend yield by the square root of the stock price, ranks DJIA stocks from highest to lowest using this ratio, drops the stock with the highest ratio, and buys the next four stocks in equal dollar amounts. The underlying rationale is that high yield is positively correlated with better performance. TMF also cites academic studies that suggest beta is inversely correlated with price but more strongly related with the square root of the price. By selecting stocks with high yields, TMF selects stocks whose price movement is more likely to be favorable. By selecting high beta DJIA stocks, the magnitude of anticipated upward movement is increased.[13]

TMF's real-money demonstration portfolio for the Foolish Four strategy started with $4000 on December 23, 1998, although a virtual version of the portfolio began earlier. With annual portfolio rebalancing near the end of December, there is only one buy announcement per year and little fanfare tied to Foolish Four buy–sell decisions.

TMF's Dividend Reinvestment Plan Portfolio, or DRIP Portfolio, was launched with $500 on July 28, 1997. It adds $100 every month, and the goal is to own $150,000 in stock by August of the year 2017. Due to the slow nature of dollar-cost-averaging and relatively significant starting costs, TMF does not expect the DRIP Portfolio to seriously challenge the S&P 500 for its first three to five years as it builds an investment base. Still, TMF expects long-term advantages of dollar-cost-averaging to overcome the short-term disadvantage tied to DRIP investing. Given modest regular coverage, there is little fanfare tied to DRIP Portfolio buy decisions. No DRIP Portfolio sell announcements have been made yet, given the long-term nature of this strategy.

The fifth TMF portfolio, the Boring Portfolio, began trading on January 29, 1996. The Boring approach differs from other TMF portfolios in many respects.

[13]McQueen and Thorley (1999) investigate the investment experience of the Foolish Four strategy and find that it produces below-market results.

Investors find high-tech, high-risk companies in the Rule Breaker Portfolio. Several giant companies in the Rule Maker Portfolio are bought without concern for near-term valuation. The Boring Portfolio favors stringent financial analysis in order to find the most compelling valuations in the market. The Boring Portfolio searches for exceptional companies at reasonable to highly attractive valuations. The Boring Portfolio column runs on TMF three times a week (Monday, Wednesday, and Friday). Discussions on other days are confined to the message boards.

VI. METHODOLOGY

Every weekday, by 8:00 PM EST, TMF posts updated market values for the Rule Breaker Portfolio online. Each day's market action, with special emphasis on portfolio companies, is dissected in a detailed Nightly Recap. TMF also writes regular updates on each Rule Breaker Stock every couple of weeks or whenever a significant bit of news hits the wire. Because buy–sell decisions for individual TMF portfolios are clearly announced and archived, it is possible to assess the market-price influences of TMF's portfolio buy–sell decisions. When announcements of TMF buy decisions are associated with unusually strong positive stock returns, it becomes possible to argue that TMF buy decisions are mimicked by other investors. Similarly, when announcements of TMF sell decisions are associated with unusually strong negative stock returns, evidence is generated that TMF sell decisions are repeated by other investors. Therefore, studying the share-price effects of TMF buy–sell decisions allows one to assess the "newsworthiness" of such decisions and the ability of TMF to encourage Internet investors to act in a herd-like manner. This study begins by estimating the market response to TMF buy–sell announcements in all portfolios. Then, the possibility of differences across portfolios is considered.

To test for robustness, it is worth considering a variety of estimates of abnormal stock returns surrounding TMF buy–sell announcements. First, assume that security returns follow a conventional single factor market model:

$$R_{jt} = \alpha_j + \beta_j R_{mt} + \varepsilon_{jt}, \qquad (3.1)$$

where R_{jt} is the rate of return on the common stock of the jth firm on day t; R_{mt} is the market rate of return using a market index on day t; and ε_{jt} is a random variable with an expected value of zero, uncorrelated with R_{mt} and R_{jt}, not autocorrelated, and homoscedastic. α_j is an intercept, and β_j is a slope parameter that measures the sensitivity of R_{jt} to the market index. The ordinary least squares (OLS) market model is employed to estimate the market-model adjusted abnormal return, AR, (or prediction error) for the common stock of firm j on day t, such that

$$AR_{jt} = R_{jt} - (\alpha_j + B_j R_{mt}). \qquad (3.2a)$$

Abnormal returns are estimated using three alternative market indexes. Because some TMF portfolios are centered on small-cap growth stocks, the Russell 2000 can be employed as a value-weighted market index that presents a valid perspective on the risk-return tradeoff involved with small-cap growth stocks. Findings are also shown based upon the S&P 500 and the Wilshire 5000 value-weighted market indexes.

Abnormal returns are also estimated using two alternative estimation techniques. In a second approach, abnormal returns are estimated using market-adjusted returns computed by subtracting the observed return on each market index for day t, R_{mt}, from the rate of return of the common stock of the jth firm on day t. Abnormal returns estimated using market-adjusted returns are

$$AR_{jt} = R_{jt} - R_{mt}. \tag{3.2b}$$

In a third approach, abnormal returns are estimated using comparison period mean-adjusted returns. Abnormal returns using comparison period mean-adjusted returns are computed by subtracting the arithmetic mean return of the common stock of the jth firm computed over the estimation period $\overline{R}_j$, from its return on day t:

$$AR_{jt} = R_{jt} - \overline{R}_j. \tag{3.2c}$$

In all instances, a 250-day estimation period is used that begins 295 trading days before the event date, $t = -295$, and ends 46 trading days before the event date, $t = -46$. The event date, $t = 0$, is assumed to be the first trading day following the trade decision announcement.

Daily abnormal returns are averaged over the sample of c firms to yield average abnormal returns, AAR, (or average abnormal returns):

$$AAR_t = \frac{\sum_{j=1}^{c} AR_{jt}}{c}. \tag{3.3}$$

Cumulative average abnormal returns, CAR, (or cumulative average prediction errors) are then calculated over various event interval periods from $(-1,+1)$:

$$CAR_{T_1,T_2} = \frac{\sum_{j=1}^{c} \sum_{t=T_1}^{T_2} AR_{jt}}{c}. \tag{3.4}$$

Following Haw, Pastena, and Lilien (1990), among others, a t-test is applied to examine the hypothesis that the CAR_{T_1,T_2} are not significantly different from zero. Under the null hypothesis, each AR_{jt} has mean zero and constant variance $\sigma^2_{AR_{jt}}$. The maximum likelihood estimate of the variance is

$$S^2_{AR_{jt}} = S^2_{AR_j}\left[1 + \frac{1}{D_j} + \frac{(R_{mt} - \overline{R}_m)^2}{\sum_{k=1}^{D_j}(R_{mk} - \overline{R}_m)^2}\right], \tag{3.5}$$

where

$$S_{AR_j}^2 = \frac{\sum_{k=1}^{D_j} AR_{jk}^2}{D_j - 2},$$ (3.6)

R_{mt} is the observed return on the market index on day t, $\bar{R}_m$ is the mean market return over the estimation period, and D_j is the number of nonmissing trading day returns used to estimate the parameters for firm j.

Define the standardized abnormal return as

$$SAR_{jt} = \frac{AR_{jt}}{S_{AR_{jt}}}.$$ (3.7)

Under the null hypothesis, each SAR_{jt} follows the student's t distribution with $D_j - 2$ degrees of freedom. Summing the SAR_{jt} across the sample gives

$$TSAR_t = \sum_{j=1}^{c} SAR_{jt}.$$ (3.8)

The expected value of $TSAR_t$ is zero. The variance of $TSAR_t$ is

$$Q_t = \sum_{j=1}^{c} \frac{D_j - 2}{D_j - 4}.$$ (3.9)

The test statistic for the null hypothesis that $CAPE_{T_1,T_2} = 0$ is

$$Z_{T_1,T_2} = \frac{1}{\sqrt{c}} \sum_{j=1}^{c} Z_{T_1,T_2}^j,$$ (3.10)

where

$$Z_{T_1,T_2}^j = \frac{1}{\sqrt{Q_{T_1,T_2}^j}} \sum_{t=T_1}^{T_2} SAR_{jt},$$ (3.11)

and

$$Q_{t_1,T_2}^j = (T_2 - T_1 + 1)\frac{D_j - 2}{D_j - 4}.$$ (3.12)

Under cross-sectional independence of the Z_{T_1,T_2}^j and other conditions (see Linn and McConnell, 1983), Z_{T_1,T_2} follows the standard normal distribution under the null hypothesis.

Given the relatively small number of buy–sell decisions in some portfolios, a nonparametric rank test statistic is also considered that is based upon median abnormal returns that extends a similar test suggested by Corrado (1989). This rank test treats the estimation period and the event period as a single time series and assigns a rank to each daily (or multiple-day event period) return for each firm. Let K_{jt} represent the rank of abnormal return AR_{jt} in the time series of $D_j + E_j$ abnormal returns of stock j. E_j is the number of nonmissing returns on stock j in the event period. If there are no missing returns, $E_j = E$ (for event periods of one, two, or three days), and $D_j = D = 250$ days. Rank one signifies the smallest abnormal return, and the median rank across the combined estimation and event period is

$$\hat{K} = \frac{D+E+1}{2},$$ (3.13)

The rank test statistic for the event window composed of days T_1 through T_2 is

$$z_r = (T_2 - T_1 + 1)^{1/2} \left\{ \frac{\overline{K_{T_1,T_2}} - \hat{K}}{\left[\sum_{t=1}^{D+E} (\overline{K}_r - \hat{K})^2 / (D+E) \right]^{1/2}} \right\},$$ (3.14)

where

$$\overline{K_{T_1,T_2}} = \frac{1}{T_2 - T_1 + 1} \sum_{t=T_1}^{T_2} \frac{1}{c} \sum_{j=1}^{c} K_{jt}$$ (3.15)

is the average rank across a sample of c stocks, and $T_2 - T_1 + 1$ days of the event window and $\overline{K}_t = (1/c)\sum_{j=1}^{c} K_{jt}$ is the average rank across c stocks on day t of the combined estimation and event period. Notice that the expected rank is still $\hat{K}$ for event windows shorter than E days, because the full $D + E$ time series is used for the assignment of ranks.

VII. ALL PORTFOLIO RETURNS

Table 3.3 shows cumulative abnormal returns (CARs) for $c = 96$ TMF buy announcements in all portfolios over the August 4, 1994, (inception) to September 30, 1999, period. On average, TMF buy announcements have statistically significant positive wealth effects over the (0) event period ranging from 1.79 ($t = 5.89$) to 1.51% ($t = 4.70$), depending upon the estimation method. Positive but less statistically significant valuation effects on (+1) suggest that the influence of TMF buy announcements is quickly incorporated into target-company stock prices. Weakly significant positive returns on (−1)

TABLE 3.3   Cumulative Abnormal Returns for All Motley Fool Portfolios Buy Announcements

Event period: n = 96	−1	0	+1	0, +1	−1,+1
		Mean CAR (*t*-statistic)			
Mean-adjusted returns[a]					
	0.44%	1.51%	0.45%	1.96%	2.41%
	(1.37)[b]	(4.70)[c]	(1.39)[b]	(4.31)[c]	(4.31)[c]
Market-adjusted returns					
Russell	0.48%	1.79%	0.55%	2.35%	2.84%
	(1.61)[b]	(5.89)[c]	(1.84)[d]	(5.47)[c]	(5.39)[c]
S&P	0.46%	1.73%	0.57%	2.30%	2.77%
	(1.60)[b]	(5.91)[c]	(1.96)[d]	(5.57)[c]	(5.47)[c]
Wilshire	0.46%	1.74%	0.56%	2.31%	2.77%
	(1.57)[b]	(5.93)[c]	(1.92)[d]	(5.55)[c]	(5.44)[c]
Market-model adjusted returns[a]					
Russell	0.35%	1.66%	0.36%	2.02%	2.37%
	(1.17)	(5.55)[c]	(1.21)	(4.78)[c]	(4.58)[c]
S&P	0.32%	1.62%	0.45%	2.07%	2.40%
	(1.13)	(5.62)[c]	(1.56)[b]	(5.07)[c]	(4.79)[c]
Wilshire	0.31%	1.65%	0.41%	2.07%	2.39%
	(1.09)	(5.70)[c]	(1.43)[b]	(5.04)[c]	(4.74)[c]
		Median CAR (*z*-score)			
Mean-adjusted returns[a]					
	0.44%	0.82%	0.03%	1.43%	0.97%
	(1.15)	(2.99)[c]	(0.74)	(3.4)[c]	(1.56)[b]
Market-adjusted returns					
Russell	0.03%	1.11%	0.18%	1.33%	1.12%
	(0.4)	(2.85)[c]	(0.81)	(3.26)[c]	(2.03)[d]
S&P	0.13%	1.02%	0.22%	1.50%	1.73%
	(0.72)	(3.78)[c]	(1.74)[d]	(3.37)[c]	(2.55)[c]
Wilshire	0.05%	0.93%	0.24%	1.37%	1.71%
	(0.11)	(3.58)[c]	(1.54)[b]	(3.37)[c]	(2.15)[d]
Market-model adjusted returns[a]					
Russell	0.09%	0.86%	0.00	1.07%	0.70%
	(0.95)	(3.6)[c]	(0.33)	(3.4)[c]	(1.97)[d]
S&P	0.24%	0.72%	0.15%	1.17%	0.91%
	(1.32)[b]	(4.18)[c]	(1.73)[d]	(3.57)[c]	(2.95)[c]
Wilshire	0.16%	0.89%	0.11%	1.09%	0.85%
	(1.16)	(4.02)[c]	(1.36)[b]	(3.81)[c]	(2.38)[c]

Note: This table presents cumulative abnormal returns (CARs) for five event periods surrounding announcements of the intent to purchase in *The Motley Fool's* portfolios. Three methods are used to estimate CARs: mean-adjusted returns, market-adjusted returns, and market-model adjusted returns. Market-adjusted and market-model CARs are estimated using three stock indexes: the Russell 2000, the S&P 500, and the Wilshire 5000. Mean (median) CARs and *t*-statistics (*z*-scores) are presented.
[a]Estimation period is day −295 to day −46 when returns are available.
[b]Indicates significance at the $\alpha = 0.10$ level.
[c]Indicates significance at the $\alpha = 0.01$ level.
[d]Indicates significance at the $\alpha = 0.05$ level.

suggest that there may be some preannouncement "leakage" of TMF buying intentions. In any event, average CARs over the entire $(-1,+1)$ event period average a quite high 2.84 ($t = 5.39$) to 2.37% ($t = 4.58$), depending on the estimation method.

Nonparametric estimates of wealth effects tied to TMF buy announcements tend to be somewhat smaller than the parametric results, but generally corroborate mean results. Median wealth effects over the (0) event window are highly significant, ranging from 1.11 (z-statistic = 2.85) to 0.72% (z-statistic = 4.18). Results for (+1) are positive too, although smaller and less significant, while the effects on day (-1) are nearly all insignificant. Median CARs over the entire $(-1,+1)$ event period range from a high of 1.73% (z-statistic = 2.55) to a low of 0.70% (z-statistic = 1.97), depending on the estimation method.

Table 3.4 shows CARs for $c = 60$ TMF sell announcements in all portfolios over the August 4, 1994, to September 30, 1999, period. Again, to test for robustness, both mean and median CARs are derived using three alternative abnormal return estimation methods and three alternative market indexes.

On average, TMF sell announcements have significant negative wealth effects over the (0) event period of -1.58 ($t = -3.92$) to -1.35% ($t = -3.13$). Effects on day (-1) are also highly significant and nearly as large as on day (0), ranging from -1.48 ($t = -3.60$) to -1.14% ($t = -2.44$). On the other hand, the (+1) window shows smaller and less robust CARs, from -0.74 ($t = -1.60$) to -0.44% ($t = -1.06$), depending on the estimation method. This differs from buy announcement estimation results where the (+1) window showed generally larger, more significant effects relative to the day (-1) window. Results over the entire $(-1,+1)$ event window are -3.71 ($t = -5.31$) to -3.19% ($t = -4.20$), depending on the estimation method.

Median results for TMF sell announcements on day (0), while still negative, are generally insignificant. Only over the longer windows, (0,+1) and $(-1,+1)$ are highly significant median stock-price effects noted following TMF sell announcements. The median negative $(-1,+1)$ stock-price reaction tied to sell announcements is -1.92 (z-statistic = -2.43) to -1.26% (z-statistic = -3.01), depending on the estimation method.

In sum, both TMF buy and sell announcements have significant wealth effects on (0). However, patterns for the (-1) and (+1) windows differ. Buy announcements maintain fairly significant positive effects on day (+1), but show only weak evidence of small positive returns on day (-1), while the pattern for sell announcements is reversed. Also, sell announcement results show less consistency between the mean and median results than do buy announcements, suggesting that the sell effects are more influenced by a relatively few observations. To provide additional insights into these distinctions, the next section breaks out the effects of buy and sell announcements for each of the five TMF portfolios.

TABLE 3.4   Cumulative Abnormal Returns for All Motley Fool Portfolios Sell Announcements

Event period: n = 60	−1	0	+1	0,+1	−1,+1
			Mean CAR (*t*-statistic)		
Mean-adjusted returns[a]					
	−1.14%	−1.52%	−0.74%	−2.27%	−3.41%
	(−2.44)[b]	(−3.27)[b]	(−1.60)[c]	(−3.44)[b]	(4.22)[b]
Market-adjusted returns					
Russell 2000	−1.35%	−1.45%	−0.57%	−2.02%	−3.37%
	(−3.17)[b]	(−3.39)[b]	(−1.34)[c]	(−3.35)[b]	(−4.56)[b]
S&P 500	−1.28%	−1.41%	−0.50%	−1.91%	−3.19%
	(−2.91)[b]	(−3.22)[b]	(−1.14)	(−3.08)[b]	(−4.20)[b]
Wilshire 5000	−1.33%	−1.35%	−0.59%	−1.95%	−3.28%
	(−3.08)[b]	(−3.13)[b]	(−1.37)[c]	(−3.19)[b]	(−4.38)[b]
Market-model adjusted returns[a]					
Russell 2000	−1.47%	−1.58%	−0.64%	−2.23%	−3.71%
	(−3.66)[b]	(−3.92)[b]	(−1.61)[c]	(−3.91)[b]	(−5.31)[b]
S&P 500	−1.39%	−1.49%	−0.44%	−1.93%	−3.33%
	(−3.35)[b]	(−3.57)[b]	(−1.06)	(−3.27)[b]	(−4.60)[b]
Wilshire 5000	−1.48%	−1.38%	−0.60%	−1.99%	−3.47%
	(−3.60)[b]	(−3.38)[b]	(−1.47)[c]	(−3.43)[b]	(−4.88)[b]
			Median CAR (*z*-score)		
Mean-adjusted returns[a]					
	−0.25%	−0.65%	−0.69%	−1.09%	−1.41%
	(−0.41)	(−1.18)	(−1.44)[c]	(−2.74)[b]	(−2.74)[b]
Market-adjusted returns					
Russell 2000	−0.38%	−0.63%	−0.61%	−1.42%	−1.26%
	(−1.2)	(−0.94)	(−1.72)[d]	(−2.75)[b]	(−3.01)[b]
S&P 500	−0.08%	−0.52%	−0.49%	−1.42%	−1.45%
	(−0.59)	(−1.62)[c]	(−1.62)[c]	(−2.91)[b]	(−2.14)[d]
Wilshire 5000	−0.11%	−0.45%	−0.52%	−1.43%	−1.50%
	(−0.62)	(−1.13)	(−1.91)[d]	(−2.94)[b]	(−2.43)[b]
Market-model adjusted returns[a]					
Russell 2000	−0.42%	−0.74%	−0.58%	−1.48%	−1.92%
	(−1.14)	(−1.14)	(−1.39)[c]	(−2.95)[b]	(−2.43)[b]
S&P 500	−0.24%	−0.66%	−0.48%	−1.37%	−1.81%
	(−0.34)	(−0.85)	(−0.85)	(−2.41)[b]	(−2.15)[d]
Wilshire 5000	−0.30%	−0.50%	−0.51%	−1.39%	−1.88%
	(−0.59)	(−0.59)	(−1.37)[c]	(−2.92)[b]	(−2.4)[b]

Note: This table presents cumulative abnormal returns (CARs) for five event periods surrounding announcements of the intent to sell in *The Motley Fool's* portfolios. Three methods are used to estimate CARs: mean-adjusted returns, market-adjusted returns, and market-model adjusted returns. Market-adjusted and market-model CARs are estimated using three stock indexes: the Russell 2000, the S&P 500, and the Wilshire 5000. Mean (median) CARs and *t*-statistics (*z*-scores) are presented.
[a]Estimation period is day −295 to day −46 when returns are available.
[b]Indicates significance at the $\alpha = 0.01$ level.
[c]Indicates significance at the $\alpha = 0.10$ level.
[d]Indicates significance at the $\alpha = 0.05$ level.

VIII. INDIVIDUAL PORTFOLIO RETURNS

Table 3.5 shows buy announcement CARs for each of the TMF portfolios over the August 4, 1994, to September 30, 1999, period. Mean and median estimates are presented using the market-model adjusted estimation method and the S&P 500 Index. Similar results were also derived using alternative estimation methods and market indexes and are available on request. As before, CARs are reported for five event-period windows: (−1), (0), (+1), (0,+1), and (−1, +1). Results for all portfolios are repeated from Table 3.3 for comparison purposes.

Estimation results indicate that wealth effects reported for TMF buy announcements in Table 3.5 are mainly attributable to transactions in the Rule Breaker Portfolio, Boring Portfolio, and (weakly) Foolish Four Portfolio. Neither Rule Maker nor DRIP portfolio announcements engender meaningful market reactions. Buy announcements for the Rule Breaker Portfolio cause the strongest mean effect on day (0), 2.22% ($t = 3.93$). Buy announcement returns for the Boring Portfolio on (0) are somewhat smaller, at 1.78%, but still highly significant ($t = 3.29$). Nonparametric results are consistent with mean effects. The Foolish Four Portfolio's mean buy announcement return on the announcement day, or for day (0) is only weakly significant at 1.18% ($t = 1.56$), although the median effect of 1.90% is quite strong (z-statistic = 2.44).

Each of these three portfolios show positive and statistically significant returns over the (0,+1) and (−1,+1) announcement period windows. Mean results are greatest for the Rule Breaker Portfolio (3.36%, $t = 3.44$); median returns are greatest for the Foolish Four Portfolio (3.95%, z-statistic = 2.44). Results for the (−1) and (+1) event days vary on a portfolio-by-portfolio basis. Mean portfolio returns of 1.09% ($t = 1.94$) are statistically significant for the Rule Breaker Portfolio on day (−1). Such positive preannouncement effects are consistent with some information leakage, or "front running," prior to TMF buy announcements for the Rule Breaker Portfolio. The Boring Portfolio enjoys statistically significant positive returns on day (+1) of 1.14% ($t = 2.10$), implying that returns continue to be positive after Boring Portfolio buy announcements. Day (+1) parametric results for the Foolish Four Portfolio suggest fairly weak positive effects tied to buy announcements (1.04%, $t = 1.39$), and these influences are inconsistent with nonparametric results.

Mean cumulative abnormal returns for all TMF sell announcements are shown by portfolio in Table 3.6. Statistically significant negative returns are shown on day (0) for each of the three portfolios that announced sell transactions during the time frame covered by this study. While the Rule Breaker, Boring, and Foolish Four portfolios announced sell decisions, neither the Rule Maker nor DRIP portfolios announced any portfolio sales. Negative sell announcement returns are most obvious in the case of the Boring Portfolio, −2.06% ($t = −2.96$); negative sell announcement returns are smallest and weakest for the Rule Breaker Portfolio, −0.95% ($t = −1.35$). Nonparametric sell announcement results for other windows vary by portfolio. There is some evidence of a significantly negative

TABLE 3.5   Cumulative Abnormal Returns for Each Portfolio Buy Announcements

Event period:	−1	0	+1	0,+1	−1,+1
		Mean CAR (*t*-statistic)			
Rule breaker portfolio					
(*n* = 40)	1.09%	2.22%	0.04%	2.26%	3.36%
	$(1.94)^a$	$(3.93)^b$	(0.08)	$(2.83)^b$	$(3.44)^b$
Rule maker portfolio					
(*n* = 17)	−1.02%	0.58%	0.21%	0.80%	−0.22%
	$(-2.14)^a$	(1.23)	(0.44)	(1.19)	(−0.27)
Foolish four portfolio					
(*n* = 9)	0.62%	1.18%	1.04%	2.22%	2.85%
	(0.82)	$(1.56)^c$	$(1.39)^c$	$(2.09)^a$	$(2.18)^a$
DRIP portfolio					
(*n* = 4)	−0.09%	0.00%	−0.29%	−0.28%	−0.38%
	(−0.11)	(0.01)	(−0.35)	(−0.24)	(−0.26)
Boring portfolio					
(*n* = 26)	−0.01%	1.78%	1.14%	2.92%	2.90%
	(−0.03)	$(3.29)^b$	$(2.10)^a$	$(3.81)^b$	$(3.09)^b$
All portfolios					
(*n* = 96)	0.32%	1.62%	0.45%	2.07%	2.40%
	(1.13)	$(5.62)^b$	$(1.56)^c$	$(5.07)^b$	$(4.79)^b$
		Median CAR (*z*–score)			
Rule breaker portfolio					
(*n* = 40)	0.28%	0.62%	−0.19%	0.77%	0.85%
	(1.25)	$(2.83)^b$	(0.30)	$(2.19)^a$	$(1.56)^c$
Rule maker portfolio					
(*n* = 17)	−0.38%	0.34%	0.13%	0.72%	−0.14%
	(−0.59)	(0.87)	(0.87)	(0.38)	(−0.10)
Foolish four portfolio					
(*n* = 9)	0.52%	1.90%	0.52%	2.75%	3.95%
	$(1.77)^a$	$(2.44)^b$	(1.11)	$(2.44)^b$	$(2.44)^b$
DRIP portfolio					
(*n* = 4)	0.90%	0.11%	−0.10%	−0.39%	0.35%
	(1.13)	(0.13)	$(-1.87)^a$	(−0.87)	(1.13)
Boring portfolio					
(*n* = 26)	−0.11%	1.05%	0.77%	1.87%	2.09%
	(−0.02)	$(2.34)^b$	$(2.34)^b$	$(2.73)^b$	$(1.94)^a$
All portfolios					
(*n* = 96)	0.24%	0.72%	0.15%	1.17%	0.91%
	$(1.32)^c$	$(4.18)^b$	$(1.73)^a$	$(3.57)^b$	$(2.95)^b$

Note: This table presents cumulative abnormal returns (CARs) for five event periods surrounding announcements of the intent to purchase in each of *The Motley Fool's* portfolios. The market-model method and the S&P 500 Index are used to estimate the CARs. Mean (median) CARs and *t*-statistics (*z*-scores) are presented. Results using the mean-adjusted and market-adjusted return methods and the Russell 2000 and Wilshire 5000 indexes (not shown) are similar.

[a]Indicates significance at the $\alpha = 0.05$ level.
[b]Indicates significance at the $\alpha = 0.01$ level.
[c]Indicates significance at the $\alpha = 0.10$ level.

TABLE 3.6 Cumulative Abnormal Returns for Each Motley Fool Portfolio Sell Announcements

Event period:	−1	0	+1	0,+1	−1,+1
		Mean CAR (*t*-statistic)			
Rule breaker portfolio					
(*n* = 30)	−0.61%	−0.95%	−0.21%	−1.16%	−1.78%
	(−0.87)	(−1.35)[a]	(−0.30)	(−1.17)	(−1.46)[a]
Foolish four portfolio					
(*n* = 9)	0.45%	−1.95%	0.07%	−1.88%	−1.42%
	(0.61)	(−2.63)[b]	(0.10)	(−1.78)[c]	(−1.10)
Boring portfolio					
(*n* = 21)	−3.31%	−2.06%	−0.99%	−3.05%	−6.36%
	(−4.76)[b]	(−2.96)[b]	(−1.43)[a]	(−3.10)[b]	(−5.28)[b]
All portfolios[d]					
(*n* = 60)	−1.39%	−1.49%	−0.44%	−1.93%	−3.33%
	(−3.35)[b]	(−3.57)[b]	(−1.06)	(−3.27)[b]	(−4.60)[b]
		Median CAR (*z*-score)			
Rule breaker portfolio					
(*n* = 30)	−0.16%	−0.38%	−0.20%	−1.18%	−1.33%
	(−0.06)	(−0.06)	(0.31)	(−0.79)	(−0.79)
Foolish four portfolio					
(*n* = 9)	0.39%	−1.72%	−0.28%	−0.87%	−0.69%
	(1.76)[c]	(−1.57)[a]	(−0.24)	(−2.24)[c]	(−0.91)
Boring portfolio					
(*n* = 21)	−1.15%	−0.74%	−0.88%	−1.71%	−2.97%
	(−1.65)[c]	(−0.34)	(−1.65)[c]	(−1.65)[c]	(−2.09)[c]
All portfolios[d]					
(*n* = 60)	−0.24%	−0.66%	−0.48%	−1.37%	−1.81%
	(−0.34)	(−0.85)	(−0.85)	(−2.41)[b]	(−2.15)[c]

Note: This table presents cumulative abnormal returns (CARs) for five event periods surrounding announcements of the intent to sell in each of *The Motley Fool's* portfolios. The market-model method and the S&P 500 Index are used to estimate the CARs. Mean (median) CARs and *t*-statistics (*z*-scores) are presented. Results using the mean-adjusted and market-adjusted return methods and the Russell 2000 and Wilshire 5000 indexes are similar.
[a]Indicates significance at the $\alpha = 0.10$ level.
[b]Indicates significance at the $\alpha = 0.01$ level.
[c]Indicates significance at the $\alpha = 0.05$ level.
[d]The Rule Maker Portfolio and the DRIP Portfolio do not have any sell transactions.

reaction to sell announcements on day (−1) for the Boring Portfolio (−3.31%, $t = -4.76$), but not for the Rule Breaker or Foolish Four portfolios. The Boring Portfolio is alone in having highly significant negative effects for sell announcements over the entire (1,+1) event window for both mean (−6.36%, $t = -5.28$) and median (−2.97%, *z*-statistic = −2.09) estimation methods.

Disparate results for individual TMF portfolios may be attributed to several factors, including the relative prominence of the portfolio measured by the amount of TMF coverage, differences in investment strategies, and the number of transactions in each portfolio. For example, the lack of a stockmarket reaction to buy decisions for the Rule Maker Portfolio may stem from the fact that this portfolio invests only in large-cap "blue-chip" companies that are not apt to be affected by the buy–sell decisions of TMF readers. Significant wealth effects tied to the $n = 9$ buy–sell announcements for the Foolish Four Portfolio are surprising because such decisions are based upon a closely followed algorithm that is widely discussed prior to when actual buy–sell decisions are made. Significant day (0) effects suggest that adherents to the Foolish Four strategy follow TMF's lead even to the timing of buy–sell decisions. Managers of the DRIP Portfolio discuss investment opportunities through a series of nightly columns, narrow their selection down to two investment alternatives, and make their final determination only after widely soliciting reader opinions. Thus, there is little newsworthiness or surprise attached to DRIP Portfolio buy decisions. Moreover, with only four buy decisions and no sell decisions from the inception through September 1999, there is little basis upon which to judge the strength of the stock market reaction to DRIP Portfolio announcements.

Significant wealth effects are noted for both buy and sell announcements for the Boring Portfolio. From the inception through September 1999, the Boring Portfolio announced 47 transactions, including 26 buy decisions and 21 sell decisions. It invested in a wide variety of companies, from volatile technology issues, such as Cisco and Gateway, to obscure fertilizer and plastics producers, such as the Potash Corporation and the Carlile Companies. Perhaps most unusual for the Boring Portfolio is a statistically significant negative wealth effect noted on day (−1) for sell announcements. The mean sell announcement effect is −3.31% ($t = -4.76$). During this period, managers of the Boring Portfolio clearly displayed a preference for selling into weakness. Negative market effects on day (−1) are also consistent with the possibility of information leakage, or front running, during the period just prior to Boring Portfolio sell decisions. Archived information at the TMF Web site suggests that sell decisions for the Boring Portfolio were often triggered by negative news stories. For example, the decision to sell Kulicke & Soffa on March 14, 1996, was attributed to an earnings warning on day (−1). A review of sell announcements indicates that this type of rationale was common, especially during the early days of the Boring Portfolio.

TMF's flagship portfolio, the Rule Breaker Portfolio, shows significant wealth effects for buy announcements on day (0), but only weak effects tied to its sell announcements. As mentioned previously, the Rule Breaker Portfolio follows a two-part strategy. Most of the Rule Breaker Portfolio is invested in small-cap, high-tech stocks that capture the imagination of TMF followers. While many such investments now rival or exceed the market capitalization of industry leaders, such as those contained in the DJIA, they were truly small cap in nature at the time of TMF's initial investment. A modest share (less than 10%) of the Rule

Breaker Portfolio is invested in large-cap members of the DJIA using TMF's Foolish Four algorithm.

Table 3.7 isolates stock market effects for buy–sell announcements for the small-cap/high-tech and Foolish Four strategy portions of the Rule Breaker Portfolio. Announcement-related CARs are estimated using the market-model method and the S&P 500 Index. Mean and median CARs derived using the two alternate estimation methods and two alternate market indexes described above

TABLE 3.7   Cumulative Abnormal Returns for the Rule Breaker Portfolio

Event period:	−1	0	+1	0,+1	−1,+1
		Mean CAR (t-statistic)			
Buy announcements					
Rule breaker portfolio small-cap buys					
(n = 22)	2.02%	3.66%	0.46%	4.13%	6.15%
	(1.92)^a	(3.49)^b	(0.44)	(2.78)^b	(3.38)^b
Rule breaker portfolio foolish four buys					
(n = 18)	−0.02%	0.45%	−0.47%	−0.01%	−0.04%
	(−0.08)	(1.19)	(−1.23)	(−0.03)	(−0.07)
Rule breaker portfolio all buys					
(n = 40)	1.09%	2.22%	0.04%	2.26%	3.36%
	(1.94)^a	(3.93)^b	(0.08)	(2.83)^b	(3.44)^b
Buys excluding rule breaker small-cap buys					
(n = 74)	−0.14%	1.00%	0.51%	1.51%	1.36%
	(−0.57)	(3.86)^b	(1.97)^a	(4.13)^b	(3.04)^b
Sell announcements					
Rule breaker portfolio small-cap sells					
(n = 18)	−0.79%	−1.56%	−0.15%	−1.72%	−2.51%
	(0.69)	(−1.35)^c	(−0.13)	(−1.05)	(−1.25)
Rule breaker portfolio foolish four sells					
(n = 12)	−0.34%	−0.03%	−0.30%	−0.33%	−0.68%
	(−0.82)	(−0.07)	(−0.72)	(−0.56)	(−0.93)
Rule breaker portfolio all sells					
(n = 30)	−0.61%	−0.95%	−0.21%	−1.16%	−1.78%
	(−0.87)	(−1.35)^c	(−0.30)	(−1.17)	(−1.46)^c
Sells excluding rule breaker small-cap sells					
(n = 42)	−1.65%	−1.45%	−0.56%	−2.02%	−3.68%
	(−4.21)^b	(−3.71)^b	(−1.44)^c	(−3.64)^b	(−5.40)^b

Note: This table presents cumulative abnormal returns (CARs) for five event periods surrounding announcements of the intent to purchase in the Rule Breaker Portfolio. Results are presented separately for the small-cap announcements and the DJIA announcements. The market-model method and the S&P 500 Index are used to estimate the CARs. Mean CARs and t-statistics are presented. Nonparametric results and results using alternative estimation methods and indexes are similar.
[a]Indicates significance at the α = 0.05 level.
[b]Indicates significance at the α = 0.01 level.
[c]Indicates significance at the α = 0.10 level.

are similar to shown estimates and are available on request. Results clearly show that significant announcement effects for the day (0) period are attributable to small-cap buy (3.66%, $t = 3.49$) and sell (-1.56%, $t = -1.35$) announcements. No such effects are noted for Foolish Four buy–sell announcements. Another clear implication is that TMF small-cap buy announcements are more meaningful than corresponding sell announcements. A simple explanation for the lack of a strong negative stock-price reaction following Rule Breaker Portfolio sell announcements is that such decisions are often communicated with a great deal more ambiguity than buy announcements.

In 4 of 18 instances, Rule Breaker Portfolio sell announcements involve only partial liquidations. For example, in a recent partial sale of its burgeoning positions in AOL and amazon.com, TMF wrote: "At present, America Online and amazon.com make up more than 60 per cent of our assets. This has been a great problem to have, because the only way THAT ever happened is because they were superb investments.... We must note here, since people across the Internet tend to read our buy and sell reports and sometimes put [their] own spin on them, that in no way does our partial sale indicate any lack of enthusiasm for the long-term potential of both of these stocks. We will continue to maintain large holdings of them over the long term. This sell announcement demonstrates that we're only trimming these positions down by 20%. At present prices, that means we'll still have roughly half the Rule Breaker Portfolio in these two fine companies."[14]

Clearly, TMF's opinion regarding AOL and amazon.com was more favorable than that toward three other positions sold on that date: "3Com, Innovex, and KLA-Tencor are three good companies with bad stocks. These are among our biggest losers in the portfolio, and ... we think we can invest this money better elsewhere."[15] Other sell announcements have been accompanied by praise so compelling that they sound like buy announcements. In the case of The Gap, TMF wrote: "Gap apparel is out there on the heads, shoulders, legs, and feet of Americans of all shapes, sizes, and ages. This is a preeminent consumer company and brand. It has designed products to meet all-inclusive price points. And it has branded the entire production with a commitment to casual clothing for everyone, from CEOs to students, from toddlers to retirees."[16] In sum, whereas TMF small-cap buy announcements are uniformly bullish and compelling, sell announcements tend to convey much more ambiguous signals to investors.

To clarify the relative importance of the Rule Breaker Portfolio's small-cap segment, Table 3.7 also shows buy–sell announcement wealth effects for all

[14]See "Fool To Sell COMS, INVX, KLAC, and portions of AOL & AMZN," November 25, 1998; http://fool.com/portfolios/RuleBreaker/trades/RuleBreakerTrade_bigsell981125.htm.
[15]See "Fool To Sell COMS, INVX, KLAC, and portions of AOL & AMZN," November 25, 1998; http://fool.com/portfolios/RuleBreaker/trades/RuleBreakerTrade_bigsell981125.htm.
[16]See "Fool Sells Gap," August 13, 1996; http://fool.com/portfolios/RuleBreaker/Trades/RuleBreakerTrade_gps960813.htm.

transactions *except* Rule Breaker Portfolio small-cap transactions. CARs for this set of other buy–sell announcements for day (0) are highly significant but smaller in magnitude than the reaction to small-cap buy–sell announcements. The estimated day (0) effect for non-small-cap buy announcements is 1.00% ($t = 3.86$) versus 3.66% ($t = 3.49$) for the Rule Breaker Portfolio's small-cap tech stocks. For the entire ($-1,+1$) event window, the estimated share-price effect for all non-small-cap buy announcements is 1.36% ($t = 3.04$) compared to 6.15% ($t = 3.38$) for Rule Breaker Portfolio small-cap tech stocks.

IX. CONCLUSION

There has been a recent explosion of investor interest in buy–sell advice given on the Internet. At the same time, there is an emerging body of research in financial economics on print newsletters and the stock-price effects of buy–sell advice published in the print and electronic media. Such studies document stock returns of 2.35% tied to stock recommendations in *Business Week* magazine's "Inside Wall Street" column (Mathur and Waheed, 1995), average positive abnormal returns of 4.06% in the period surrounding publication of analyst recommendations in the *Wall Street Journal's* "dartboard" column (Barber and Loeffler, 1993), an average stock-price increase of 1.1% on the first trading day after a stock purchase is recommended on PBS's *Wall $treet Week* television program (Griffin, Jones, and Zmijewski, 1995), and significant abnormal returns of 1.91% from the recommendation day to the publication day for common stock recommendations made by prominent money managers at *Barron's* Annual Roundtable (Desai and Jain, 1995).

To test the power of Internet stock advice, this chapter considers ramifications tied to buy–sell announcements made on the Internet by TMF. TMF is perhaps the best known site on the Internet for investment advice and "chat." TMF has also extended its reach beyond the Internet with regular columns of stock market advice in daily newspapers and a syndicated weekly radio program. TMF founders David and Tom Gardner are also regular contributors to the financial news broadcast media on cable and network television. In all of these venues, the focus of TMF advice centers around five real-money portfolios and their related buy–sell decisions. TMF promises advertisers 26 million advertising exposures (banner views) per month to wealthy, tech-savvy readers. As such, it is plausible that TMF's buy–sell advice would have the ability to move stock prices.

On average, TMF buy announcements have statistically significant positive wealth effects over the day (0) event period of 0.72–1.79%, depending on the estimation method. Buy announcement CARs over the entire ($-1,+1$) event period average 0.70–2.84%. TMF sell announcements also tend to have statistically significant negative wealth effects over the (0) event period of -0.50 to -1.58%, depending on the estimation method. Sell announcement CARs over the entire ($-1,+1$) event period average -1.26 to -3.71%, depending on the estimation method.

Such effects are particularly noteworthy for small-cap tech stock buy–sell announcements for TMF's high-profile Rule Breaker Portfolio. TMF small-cap tech stock buy announcements have statistically significant positive wealth effects that average 3.66% over the (0) event day and 6.15% over the entire (−1,+1) event period. TMF small-cap tech stock sell announcements also tend to have variable and statistically insignificant average negative wealth effects over the (0) event day of −1.56% and average −2.51% over the entire (−1,+1) event period. This lesser impact of TMF sell announcements may be due to the fact complete and partial liquidations are often accompanied by bullish information on the companies whose stock is sold. Thus, it is fair to conclude that TMF sell announcements present mixed messages to investors that have a less discernable impact than buy announcements.

The magnitude of stock-price effects tied to TMF buy–sell recommendations on the Internet, particularly TMF small-cap tech stock announcements, suggest that such announcements are at least as newsworthy as the types of second-hand buy–sell recommendations published in the traditional print and electronic media. These results suggest that Internet investors heed and quickly following the buy–sell advice given on TMF, perhaps in a herd-like manner.

X. REFERENCES

Barber, B. M. and Loeffler, D. (1993). The "Dartboard" Column: Second-Hand Information and Price Pressure. *Journal of Financial and Quantitative Analysis* 28, 273–284.

Corrado, C. J. (1989). A Nonparametric Test for Abnormal Security-Price Performance in Event Studies. *Journal of Financial Economics* 23, 385–396.

Desai, H. and Jain, P. C. (1995). An Analysis of the Recommendations of the "Superstar" Money Managers at *Barron's* Annual Roundtable. *Journal of Finance* 50, 1257–1273.

Graham, J. R. (1999). Herding Among Investment Newsletters: Theory and Evidence. *Journal of Finance* 54, 237–268.

Graham, J. R. and Harvey, C. R. (1996). Market Timing Ability and Volatility Implied in Investment Newsletters' Asset Allocation Recommendations. *Journal of Financial Economics* 42, 397–421.

Gardner, D. and Gardner, T. (1996). *The Motley Fool Investment Guide*. New York: Simon & Schuster.

Griffin, P. A., Jones, J. J., and Zmijewski, M. (1995). How Useful Are Wall $Treet Week Stock Recommendations? *Journal of Financial Statement Analysis* 1, 33–52.

Haw, I., Pastena, V. S., and Lilien, S. B. (1990). Market Manifestation of Nonpublic Information Prior to Mergers: The Effect of Capital Structure. *Accounting Review* 65, 432–451.

Hirschey, M. (1998). How Much Is a Tulip Worth? *Financial Analysts Journal* 54, 11–17.

Hirschey, M., Richardson, V. J., and Scholz, S. (2000a). How 'Foolish' Are Internet Investors? *Financial Analysts Journal* 56, 62–69.

Hirschey, M., Richardson, V. J., and Scholz, S. (2000b). Stock-Price Reactions to Buy-Sell Recommendations on the Internet: The Motley Fool Case. *Financial Review* 35, 147–174.

Jaffe, J. F. and Mahoney, J. M. (1999). The Performance of Investment Newsletters. *Journal of Financial Economics* 53, 289–307.

Linn, S. C. and McConnell, J. J. (1983). An Empirical Investigation of the Impact of 'Antitakeover' Amendments on Common Stock Prices. *Journal of Financial Economics* 11, 361–399.

Mathur, I. and Waheed, A. (1995). Stock Price Reactions to Securities Recommended in *Business Week's* Inside Wall Street. *Financial Review* 30, 583–604.

McQueen, G. and Thorley, S. (1999). Mining Fool's Gold. *Financial Analysts Journal* 55, 61–72.

Metrick, A. (1999). Performance Evaluation with Transactions Data: The Stock Selection of Investment Newsletters. *Journal of Finance* 54, 1743–1775.

Scharfstein, D. and Stein, J. (1990). Herding Behavior and Investment. *American Economic Review* 80, 465–479.

Trueman, B. (1994). Analyst Forecasts and Herding Behavior. *Review of Financial Studies* 7, 97–124.

Welch, I. (1992). Sequential Sales, Learning, and Cascades. *Journal of Finance* 47, 695–732.

4

A DISSERTATION ON TULIPS AND AMERICA ONLINE

More than 350 years ago, a passion to possess beautiful tulip blossoms, commonly referred to as the "tulip mania," took hold in Holland. This chapter documents a present-day equivalent price of the amount paid for a typical tulip bulb in Holland during the height of this tulip mania. As unbelievable as it now sounds, careful examination of pricing records from 17th century Holland confirms that many otherwise sensible persons "invested" the present-day equivalent of roughly $35,000 in the purchase of a *single* tulip bulb. That $35,000 price for a single tulip bulb is not a misprint. It is a crazy price to pay for a tulip.

Like all hardy flowering plants, tulips are essentially an agricultural commodity. This makes it easy for growers to quickly respond to changing demand and supply conditions. Within a growing season or two, the demand for especially sought-after tulip varieties can be quickly sated. Similarly, falling tulip demand quickly leads to a downturn in production and a redeployment of agricultural resources to the production of more sought-after commodities. In retrospect, it is not surprising that the inevitable crash in Holland tulip prices became permanent. Within 6 months of the market peak, tulip prices in Holland and throughout the rest of the world fell to less than the present-day equivalent of $1, a price level that has been maintained for more than 350 years. What remains surprising is that tulip prices rose to such unbelievable heights in once tulip-crazy 17th century Holland.

For some, documenting 17th century tulip prices in Holland will be nothing more than substantiating an interesting historical artifact. For others, confirming the extremes of the Dutch tulip mania will provide useful evidence on the occasional role played by social psychology in asset pricing. Silly as this tulip mania now appears, recent market prices for tech stocks, especially Internet stocks during the late 1990s, suggest that extraordinary popular delusions and the madness of crowds is not confined to the Dutch people of the 17th century.

I. HOW MUCH IS A TULIP WORTH?[1]

To present-day investors, the tulip is nothing more and nothing less than a lovely garden flower. They grow from bulbs with leaves and stems that range from 4 to over 30 inches tall. The tulip usually develops one large, bell-shaped flower at the tip of its stem. The flowers may be almost any solid color; some tulips have flowers with two colors. Some tulip flowers become streaked with other colors because of viral diseases that affect the plant's color but not its health.

Thousands of varieties of tulips have developed from a few species. Almost all the cultivated kinds of tulips were developed from tulips of Asia Minor that were brought to Vienna, Austria, from Constantinople, Turkey (now Istanbul), in the 1500s. The name tulip comes from a Turkish word meaning turban, because their beautiful blossoms look a little like turbans. Popular garden varieties of tulips include the Darwin hybrids and the Triumphs, Lily-flowered, Fringed, and Parrot tulips. Tulips belong to the lily family, Liliaceae. The tulip brought to Europe in the 1500s is *Tulipa gesneriana*. Although tulips grow in many parts of the world, they are generally associated with the Netherlands where tulip cultivation remains an important industry today. It is also important in the northwestern part of the United States. Billions of tulip bulbs are produced every year. Dutch growers produce nearly 2000 varieties (see De Hertogh, 1994).

After the tulip was brought to Europe, it became the most fashionable flower in both England and Holland. Interest in the flower developed into a craze in Holland, called the tulip mania, between 1634 and 1637. Individual bulbs sold for huge prices. While many present-day investors are vaguely familiar with this so-called tulip mania, it is not generally recognized just how high tulip prices became during this period and how destructive the mania had become by its conclusion.

A fascinating early account of Holland's tulip mania can be found in Charles Mackay's (1841) classic *Memoirs of Extraordinary Popular Delusions and the Madness of Crowds*. In that book, Mackay relates details of the tulip mania along with his account of the Mississippi Scheme, the South-Sea bubble, the witch mania, the slow poisoners, and other popular manias. Mackay's objective was to recount remarkable instances of "moral epidemics which have been excited,

---

[1]For a more complete discussion of this topic, see Hirschey (1998).

sometimes by one cause and sometimes by another, and to show how easily the masses have been led astray, and how imitative and gregarious men are, even in their infatuations and crimes" (Mackay, 1841, p. xvii). Mackay's underlying presumption is clearly that aberrant crowd behavior in the world of investing bears resemblance to aberrant crowd behavior in the noninvesting world.

II. THE TULIP MANIA

During the 1600s, the Netherlands was a major sea power, accounting for roughly one-half of Europe's shipping trade. In 1602, Dutch firms trading with the East Indies combined to form the Dutch East India Company. The Dutch West India Company, founded in 1621, opened trade with the New World and western Africa. In 1624, the company colonized New Netherland, which consisted of parts of present-day New York, New Jersey, Connecticut, and Delaware. In 1626, Dutch colonists bought Manhattan Island from the Indians for goods worth about $24. They had established New Amsterdam (now New York City) the year before. Expanding trade and the international influence of a great colonial empire made Amsterdam a major commercial city and gave the Dutch one of the highest standards of living in the world (see de Vries, 1994). It was during this "golden age" that tulips were introduced to the Netherlands.

Conrad Gesner is credited with bringing the first tulip bulbs from Constantinople to Holland and Germany in 1559, where they became much sought after among the rich and well-to-do. By 1634, the rage for possessing tulips had spread to the middle classes of Dutch society. Merchants and shop-keepers began to vie with one another in the preposterous prices paid for simple tulip bulbs. Men became known to pay a fortune for a single bulb, not with the idea of reselling at a profit, but simply for private admiration. Later, investors began to accumulate tulip bulbs for resale and trading profits.

Prices continued to rise until 1635 when persons were known to invest fortunes of as much as 100,000 florins in the purchase of 40 tulip bulbs. Mackay himself cites examples of various tulip bulbs fetching anywhere from 1260–5500 florins each. Of course, lending present-day meaning to 17th century prices in florins, or to any early currency, is made difficult by changing price levels and monetary systems. The florin was a coin that originated from the Italian city of Florence in 1252. Made of pure gold, the original florin weighed about an eighth of an ounce (3.5 grams). Florins became popular for trade during the economic expansion of Europe from the 1200s to the 1400s. Ironically, the coin's name comes from an Italian word meaning little flower. It refers to a lily, the symbol of Florence, which appears on one side of the coin. Florence stopped making florins in the early 1500s. Many European countries, including the Netherlands, produced their own versions. In the early 1600s, money was scarce in the American Colonies, and Dutch florins along with English shillings, Spanish dollars, and French coins all circulated here in America (see Doty, 1994).

TABLE 4.1   How Much is a Tulip Worth?

	Holland price 1635 (in florins)	U.S. price 1998 (in dollars)
Two lasts of wheat	448	440
Four lasts of rye	558	1,152
Four fat oxen	480	3,476
Eight fat swine	240	1,134
Twelve fat sheep	120	702
Two Hogsheads of wine	70	4,792
Four tons of beer	32	7,571
Two tons of butter	192	6,109
One thousand pounds of cheese	120	6,980
A complete bed	100	1,410
A suit of clothes	80	750
A silver drinking cup	60	68
Total	2500	34,584

III. ESTIMATING 17TH CENTURY TULIP PRICES

Happily, a present-day equivalent of 17th century Dutch tulip prices can be estimated because Mackay gives an example of a typical price paid for a single bulb
of a species called the *Viceroy*, where the price paid is measured both in terms of
florins and in terms of real goods received in trade. This example, shown in
Table 4.1, provides an opportunity to calculate a present-day equivalent price of
the amount paid. Keep in mind throughout this example that one single tulip bulb
was received in trade for *all* items listed in Table 4.1.

The first item received in trade is two lasts of wheat. A last is a unit of weight
or cubic measure that typically equals 4000 pounds, but can vary in different
localities and for different loads.[2] Let us assume that 4000 pounds is indeed the
correct weight and that a bushel of wheat weighs 60 pounds, where the current
price of wheat is roughly $3.30 per bushel. This gives a price of $440 for two lasts
of wheat. Similarly, four lasts of rye at a price of $144.60 per ton, given 2000
pounds per ton, is worth $1152.

In 17th century Holland, oxen were a valuable source of power in an agrar-
ian economy. In present-day America, oxen have been replaced by a different
kind of animal, the *John Deere* tractor. To measure the current value in use of four
fat oxen one might reasonably measure the cost of a modest farm tractor or a
commensurate value of four fat beef animals, say white-faced Herefords. Four
Herefords are cheaper than a modest *John Deere* tractor and thus represent a conservative measure of the value represented by four fat oxen. With a typical weight
of 1100 pounds, and an on-the-hoof price of $0.79 per pound, a conservative

[2]See *The World Book Dictionary, Volume 2* (Chicago, IL: Scott Fetzer, 1994, p. 1182).

estimate of the value of four fat Herefords is $3476. Similarly, the value of eight fat swine with an average weight of 225 pounds, and a on-the-hoof price of $0.63 per pound, is $1134. The value of twelve fat sheep with an average weight of 65 pounds, and an on-the-hoof price of $0.90 per pound, is $702.

According to *The World Book Dictionary*, a hogshead is a large barrel or cask. In the United States, a hogshead contains from 63–140 gallons; in Great Britain it contains from 50–100 gallons.[3] Taking 75 gallons as a reasonable average, two Hogsheads represents 150 gallons of wine. As a proxy for the cost of a medium-grade table wine, consider the $5.99 per bottle price for the 1996 *Fetzer Vineyards Sundial Chardonnay (California)*. Each bottle holds 750 milliliters, where each liter equals roughly 1 quart. Taking 4 quarts to the gallon, this gives $4792 as the present-day value of 150 gallons of wine.

Of course, a ton is a standard measure of weight equal to 2000 pounds (short ton) in the United States and Canada and equal to 2240 pounds (long ton) in Great Britain. Thus, two long tons of butter, at a retail price of $1.69 per pound, has a value of $7571. Popularly priced beer in 12-ounce cans, such as *Budweiser*, weighs 22 pounds per case. Given a typical retail price of $15 per case, this gives a price of $6109 for 4 tons of beer.[4] A typical retail price for an 8-ounce brick of *Kraft Sharp Cheddar* cheese is $3.49. This means the present-day value of 1000 pounds of cheese is roughly $6980.

The present-day value of a complete bed, a suit of clothes, and a silver drinking cup can vary widely, depending upon personal preferences. For example, a typical retail price for a popular *Serta Masterpiece Worthington* queen-size foundation and mattress is $576. A frame usually runs $59, with a headboard and footboard costing anywhere between $400 and $600, say $500. Sheets, pillows, pillow cases, and a comforter might run an additional $275. This brings the present-day value of a complete bed to roughly $1410. A moderately priced suit of clothes for a businessman or businesswoman might run between $500 and $1000, say $750. And finally, a moderately priced hand-made *Alesandro* drinking cup made of sterling silver has a typical retail price of $68.

In sum, a representative calculation of the present-day price paid for a single *Viceroy* tulip bulb during 1635, near the height of the tulip mania in Holland, totals a whopping $34,584. Therefore, Mackay's example of individual tulip bulbs fetching anywhere from 1260–5500 florins implies a present-day price range from $17,430–$76,085 each.[5]

---

[3]See *The World Book Dictionary, Volume 1* (Chicago, IL: Scott Fetzer, 1994, p. 1007).

[4]When used to measure liquids, a ton is sometimes measured by the volume of water a ship will displace at sea level. The volume of a long ton of seawater is 35 cubic feet.

[5]As an interesting check on these numbers, consider the fact that if each florin represented the buying power of 3.5 grains of gold (or about one-eighth ounce), then a *Viceroy* tulip bulb price of 2500 florins would be roughly equivalent to 365 ounces of gold. With a present-day gold price of roughly $280 per ounce, 2500 florins translates into a present-day equivalent of roughly $102,083 worth of gold. Measured in terms of gold, Mackay's example of individual tulip bulbs fetching anywhere from 1260–5500 florins translates into a present-day price range from $51,450 to $224,583. Note that the present-day gold-equivalent tulip prices exceed the product-equivalent (or "real") prices calculated in

Mackay (1841, p. 93) relates that interest in tulips grew so much that by 1636 regular marts for their sale were established on the Amsterdam Stock Exchange and in Rotterdam, Harlaem, Leyden, Alkmar, Hoorn, and other towns. Popular interest in tulips shifted from hobbyists and collectors to stock-jobbers (security analysts), speculators, and gamblers. People from all walks of life liquidated homes and real estate at ridiculously low prices in order to garner funds for tulip speculation. Tulip-notaries and clerks were appointed to record transactions; intricate public laws and regulations were developed to control the tulip trade.

It was during the early autumn of 1636 that the more prudent began to liquidate their tulip holdings. Tulip prices began to weaken, slowly at first, but then more rapidly. Soon, confidence was destroyed, and panic seized the market. Within 6 weeks, tulip prices crashed by 90% or more; widespread defaults on purchase contracts and liens were experienced. At first, the Dutch government refused to interfere and advised tulip holders to agree among themselves to some plan for stabilizing tulip prices and restoring public credit. All such plans failed. After much bickering, assembled deputies in Amsterdam agreed to declare null and void all contracts made at the height of the mania, or prior to November 1636. Tulip contracts made subsequent to that date were to be settled if buyers paid 10% of earlier agreed upon prices. However, this decision gave no satisfaction as tulip prices continued to fall, and the Provincial Council in the Hague was asked to invent some measure to stabilize tulip prices and public credit. Again, all such efforts failed. Tulip prices continued to crash even further. In Amsterdam, judges unanimously refused to honor tulip contracts on the grounds that gambling debts were not debts in the eyes of the law. No court in Holland would enforce payment. Dutch tulip collectors, stock-jobbers, speculators, and gamblers who held tulips at the time of the collapse were left to bear ruinous losses; those lucky enough to have profited were allowed to keep their gains. Tulip prices plunged to less than the present-day equivalent of $1 each (or 10 guineas), and many of those who profited from the mania and the ensuing collapse apparently converted their gains into English or other funds to hide them from enraged countrymen. When tulip profiteers converted their gains to foreign currency and left the country, the money supply shrank in Holland, and Dutch commerce suffered a severe shock from which it took many years to recover.

All subsequent stock-jobber attempts to recreate another tulip mania in Holland, England, and Paris proved fruitless. While tulips are still more popular in Holland than elsewhere, tulip prices have never again approached levels seen during the height of the tulip mania of 1634–36. Today, serious horticulturists might buy rare "collections" of *Emperor Tulips, Mid-Season Tulips,* or *Darwin Hybrid Tulips* at prices from $0.30–0.40 each, or at levels similar to postmania tulip prices in Holland.[6]

Table 4.1. This is consistent with a decline in the price of real goods over time and a generally rising standard of living. Importantly, there is ample reason to believe that the price estimated in Table 4.1 is a conservative estimate of the present-day equivalent price paid for a single bulb at the height of Holland's tulip mania.

[6]See Van Engelen, Inc., Wholesale Price List, 23 Tulip Drive, Bantam, CN 06750.

IV. PSYCHOLOGY OF MANIAS

Mackay, like other popular accounts of tulip bulb pricing in Holland during the 1634–36 period, refers to the word "mania" when describing that episode. It is well-worth noting that mania is a kind of insanity characterized by great excitement, extremes of joy or rage, and uncontrolled and often violent activity.[7] Sometimes referred to as a "bipolar disorder," mania is a serious mental illness in which a person alternates between periods of severe depression and periods of intense joy. The illness is also called manic-depressive illness or manic depression. Approximately 3 million people in the United States suffer from bipolar disorder. If treated inadequately, the illness can have tragic consequences, such as suicide.

During periods of depression, a person suffering from bipolar disorder may feel sad, anxious, irritable, hopeless, or unmotivated. Depressed patients may experience insomnia or excessive sleeping, decreased or increased appetite, weight loss or weight gain, slowing of thought and movement, and poor memory and concentration. During periods of mania, a person may experience euphoria (indescribable happiness) or may alternate between euphoria and irritability. Manic patients sometimes behave inappropriately. For example, they may laugh uncontrollably at funerals. Periods of mania also are characterized by increased energy, racing thoughts, increased rate of speech, decreased need for sleep, exaggerated sense of self-worth, and poor judgment. Treatment for the disorder includes drugs and psychotherapy (see Dilsaver, 1994).

In commenting on Mackay's book, noted Wall Street speculator Bernard M. Baruch (1932, p. xiii) wrote, "without due recognition of crowd-thinking (which often seems crowd-madness) our theories of economics leave much to be desired." Given the foibles of human nature, Baruch offered no hope that manias would cease. However, Baruch (1932, p. xiv) wrote that "popular recognition of them and their early symptoms should lighten and may even avoid their more harmful effects."

Today, it is safe to characterize a tulip price of roughly $35,000 as "crazy." Not only is there the "proof" of historical tulip prices, no living persons have any financial or emotional capital invested in the notion that it can be wise to pay $35,000 for a tulip bulb. While the separation of time and space makes it safe to characterize the behavior of certain anonymous persons as acting crazy during the Dutch tulip mania, it is less safe to regard the recently popular behavior of known persons as crazy.

It is plausible that during the late-1990s stock-jobbers, speculators, and gamblers devoted significant time and energy to justify what may be later regarded as crazy prices for tech stock, especially those for companies tied directly to the Internet. In retrospect, extreme prices appear to have been paid at various times in recent years for computer ("tronics") stocks, "Nifty Fifty" companies, oil

---

[7]*The World Book Dictionary, Volume 2* (Chicago, IL: Scott Fetzer, 1994, p. 1265).

stocks, gold, silver, Japanese stocks, and biotech companies. In retrospect, everyone would agree that the prices paid for such assets at market peaks were very "high." Still, confidence in the conventional reasonableness of stock market valuations would cause some to dispute the notion that such high prices were crazy. Among those who view the market as perfectly efficient, stock prices are never "too high" or "too low," they are always "just right."

V. THE LATE-1990s INTERNET STOCK MANIA

To cite a recent, and therefore sure to be controversial, example of bubble-like behavior in the stock market, consider the late-1990s pricing of Internet stocks. Table 4.2 shows late-1990s prices and market capitalizations for 20 well-known Internet and online service companies. Also shown is conventional accounting information concerning sales, book values, and projected earnings data that were widely available and known to stock market investors at that time.[8] Notice how data for this sample is drawn from a period well before the ultimate market peak in 2000 and after many seasoned observers of the stock market reasoned that Internet stock prices had reached unsustainable heights.

On average, notice how these 20 generally recognized leaders in the late-1990s Internet space sold at a share price of $34.35 despite feeble sales of only $4.07 per share and an anemic book value of only $2.40 per share. Also observe that these were not insignificant companies with immaterial stock market capitalizations. Given the enormous popularity of tech stock investing in the late-1990s and the growing hype surrounding any company with ties to the Internet, these 20 Internet stocks boasted an average stock market capitalization that was a whopping $1.9 billion. These stock market darlings were accorded such elevated stock market capitalizations despite the fact that they were losing an average $1.43 per share during the preceding 12-month period. At the time, enthusiastic investors argued that companies able to secure an early foothold in the Internet space would translate durable "first mover" advantages into lasting business and stock market success.

Would a rational investor pay an extravagant price–sales ratio of 8.4 and a heroic price–book ratio of 14.3 for such a basket of money-losing stocks? Sure, so long as those companies indeed held the ready prospect for enormous future revenues, cash flow, and profits. Unfortunately, few did. As shown in Table 4.2, 15 of these 20 companies had crashed and burned by mid-2002, roughly 4 years later. The still-struggling survivors include Amazon.com, Inc., a leading Internet retailer; AOL Time Warner, Inc., an Internet service provider and publishing juggernaut; Doubleclick, Inc., a digital marketing enterprise; Earthlink, Inc., an

[8]All data are from Yahoo! after the market close on 3/37/98. See http://quote.yahoo.com/q?s=AMZN+AOL+CNWK+CYCH+DBCC+DCLK+EGRP+ELNK+XCIT+ATHM+IDTC+SEEK+LCOS+MECK+NTKI+NSCP+OTEXF+PSIX+SPYG+YHOO&d=v1.

TABLE 4.2 Internet Stock Prices: Late-1990s and Today

Company	Ticker	Price[a] (6/04/98)	52-week low	52-week high	Sales ($ per share)	Book value ($)	EPS ($)	1999 EPS estimate ($)	1999 P/E	Shares	Market capitalization (in millions $)	Analyst opinion[b]	Price (9/12/02)	Splits[c]	Split-adjusted annual return (%)[c]
Amazon.com, Inc.	AMZN	43.88	8.25	50.00	4.84	0.41	(0.75)	(0.55)	NA	49.4	2,167.4	1.9	16.75	6:1	21.5
America Online	AOL	81.25	26.69	92.25	10.70	2.09	0.34	0.90	90.3	216.2	17,566.3	1.4	12.54	8:1	5.1
CNET Inc.	CNWK	32.94	19.31	46.50	2.64	2.42	-1.25	0.68	48.4	14.9	490.8	2.0			
CyberCash Inc.	CYCH	15.13	10.13	27.75	0.50	1.96	-2.11	1.24	12.2	12.2	184.5	3.0			
Data Broadcasting Corp.	DBCC	5.94	4.25	9.13	2.74	2.99	0.08			34.0	201.9				
DoubleClick, Inc.	DCLK	32.50	26.13	49.25	3.47	4.12	-1.04	-0.48		16.4	533.0	2.0	5.68	4:1	-8.1
e-TRADE Group, Inc.	EGRP	22.00	17.38	47.88	5.05	7.39	0.52	0.90	24.4	39.0	858.0	1.6			
EarthLink Network, Inc.	ELNK	58.50	10.00	77.00	8.77	0.54	-2.67	1.51	38.7	12.0	702.0	2.0	5.89	2:1	-31.4
Excite, Inc.	XCIT	55.97	10.13	93.31	4.08	1.28	-1.84	0.91	61.5	23.4	1,309.7	2.2			
At Home Corp.	ATHM	34.63	16.63	47.00	0.12	0.93	-2.86	0.05	692.5	118.7	4,110.0	2.3			
IDT Corp.	IDTC	26.50	7.38	40.25	9.71	2.99	0.40	0.81	32.7	14.0	371.0	1.2			
Infoseek Corp.	SEEK	22.56	4.38	45.00	1.55	1.00	-0.82	0.28	80.6	30.9	697.2	2.4			
Lycos Inc.	LCOS	51.50	11.19	79.13	3.08	2.51	-5.91	0.16	321.9	15.6	803.4	1.8			
Mecklermedia Corp.	MECK	19.38	17.75	29.88	7.07	2.12	0.73	1.52	12.7	8.3	160.8	1.0			
N2K Inc.	NTKI	19.81	12.25	34.63	2.56	3.26	-6.22	-2.67		14.2	281.3	1.8			
Netscape Communications	NSCP	24.38	14.88	49.50	5.89	4.38	-1.29	0.39	62.5	98.5	2,400.9	2.6			
Open Text Corp.	OTEXF	17.00	8.00	23.50	2.02	1.93	-0.57	0.65	26.2	17.6	299.2	1.5			
PSINet Inc.	PSIX	10.50	4.25	15.25	3.40	0.39	-1.58	-1.38		51.1	536.6	2.3			
Spyglass, Inc.	SPYG	10.06	4.06	15.25	1.15	2.47	-1.31	0.08	125.8	13.1	131.8	2.0			
Yahoo! Inc.	YHOO	102.63	20.56	129.63	2.06	2.74	-0.45	0.74	138.7	46.3	4,751.5	2.0	10.35	8:1	-4.9
Average		**34.35**	**12.68**	**50.10**	**4.07**	**2.40**	**-1.43**	**0.30**	**113.7**	**42.3**	**1,927.9**	**1.9**			

[a] All data are from Yahoo! after the market close on June 4, 1998, and September 12, 2002.

[b] Analyst rating. 1 = strong buy, 5 = strong sell.

[c] Over the 6/04/02 to 9/12/02 period.

Internet access and related services company; and Yahoo!, an Internet business and consumer services organization. In short, only 5 of these 20 late-1990s leaders in the Internet space survived in recognizable form over the ensuing 4-year period. The rest had either gone out of business or been merged out of existence.[9] Of the five late-1990s leaders shown in Table 4.2 that survived until mid-2002, only Amazon.com and AOL turned in positive stock price performance over the ensuing four-plus years. Suffice to say, this is not the type of stock market performance foreseen by late-1990s advocates of tech stocks, especially those closely tied to the Internet.

When measured against popular benchmarks, everyone would agree that late-1990s valuations in this sector were at least "very high." However, despite the carnage in the tech sector since the 2000 market peak, some would still dispute the notion that such valuations were crazy. To be fair, given the high degree of uncertainty regarding the sector's future growth prospects, it was indeed difficult to distinguish whether or not Internet valuations were crazy or just very high during the period leading up to the 2000 market peak.

An interesting case study of extreme market expectations for Internet stocks near the 2000 market peak is provided by a detailed valuation analysis of AOL, then dubbed the "King of Cyberspace."[10] AOL's late-1990s market capitalization of roughly $14.5 billion approached the *combined* value of all the other widely followed cyberstars shown in Table 4.2. Near the start of the new millennium, individual and institutional investor attention was riveted on AOL as the company completed a much discussed merger with traditional print media powerhouse Time-Warner, Inc. AOL was widely praised at the time for using its "inflated" stock price to buy "real" businesses with meaningful revenues, earnings, and book values. Less widely understood was why shareholders in Time-Warner would swap their shares for such an inflated currency, or why other investors and stock analysts praised the merger as a means for tapping untold synergies between the companies. It is worth emphasizing that the ensuing discussion is based upon conventional accounting data and other business information concerning AOL that were broadly available and understood by stock market investors at the time.

VI. AOL AS A GROWTH STOCK

Investors in AOL and Microsoft Corp. enjoyed stellar stock market returns over the 1995–99 period. Both were among the top performers in a robust stock market environment. In evaluating the forward-looking investment potential for AOL, it

---

[9]For example, Netscape was merged into AOL prior to that company's combination with Time-Warner, Inc. While Netscape shareholders were thus able to salvage some value for their once highly sought after shares, it is safe to say that Netscape investors fared poorly during the ensuing market rout.

[10]For an early examination of the valuation issues surrounding AOL, see Hirschey (2001, pp. 412–417 and 466–470).

is interesting to compare AOL to Microsoft, clearly the most successful technology stock of this generation (see Hirschey, 2001).

After considering the effects of stock splits, but ignoring nonrecurring charges AOL had an earnings per share (EPS) of $0.20 during 1999 (see Fig. 4.1). AOL's 1999 EPS of $0.20 was very similar to 1993 earnings results achieved by Microsoft. As shown in Fig. 4.2, Microsoft also made $0.20 per share in 1993. Also notice that AOL sales revenue in 1999 of $4.8 billion was much higher than Microsoft's $3.8 billion in revenues during 1993. This reflects the fact that Microsoft typically earns much higher profit margins than does AOL.

For argument's sake, let us assume that AOL enjoys stellar EPS growth over the 1999–2006 7-year period. In fact, let us assume that AOL duplicates the unprecedented success that Microsoft enjoyed during the 1993–2000 period. If AOL grows at a Microsoft-like rate, AOL will report 2006 EPS of $1.65, a level that coincides with Microsoft's estimated earnings during 2000.

On a split-adjusted basis, AOL sold as high as 95-13/16 during December 1999. At that price, AOL was trading at a price–earnings (P/E) ratio of 479:1 when measured against 1999 earnings. Assuming that AOL is as successful in growing its earnings over the 1999–2006 period as Microsoft was at a similar stage in its life, a 1999 price of 95-13/16 for AOL implies a P/E ratio of 58:1 against expected earnings of $1.65 in 2006.

At its share-price peak of 95-13/16 in December 1999, AOL's valuation looks expensive when compared with Microsoft. Over the 1993–2000 period, Microsoft's P/E ratio climbed with growing investor optimism regarding the company's future growth prospects. From an average P/E of roughly 26.8:1 in 1993, Microsoft's P/E reached roughly 55.6:1 by late 1999.

For argument's sake, let us assume that this optimistic valuation for Microsoft represents an appropriate valuation for a dominant high-tech leader. Let us also assume that such a valuation is appropriate for AOL. This means that one might assume that a P/E in the range of 55:1 will be appropriate for AOL in 2006. In the late-1999 opinion of *The Value Line Investment Survey*, an appropriate 2002–04 P/E for AOL is, in fact, 55:1. At a 1999 price of 95-13/16, and a P/E ratio of 58:1 against 2006 earnings, AOL was selling for more than its appropriate valuation in 2006 for a dominant high-tech leader. In other words, over the 1999–2006 period, AOL would have to grow its EPS faster than Microsoft grew its earnings over the 1993–2000 period to justify a 2006 stock price of 95-13/16!

Of course, current investors in AOL would be disappointed if its stock price failed to advance over the 1999–2006 time frame. If a typical AOL investor was looking for a 20% annual rate of return from such a high-risk stock, an investment in AOL at 95-13/16 in 1999 would need to grow to roughly $345 by 2006 to provide a satisfactory return. To justify such a price, AOL's earnings would have to grow at roughly 77% per year over the 1999–2006 time period. This is a substantial premium over the 42.1% annual earnings growth achieved by Microsoft over the 1993–2000 time frame or at a similar stage in its development.

AMERICA ONLINE NYSE-AOL | RECENT PRICE **58** | P/E RATIO **NMF** (Trailing: NMF / Median: NMF) | RELATIVE P/E RATIO **NMF** | DIV'D YLD **Nil** | **VALUE LINE**

TIMELINESS **2** Lowered 3/3/00	High: 0.2 0.5 0.9 2.9 4.4 5.7 40.0 95.8	Target Price Range 2002 2003 2004
SAFETY **3** Raised 3/3/00	Low: 0.1 0.1 0.4 0.8 1.4 2.0 5.2 32.5	
TECHNICAL **2** Raised 1/21/00		
BETA 1.75 (1.00 = Market)		

LEGENDS
45.0 x "Cash Flow" p sh
Relative Price Strength
2-for-1 split 11/94
2-for-1 split 4/95
2-for-1 split 11/95
2-for-1 split 3/98
2-for-1 split 11/98
2-for-1 split 2/99
2-for-1 split 11/99
Options: Yes
Shaded area indicates recession

2002-04 PROJECTIONS
	Price	Gain	Ann'l Total Return
High	115	(+100%)	19%
Low	75	(+30%)	7%

Insider Decisions
	A M J J A S O N D
to Buy	0 0 0 0 0 0 0 0 0
Options	0 0 0 5 5 0 0 0 1
to Sell	0 0 0 10 5 0 8 0 0

Institutional Decisions
	1Q1999	2Q1999	3Q1999
to Buy	501	432	497
to Sell	217	315	278
Hld's(000)	1106700	925844	980618

Percent 90.0 / 60.0 / 30.0 shares traded

America Online was incorporated in Delaware in 1985. The company was listed on the Nasdaq in March, 1992 in connection with an initial public offering co-managed by Alex. Brown and Robertson, Stephens; two million common shares were tendered to the public at $0.09 apiece. In December, 1996, the company adopted a simplified, competitive pricing structure (currently $21.95 per month for unlimited access) and user-friendly interface, which helped to accelerate already-rapid revenue growth.

CAPITAL STRUCTURE as of 12/31/99
Total Debt $1581.0 mill. Due in 5 Yrs $800.0 mill.
LT Debt $1581.0 mill.   LT Interest $70.0 mill.
(20% of Cap'l)

Leases, Uncapitalized Annual rentals $262.0 mill.
Pension Liability None - No defined benefit plan.

Common Stock 2,281,767,899 shs. (80% of Cap'l) as of 1/31/00

MARKET CAP: $132.3 billion (Large Cap)

CURRENT POSITION
(SMILL.)	1998	1999	12/31/99
Cash Assets	631.0	1424.0	3053.0
Receivables	104.0	402.0	483.0
Other	195.0	153.0	280.0
Current Assets	930.0	1979.0	3816.0
Accts Payable	87.0	74.0	65.0
Debt Due	--	--	--
Other	807.0	1651.0	2097.0
Current Liab.	894.0	1725.0	2162.0

ANNUAL RATES
of change (per sh)	Past 10 Yrs.	Past 5 Yrs	Est'd '97-'99 to '02-'04
Revenues	--	87.5%	33.0%
"Cash Flow"	--	98.0%	68.0%
Earnings	--	76.5%	90.0%
Dividends	--	--	Nil
Book Value	--	61.0%	55.0%

Fiscal Year Ends	**QUARTERLY REVENUES ($ mill.)**				Full Fiscal Year
	Sep.30	Dec.31	Mar.31	Jun.30	
1996	197.9	249.2	312.3	334.5	1093.9
1997	350.0	409.4	450.1	475.7	1685.2
1998	522.0	592.0	694.0	792.0	2600.0
1999	999.0	1147	1253	1378	4777
2000	1467	1510	1743	1930	6650

Fiscal Year Ends	**EARNINGS PER SHARE A**				Full Fiscal Year
	Sep.30	Dec.31	Mar.31	Jun.30	
1996	d.01	.01	.01	.01	.02
1997	.01	d.06	--	--	d.05
1998	.01	.01	.02	.03	.07
1999	.04	.05	.05	.06	.20
2000	.08	.09	.10	.11	.38

Cal- endar	**QUARTERLY DIVIDENDS PAID**				Full Year
	Mar.31	Jun.30	Sep.30	Dec.31	
1996					
1997		NO CASH DIVIDENDS			
1998		BEING PAID			
1999					
2000					

	1989	1990	1991	1992	1993	1994	1995	1996	1997	1998	1999	2000	© VALUE LINE PUB., INC.	02-04
	--	--	.14	.04	.05	.11	.33	.74	1.05	1.48	2.17	2.90	Revenues per sh A	6.40
	--	--	.02	.00	.01	.01	.03	.04	.00	.13	.35	.55	"Cash Flow" per sh	2.10
	--	--	.00	.00	.01	.01	.01	.02	d.05	.07	.20	.38	Earnings per sh A	1.75
	--	--	--	--	--	--	--	--	--	--	--	Nil	Div'ds Decl'd per sh	Nil
	--	--	d.06	.03	.03	.11	.18	.35	.08	.34	1.38	1.75	Book Value per sh B	5.40
	--	--	155.51	701.54	754.18	927.42	1201.8	1482.0	1603.0	1757.1	2201.8	2300.0	Common Shs Outst'g C	2600.0
	--	--	--	32.3	48.7	79.8	60.7	NMF	NMF	NMF	NMF		Avg Ann'l P/E Ratio	55.0
	--	--	--	1.96	2.88	5.23	4.06	NMF	NMF	NMF	NMF		Relative P/E Ratio	3.65
	--	--	--	--	--	--	--	--	--	--	--		Avg Ann'l Div'd Yield	Nil
	--	--	21.4	26.6	40.0	104.4	394.3	1093.9	1685.2	2600.0	4777.0	6650	Revenues ($mill) A	16700
	--	--	14.9%	17.1%	14.9%	10.1%	11.1%	9.0%	NMF	11.9%	17.9%	24.5%	Operating Margin	50.0%
	--	--	1.7	1.2	1.5	2.5	11.1	33.4	64.6	100.0	287.0	300	Depreciation ($mill)	530
	--	--	.9	2.2	3.1	6.2	18.9	29.8	d71.5	132.6	486.0	970	Net Profit ($mill)	5000
	--	--	38.2%	38.1%	38.2%	38.1%	44.5%	52.2%	41.0%	39.8%	39.3%	38.0%	Income Tax Rate	38.0%
	--	--	4.4%	8.3%	7.7%	5.9%	4.8%	2.7%	NMF	5.1%	10.2%	14.5%	Net Profit Margin	30.0%
	--	--	.2	1.8	16.8	64.9	d.4	d19.3	d231.0	36.0	254.0	595	Working Cap'l ($mill)	7850
	--	--	.2	--	5.8	19.5	19.3	50.0	372.0	348.0	390	Long-Term Debt ($mill)	510
	--	--	3.5	18.9	28.9	98.9	217.9	512.5	128.0	598.0	3033.0	4000	Shr. Equity ($mill)	14000
	--	--	25.3%	11.7%	12.9%	5.9%	8.2%	5.7%	NMF	14.1%	14.6%	22.5%	Return on Total Cap'l	34.5%
	--	--	26.6%	11.7%	12.9%	6.3%	8.7%	5.8%	NMF	22.2%	16.0%	24.5%	Return on Shr. Equity	35.5%
	--	--	--	NMF	12.9%	6.3%	8.7%	5.8%	NMF	22.2%	16.0%	24.5%	Retained to Com Eq	35.5%
	--	--	--	NMF	--	--	--	--	--	--	--	Nil	All Div'ds to Net Prof	Nil

% TOT. RETURN 1/00
	THIS STOCK	VL ARITH. INDEX
1 yr.	29.8	7.0
3 yr.	2439.1	40.2
5 yr.	6795.3	117.2

BUSINESS: America Online, Inc. is the leading provider of online information services, with over 21 million subscribers (includes AOL and CompuServe). Offers electronic mail and conferencing, online forums and classes, interactive newspapers and magazines, and access to the Internet. Has strategic alliances with dozens of cos. incl. ABC, Viacom, American Express, IBM, and Bertelsmann. Has about 8500 employees, 240,000 shareholders. Acq'd WAIS, Inc., 5/95; Medior, Inc., 5/95; GNN, 6/95; Ubique Ltd., 9/95; Compuserve, 2/97; Netscape, 3/99. Officers and Directors own 2.4% of common (9/99 Proxy). Chairman & CEO: Stephen M. Case. Incorporated: DE. Address: 8619 Westwood Center Dr., Vienna, VA. 22182. Telephone: 703-448-8700. Internet: www.aol.com.

America Online is on track to acquire Time Warner. The deal would provide Time Warner shareholders 1.5 AOL shares for each share of TWX (AOL stockholders would receive 1.0 shares in the new company). Subject to normal shareholder and regulatory approval, the acquisition — the second-largest in history — will likely be finalized late this year.

Combined, the companies have much to offer each other. One major benefit is that AOL would be able to offer high-speed Internet services over television cables. This should provide a more enjoyable Internet experience; enable the digital distribution of new services for interactive entertainment, information, and e-commerce; and facilitate the operation of these services on everything from desktop computers to television sets and handheld devices. Another benefit should come from gains in advertising. Linking AOL's strength in this area to Time Warner's entertainment sites holds sizable potential. And AOL's services should benefit Time Warner's operations as well. The CNN cable network, owned by Time Warner, stands to gain from the promotional strength provided by

AOL's 24 million subscribers. And Time Warner's music division would gain from AOL's ability to deliver music online.

The company's Internet prospects remain substantial. Over the past year, AOL's net subscriber base has increased over 55%, to 24 million. Currently, about a third of all U.S. households use Internet access, and penetration appears likely to double by 2003. Meanwhile, advertising and commerce revenues should climb at an even higher rate, reaching about five times current levels, benefiting from the overwhelming size of AOL's audience.

The pending acquisition should modestly enhance appreciation potential from timely AOL stock's standalone prospects. The investment community has largely shied away from shares in AOL, as it hitches its growth possibilities to Time Warner's tangible, more mature assets. The combination would generate large amounts of cash flow, though, and, as noted, would have significant avenues for business investment. (Note: we will update our projections once the acquisition has been completed.)
                          Stephen E. Jones   March 3, 2000

(A) Fiscal year ends June 30th. Based on diluted earnings, primary through '95. Excludes gains arising from net operating loss carryforward: '91, 1¢; '92, 1¢; '93, 1¢. Excludes nonrecurring charges: '97: 30¢; '98, 2¢; '99, 14¢. Next earnings report due early May. (B) Includes intangibles. In '99: $454.0 million, 20¢/share. (C) In millions, adjusted for stock splits.

Company's Financial Strength	A
Stock's Price Stability	10
Price Growth Persistence	100
Earnings Predictability	10

FIGURE 4.1   The late-1990s rise of AOL is one of the most amazing stories in stock market history.

MICROSOFT NDQ-MSFT

RECENT PRICE	94	
P/E RATIO	56.0	(Trailing: 58.7 / Median: 28.0)
RELATIVE P/E RATIO	4.18	
DIV'D YLD	Nil	

VALUE LINE

TIMELINESS	2	Lowered 6/4/99	High:	1.0	1.2	2.2	4.7	5.9	6.1	8.1	13.7	21.5	37.7	72.0	119.9
			Low:	0.6	0.6	1.2	2.0	4.1	4.4	4.9	7.3	10.0	20.2	31.1	68.0
SAFETY	2	Raised 12/6/96													
TECHNICAL	2	Raised 2/4/00													
BETA	1.10	(1.00 = Market)													

Target Price Range
2002 | 2003 | 2004

LEGENDS
30.0 x "Cash Flow" p sh
Relative Price Strength
2-for-1 split   9/87
2-for-1 split   4/90
3-for-2 split   6/91
3-for-2 split   6/92
2-for-1 split   5/94
2-for-1 split   12/96
2-for-1 split   2/98
2-for-1 split   3/99
Options: Yes
Shaded area indicates recession

2002-04 PROJECTIONS
	Price	Gain	Ann'l Total Return
High	130	(+40%)	9%
Low	95	(Nil)	1%

Insider Decisions
	A	M	J	J	A	S	O	N	D
to Buy	0	0	0	0	0	0	0	0	0
Options	2	2	0	2	4	0	0	1	2
to Sell	3	3	0	5	6	0	2	0	0

Institutional Decisions
	1Q1999	2Q1999	3Q1999
to Buy	612	633	628
to Sell	499	449	435
Hld's(000)	1911464	2011456	2118434

Percent 30.0 / shares 20.0 / traded 10.0

1983	1984	1985	1986	1987	1988	1989	1990	1991	1992	1993	1994	1995	1996	1997	1998	1999	2000	© VALUE LINE PUB., INC.	02-04
.02	.03		.05	.06	.09	.15	.20	.29	.44	.83	1.00	1.26	1.84	2.36	2.93	3.87	4.60	Sales per sh A	8.80
--	--	.01	.01	.02	.04	.05	.08	.13	.19	.24	.31	.37	.56	.83	1.17	1.68	1.95	"Cash Flow" per sh	3.35
--	--	.01	.01	.02	.03	.04	.07	.10	.15	.20	.25	.29	.43	.66	.89	1.39	1.68	Earnings per sh B	3.00
--	--	--	--	--	--	--	--	--	--	--	--	--	--	--	--	Nil	Nil	Div'ds Decl'd per sh	Nil
--	.01	.02	.04	.06	.10	.14	.22	.32	.50	.72	.96	1.13	1.47	2.03	3.17	5.37	7.00	Book Value per sh	14.65
3077.1	3061.5	3100.8	3674.9	3795.3	3863.7	3930.2	4093.2	4181.8	4354.2	4512.0	4648.0	4704.0	4704.0	4816.0	4940.0	5109.0	5200.0	Common Shs Outst'g C	5000.0
--	--	17.7	19.6	19.9	25.2	17.8	19.9	22.6	28.5	26.8	21.4	28.2	29.1	33.0	42.8	49.8		Avg Ann'l P/E Ratio	38.0
--	--	1.44	1.33	1.33	2.09	1.35	1.48	1.44	1.73	1.58	1.40	1.89	1.82	1.90	2.23	2.73		Relative P/E Ratio	2.55
--	--	--	--	--	--	--	--	--	--	--	--	--	--	--	--	--		Avg Ann'l Div'd Yield	Nil

% TOT. RETURN 1/00
	THIS STOCK	VL ARITH. INDEX
1 yr.	119.9	7.0
3 yr.	283.8	40.2
5 yr.	1218.7	117.2

CAPITAL STRUCTURE as of 12/31/99

Total Debt None					803.5	1183.4	1843.4	2758.7	3753.0	4649.0	5937.0	8671.0	11358	14484	19747	23800	Sales ($mill)	44000
					33.2%	37.1%	39.4%	40.2%	39.4%	42.2%	38.9%	41.0%	50.1%	55.0%	56.0%	55.5%	Operating Margin	51.5%
Leases, Uncapitalized $85.0 mill.					24.2	46.3	75.8	112.3	151.0	237.0	269.0	480.0	557.0	1024.0	1010.0	1025	Depreciation ($mill)	1290
Pension Liability None - No defined benefit pension plan.					170.5	279.2	462.7	708.1	953.0	1210.0	1453.0	2176.0	3454.0	4786.0	7625.0	9235	Net Profit ($mill)	15515
					32.0%	32.0%	32.0%	32.0%	32.0%	33.2%	32.9%	35.0%	35.0%	35.4%	35.0%	35.0%	Income Tax Rate	35.0%
Pfd Stock None					21.2%	23.6%	25.1%	25.7%	25.4%	26.0%	24.5%	25.1%	30.4%	33.0%	38.6%	38.8%	Net Profit Margin	35.3%
					310.1	533.1	735.1	1322.8	2287.0	3399.0	4273.0	5414.0	6763.0	10159	11515	19465	Working Cap'l ($mill)	57895
Common Stock 5,204,853,333 shs. (100% of Cap'l)					--	--	--	--	--	--	--	--	--	--	--	Nil	Long-Term Debt ($mill)	Nil
					561.8	918.6	1350.8	2193.0	3242.0	4450.0	5333.0	6908.0	10777	16627	28438	36340	Shr. Equity ($mill)	73240
MARKET CAP: $490 billion (Large Cap)					30.3%	30.4%	34.3%	32.3%	29.4%	27.2%	27.2%	31.5%	32.0%	28.8%	26.8%	25.5%	Return on Total Cap'l	21.0%
					30.3%	30.4%	34.3%	32.3%	29.4%	27.2%	27.2%	31.5%	32.0%	28.8%	26.8%	25.5%	Return on Shr. Equity	21.0%
					30.3%	30.4%	34.3%	32.3%	29.4%	27.2%	27.2%	31.5%	35.1%	30.4%	27.7%	25.5%	Retained to Com Eq	21.0%
					--	--	--	--	--	--	--	--	1%	NMF	Nil	Nil	All Div'ds to Net Prof	Nil

CURRENT POSITION
	1998	1999	12/31/99
(SMIL.)			
Cash Assets	13927	17236	17843
Receivables	1460	2245	3284
Inventory	--	--	--
Other	502	752	893
Current Assets	15889	20233	22020
Accts Payable	759	874	1233
Debt Due	--	--	--
Other	4971	7844	9271
Current Liab.	5730	8718	10504

ANNUAL RATES
of change (per sh)	Past 10 Yrs.	Past 5 Yrs.	Est'd '97-'99 to '02-'04
Sales	35.0%	30.0%	24.5%
"Cash Flow"	42.5%	37.5%	25.5%
Earnings	41.5%	37.5%	29.0%
Dividends	--	--	Nil
Book Value	42.5%	37.0%	37.0%

Fiscal Year Ends	QUARTERLY SALES ($ mil.) A			Full Year
	Sep.30	Dec.31	Mar.31	Jun.30	
1996	2016	2195	2205	2255	8671
1997	2295	2680	3208	3175	11358
1998	3130	3585	3774	3995	14484
1999	4193D	5195D	4595D	5764	19747
2000	5384	6112	5800	6504	23800

Fiscal Year Ends	EARNINGS PER SHARE A B			Full Fiscal Year
	Sep.30	Dec.31	Mar.31	Jun.30	
1996	.10	.11	.11	.11	.43
1997	.12	.14	.20	.20	.66
1998	.18	.21	.25	.25	.89
1999	.28	.36	.35	.40	1.39
2000	.38	.47	.41	.42	1.68

Cal-endar	QUARTERLY DIVIDENDS PAID			Full Year
	Mar.31	Jun.30	Sep.30	Dec.31	
1996					
1997	NO CASH DIVIDENDS			
1998	BEING PAID			
1999					
2000					

BUSINESS: Microsoft Corp. is the largest independent maker of software. Revenue sources in fiscal 1999: Windows Platforms 43% (operating systems and server applications and Internet products). Productivity Applications and Developer 45% (desktop applications, server applications, and developer tools). Consumer, Commerce, and Other 12% (learning and entertainment software, PC input devices, fees, consulting, and online services). R&D: 15.1% of sales. Has 31,400 employees and 92,170 stockholders. William H. Gates owns 15.3% of stock, other officers & directors 10.2% (9/99 proxy). Chairman: William H. Gates. President and CEO: Steven A. Ballmer. Inc.: WA. Address: One Microsoft Way, Redmond, WA 98052-6399. Tele.: 425-882-8080. Internet: www.microsoft.com.

Microsoft finally rolled out its next generation operating system (OS), Windows 2000. The upgrade to the company's Windows NT OS was released February 17th to generally favorable reviews. It offers better performance, scalability, security, and resource management than Windows NT. The new system is at the center of Microsoft's effort to extend its operating system hegemony from the desktop to high-end servers. Businesses are likely to take their time, and not rush to embrace the new OS. There reportedly will be a steep learning curve for information support personnel, and there may be incompatibility problems with some existing applications. Still, we expect the product to be very popular, given its improvements over Windows NT, and it should help boost the company's revenues and earnings for the next two or three years. **A further wave of new products should lead to continued good earnings gains.** Windows 2000 will be the base on which Microsoft builds a whole group of products. In April, it is scheduled to unveil its blueprint for Internet services. And, this summer, the company is

scheduled to roll out upgrades for its database product, SQL Server 2000 and its Exchange Server 2000 messaging server, as well as an upgrade (Millennium) to the Windows 98 OS. Then, too, the company is moving into new areas, such as television set-top boxes, and is investing in other businesses, such as cable operators. Now, there is the possibility that Internet appliances, which access the Internet without the need for a personal computer, will become more common, cutting into Microsoft's sales. All told, though, we think the company's broad, growing product line and marketing efforts will lead to strong annual share-net growth out to 2002-2004. **Microsoft shares are timely.** But the current price largely discounts the good earnings gains we forecast for the years ahead. Too, the company is the subject of several lawsuits, including one brought by the Department of Justice. Microsoft does not expect the actions to lead to any material adverse effects on it or its financial condition, but the uncertainties caused by the actions could lead to greater-than-usual stock-price volatility.

George A. Niemond   March 3, 2000

(A) Fiscal year ends June 30th. (B) Primary earnings through fiscal '97, then diluted. Excludes nonrecurring losses: '94, 1¢; '98, 6¢; (C) In millions, adjusted for stock splits and dividends. (D) Restated   '00, 3¢; gains, '99, 3¢; '00, 2¢. Next earnings report due mid-April.

Company's Financial Strength   A++
Stock's Price Stability   60
Price Growth Persistence   95
Earnings Predictability   85

FIGURE 4.2   Microsoft has enjoyed stunning long-term success.

Of course, whether AOL will be able to achieve such stunning levels of earnings growth is a matter for conjecture. One thing is for certain, however. Investors in AOL are counting on truly unprecedented success in terms of AOL's future earnings growth.

VII. AOL RISK ASSESSMENT

Another straightforward way of valuing AOL is to look at the company's projected EPS growth and attempt to discount such earnings at an appropriate risk-adjusted discount rate (Hirschey, 2001).

For argument's sake, let us assume that AOL is more risky than the typical stock. *The Value Line Investment Survey* projects a β = 1.75 for AOL, meaning that the company has 175% of the risk of the overall market. This means that AOL is roughly 75% more risky than the overall market, when risk is measured in terms of stock-price volatility. With a risk premium of 8%, a stock that is 1.75 times as risky as the market as a whole would command 1.75 times the market risk premium. Under these circumstances, an appropriate risk premium for AOL would not be 8%, but 1.75 times 8%, or 14% (= 8% × 1.75). If you add the required risk premium of 14% to 5%, the risk-free rate of interest, you would get a reasonable discount rate for AOL in the range of 19% (= 5% + 1.75 × 8%).

Keep in mind that a 19% expected rate of return for AOL represents a fairly low expectation, given that the stock has virtually skyrocketed during recent years. It is reasonable to expect that many of AOL's present shareholders would be very disappointed with a 19% annual rate of return. They are looking at the recent history of AOL in which it split its stock several times and jumped more than 20:1 over the 1997–98 time frame.

VIII. AOL GROWTH EXPECTATIONS

The Value Line Investment Survey projects stunning EPS growth of 90% per year over the 3- to 5-year period ending in 2002–04. From 1999 levels, the consensus forecast earnings growth rate for AOL falls in a range near 50% per year.

Two things make it difficult to estimate EPS growth for AOL. First, EPS projection requires an accurate forecast of revenues and costs. Second, in the light of future earnings, an accurate estimate of EPS requires an accurate forecast of the likely growth in the number of outstanding shares. In early 2000, AOL had about 2.2 billion shares outstanding. *After* adjusting for splits, the number of outstanding shares for AOL has gone up by a factor of more than 14:1 since AOL first went public. Since first going public, AOL has used its stock for mergers, such as the merger with Netscape Communications in 1999, and for newly issued stock tied to options granted to top executives and other employees. A tremendous number of new shares will also be issued when the merger with Time Warner, Inc. goes through as planned.

Over the 1991–99 period, the number of AOL's split-adjusted shares outstanding grew from 155 million to 2.2 billion, or at a rate of roughly 39% per year. Of course, just because AOL has grown the number of shares outstanding by 39% a year for the last decade does not mean that they are going to grow the number of shares outstanding by 39% per year going forward. Still, it seems fair to suggest that AOL will, in fact, be issuing more shares over the coming decade to reward top-performing employees and executives and to pay for mergers in the ever-escalating telecommunications industry mating game. Given AOL's history, it seems conservative to assume that the company will increase the number of outstanding shares by at least 10% per year. Over the 3-year 1996–99 period, the number of AOL's split-adjusted shares outstanding grew from 1.5 billion to 2.2 billion or at a rate of roughly 14% per year. If AOL is able to grow earnings by 50% per year, but the number of outstanding shares grows by 14% per year, the net growth in EPS will average much less than 50% per year. In fact, with earnings growth of 50% per year and annual growth in the number of shares outstanding of 14%, EPS growth will average only 31.5% (= 1.50/1.14) per year.

If AOL is, in fact, able to grow its earnings by 50% per year and only suffers dilution of 10% per year from new stock issues, AOL's EPS will grow by roughly 36% (= 1.5/1.1) per year. That is an optimistic EPS growth rate because it discounts the onslaught of competition that AOL is going to face.

IX. AOL VALUATION AS A GROWTH STOCK

With optimistic EPS growth of 36% per year from a 1999 base of $0.20, AOL's expected EPS in 2006 would total $1.72 (= $1.36^7 \times 20¢$). To project a reasonable price for AOL in 2006, it is simply necessary to multiply that amount by a reasonable P/E ratio.

Fidelity Mutual Fund guru Peter Lynch is famous for saying that an appropriate P/E ratio should be no higher than the EPS growth rate. Using a P/E ratio of 36, a reasonable price for AOL in 2006 would be roughly $61.92 (= 36 × $1.72). However, today's stock market seems willing, if not eager, to pay premium P/E multiples for what many regard as "bulletproof" franchises. Microsoft has enjoyed a bulletproof software franchise for the desktop computer and enjoys a P/E multiple in the range of 55:1. If AOL is accorded a similar multiple, a reasonable price for AOL in 2006 would be roughly $94.60 (= 55 × $1.72). Therefore, based on admittedly rough assumptions regarding what might constitute an appropriate P/E multiple for AOL, a broad range from $61.92 to $94.60 is calculated as a reasonable AOL price in 2006.

How much is a stock that might sell for $61.92 to $94.60 in the year 2006 worth in the year 1999? The answer depends on the appropriate risk-adjusted discount rate. Using a 19% risk-adjusted rate of return, $1 will grow to $3.38 in

7 years. In other words, the future value of a present sum of $1 growing at 19% for 7 years is $3.38. Therefore, the present value of $3.38 to be received in 7 years is $1, when the interest rate is 19%.

In the case of AOL, the present value of a $61.92 stock price in 2006 is $18.32 [= $61.92/(1.19^7)] when an appropriate risk-adjusted discount rate is 19%. Similarly, the present value of a $94.60 stock price in 2006 is $27.99 [= $94.60/(1.19^7)] when the appropriate risk-adjusted discount rate is 19%. Based on a reasonable assessment of AOL's future growth prospects and after adjusting for the above-average risk tied to Internet stocks, in general, and AOL, in particular, a reasonable 1999 price range for AOL would fall in the range between $18.32 and $27.99.

In light of these numbers, how is one to interpret a 1999 stock price for AOL of 95-13/16? Two possibilities exist. On the one hand, widely accepted estimates of AOL's EPS growth prospects may have been far too conservative. Alternatively, AOL's stock price of 95-13/16 may simply have been too high. To be sure, AOL's stock did spectacularly well during the 1995–99 period. Going forward, it will be interesting to learn if AOL bulls or bears were right about its 1999 stock price being too low (the bull case) or too high (the bear case). It might well be the case that buying AOL for 95-13/16 in 1999 was like buying the best farm land in Iowa and paying $7500 per acre when interest rates are 6–8% per year; it is an obvious no-win situation if you pay $7500 an acre for farm land that generates only $150 per year in profits. In Iowa, anyone who pays $7500 per acre for land to grow corn is going to get shelled. Similarly, in the stock market, anyone who pays 95-13/16 for stock worth $18.32 to $27.99 is going to get shelled. Within months of reaching 95-13/16, AOL stockholders did, in fact, get shelled. AOL's mid-2000 stock price plummeted to less than $50 per share, a mind-numbing loss of roughly $100 billion in market capitalization. By 2002, AOL traded for as little as $8.70 per share, reflecting a price decline of more than 90% from the market peak.

X. AOL AS A VALUE STOCK

Another sensible way for arriving at a reasonable economic value per share for AOL during the late-1990s was to consider the prices paid for related businesses by knowledgeable industry insiders.

For example, on May 5, 1999, AT&T Corp. won the takeover fight to become the nation's largest cable television company, with a complicated $54 billion bid to acquire MediaOne Group Inc., the nation's fourth largest cable company. In the deal, AT&T, whose initial $62 billion bid topped Comcast's $48 billion offer, swapped cable systems that could result in Comcast gaining an extra 2 million customers and AT&T receiving up to $9.2 billion. Like AT&T, Comcast agreed to pay roughly $4600 per subscriber for the cable customers being acquired. The amount paid per subscriber was a huge premium to the level paid only months earlier by AT&T for the cable operations of Tele-Communications, Inc., the second largest cable provider. In 1998, the going rate was $2500 per subscriber.

To justify such a premium price, AT&T planned to offer its 16 million cable TV customers a broad array of telephone, Internet, and TV services. In that vision, customers would only need one cable into their homes and would receive one lower priced bill, according to the company. AT&T claimed it could save consumers 20–25% off their cable and telephone bills. The expanded service would include local, intrastate, and long-distance phone calls; cable; and Internet access for a flat, monthly fee. Extra services, such as call waiting and caller ID, would also be included. AT&T said it would only charge customers between $4 and $6 for an extra line for a fax or dial-up access to the Internet on computer, compared with the $17 charged by some phone companies.

For purposes of illustration, let us assume that a typical AT&T customer is used to paying $30 per month for local phone service and another $70 per month for intrastate and long-distance phone calls. Let us also assume that 60% of these phone customers pay another $30 per month for cable TV service and that the market will grow to the point at which a similar 60% would be willing to pay $20 per month for Internet access. Of course, Internet access penetration of the overall market is presently way behind cable TV's penetration, but the number of residences logging onto the Internet is growing fast. Before discounting, this all adds up to $130 per month for a "typical" AT&T "service package" customer. After discounting, let us assume $110 per month, or $1320 per year, for a typical AT&T service-bundle customer. This means that AT&T and Comcast were willing to pay in the neighborhood of 3.5 times anticipated annual revenue per customer. Remember, customer revenues are before variable and fixed charges, which can be substantial.

In late-1999, Merrill Lynch projected that a typical monthly bill in 2002 could read as follows: $44 for basic cable, $12 for premium channels, $16 for digital channels, $35 for Internet access, and $70 for phone service. This adds up to $177 per month, or $2124 per year in 2002. Under these assumptions, AT&T and Comcast were willing to pay in the neighborhood of two times anticipated annual revenue per customer in the year 2002.

This means that a reasonable private-market value estimate of the value of AOL customers should be based on a number that is between 2 and 3.5 times anticipated annual revenue per customer.

XI. AOL CUSTOMER VALUE

In late-1999, AOL operated two worldwide Internet services: the AOL service, with more than 20 million members, and the CompuServe service, with approximately 2.2 million members. Customers paid AOL under a variety of different plans anywhere from $4.95 per month to as high as $24.95 per month. AOL's most popular plans cost $21.95 per month. In addition to online service revenues,

AOL generates revenue from advertising and online commerce. In late-1999, such revenues were about 25% of online service revenues but growing fast. Let us take the optimistic view that AOL will be able to maintain online service revenue of roughly $20 per month despite heightening competition. Being optimistic, let us also assume that advertising, commerce, and other revenue will soon grow to 50% of online revenues, or $10 per month per AOL subscriber. This allows AOL to expect total revenue of $30 per month, or $360 per year, for each of some 22.2 million subscribers. This means that the anticipated annual revenue from AOL's 1999 customer base of roughly 22.2 million customers was $8 billion (= $360 × 22.2 million).

At a conservative two times anticipated annual revenue, the total value of AOL's 1999 customer base was $16 billion (= 2 × $8 billion). Using a more aggressive 3.5 times anticipated annual revenue, the total value of AOL's customer base in 1999 was $28 billion (= 3.5 × $8 billion).

XII. PRIVATE-MARKET VALUE

In addition to its customer or subscriber base, in late-1999 AOL also operated AOL Studios, a leading creator of original interactive content; AOL.com, the world's most accessed Web site from home; Digital City, Inc., a leading local content network and community guide on AOL and the Internet; AOL NetFind, AOL's comprehensive guide to the Internet; AOL Instant Messenger, an instant messaging tool available on both the AOL service and the Internet; and ICQ, an instant communications and chat technology on the Internet and Netscape Communications, Inc.

Placing a value on such disparate operations is made difficult by the fact that they presently generate little in the way of revenues and profits. Optimistically, let us assume that these ancillary operations are worth $5 billion in total.

Taken as a whole, the analysis presented here suggests that an optimistic private-market value estimate for AOL at the end of 1999 would fall in the range between $21 billion (= $5 + $16) and $33 billion (= $5 + $28). With roughly 2.28 billion outstanding shares, this implies an optimistic private-market value for AOL of between $9.21 (= $21/2.28) and $14.47 (= $33/2.28) per share. Admittedly, this is a broad range and reflects the difficulties involved with valuing such a dynamic business. Still, these numbers can become useful when compared with AOL's December 1999 price of 95-13/16. Based on evidence from recent industry mergers, AOL seemed way overpriced at that level.

XIII. VALUE OF AOL–TIME WARNER

Several high-profile mergers have involved Internet companies, and more such mergers are sure to follow. However, few are apt to capture the imagination of investors like the marriage between AOL, the largest Internet-access provider, and media powerhouse Time Warner, the world's leading media and entertainment company. Time Warner had business interests in four fundamental areas: cable network programming (CNN), book and magazine publishing (Time), entertainment (Warner film studios), and cable services. This merger greatly excited investors because it held the promise of allowing AOL to provide high-speed Internet access over Time Warner's television cable systems, while enabling Time Warner to feed its film library and news content to AOL's large customer base. At the same time, the proposed merger between AOL and Time Warner raised some concern among Internet investors because they feared that the combined company would tend to be valued by using the metric of a large and mature media conglomerate rather than a New Economy superstar.

In the time surrounding the January 2000 merger announcement, Time Warner's stock spiked up from the high 60s to 102, while AOL's stock jumped from near 70 to 95-13/16. However, in the ensuing period, both stocks embarked on a sharp correction as investors scrambled to value the new company. During recessions when advertising revenues taper off and earnings turn soft, media stocks have been traditionally valued in the stock market at roughly 8–10 times cash flow. During economic booms, such as that experienced during the late 1990s, advertising revenues and earnings jump, and media stocks can sell for premium prices of 12–15 times cash flow.

In the case of AOL–Time Warner, the $250 billion question was: What is a reasonable cash flow expectation, and what is an appropriate multiple? Merrill Lynch's Internet software and services analyst Henry Blodget was famous for being an early bull on AOL. On February 23, 2000, Blodget put out a wildly bullish report on the proposed merger titled "AOL Time Warner: You've Got Upside!" In that report, Blodget wrote: "We also do not believe that an appropriate comparable or valuation metric for this company exists—and it could be that new valuation metrics arise that justify much higher targets than we are contemplating." Blodget argued that the combined company would be able to grow EBITDA at an annual rate of 20% per year over the 2000–05 5-year period, and that a target EBITDA multiple could reach 28 times cash flow, if not higher. Within two trading days, AOL shot up to over 60, a gain of more than 20%!

Of course, it will be years before investors know if the AOL–Time Warner merger was able to capture all the synergies envisioned by investors during December 1999. Table 4.3 shows valuation scenarios for the combined company based on various EBITDA estimates and price-EBITDA multiples. With 22% growth and a cash flow multiple of 28:1, Blodget foretold a stock price for the combined company of 90 per share by the end of 2002. Notice from Table 4.3 that Blodget's assumptions are at the most optimistic end of the cash flow growth and price-cash flow multiple spectrums. Also notice how more modest expectations yield much lower stock-price estimates.

With the benefit of 20/20 hindsight, we now know that Henry Blodget was far too optimistic about AOL's future growth prospects back in February 2000. In fact, Henry Blodget is now a former stock analyst who is no longer employed by

TABLE 4.3   Cash-Flow and Stock-Price Estimates for the Combined AOL–Time-Warner

	Conservative			Aggressive	
	10%	15%	20%	25%	30%
A. EBIDTA cash flow estimates (in $ billions)					
EBIDTA growth rate					
2000	7.7	8.1	8.4	8.8	9.1
2001	8.5	9.3	10.1	10.9	11.8
2002	9.3	10.6	12.1	13.7	15.4
2003	10.2	12.2	14.5	17.1	20.0
2004	11.3	14.1	17.4	21.4	26.0
2005	12.4	16.2	20.9	26.7	33.8
B. AOL–Time Warner stock-price estimates with various EBIDTA multiples					
EBIDTA multiple					
2000	15.4	24.2	33.6	43.8	54.6
2001	16.9	27.8	40.3	54.7	71.0
2002	18.6	31.9	48.4	68.4	92.3
2003	20.5	36.7	58.1	85.4	120.0
2004	22.5	42.2	69.7	106.8	155.9
2005	24.8	48.6	83.6	133.5	202.7

Merrill Lynch. What remains a mystery is why late-1990s investors were so gullible as to believe that AOL was then worth so much more on a relative basis than Microsoft Corp., the most successful tech stock of our time. In retrospect, it seems quite plausible that investors as a whole fell victim to the "believing is seeing" problem when it came to AOL. Wanting desperately to believe in the possibility of untold future riches, AOL investors apparently convinced themselves that the purchase of even the most ridiculously overpriced stock could be justified given sufficiently optimistic underlying assumptions. Rather than basing their investment beliefs upon economic reality and historical market experience, overly enthusiastic AOL investors let their beliefs cause them to "see" investment merit in an obviously overpriced AOL. During the late-1990s, it now seems quite clear that there was a basic disconnect between stock market valuations and economic fundamentals for a wide range of tech stocks, especially for tech stocks with business prospects directly tied to the Internet.

XIV.   CONCLUSION

The tulip mania of 17th century Holland seems to offer proof that prices for mundane, everyday items can sometimes reach truly exceptional levels that cannot be supported by any reasonable reading of underlying economic fundamentals. Of course, if the Dutch tulip mania was the only telling example of such pricing behavior in a widely traded market, then there would be scant reason to consider the possibility of pricing bubbles in modern and efficient securities markets.

Bubbles simply do not exist in perfectly efficient securities markets. According to the efficient market hypothesis, current stock prices *always* and perfectly reflect relevant risk and return information. The efficient markets hypothesis implies that near-term stock-price changes are random and independent. In such a rational pricing environment, investing is a "fair game" where the expected excess return for each security or investment asset is zero. Taken literally, this means that every stock at every point in time is an equally good buy or sell.

A careful reading of the late-1990s stock evidence concerning the pricing of tech stocks, especially tech stocks with business prospects tied directly to the Internet, suggests that bubbles do in fact sometimes emerge in modern and *typically* efficient securities markets. In the last 50 years, well-documented episodes of aberrant pricing behavior have emerged for assets as diverse as computer (tronics) stocks, Nifty Fifty companies, oil stocks, sugar, gold, silver, Japanese stocks, and biotech companies. Indeed, Kindleberger (1989) documents that the history of our typically well-functioning financial system has been punctuated by an unpredictable series of manias, panics, and crashes.

Within this context, it becomes reasonable to regard the efficient market hypothesis as a "working premise" regarding *primarily* rational investors that *typically* price securities in a rational fashion. However, a careful reading of history seems to prove that outbreaks of abnormal crowd behavior, typified by "extraordinary popular delusions and madness," are occasionally observed in typically rational corners of the world, such as the stock market.

XV. REFERENCES

Baruch, B. M. and Mackay, C. (1932). *Memoirs of Extraordinary Popular Delusions and the Madness of Crowds*. London: Bentley.
De Hertogh, A. A. (1994). The World Book Encyclopedia, Volume 19. Chicago, IL: Scott Fetzer, p. 482.
de Vries, J. (1994). *The World Book Encyclopedia, Volume 14*. Chicago, IL: Scott Fetzer, p. 148.
Dilsaver, S. C. (1994). *The World Book Encyclopedia, Volume 2*. Chicago, IL: Scott Fetzer, pp. 326–327.
Doty, R. G. (1994). *The World Book Encyclopedia, Volume 7*. Chicago, IL: Scott Fetzer, p. 266.
Hirschey, M. (1998). How Much Is a Tulip Worth? *Financial Analysts Journal* 54, 11–17.
Hirschey, M. (2001). *Investments: Theory & Applications*. Mason, OH: Thompson Learning, Inc.
Kindleberger, C. P. (1989). *Manias, Panics, and Crashes: A History of Financial Crises, Revised Edition*. New York: Basic Books.
Mackay, C. (1841). *Memoirs of Extraordinary Popular Delusions and the Madness of Crowds*. London: Bentley.

5

THE CRASH OF 2000–2002 AND IMMINENT REBOUND

Experienced investors know that competitor entry in highly profitable, high-growth industries causes above-normal profits to regress toward the mean. Conversely, bankruptcy and exit allow the below-normal profits of depressed industries to rise toward the mean. However, in an efficient market, current prices incorporate all relevant evidence, including information about the mean reversion in business profits, and stock market rates of return are expected to follow a random walk. In fact, the distribution of annual rates of return for the stock market closely resembles a normal distribution, or bell-shaped curve.

A different pattern in stock market returns emerges, however, when one considers the sequence of long-term market returns. Strong evidence of return reversal in stock market returns is suggested by the unfolding of annual returns. Statistically speaking, there appears to be high negative autocorrelation in annual returns. Sharp reversals of extreme negative returns in the stock market are common. Bear markets with sharply negative annual rates of return tend to be followed by bull markets with robust positive returns. In the period following booming bull markets, market returns tend to revert toward long-term norms.

The purpose of this chapter is to document evidence of return reversals in U.S. equity market returns over time. Following periods where the equities market has significantly outperformed long-term norms, periods of significant underperformance are observed. Conversely, after periods where the U.S. equities market has significantly underperformed long-term market norms, periods of significant outperformance are observed. Importantly, the degree by which above-normal market performance reverts to below-market performance during subsequent periods cannot be explained by conventional statistical theories describing the well-known process of regression to the mean. Similarly, the extent to which below-normal market performance reverses to above-market performance during subsequent periods cannot be explained as a simple manifestation of the regression to the mean phenomenon. Rather, the return reversal in stock market returns phenomenon offers added support for the overreaction hypothesis as explained by theories from the field of psychology.

I. MEAN REVERSION IN BUSINESS PROFITS

Economic theory explains the often-observed mean reversion in business profits over time as a typical characteristic of the competitive environment. Unexpected good fortune in the form of rising prices or falling costs translates into above-normal profits that act as a magnet for new competition. Favorable imbalances of demand and supply tend to be quickly remedied by increasing competitor supply, which leads to a reduction in firm demand, falling prices, and diminishing profits. This process continues until equilibrium quantities and prices are restored and business profits reflect only a risk-adjusted normal rate of return. At that point, competitors and potential entrants expect only a fair rate of return on investment. Similarly, when unfavorable imbalances of demand and supply exist, a decrease in supply leads to an increase in firm demand, rising prices, and rising profits. Again, this process continues until equilibrium quantities and prices are restored, and both established competitors and potential entrants are promised the opportunity for a fair risk-adjusted rate of return on investment.

Economic theory that describes a mean reversion in business profits over time is broadly accepted because of its simple and compelling logic. Such theory also enjoys broad acceptance because it has telling real-world predictive capability. High business profits often lead to booming capital expenditures and higher employment. Eventually, such expansion in an industry causes the marginal rate of return on investment to fall. Conversely, low business profits typically lead to falling capital expenditures, layoffs, and plant closings. Eventually, such industry contraction leads to rising rates of return for survivors. In short, economic theory that describes a mean reversion in business profits over time has compelling descriptive and predictive capability.

At the same time, economic theory is incapable of describing or predicting a similar mean reversion in investor profits over time. In a perfectly efficient capital market, knowledgeable investors always accurately price equities in light of all relevant economic considerations, including the expected mean reversion in business profits over time. Despite business-cycle-dependent business profits, there would be no effect on investor profits from a perfectly anticipated business cycle. Only the unexpected effects of business cycles, and the unexpected mean reversion of business profits, would influence investor profits in a perfectly efficient capital market. If mean reversion in market returns (investor profits) over time were prevalent in the securities markets, theory from the fields of statistics and/or psychology might offer relevant explanation.

II. BUSINESS CYCLES VS. MARKET CYCLES

Business cycles are a much-studied characteristic of the macroeconomy. The National Bureau of Economic Research defines recession as a period of significant decline in total output, income, employment, and trade. Usually lasting from 6 months to 1 year, recessions are marked by widespread contractions in many sectors of the economy. A growth recession is a recurring period of slow growth in total output, income, employment, and trade, usually lasting a year or more. These two concepts are often observed in tandem. For example, a growth recession may encompass a recession. In such instances, the economic slowdown usually begins before the recession starts, but ends at about the same time. Slowdowns also may occur without recession, in which case the economy continues to grow, but at a pace significantly below its long-run growth potential. While economists are not very good at predicting when recessions or business expansions will develop, they are very good at explaining the dynamic process that occurs over the course of the business cycle.

During recessions and business slowdowns, profits typically fall. Layoffs and losses mount, especially for fringe competitors. Through bankruptcies and plant closings, industry output shrinks to meet lower demand, and the seeds of the next business recovery are sown. As business recovers, losses disappear and profits resume at levels sufficient to maintain capital investment. Just the opposite occurs when an unexpected burst in demand causes an unforeseen burst in business profits. During economic expansions, entry and nonleading firm growth eat into the high profit margins of industry leaders, and company rates of return on investment fall toward long-time industry norms.

For both companies and industries, expansion and contraction occurs based upon the relationship between the internal rate of return on investment and the marginal cost of capital. Capital expenditures rise when the internal rate of return on investment exceeds the marginal cost of capital. Capital expenditures fall when the internal rate of return on investment is less than the marginal cost of capital. In the language of finance, an increase in investment is suggested whenever the net present value of individual projects exceeds zero.

At any point in time, firm and industry profit rates vary widely. Over time, however, these profit rates tend to converge toward the overall average annual rate of return on invested capital. During the 20th century, the overall average annual rate of return on invested capital averaged roughly 10% per year. During the post-World War II period, the overall average annual rate of return on invested capital averaged roughly 12–14% per year. Experienced investors know that competitor entry and growth in highly profitable industries causes above-normal profits to regress toward the mean. Conversely, bankruptcy and exit allow the below-normal profits of depressed industries to rise toward the mean. For example, drugs, health care services, and medical supplies were among the most profitable U.S. industries during the late 1980s as an aging population and government-sponsored health programs caused the demand for health care to skyrocket. In the late-1990s, however, a proliferation of new drug therapies, cost-containment measures, and government regulations conspired to limit profit-making opportunities in health care. As a result, profit and sales growth in health care turned downward. Over the next decade, it is not likely that health care industry profits will dramatically exceed all-industry averages. In that event, they will have regressed toward the mean profit level. At the same time, major air carriers such as United, American, and Delta typically earn meager profits, at best, because they operate in an industry with a homogeneous product (safe air travel) and huge fixed costs. As a result, price competition is vicious. Nevertheless, profit rates for the airlines were bound to rise during the late-1990s because the industry could not continue to sustain the enormous losses incurred during the early-1990s. Bankruptcy and exit allow prices and profits to rise toward a risk-adjusted normal rate of return for survivors.

For some investors, especially those with a strong background in statistics, the idea of return reversal in market returns might be misinterpreted as a simple "regression to the mean." However, the regression to the mean concept fails to explain return reversals in the Standard & Poor's (S&P) 500, where returns following vicious bear markets substantially exceed long-term averages rather than regress toward long-term market norms. The regression to the mean concept also fails to explain return reversals in the Nasdaq following vicious bear markets and boisterous bull markets (see Hirschey, 2003).

III. RETURN REVERSAL IN THE S&P 500 AND THE NASDAQ

Champions of the efficient market hypothesis argue that economic theory and evidence consistent with mean reversion in business profits have no meaningful implications for investment analysis and portfolio management. The efficient market hypothesis states that security prices fully reflect all available information for all securities at every point in time. Individual and professional investors buy and sell stocks under the assumption that they have discovered a divergence between intrinsic value and market price. When market price is below perceived intrinsic value, buyers aggressively acquire and bid up the price of such securities. When market price is above perceived intrinsic value, sellers aggressively abandon such securities and prices fall. Through their market activity, each buyer and each seller is behaving in such a way as to imply that they somehow know more than the person acting on the other side of each transaction. However, if the stock and bond markets are perfectly efficient and current prices fully reflect all available information, then neither buyers nor sellers have an informational advantage. In an efficient market, both buyers and sellers have the same exact set of information. Everyone knows that the business cycle is apt to affect business profits, but nobody knows how to make investment profits based upon that information.

On an empirical basis, the efficient market hypothesis is closely tied to the random walk concept. With respect to the stock market, random walk theory simply asserts that stock-price movements do not follow any patterns or trends over time. Past price action cannot be used to predict future price movements. All subsequent price changes represent arbitrary departures from previous prices. When information arises about a stock or the market as a whole, the news spreads very quickly and tends to be quickly reflected in security prices. The logic of the random walk idea is not that market prices are erratic. It is simply that when the flow of information is unimpeded, all of today's news is reflected in today's stock prices. Tomorrow's price changes reflect only tomorrow's news. By definition, news is unpredictable and random. Thus, price changes that result when news is released must also be unpredictable and random.

Although stocks can be expected to advance over long periods of time, it is well accepted that day-to-day rates of return in the stock market exhibit what might be called a random walk with drift. Daily rates of return on common stocks have a slight upward bias, or upward drift, given the long-term positive expectation for investor rates of return. Random walk theory asserts that the overwhelming characteristic of short-term rates of return in the stock market is their unpredictability.

As shown in Fig. 5.1, the distribution of rolling 12-month rates of return for the S&P 500 from 1950 to October 2002 closely resembles a normal distribution, or bell-shaped curve, with an average annual return around 9.7% and a standard deviation of annual returns of 15.5%.[1] Over this roughly 50-year period, there were 609 rolling 12-month return periods. A similar pattern emerges when annual rates of return are depicted for other major stock market indexes, such as the Nasdaq Composite Index. Stock market indexes tend to move together over extended time frames.[2] The distribution of rolling 12-month annual rates of return for the Nasdaq

[1]The same normal distribution, or bell-shaped curve, is evident when data for the overall market are captured using the Dow Jones Industrial Average and when the Nasdaq 100 Index is used to capture returns in the tech stock sector. The 500-stock S&P 500 is relied upon in this chapter as an index for the overall market because it provides somewhat broader coverage of the overall market than the 30-stock Dow Jones Industrial Average. Similarly, the broader Nasdaq Composite Index is used to measure return reversal in the tech stock sector because it has a longer price history and wider coverage than the Nasdaq 100 which dates only from January 31, 1985.

[2]For example, over the 357 rolling 12-month return periods between the initiation of the Nasdaq Index on February 5, 1971, and August 1, 2001, the degree of correlation between the S&P 500 and the Nasdaq is a very high 82.6%. The S&P 500 and the Nasdaq capture important dimensions of trends in the overall equity market and include a number of common component companies. Nevertheless, the Nasdaq is more greatly influenced by prices for small-cap and technology stocks. The correlation between the S&P 500 and other large-cap stock indexes, such as the Dow Jones Industrial Average, tends to be much higher (94.4% over this period).

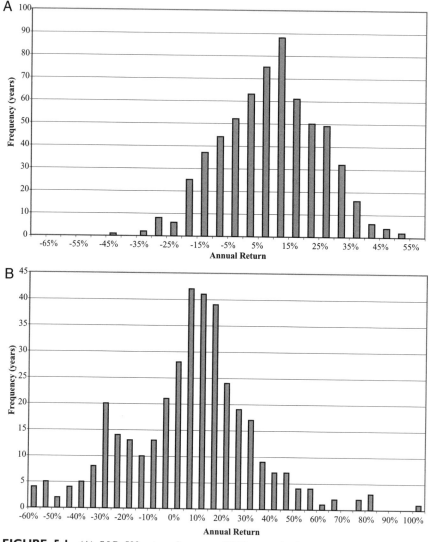

FIGURE 5.1 (A) S&P 500 return frequency (1950–present); (B) Nasdaq return frequency (1971–present).

Index from its founding on February 5, 1971, to the present (357 periods) also resembles a normal distribution, or bell-shaped curve, with an average annual return around 13.6% and a standard deviation of annual returns of 25.6%. These distributions depict the conceptual predictions of random walk theory.

A different pattern in stock market returns, and one that provides strong evidence of return reversal in stock market returns, is provided when one considers the pattern of long-term market returns. Evidence on the degree of return

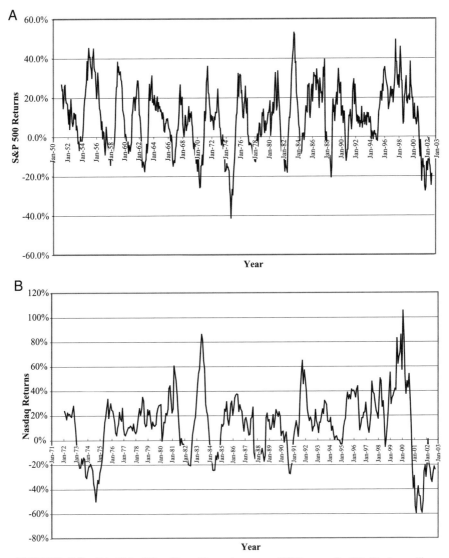

FIGURE 5.2 (A) S&P 500 rolling 12-month returns (1950–present); (B) Nasdaq rolling 12-month returns (1971–present).

reversal as revealed by the sequence of annual returns is shown in Fig. 5.2. Notice that while rolling 12-month annual rates of return on the S&P 500 and the Nasdaq are noisy, both converge over time toward long-term averages. Statistically speaking, this is caused by negative autocorrelation in annual returns. For the S&P 500, the degree of negative autocorrelation in annual returns is a statistically significant −7.2%; for the more volatile Nasdaq, the degree of negative autocorrelation in annual returns is a statistically significant −10.2%.

Strong further evidence of return reversal in market returns is given in Table 5.1. In the last half of the 20th century, the worst 12-month period for the S&P 500 ended in September 1974. Experienced investors remember the fall of 1974 as the culmination of one of the worst bear market of our lifetimes. Brutal bear markets were also experienced in the 12-month period ending May 1970 and August 2001. Notice how these worst 10 bear market periods, where the S&P 500 fell by an average –29.2%, were followed by periods with robust positive returns

TABLE 5.1   Worst and Best Historical 12-Month Returns

Month ending	Historical 12-month returns (%)	Forward-looking 12-month returns (%)	Month ending	Historical 12-month returns (%)	Forward-looking 12-month returns (%)
Ten worst historical S&P 500 returns			*Ten worst historical Nasdaq returns*		
September-74	–41.4	32.0	March-01	–59.8	0.3
October-74	–31.8	20.5	September-01	–59.2	–21.8
August-74	–30.8	20.4	August-01	–57.1	–27.2
December-74	–29.7	31.5	February-01	–54.2	–19.5
September-01	–27.5	–21.7	September-74	–49.9	33.5
November-74	–27.1	30.4	October-01	49.8	–24.1
July-74	–26.7	11.9	July-01	–46.2	–34.5
May-70	–26.0	30.2	June-01	–45.5	–32.3
October-01	–25.9	–16.8	April–01	–45.2	–20.2
June-70	–25.6	35.7	October-74	–40.8	18.0
Worst 10	**–29.2**	**17.4**	**Worst 10**	**–50.8**	**–12.8**
Worst 30	**–21.8**	**13.6**	**Worst 30**	**–36.4**	**0.6**
Worst 10%	**–17.5**	**14.2**	**Worst 10%**	**–34.3**	**0.0**
Ten best historical S&P 500 returns			*Ten best historical Nasdaq returns*		
June-83	52.9	–8.6	February-00	105.3	–54.2
July-83	51.8	–7.3	June-83	86.0	–24.8
July-97	49.1	17.4	March-00	85.8	–59.8
March-98	45.5	16.8	December-99	85.6	–39.3
May-83	45.1	–7.3	August-99	82.7	53.6
December-54	45.0	26.4	July-83	81.6	–24.4
August-55	44.8	10.0	May-83	72.9	–24.6
April-83	41.2	–2.7	November-99	71.1	–22.1
July-55	40.9	13.5	October-99	67.5	13.6
February-55	40.6	23.3	October-91	64.6	11.5
Best 10	**45.7**	**8.2**	**Best 10**	**80.3**	**–17.1**
Best 30	**40.1**	**9.3**	**Best 30**	**62.7**	**–7.0**
Best 10%	**35.2**	**10.6**	**Best 10%**	**56.4**	**–2.6**
Overall averages (1950–present)	**9.7**		**Overall averages (1971–present)**	**13.6**	
S.D.	**15.5**		**S.D.**	**25.6**	
Correlation	**–7.2**		**Correlation**	**–10.2**	
Number of 12-month returns	**609**		**Number of 12-month returns**	**357**	

that averaged 17.4%. However, it is important to note that these worst 10 bear market periods are not fully independent. This makes consideration of larger samples of poorly performing markets interesting. In this vein, it is interesting to note that returns for the worst 30 bear market periods, where negative historical 12-month returns of −21.8% for the S&P 500, are followed by above-normal returns in the following year of 13.6%. For the worst 10% (or 60) bear market environments for the S&P 500, large negative market returns of −17.5% are followed by above-normal market returns of 14.2% in the subsequent 12 months.

As shown in Table 5.1, mean reversion in S&P 500 returns is evident in the period following robust bull market expansions, but this influence is weaker than that seen following severe bear market contractions. In the last half of the 20th century, the best 12-month period for the S&P 500 ended in June 1983. Experienced investors remember 1982 as the start of the greatest bull market in stock market history, and that bull market got off to a wonderful start. Splendid bull markets were also experienced in the 12-month periods ending July 1997 and March 1998. Notice how these booming best 10 bull markets saw the S&P 500 rise by an average 45.7%. On average, subsequent 12-month returns were a more conventional 8.2% per year. It is also interesting to note that the best 30 bull market periods depict mean reversion in market returns with historical 12-month returns of 40.1% followed by an average 9.3% in the following year. For the best 10% (or 60) bull market environments for the S&P 500, above-average market returns of 35.2% reverted toward market norms of 10.6% in the subsequent 12-month period.

Robust evidence of return reversal in market returns is evident in the more volatile Nasdaq Stock Market. In timing and relative magnitude, return reversal for the Nasdaq tends to amplify the S&P 500 experience. Since the February 1971 introduction of the Nasdaq Index, but prior to the most recent experience since the market peak in March 2000, the worst 12-month period for the Nasdaq ended in September 1974. Notice how the worst 10 bear market periods for the Nasdaq, where the index fell by an average −50.8%, were followed by periods with much more modest returns that averaged −12.8%. The worst 30 bear market periods for the Nasdaq also depict return reversal in market returns with historical 12-month returns of −36.4% followed by positive returns in the following year of 0.6%. For the worst 10% (or 35) bear market environments for the Nasdaq, sharply negative market returns of −34.3% were followed by flat market returns of 0.0% in the subsequent 12-month period.

Potent evidence of return reversal in market returns is also evident for the Nasdaq in the period following vigorous bull market expansions. Notice how the best 10 bull markets saw the Nasdaq rise by an average 80.3%. On average, subsequent 12-month returns were a sharply negative −17.1% per year. It is also interesting to note that the best 30 bull market periods for the Nasdaq depict return reversal in market returns with historical 12-month returns of 62.7% followed by an average −7.0% in the following year. For the best 10% (or 35) bull market environments for the Nasdaq, above-average market returns of 56.4% reverted to below-market norms of −2.6% in the subsequent 12-month period.

IV. NONOVERLAPPING PERIOD ANALYSIS

An obvious advantage of the overlapping period analysis described in Table 5.1 is that it uses all available data to consider the possibility of extreme return reversals following extraordinary 12-month market returns. These data strongly suggest that extraordinary historical returns give rise to a reversal in forward-looking returns. Extreme return reversal appears especially prevalent in the case of unusually negative historical returns. When historical returns on the S&P 500 and the Nasdaq fall below arbitrary popular benchmarks of −10% (signifying a 12-month correction) or −20% (signifying a 12-month bear market), above-average market returns are consistently observed during the subsequent 12-month period.

A possible concern with the data reported in Table 5.1 is that such a rolling 12-month period analysis involves overlapping periods. However, this is not an overwhelming concern. Table 5.2 shows that extreme return reversal is also prevalent when nonoverlapping periods are analyzed.

Since 1950, there have been 16 unique instances when the overall market, as measured by the S&P 500, has suffered a sustained market correction of at least −10% in historical 12-month returns. On average, such corrections in the S&P 500 last 4.25 months and involve a decline of −14.1%. During the subsequent 12-month period, forward-looking investors consistently earn above-average market returns of 14.3% per year. Since 1950, there have only been 5 unique periods when the overall market, as measured by the S&P 500, has suffered a sustained bear market of at least −20% in 12-month returns. On average, these bear markets in the S&P 500 last 3 months and involve a decline of −24.7%. During the subsequent 12-month period, forward-looking investors consistently earn above-average market returns of 14.1% per year.

A similar pattern of extreme return reversal is also obvious for the more volatile Nasdaq. Since 1971, there have been 9 unique instances when the Nasdaq has suffered a sustained market correction of at least −10% in historical 12-month returns. On average, Nasdaq corrections last 7.11 months and involve a decline of −20.0%. During the subsequent 12-month period, forward-looking Nasdaq investors consistently earn above-average market returns of 21.0% per year. Since 1971, there have been 7 unique periods when the Nasdaq has suffered a sustained bear market of at least −20% in 12-month returns. Nasdaq bear markets average 5.43 months in duration and involve a decline of −28.2%. During the subsequent 12-month period, forward-looking Nasdaq investors earn above-average market returns of 15.7% per year.

Thus, it seems fair to conclude that the extreme return reversal phenomenon described in Table 5.1 is not caused by any distortion or bias due to the use of overlapping time periods.[3]

[3]Table 5.2 shows that extreme return reversal is prevalent over the entire period despite sharply negative forward-looking returns for the S&P 500 and the Nasdaq during the present bear market. These data illustrate how atypical present market returns are when compared with market norms and the potential for a sharp reversal of returns in the coming period.

TABLE 5.2 Recent Bear Markets and Subsequent 12-Month Returns

Time period	Duration (in months)	Average historical 12-month returns (%)	Average forward-looking 12-month returns (%)	Time period	Duration (in months)	Average historical 12-month returns (%)	Average forward-looking 12-month returns (%)
S&P 500 –10% 12-month corrections (1950–present)				*Nasdaq –10% 12-month corrections (1971–present)*			
December 1957	1	–14.3	38.1	April 1973–March 1975	24	–26.0	–5.8
May–December 1962	8	–13.7	22.7	March–July 1982	5	–18.6	70.7
August–December 1966	5	–13.0	20.2	April–December 1984	9	–17.2	22.4
November 1969–January 1970	3	–14.1	1.9	October–November 1987	2	–12.8	20.0
March–August 1970	6	–19.1	24.9	January–March 1988	3	–12.9	11.3
October 1970	1	–14.3	13.2	May 1988	1	–11.1	20.5
November 1973–March 1975	17	–21.5	7.7	September 1988	3	–13.6	21.3
October 1977	1	–10.3	0.9	August 1990–December 1990	5	–22.5	51.6
December 1977–February 1978	3	–12.3	7.9	November 2001–October 2001 (?)	12	–45.5	–23.3
November 1981	1	–10.1	9.6				
February–July 1982	6	–15.7	43.1				
March 1988	1	–11.2	13.9				
June–October 1988	4	–15.2	26.6				
September–October 1990	2	–11.5	27.9				
December 2000	1	–10.1	–13.0				
March–October 2001 (?)	8	–19.8	–16.4				
Averages	**4.25**	**–14.1**	**14.3**	**Averages**	**7.11**	**–20.0**	**21.0**
S&P 500 –20% 12-month bear markets (1950–present)				*Nasdaq –20% 12-month bear markets (1971–present)*			
April–June 1970	3	–24.3	31.1	May–June 1973	2	–22.5	–23.3
July 1974–January 1975	7	–29.7	25.4	November 1973–March 1974	5	–26.0	–27.0
August 1988	1	–20.7	34.4	May 1974–February 1975	10	–33.0	21.9
March 2001	1	–22.6	–1.1	May–July 1982	3	–20.5	80.2
August–October 2001	3	–26.2	–19.2	May–July 1984	3	–24.6	26.6
				September–November 1990	3	–25.3	54.5
				November 2001–October 2001 (?)	12	–45.5	–23.3
Averages	**3.00**	**–24.7**	**14.1**	**Averages**	**5.43**	**–28.2**	**15.7**

V. RETURN REVERSAL OR SIMPLY REGRESSION TO THE MEAN?

For some investors, especially those with a strong background in statistics, the idea of extreme return reversal in the stock market might be misinterpreted as a simple manifestation of a more familiar statistical concept called "regression to the mean." In the last half of the 19th century, Sir Francis Galton was among the earliest and most respected British advocates of using statistics to study regularities in natural phenomena. During the 1860s, Galton searched for weather patterns as a means for improving weather forecasts. This was path-breaking use of the probability concept. His 1875 experiments on how specific factors affect the size and weight of fruit and sweet peas convinced Galton that important traits could be statistically isolated, and shown subject to what he called "reversion towards the average characteristics of the species." Galton's further study of inheritance patterns within leading Victorian families led him to believe that there was also a natural tendency for human characteristics, talent, and character to regress toward the population average. Because Galton equated average characteristics with mediocrity, he called this tendency "regression towards mediocrity."

Sir Francis Galton (1886) formalized his regression toward mediocrity concept in a paper titled "Regression Towards Mediocrity in Hereditary Stature." Focusing on height across generations, Galton related the height of children to the average height of their parents. After controlling for gender differences, children and parents had the same mean height. Interestingly, Galton found the average height of children from taller parents was closer to the mean height of all children than to the mean height of their parents. The same thing happened when he started with children. The average height of parents with taller children was closer to the mean height of all parents than to the mean height of their children. This is now recognized as the regression to the mean concept. It is a statistical relationship and not a genetic phenomenon.

Regression to the mean is a statistical relationship that occurs whenever one analyzes two measures that are imperfectly correlated and a nonrandom sample from the overall population of one such measure, such as historical and forward-looking stock market returns. As shown in Fig. 5.1, the frequency distributions of historical 12-month returns for both the S&P 500 and the Nasdaq appear normally distributed and look like "bell-shaped" curves. Regression to the mean theory suggests that when samples of pretest historical stock market returns for vicious bear markets are isolated, for example, posttest forward-looking market returns should have an average that is closer to the overall population mean than to the sample average for vicious bear markets. Similarly, regression to the mean theory suggests that when pretest historical samples of returns for booming bull markets are isolated, posttest forward-looking market returns should have an average that is closer to the overall population mean than to the bull market sample average. Purely on a statistical basis, market returns for the sample posttest period can be expected to wind up closer to the population mean than their bear or bull market sample pretest means were to the population mean. Purely on a statistical basis, sample means for market returns can be expected to regress toward the population mean from the pretest (historical) to the posttest (forward-looking) periods.

To see why regression to the mean might occur in the stock market, consider the fact that the sample of historical bear markets is defined simply on the basis of poor historical performance. When market returns are isolated for the worst 10% of all market environments, what are the chances that during the posttest period that exact group will once again be associated with the lowest 10% market environments? That probability is small, of course. Even if just a few posttest periods display more typical market returns, the group mean return during the post-test period will have to be closer to the population mean than to the pretest mean. The same is true at the other end of the annual return spectrum. If a sample of bull markets is isolated simply on the basis of high annual returns during the pretest historical period, market returns during the posttest forward-looking period are apt to be closer to the overall population mean than to the sample average for the pretest period.

The regression toward the mean phenomenon occurs whenever one draws an asymmetric sample from the overall population. If a sample of market returns were drawn randomly from the overall population, the sample and the population would be expected to have the same pretest and posttest average. It will happen forward in time, that is from historical to forward-looking returns. It will happen backward in time, that is from forward-looking returns to historical returns. The less correlated are historical and forward-looking returns, or any two variables, the greater is the regression to the mean. The percent of regression to the mean in any given situation is given by the formula:

$$P_{rm} = 100(1 - r)$$

where P_{rm} is the percent of regression to the mean and r is the correlation between any two measures.

For example, if $r = 0.5$, there is 50% regression to the mean. With a correlation of 0.5 between historical and forward-looking returns, the sampled group mean for forward-looking returns can be expected to move *50%* of the distance from the pretest historical mean to the population average annual rate of return during the posttest period. If the correlation is a small 0.2, the posttest average return can be expected to regress 80% of the distance toward the population mean. If there is no correlation between pretest historical market returns and posttest forward-looking market returns, posttest sample returns can be expected to "regress" all the way to the population mean. It is worth thinking about what this last case implies with respect to the efficient market hypothesis. With zero correlation between historical and forward-looking market returns, knowing historical returns gives absolutely no information about forward-looking returns. In that event, an investor's best guess as to how the market will do during any future period, irrespective of historical bear and bull markets, is the population average rate of return.

In Table 5.1, notice how S&P 500 returns during the 12 months following robust bull markets conform closely with long-term market norms. As a result, the regression to the mean concept offers a valid explanation of forward-looking market returns for the S&P 500 during the period immediately following robust bull markets. However, also notice how the regression to the mean concept fails to explain why S&P 500 returns in the 12 months following vicious bear markets substantially exceed rather than regress toward long-term market norms. The regression to the mean concept also fails to explain why Nasdaq returns in the 12 months following vicious bear markets substantially exceed rather than regress toward long-term market norms. Also observe how Nasdaq returns in the 12 months following boisterous bull markets are highly negative, rather than simply regress toward market averages.

It is fair to conclude that the regression to the mean concept fails to provide adequate explanation of the return reversal patterns evident in Table 5.1. As a result, alternate explanation(s) must be sought.

VI. OVERREACTION HYPOTHESIS

The return reversal in S&P 500 and Nasdaq returns reported in this chapter is consistent with the market overreaction hypothesis proposed by Werner F. M. DeBondt and Richard Thaler. In an early article, DeBondt and Thaler (1985) report that the stock market appears to be highly efficient in rapidly incorporating information that affects prices in the short run, but systematically fails to process more complex and longer run information in an efficient manner. Even some of the most staunch defenders of the efficient market hypothesis and the earliest critics of "behavioral" research in finance tend to agree with this basic premise. For example, in his discussion of DeBondt and Thaler's original research, Peter L. Bernstein (1985, p. 807) wrote: "… let us give the efficient Market Hypothesis its due as an explanation of how markets work in the short run, even if we can reject the hypothesis in the long run."

In a follow-up article, DeBondt and Thaler (1990) observe that although most economists recognize that not everyone is fully rational, the existence of irrational agents in the stock market is often dismissed as irrelevant. They investigate security analysts as one possible source of irrationality in financial markets and find that security analysts have a tendency to make forecasts that are too extreme, given the predictive value of the information available to the forecaster. In fact, forecasted changes are simply too extreme to be considered rational. They suggest the behavior of the security analyst community as one possible source of long-term overreaction in the equity markets.

DeBondt and Thaler's path-breaking research has given rise to a broadening stream of academic inquiry that gives strong support to the premise of long-term overreaction in the stock market. For example, Michaely, Thaler, and Womack (1995) find that the magnitude of short-run price reactions to dividend omissions are greater than for dividend initiations. Contrary to the efficient market hypothesis, in the year following such announcements, stock prices continue to drift in the same direction, though the drift following omissions is stronger and more robust. This postdividend initiation/omission price drift is distinct from and more pronounced than that following earnings surprises. Dreman and Berry (1995) examine the importance of earnings surprises within the context of contrarian investment strategies. They report that positive and negative earnings surprises affect "best" and "worst" stocks in an asymmetric manner that favors worst stocks. They demonstrate that stocks are not immediately priced at an appropriate level after an earnings surprise. Rather, over a prolonged period of time (at least five years), stock prices revert to the mean, with low P/E stocks outperforming and the high P/E stocks underperforming the market. This evidence is consistent with the overreaction hypothesis that investors misprice best and worst stocks because their expectations are too one sided. More recently, Nam, Pyun, and Avard (2001) investigate the mean reverting pattern of monthly returns for the New York Stock Exchange (NYSE), the American Stock Exchange (AMEX), and the Nasdaq indexes using asymmetric, non linear, smooth-transition GARCH models. These models illustrate a pattern of asymmetric mean reversion and risk decimation, support the market overreaction hypothesis, and corroborate arguments for contrarian portfolio strategies.

In a comment on Internet stock pricing in the spring of 1999, Thaler (1999) wrote that his survey of professional investors revealed that the median respondent thought that the intrinsic value of a portfolio of five Internet stocks (America Online, Amazon.com, eBay, Priceline.com, and Yahoo!) was only 50% of the market price. "Suppose," Thaler (1999) wrote, " the 'professionals' are right and these multibillion dollar companies are worth only half of their current prices. Suppose further that this valuation is the consensus of Wall Street experts. How can such a situation exist? The answer is that it may be an equilibrium (although not a "rational equilibrium") as long as the Wall Street experts are not the marginal investors in these stocks." A number of other authors also questioned peak valuations of Internet and "new era" growth stocks. In an earlier paper, I likened the pricing of Internet stocks to an earlier craze for tulips, the tulip mania (Hirschey, 1998). I argued that the efficient market hypothesis is a useful working hypothesis and that investors may be primarily rational and typically price securities in a rational fashion. Nevertheless, outbreaks of crowd behavior, typified by extraordinary popular delusions and madness, are a possibility. In a similar vein, Chan, Karceski, and Lakonishok (2000) and Hirschey (2001) describe the excessive pricing of large-cap growth stocks in the late-1990s as reflective of investor overreaction.

That investors sometimes overreact seems clear, *why* investors overreact is yet uncertain. Progress on this front has been slow, perhaps because many researchers in the investments field are better schooled in economics and statistics than in psychology. DeBondt and Thaler (1985) submit that stock market overreaction can be explained by research in experimental psychology that shows people often overreact to unexpected dramatic events. In revising their beliefs, individual investors may overweigh recent information and underweigh prior base-rate data on an ongoing basis. For example, momentum-based trading strategies are a formalization of the recency effect; speculators simply buy what seems to be working. In the period up to the March 2000 peak, so long as Internet stocks were rising, speculators kept buying and did not stop to worry about fundamental valuation.[4]

The practical usefulness of information about return reversal in stock market returns, and theory from the field of behavioral finance, is documented to the extent that it helps investors understand and predict stock market behavior. The hypothesis that a cognitive bias, or investor overreaction to a long series of bad news, could produce predictable mispricing is inherently testable. While the data presented in this chapter suggest support for the overreaction hypothesis, this support would be strengthened considerably with corroborative future evidence. For example, Table 5.3 depicts recent historical returns for the S&P 500 and the Nasdaq. Clearly, the new millennium has been rough on investors. Many previous adherents of new era growth stock investing now decry the "obvious" excesses of speculators participating in the recent Internet stock bubble. However, when one considers the magnitude of recent declines in light of the long-term (base-rate) data provided in Tables 5.1 and 5.2, it seems quite plausible that present investors who dump equities in favor of fixed-yield instruments may be making a similar mistake. Data in Tables 5.1 and 5.2 suggest that forward-looking returns on the S&P 500 and the Nasdaq are apt to be strongly positive. According to the overreaction hypothesis, a vigorous new bull market would appear to be just around the corner.

VII. WHAT ABOUT THE JAPANESE EXPERIENCE?

The extreme reversal in stock market returns evident in stock market history is consistent with the market overreaction hypothesis. While the stock market appears to be efficient in rapidly incorporating information that affects prices in the short run, it systematically fails to process more complex and longer run information in an efficient manner. Stock market overreaction can be explained by research in experimental psychology that shows people often overreact to unexpected dramatic events. In revising their beliefs, individual investors may overweigh recent information and underweigh prior base-rate data on an ongoing basis. Information about return reversal in stock market returns, and theory from the field of behavioral finance, is useful to investors if it helps them understand

---

[4]In March 2000, a well-known security analyst admitted to me in a private conversation that he could not recommend purchase of America Online on the basis of it representing an attractive value (i.e., "value stock") or argue that it was reasonably priced on the basis of its growth prospects (i.e., "growth at a reasonable price"). Yet, he rated the stock a Strong Buy. "Why?", I asked. "People seem willing to pay these prices," he replied.

TABLE 5.3　The New Millenium Has Been Rough on the S&P 500 and the Nasdaq

Month ending	S&P 500 historical 12-month returns (%)	Nasdaq historical 12-month returns (%)
January-00	9.0	57.2
February-00	10.3	105.3
March-00	16.5	85.8
April-00	8.8	51.8
May-00	9.1	37.7
June-00	6.0	47.7
July-00	7.7	42.8
August-00	14.9	53.6
September-00	12.0	33.7
October-00	4.9	13.6
November-00	−5.3	−22.1
December-00	−10.1	−39.3
January-01	−2.0	−29.6
February-01	−9.3	−54.2
March-01	−22.6	−59.8
April-01	−14.0	−45.2
May-01	−11.6	−37.9
June-01	−15.8	−45.5
July-01	−15.3	−46.2
August-01	−25.3	−57.1
September-01	−27.5	−59.2
October-01	−25.9	−49.8
November-01	−13.3	−25.7
December-01	−13.0	−21.1
January-02	−17.3	−30.2
February-02	−10.7	−19.5
March-02	−1.1	0.3
April-02	−13.8	−20.2
May-02	−15.0	−23.4
June-02	−19.2	−32.3
July-02	−24.7	−34.5
August-02	−17.0	−23.5
September-02	−21.7	−21.8
October-02	−16.8	−24.1
Overall Averages	**9.7**	**13.6**
S.D.	**15.5**	**25.6**

and predict stock market behavior. Given the magnitude of recent stock market declines and the sharply negative stock market reaction following the devastating terrorist attacks in New York City and Washington, D.C., the overreaction hypothesis predicts that a vigorous new bull market is imminent.

A contrary viewpoint might be expressed by those who point to the Japanese experience of the late-1990s and argue that the U.S. stock market is destined to

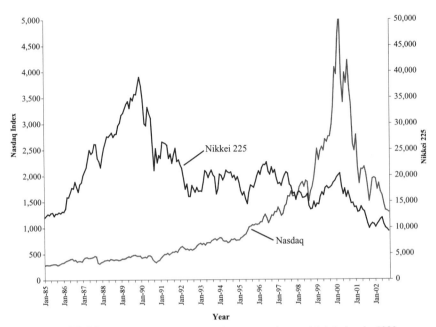

FIGURE 5.3   The Nasdaq soared while Japanese stocks crumbled during the 1990s.

languish for a decade or more at current levels. Within this context, it becomes interesting to compare the recent stock market performance of Japanese stocks with the performance of the Nasdaq.

As shown in Fig. 5.3, the Nasdaq soared during the 1990s while Japan's Nikkei 225 Index crumbled. From a January 2, 1985, start at 11,543, the Nikkei soared to a closing high of 38,916 on December 29, 1989. This represents a 5-year gain of 237.1% in the Nikkei, and a stunning compound annual return of 27.5% per year. Then, the Nikkei bubble burst and the Japanese equity market crashed. On October 8, 1998, the Nikkei hit 12,880, representing a stunning drop of 66.9% from the peak reached roughly *9 years* earlier. Following a modest recovery to 18,934.34 on December 30, 1999, the Nikkei closed out the 1990s a stunning 51.3% off the high reached more than a decade earlier. Worse yet, the Nikkei headed south at the start of the new millennium and reached a new low of 8995.2 on September 4, 2002, or roughly 76.9% off the market peak reached more than 12 years earlier.

The contrast between the 1990s performance of the crumbling Nikkei and the soaring Nasdaq indexes is stark. From a beginning level of 247.1 on January 2, 1985, the Nasdaq soared to 5132.52 on March 10, 2000. This represents a 15-1/4-year return on the Nasdaq of 2077.1% and an astounding compound return of 22.0% per year.[5] Therefore, the high point reached by the Japanese Nikkei in

[5]From a beginning split-adjusted level of 125 on January 31, 1985, the Nasdaq 100 soared to 4816.35 on March 24, 2000. This represents a 15-1/4-year return of 3753.3%, and an amazing compound return of 27.1% per year.

FIGURE 5.4   The 2000–02 Nasdaq crash matches the 1990s crash in Japanese stocks.

1989 and the pinnacle reached by the Nasdaq Stock Market in 2000 are quite comparable with respect to the above-normal annual rates of return that were sustained in the 5 years prior to their respective market peaks. They are also comparable with respect to a peak market capitalization of roughly $6 trillion each. An important difference lies in the fact that the greater length of the Nasdaq bull market has led to P/E ratios for the Nasdaq that were somewhat higher than the historic highs near 100 seen for the Nikkei in 1989 because many late-1990s tech stock favorites had no earnings or were reporting large losses.[6] The similarities in market returns during the bubble formation period and the valuation extremes reached during the peak of each market bubble suggest that the ensuing correction in tech stocks on the Nasdaq may indeed mirror the epic recent correction in Japanese stocks (see Shiller, Fumiko, and Tsutsui, 1996).

Figure 5.4 gives an interesting perspective on what might lie in store for the overall Nasdaq market. Nasdaq investors can take both good and bad news from this comparison. The good news is that the historic crash on the Nasdaq has already traced out a retrenchment that is remarkably similar to the crash in the Japanese market. From an all-time closing high of 38,916 on December 29, 1989, the Nikkei reached a new low of 8995.2 on September 4, 2002. An identical retrenchment of 76.9% from Nasdaq's 5132.52 market peak on March 10, 2000,

---

[6]As mentioned in Chapter 1, at the 2000 market peak, the Nasdaq Composite reached an average P/E of 245.7. In February 2000, the Nasdaq 100 P/E reached 134.7.

would put the Nasdaq at 1185.6, a level that is virtually identical to the 1192.42 reached by the Nasdaq on July 24, 2002. Therefore, the good news is that the correction on the Nasdaq may have already hit bottom. Nasdaq investors have little reason to fear a continuing crash in stock prices. Now is the time to begin preparing for the next bull market.

The bad news implicit in a comparison between the crash experience on the Nasdaq and in the Japanese market is that if Nasdaq performance continues to follow a pattern similar to that followed by the Nikkei, Nasdaq investors can look forward to an extended period of anemic capital appreciation. Prior to the historic recent crash in tech stocks, I wrote that new highs for the Nasdaq may be a long time in coming (see Hirschey, 2001). For example, as shown in Fig. 5.4, if the Nasdaq performance were to precisely mimic the pattern set by the Nikkei, it would not be surprising to see the Nasdaq trade in a broad range from 1000–2000 for as long as a decade. While taking 10 years to recover from 2002 levels of roughly 1200–2000 on the Nasdaq suggests anemic market returns, such a recovery would still represent an expected average rate of return in excess of 5.2% per year for the Nasdaq market. There is reason to hope for more.

The crash on the Nasdaq was "accomplished" in a far shorter period of time than the crash in Japanese stock prices, and there is every reason to expect a somewhat faster recovery. The Japanese economy suffers from basic structural difficulties and policy missteps that leave it far more troubled that the U.S. economy. In Japan, the 1989 inflation that was evident in a stock market bubble spilled over into an explosion in real estate prices, a much larger bubble that continues to be unwound. Restriction on trade and capital flows in Japan also led to misallocations that will be corrected only slowly. In the United States, capital markets tend to adjust quickly following changes in underlying economic conditions. Enlightened monetary, tax, and regulatory policy can also be expected to help spur economic recovery in the United States and higher Nasdaq 100 stock prices.

How long it will take for Nasdaq stock prices to recover and grow beyond their recent market peak is a matter for conjecture. During the post-World War II period, the annual rate of return in stock prices has averaged roughly 12–14% per year. With a market return of 13% per year, for example, it would take roughly *11.9 years* to make a sustained recovery from the post-crash Nasdaq low of 1192.42 (reached on July 24, 2002) and reclaim the market peak of 5132.52 (first reached on March 10, 2000). Thus, while market experience suggests that much, if not all, of the crash on the Nasdaq is over, it may be some years before tech stock favorites reclaim prior peak valuations.

In considering recent experience, tech stock investors should not base their present investment decision on the premise that market P/E ratios in excess of 100 times earnings will again be deemed reasonable during their lifetime. Nasdaq and tech stock favorites may never again reach the relative valuations evident at the 2000 peak. Still, it is worth emphasizing that economic growth, not reinflation of a stock market bubble, can be expected to push Nasdaq and tech stocks higher from present levels. Going forward, Nasdaq and tech stock investors should expect a sharp reversal of negative returns. Positive expected returns of between 5.2% to market norms of 12–14% seem reasonable and should provide a fertile market environment for tech stock investing in the coming decade.

VIII. CONCLUSION

Well-accepted economic theory and evidence documents the mean reversion in business profits over time. At the same time, the efficient market hypothesis posits that this predictable reversion to the mean in business profits holds no importance for investors. In a perfectly efficient market, all relevant information, including trends in business profits, are fully incorporated in stock prices. Both short- and long-run rates of return in a perfectly efficient stock market follow a random walk. From an efficient markets perspective, any perceived tendency for mean reversion in stock market returns can be dismissed as a simple manifestation of the well-known regression to the mean concept from the field of statistics.

In contrast, stock market evidence and behavioral finance research on the overreaction hypothesis are consistent with a predictable process of long-term return reversal in stock market returns. If investors systematically overweigh recent bad news about negative market returns, investor fear can push stock prices far below fundamental economic values. Similarly, if investors systematically overweigh recent good news about positive market returns, investor greed can push stock prices above fundamental economic values. In both instances, cognitive bias among investors can lead to predictable mispricing.

The high degree of negative autocorrelation evident in annual rates of return for the S&P 500 and the Nasdaq suggest that long-term returns in the stock market are not random. Instead, this evidence is consistent with the notion that, in the short run, stock prices may, in fact, be susceptible to extraordinary swings driven by investor sentiments of greed and fear. In the long run, however, trends in stock prices mirror real changes in business prospects as measured by revenues, earnings, dividends, and so on. As a result, periods with extraordinary above-normal market returns tend to be followed by periods of subpar performance. Similarly, intervals of sharply below-normal market returns tend to be followed by stretches of above-normal performance.

More than a simple prescription to "buy fear" or "sell greed," evidence of return reversal in stock market returns gives strong support for the relevance of insightful fundamental analysis. In his classic book, *The Intelligent Investor*, Benjamin Graham (1973) describes the relationship between the intelligent long-term investor and market fluctuation using his now famous Mr. Market metaphor. The intelligent investor has a business partner, Mr. Market, who offers to buy or sell shares in the business at a price that varies from day to day. Sometimes, Mr. Market's idea of value is justified by business developments. At other times, Mr. Market lets his enthusiasm or fear get the best of him and proposes silly prices. Graham (1973) writes that a sensible businessmen will sell out when

Mr. Market quotes a ridiculously high price or buy when the price is ridiculously low. In Graham's (1973, p. 109) words: "… price fluctuations have only one significant meaning for the true investor. They provide him with an opportunity to buy wisely when prices fall sharply and to sell wisely when they advance a great deal. At other times, he will do better if he forgets about the stock market and pays attention to his dividend returns and the operating results of his companies."

With respect to inherently unpredictable moves in the overall market, the point of this chapter is simple but important for investment management. As suggested by the efficient market hypothesis, perhaps nobody can predict when the market will take a protracted severe drop (e.g., down 20%). However, after the market has taken such a drop, the overreaction hypothesis suggests that forward-looking returns will be above average. In response to a protracted severe drop in the overall market, such as the crash of 2000–02, the overreaction hypothesis suggests that prudent investments should adopt a fully invested and diversified position in stocks. While backward-looking investors remain shell-shocked by the historic 2000–02 crash on the Nasdaq, forward-looking tech stock investors will benefit greatly from the ensuing recovery.

IX. REFERENCES

Bernstein, P. L. (1985). Does the Stock Market Overreact?: Discussion. *Journal of Finance* 40, 806–808.

Chan, L. K. C., Karceski, J., and Lakonishok, J. (2000). New Paradigm or Same Old Hype in Equity Investing? *Financial Analysts Journal* 56, 23–36.

DeBondt, W. F. M. and Thaler, R. (1985). Does the Stock Market Overreact? *Journal of Finance* 40, 793–806.

DeBondt, W. F. M. and Thaler, R. H. (1990). Do Security Analysts Overreact? *American Economic Review* 80, 52–57.

Dreman, D. N. and Berry, M. A. (1995). Overreaction, Underreaction, and the Low-P/E Effect. =*Financial Analysts Journal* 51, 21–30.

Galton, F. (1886). Regression Towards Mediocrity in Hereditary Stature. *Journal of the Anthropological Institute* 15, 246–263.

Graham, B. (1973). *The Intelligent Investor, A Book of Practical Counsel,* Fourth Edition. New York: Harper & Row.

Hirschey, M. (1998). How Much is a Tulip Worth? *Financial Analysts Journal* 54, 11–17.

Hirschey, M. (2001). Cisco and the Kids. *Financial Analysts Journal* 57, 48–59.

Hirschey, M. (2003). Extreme Return Reversal in the Stock Market. *Journal of Portfolio Management* 29, 1–13.

Michaely, R., Thaler, R. H., and Womack, K. L. (1995). Price Reactions to Dividend Initiations and Omissions: Overreaction or Drift. *Journal of Finance* 50, 573–608.

Nam, K., Pyun, C. S., and Avard, S. L. (2001). Asymmetric Reverting Behavior of Short-Horizon Stock Returns: An Evidence of Stock Market Overreaction. *Journal of Banking & Finance* 25, 807–824.

Thaler, R. H. (1999). The End of Behavioral Finance. *Financial Analysts Journal* 55, 12–17.

Shiller, R. J., Fumiko, K., and Tsutsui, Y. (1996). Why Did the Nikkei Crash? Expanding the Scope of Expectations Data Collection. *Review of Economics & Statistics* 78, 156–164.

6

STOCK-PRICE EFFECTS OF RESEARCH AND DEVELOPMENT EXPENDITURES

This chapter provides evidence that current research and development (R&D) expenditures tend to have consistently large and positive influences on the market value of the firm. Like other operating information that helps tech stock investors form appropriate expectations concerning the size and variability of future cash flows, current R&D spending decisions appear to give investors useful insight concerning the firm's future economic performance. As a result, spending on R&D can be viewed as a form of investment in an intangible asset with predictably positive effects on future revenues, cash flows, and profits.

While significant market-value effects of R&D are generally apparent across the broad scope of the U.S. corporate environment, such aggregate evidence has the potential to obscure meaningful differences across firm size classes and industry groups. Consistent with the fact that only a handful of firms is responsible for much corporate-sponsored R&D spending in the United States, Hirschey (2003a) finds that stock-price effects of R&D are clearly apparent in the case of large domestic corporations. Consistent with previous findings reported by Chauvin and Hirschey (1993) for the late-1980s, this study reports that the stock-price effects of R&D were somewhat greater for larger as opposed to smaller firms in both manufacturing and nonmanufacturing sectors at the start of the new millennium (1997–2001). Modest size advantages in R&D effectiveness suggest that rivalry among large R&D intensive firms has the effect of reducing but not eliminating the superior long-term profitability of R&D among giant U.S. corporations. In addition, this study finds that the long-term profitability of R&D investments tends to rise with institutional stock ownership across all firm size classes in the manufacturing sector. These findings suggest that a beneficial monitoring function is being fulfilled by institutional investors.

I. R&D AS A SOURCE OF INTANGIBLE CAPITAL

An emerging body of research considers the market-value effects of a wide range of corporate investment decisions. Much of this work stems from an early study by McConnell and Muscarella (1985). In what is now broadly referred to as an "event study" (or an event-time study), McConnell and Muscarella (1985) explored the behavior of common stock prices in the period surrounding the dates on which companies publicly announced future capital expenditure plans. The authors were interested in learning whether the stock market responds to capital expenditure decision announcements by revaluing company shares in a manner consistent with the predictions of the value maximization hypothesis. McConnell and Muscarella (1985) found that unanticipated increases in planned capital expenditures tend to have a positive effect on the market value of the firm and that unanticipated decreases tend to have a negative impact. It therefore appears that managers reveal information that is relevant to the valuation of their firms through such announce-ments and that the reactions of common stock prices to capital expenditure announcements are generally consistent with the value maximization hypothesis.

In interesting early event study applications, Chan, Martin, and Kensinger (1990) and Doukas and Switzer (1992) reported evidence on the stock market reaction to a very specific type of corporate investment decision: announcements of increased R&D spending. Chan, Martin, and Kensinger (1990) and Doukas and Switzer (1992) found statistically significant R&D announcement day returns, especially in the case of large "high-tech" industrial firms that devote substantial resources to R&D. The positive share-price reaction to announce-ments of increased R&D spending discovered in these studies can be taken as evi-dence of a strong link between R&D spending and the market value of the firm, a link that is especially robust in the case of large firms. More recently, Toivanen, Stoneman, and Bosworth (2002) studied the impact of innovation on firm value for a sample of large firms from the United Kingdom. They reported that the flow of R&D expenditure announcements has significantly positive impacts on market value and that firms reporting R&D expenditures for the first time enjoy much larger impacts on market value than is typical for all reporting firms.

Chen and Ho (1997) have examined the importance of investment opportu-nities and free cash flow in explaining the market response to announcements of product strategies and capital expenditures. Using Singapore data, their research study supports the investment opportunities hypothesis that investments by firms with significant growth opportunities are worthwhile while those by firms with low growth opportunities are not. The study finds no support for the free cash flow hypothesis which suggests that firms with significant internally generated cash flow sponsor value-decreasing investments. The author's results are similar to those for R&D investments, which suggests that the availability, or lack of investment opportunities, is an important consideration in assessing the value-enhancing potential of strategic investments in general.

To further investigate this relation, this study builds upon Hirschey (1985); Morck, Shleifer, and Vishny (1988); and Chauvin and Hirschey (1993) to further investigate the cross-sectional influences of R&D expenditures on the market value of the firm. In so doing, this study contemplates how the traditionally recognized stock-price effects of current profit margins, growth, risk, and advertising expenditures are augmented when R&D is considered as a potentially important source of intangible capital. To the extent that R&D expenditures represent a type of investment expenditure that gives rise to economic benefits lasting more than one year, a type of "intangible capital" is created, and positive market-value influences can be anticipated. Of course, current profit rates may also reflect, at least in part, the positive effects of previous investments in R&D. Once the stock-price effects attributable to current profits are controlled, any *incremental* stock-price effects of R&D expenditures represent evidence of intangible capital or asset-like influences.[1]

The importance of intangible assets as an explanation for the discrepancy between accounting book values and market values has also been addressed recently by Lev and Sougiannis (1999), who argue that the superior stock-price performance of low book-to-market stocks can be explained, at least in part, by the favorable stock-price influence of intangible assets. Economic theory postulates that any difference between the market value of the firm and the accounting book value of the firm reflects the influence of future abnormal profits. When positive abnormal profits are anticipated, market values can be expected to exceed accounting book values. Conversely, when negative abnormal profits or substandard rates of return are contemplated, market values can be generally expected to fall short of accounting book values. Lev and Sougiannis (1999) show that the

---

[1]Huchzermeier and Loch (2001) consider the more general problem of investment project management under conditions of risk and uncertainty using a real options approach to evaluate the value of managerial flexibility in making R&D commitments. Huchzermeier and Loch (2001) argue that managerial flexibility has value in the context of uncertain R&D projects because management can repeatedly gather information about uncertain project and market characteristics and use that information to make appropriate R&D investment decisions. Huchzermeier and Loch (2001) argue from an options pricing theory perspective that higher uncertainty in project payoffs increases the real option value of managerial decision flexibility. Managers face uncertainty not only in R&D payoffs, but also from uncertainty in market payoffs, project budgets, product performance, market requirements, and project schedules.

effects of abnormal profits are captured for a large sample of science-based companies by estimating the value of off-balance sheet investments in R&D. Lev and Sougiannis (1999) show that R&D capital is associated with subsequent stock returns and that the association between R&D and subsequent returns appears to result from an extra-market risk factor inherent in R&D, rather than from stock mispricing. In a related study, Chan, Lakonishok, and Sougiannis (2001) argue that the market is too pessimistic about beaten-down R&D-intensive technology stocks and that companies with a high ratio of R&D expenditures relative to the market value of equity earn large excess returns. R&D intensity also appears positively associated with return volatility.

Unfortunately, each of these studies is restricted by data considerations to fairly limited samples of large firms. Data is now available that makes a much more complete analysis possible, including consideration of differences in the effectiveness of R&D across firm size classes and between manufacturing and nonmanufacturing industry groups.

II. CORPORATE GOVERNANCE, R&D, AND R&D EFFECTIVENESS

A large and growing corporate governance literature builds upon the work of Jensen and Meckling (1976), who contemplate the role of corporate control mechanisms as means for helping alleviate the potential divergence of interests between managers and stockholders.[2] Jensen and Meckling (1976) describe how a variety of monitoring mechanisms inside and outside the firm work together to establish an optimal set of restrictions on firm activity. Recently, both investors and financial economists have become interested in the corporate governance implications of institutional stock ownership and in how institutional ownership might affect managerial efficiency with respect to R&D investment decisions.

In an early paper, Graves (1988) expressed concern that an increasing level of institutional ownership of publicly held firms might lead to a reluctance to invest in R&D and other long-term spending commitments. The author's underlying premise was that a popular emphasis on short-term stock market performance might lead to a similarly myopic emphasis on investment projects that promise modest but near-term results as opposed to more profitable long-term investments in R&D. To investigate the issue, Graves (1988) analyzed the relationship between institutional ownership and R&D spending during the 10-year period from 1976–85. Over this time frame, Graves (1988) found a significant negative relationship between institutional ownership and R&D spending. Specifically, a one-percentage-point increase in institutional ownership was associated with a decline in R&D spending per employee of about $33. Since institutional ownership is likely to continue growing, Graves (1988) expressed concern

---

[2]For a detailed analysis of organization structure and corporate governance, see Hirschey (2003c).

that these results imply that the decreased spending in R&D could seriously erode the competitiveness of U.S. firms. In a later paper, Hansen and Hill (1991) sought to undermine what they called the "popular myth" that managers in high-technology industries alter critical R&D investments in response to the short-term profit pressures of large institutional stockholders. Following Graves (1988), Hansen and Hill (1991) examined the relationship between R&D spending and institutional ownership over a 10-year period (1977–87) for 129 firms in 4 research-intensive industries. *Compustat* data were used to compute R&D intensity, firm size, cash resources, and leverage. In contrast to the view that institutional investors are having a damaging effect on R&D spending, Hansen and Hill (1991) found that higher levels of institutional ownership may actually be associated with greater R&D expenditures, after controlling for intervening effects. As a possible explanation for a positive relationship between institutional stock ownership and R&D intensity, Hansen and Hill (1991) suggested that many institutions may be effectively locked in to their stockholdings. In a similar vein, Baysinger, Kosnik, and Turk (1991) found equity concentration among both individual and institutional investors to have mildly positive effects on corporate R&D spending after having controlled for industry-specific factors. Ownership concentration positively affected R&D spending per employee when measured as the cumulative equity owned by major shareholders.

Institutional stock ownership might lead to higher levels of R&D spending and more effective R&D spending if institutional investors tend to be especially savvy in their assessment of corporate investment opportunities. As Jiambalvo, Rajgopal, and Venkatachalam (2002) point out, institutional investors are often characterized as sophisticated investors who are especially capable in the use of current-period information to predict future earnings. In support of that hypothesis, Jiambalvo, Rajgopal, and Venkatachalam (2002) found that the extent to which stock prices lead earnings is positively related to the percentage of institutional stock ownership. A reasonable implication of such findings is that institutional stockholders would be especially adept at deciphering the hard-to-fathom future cash flow implications of R&D investments and, thereby, would tend to favor investments in R&D-intensive firms.

An important monitoring function for institutional investors is suggested by Ryan and Wiggins (2002), who use a system of equations to investigate the endogenous relationship between R&D investment policy and chief executive officer (CEO) compensation. These authors posit that CEO compensation should balance incentive alignment and efficient risk sharing with risk-averse managers. Their analysis suggests that institutional ownership directly influences R&D investments by providing managerial oversight and indirectly influences R&D investment policy by affecting the structure of executive compensation. Further insight concerning the monitoring function of large institutional investors is contributed by El-Gazzar (1998), who argues that institutional investors have strong incentives to search for private information about companies in their portfolios because of their fiduciary responsibilities.

El-Gazzar (1998) also suggests that institutional investors typically have access to significant economic resources with which they are able to conduct their sophisticated information search. Corporate awareness concerning the sophisticated information search incentives and capabilities of institutional investors can also affect the level of disclosed information if corporations "preannounce" important corporate information in an effort to mitigate the adverse stock-price effects of negative surprise announcements. Consistent with an important monitoring function for institutional investors, El-Gazzar (1998) provides evidence that the higher the institutional holdings, the lower the market reaction to earnings releases after controlling for security capitalization and the number of analysts following the firm.

Specific evidence concerning the effects of institutional stock ownership on R&D investment policy has been provided by Bushee (1998), who found that managers are less likely to cut R&D to reverse an earnings decline when institutional ownership is high, implying that institutions are sophisticated investors who typically serve a monitoring role in reducing pressures for myopic behavior. However, Bushee (1998) also reported that when ownership by institutions that have high portfolio turnover and engage in momentum trading strategies is high it can significantly increase the probability that managers will reduce R&D to reverse an earnings decline. These results may indicate that high turnover and momentum trading by institutional investors can encourage myopic investment behavior when such institutional investors have extremely high levels of ownership in a firm; otherwise, institutional ownership serves to reduce pressures on managers for myopic investment behavior. In a similar vein, David, Hitt, and Insead (2001) report direct evidence of instances where institutional activism increased R&D inputs over both the short and the long term.

Eng and Shackell (2001) examine whether long-term performance plans and institutional holdings are associated with the level of R&D spending. In so doing, they consider two alternative mechanisms that might be used to mitigate any inefficient short-term focus of managers and investors. While no evidence is found that the adoption of long-term performance plans has implications for R&D spending, evidence does emerge that the level of institutional holdings is positively associated with the level of R&D spending. These results indicate that the horizon of institutional investors may influence managerial planning horizons and how managers decide on long-term investments.

Finally, Szewczyk, Tsetsekos, and Zantout (1996) examine the role of investment opportunities and free cash flow in explaining R&D-induced abnormal returns for a sample of firms making R&D spending increase announcements. After controlling for firm size, financial leverage, dividend yield, ownership structure, and industry structure, the authors found a significant positive relation between R&D-induced abnormal returns and institutional ownership. In a similar vein, Hirschey (2003b) found that the long-term profitability of R&D investments tends to rise with institutional stock ownership across all firm size classes. These results suggest that institutional investors have both the resources and the incentives to fulfill a beneficial monitoring function for the firm's hard-to-evaluate investments in risky intangible capital. This latter finding is especially important because it suggests that institutional stock ownership may be important in affecting both the *level* and the *effectiveness* of R&D spending. This issue merits further consideration, but first some evidence on the economic importance of R&D spending seems appropriate.

III. R&D SPENDING BY INDUSTRY GROUP

Table 6.1 shows the distribution of R&D expenditures by *Compustat* firms organized according to broad two-digit industry groups. These data are firm averages over the five-year 1997–2001 period. While there is an average of roughly 55 firms per year in each *Compustat* two-digit industry group over this period, the number of firms in each *Compustat* industry group varies widely from roughly 350 per year in banking and business services to a small handful in coal mining, passenger transportation, and nonnatural gas pipelines. On average, industry sales are about $155 billion per year, but vary widely from more than $1 trillion dollars per year in transportation equipment (including automobiles) to less than $1 billion per year in the nonnatural gas pipelines industry. On average, *Compustat* firms generate $3.2 billion per year in sales revenue. They spend an average of about $31.9 million per year on advertising, and average roughly $27.5 million per year in R&D spending. As a percentage of sales, the overall amount spent on R&D (0.90%) is commensurate with the amount typically spent on advertising (0.97%). However, Table 6.1 documents the fact that the distribution of R&D spending across two-digit industry groups is far from uniform.

The distribution of R&D spending is highly concentrated (or skewed) across Corporate America. R&D spending is heavily concentrated in a relatively few industries; a handful of high-tech sectors account for the overwhelming share of R&D activity. R&D spending is highest in industries such as chemicals and allied products (28); measuring instruments, photography, and electronic equipment (36); transportation equipment, including autos (37); and industrial machinery and computing equipment (35). Little R&D activity takes place in most business and consumer service industries (except for SIC 73, computer software), the financial sector, and retailing. In fact, *Compustat* reports zero R&D activity for firms in 19 out of 65 two-digit industry groups.[3] By way of contrast, zero advertising activity is reported for firms in 14 out of 65 industry groups.[4]

[3] *Compustat* uses zeroes and the missing data code interchangeably with respect to R&D. However, because the Securities and Exchange Commission requires disclosure of all material R&D expenditures according to FASB guidelines, we assume that all material R&D is disclosed, and therefore, set all *Compustat* "missing" data codes for R&D (and only for R&D) equal to zero. Chauvin and Hirschey (1993) test the sensitivity of this assumption and confirm the appropriateness of setting R&D expenditures equal to zero if missing on *Compustat*.

[4] It is important to recognize that the advertising data reported in *Compustat* generally refer to national advertising in the print and broadcast media. Local media inserts and personal selling expenditures, among other types of promotional effort, are not fully reflected. Therefore, while *Compustat* advertising data are a good proxy for the amount spent on brand name advertising, they are not necessarily a good indicator of the total amount spent on promotional activity.

TABLE 6.1 The Distribution of Advertising and R&D Spending By Industry Groups (1997–2000)

Two-digit SIC code	Industry	Avg. firms per year	Avg. annual industry sales ($ million)	Avg. annual sales per firm ($ million)	Avg. annual industry advertising ($ million)	Avg. annual advertising per firm ($ million)	Avg. annual advertising intensity (AD/Sales) (%)	Avg. annual industry R&D ($ million)	Avg. annual R&D per firm ($ million)	Avg. annual R&D intensity (R&D/sales) per firm (%)
01	Agriculture Production—Crops	8.0	10,376	1,297	0.3	0.0	0.00	109.5	13.7	1.06
07	Agricultural Services	2.6	5,125	1,971	0.0	0.0	0.00	1.3	0.5	0.02
10	Metal Mining	28.6	42,119	1,473	0.0	0.0	0.00	327.1	11.4	0.78
12	Coal Mining	2.4	2,701	1,125	0.0	0.0	0.00	1.2	0.5	0.04
13	Oil and Gas Extraction	101.4	100,568	992	0.0	0.0	0.00	922.3	9.1	0.92
14	Mng, Quarry Nonmtl Minerals	7.2	10,993	1,527	2.4	0.3	0.02	25.3	3.5	0.23
15	Bldg Cnstr-Gen Contr, Op Bldr	20.2	34,399	1,703	68.4	3.4	0.20	0.0	0.0	0.00
16	Heavy Constr-Not Bldg Constr	12.2	24,368	1,997	0.0	0.0	0.00	13.1	1.1	0.05
17	Construction-Special Trade	5.8	3,726	642	4.4	0.8	0.12	1.6	0.3	0.04
20	Food and Kindred Products	81.0	455,240	5,620	17,586.4	217.1	3.86	2,334.1	28.8	0.51
21	Tobacco Products	6.4	101,295	15,827	2,705.5	422.7	2.67	661.1	103.3	0.65
22	Textile Mill Products	15.0	17,275	1,152	74.1	4.9	0.43	55.7	3.7	0.32
23	Apparel and Other Finished Pds	27.8	37,764	1,358	868.9	31.3	2.30	29.3	1.1	0.08
24	Lumber and Wood Pds, Ex Furn	20.6	35,836	1,740	3.6	0.2	0.01	72.1	3.5	0.20
25	Furniture and Fixtures	21.0	46,339	2,207	91.7	4.4	0.20	687.2	32.7	1.48
26	Paper and Allied Products	45.4	164,414	3,621	867.2	19.1	0.53	1,828.8	40.3	1.11
27	Printing, Publishing and Allied	49.4	74,396	1,506	660.0	13.4	0.89	116.2	2.4	0.16
28	Chemicals and Allied Products	213.6	607,436	2,844	12,106.8	56.7	1.99	53,386.2	249.9	8.79
29	Pete Refining and Related Inds	29.0	784,147	27,040	201.5	6.9	0.03	3,258.8	112.4	0.42
30	Rubber and Misc Plastics Prods	28.8	51,978	1,805	1,762.4	61.2	3.39	840.4	29.2	1.62
31	Leather and Leather Products	8.2	5,646	689	174.5	21.3	3.09	2.7	0.3	0.05
32	Stone, Clay, Glass, Concrete Pd	25.2	35,680	1,416	44.6	1.8	0.12	151.1	6.0	0.42
33	Primary Metal Industries	58.8	135,783	2,309	99.4	1.7	0.07	1,586.2	27.0	1.17
34	Fabr Metal, Ex Machy, Trans Eq	41.8	58,700	1,404	1,726.1	41.3	2.94	632.0	15.1	1.08
35	Indl, Comml Machy, Computer Eq	196.8	553,775	2,814	4,762.8	24.2	0.86	32,496.8	165.1	5.87
36	Electr, Oth Elec Eq, Ex Cmp	237.4	554,739	2,337	6,464.3	27.2	1.17	42,731.1	180.0	7.70
37	Transportation Equipment	73.8	1,029,680	13,952	10,983.3	148.8	1.07	36,415.0	493.4	3.54
38	Meas Instr; Photo Gds; Watches	149.2	143,662	963	1,647.6	11.0	1.15	9,963.0	66.8	6.94
39	Misc Manufacturng Industries	21.2	19,308	911	1,357.3	64.0	7.03	602.7	28.4	3.12

40	Railroad Transportation	11.6	47,529	4,097	0.0	0.0	0.00	0.0	0.0	0.00
41	Transit and Passenger Trans	2.2	2,611	1,187	0.0	0.0	0.00	0.0	0.0	0.00
42	Motor Freight Trans, Warehous	19.0	34,959	1,840	0.6	0.0	0.00	0.0	0.0	0.00
44	Water Transportation	15.8	12,942	819	314.5	19.9	2.43	0.0	0.0	0.00
45	Transportation By Air	28.6	136,954	4,789	904.9	31.6	0.66	0.0	0.0	0.00
46	Pipe Lines, Ex Natural Gas	2.2	762	346	0.0	0.0	0.00	0.7	0.1	0.01
47	Transportation Services	11.0	13,969	1,270	5.8	0.5	0.04	5,779.3	46.8	0.86
48	Communications	123.6	673,786	5,451	7,405.9	59.9	1.10	19.2	0.1	0.00
49	Electric, Gas, Sanitary Serv	156.2	528,186	3,381	0.4	0.0	0.00	104.4	1.8	0.10
50	Durable Goods-Wholesale	57.8	99,932	1,729	46.3	0.8	0.05	213.8	5.8	0.10
51	Nondurable Goods-Wholesale	36.6	213,135	5,823	31.5	0.9	0.01	28.7	4.6	0.05
52	Bldg Matl, Hardwr, Garden-Retl	6.2	53,072	8,560	392.4	63.3	0.74	0.0	0.0	0.00
53	General Merchandise Stores	22.2	334,491	15,067	5,653.7	254.7	1.69	0.4	0.0	0.00
54	Food Stores	22.8	226,888	9,951	1,396.6	61.3	0.62	0.0	0.0	0.00
55	Auto Dealers, Gas Stations	9.8	20,468	2,089	233.1	23.8	1.14	0.0	0.0	0.00
56	Apparel and Accessory Stores	35.0	65,506	1,872	1,092.3	31.2	1.67	0.0	0.0	0.00
57	Home Furniture and Equip Store	16.4	43,196	2,634	997.4	60.8	2.31	5.6	0.2	0.00
58	Eating and Drinking Places	30.6	38,063	1,244	1,374.6	44.9	3.61	40.9	0.7	0.01
59	Miscellaneous Retail	58.0	126,539	2,182	1,602.4	27.6	1.27	0.0	0.0	0.03
60	Depository Institutions	348.4	720,424	2,068	0.0	0.0	0.00	0.0	0.0	0.00
61	Nondepository Credit Instn	33.4	105,182	3,149	105.4	3.2	0.10	63.3	1.5	0.00
62	Security and Commodity Brokers	41.2	173,584	4,213	577.2	14.0	0.33	0.0	0.0	0.04
63	Insurance Carriers	134.2	590,920	4,403	268.9	2.0	0.05	27.7	1.7	0.00
64	Ins Agents, Brokers and Service	16.0	27,446	1,715	0.8	0.0	0.00	0.0	0.0	0.10
65	Real Estate	22.2	9,570	431	37.2	1.7	0.39	63.6	0.4	0.00
67	Holding, Other Invest Offices	142.2	43,716	307	853.3	6.0	1.95	0.0	0.0	0.15
70	Hotels, Other Lodging Places	13.6	28,624	2,105	58.2	4.3	0.20	0.0	0.0	0.00
72	Personal Services	10.4	10,325	993	49.0	4.7	0.47	10.5	1.0	0.10
73	Business Services	340.6	383,899	1,127	3,507.3	10.3	0.91	25,549.8	75.0	6.66
75	Auto Repair, Services, Parking	6.8	14,607	2,148	197.2	29.0	1.35	0.0	0.0	0.00
78	Motion Pictures	12.8	41,736	3,261	1,555.9	121.6	3.73	102.7	8.0	0.25
79	Amusement and Recreation Svcs	27.4	21,225	775	232.2	8.5	1.09	14.4	0.5	0.07
80	Health Services	43.4	68,240	1,572	30.1	0.7	0.04	61.5	1.4	0.09
82	Educational Services	11.4	3,074	270	31.9	2.8	1.04	0.6	0.1	0.02
83	Social Services	7.0	1,634	233	0.3	0.0	0.02	0.0	0.0	0.00
87	Engr, Acc, Resh, Mgmt, Rel Svcs	45.4	20,404	449	9.4	0.2	0.05	286.3	6.3	1.40
	Averages	53.2	155,155	3,197	1,434.3	31.9	0.97	3,409.6	27.5	0.90

It is relatively rare to find companies that report high levels of both advertising and R&D activity. Exceptions to this rule are provided by firms that offer educational services, chemicals and allied products, industrial machinery and computer equipment, electronic equipment, measuring instruments, and transportation equipment. It is more typical to find firms that employ advertising or R&D, but not both, as an effective means for product differentiation.

The most obvious implication of these data is that advertising and R&D constitute alternative means of product differentiation that have the potential to differ in their effectiveness across industry groups. It is therefore relevant to ask whether or not the stock-price effects of R&D differ for firms in manufacturing ($20 \leq$ SIC < 40) versus nonmanufacturing (SIC < 20 or SIC ≥ 40) industries. Based on spending patterns, it is clear that R&D activity is concentrated among manufacturers, whereas advertising promotion tends to be more broadly dispersed across both manufacturing and nonmanufacturing sectors. By itself, these data suggest that R&D spending may be a more effective means of new product development and product differentiation for manufacturing versus nonmanufacturing firms.

IV. CORPORATE LEADERS IN R&D SPENDING

Table 6.2 shows R&D expenditures by the 50 largest firms ranked in terms of aggregate R&D spending. Average R&D expenditures of $264.8 million by the 50 largest firms ranked by R&D spending is roughly 10 times greater than the $27.5 million average R&D spending reported for all *Compustat* firms in Table 6.1. On average, the top 50 corporate leaders in terms of R&D spending devote roughly 43% of sales to R&D. This simple average is skewed upward by the extraordinary share of sales devoted to R&D by a handful of relatively small biotech firms. On a weighted average basis, the top 50 corporate leaders in terms of R&D spending devote an average of 23.2% of sales to R&D. Still, this represents an extraordinary commitment in terms of R&D intensity and is more than 25 times the typical level of R&D intensity depicted in Table 6.1. Interestingly, the 1% of sales devoted to advertising by top R&D spending firms is roughly consistent with the 0.9% *Compustat* average shown in Table 6.1. This finding reinforces the suggestion that advertising and R&D are distinct forms of product differentiation that display little synergy.

Of course, total R&D spending is only one useful indicator of the amount of firm resources devoted to R&D. Another popular indicator is R&D intensity, where the amount of sales devoted to R&D spending is taken as a useful indicator of the relative importance of R&D. Table 6.3 shows R&D expenditures by the 50 largest firms ranked in terms of the proportion of sales devoted to R&D spending. An extraordinary average R&D intensity of 163.4% of sales is reported by the top 50 corporate leaders in terms of R&D intensity. This figure, like R&D intensity among the top firms in terms of R&D spending, is skewed upward by

TABLE 6.2 Top 50 Corporate Leaders in R&D Spending (Annual Averages, 1997–2000)

Company name	Two-digit SIC code	Sales ($ million)	R&D spending ($ million)	R&D intensity (R&D/sales) (%)	Advertising spending ($ million)	Advertising intensity (AD/sales) (%)	Number of years firm in sample (%)
Cisco Systems Inc.	35	14,030.0	2,918.7	20.8	0.0	0.0	4
Lilly (Eli) & Co.	28	10,014.4	1,869.7	18.7	0.0	0.0	5
Amgen Inc.	28	3,220.9	771.4	23.9	0.0	0.0	5
National Semiconductor Corp.	36	2,250.7	468.6	20.8	0.0	0.0	5
Lsi Logic Corp.	36	1,878.6	425.2	22.6	0.0	0.0	5
Genentech Inc.	28	1,413.9	416.8	29.5	69.6	4.9	5
Chiron Corp.	28	920.8	296.9	32.2	12.2	1.3	4
Millennium Pharmactcls Inc.	28	170.0	290.5	170.9	0.0	0.0	5
Enterasys Networks Inc.	35	1,413.7	271.9	19.2	0.0	0.0	4
Electronic Arts Inc.	73	1,099.6	232.6	21.2	64.9	5.9	5
Novell Inc.	73	1,113.2	232.4	20.9	40.2	3.6	5
Biogen Inc.	28	746.7	232.3	31.1	0.0	0.0	5
Cadence Design Sys Inc.	73	1,187.1	226.4	19.1	3.9	0.3	5
Jds Uniphase Corp.	36	499.0	217.0	43.5	0.0	0.0	4
Newbridge Networks Corp.	36	1,115.7	216.4	19.4	0.0	0.0	3
Adobe Systems Inc.	73	1,063.6	210.0	19.7	17.2	1.6	5
Cirrus Logic Inc.	35	883.4	179.3	20.3	2.4	0.3	3
I2 Technologies Inc.	73	649.1	178.7	27.5	0.0	0.0	3
Novellus Systems Inc.	35	831.7	177.1	21.3	5.6	0.7	5
Synopsys Inc.	73	697.5	174.3	25.0	0.0	0.0	5
Ascential Software Corp.	73	799.9	156.1	19.5	0.0	0.0	4
Cypress Semiconductor Corp.	36	767.8	156.0	20.3	0.0	0.0	5
Genzyme Corp.	28	728.1	154.8	21.3	0.0	0.0	5
Networks Associates Inc.	73	770.9	153.5	19.9	40.1	5.2	5

(continues)

TABLE 6.2 (*continued*)

Company name	Two-digit SIC code	Sales ($ million)	R&D spending ($ million)	R&D intensity (R&D/sales) (%)	Advertising spending ($ million)	Advertising intensity (AD/sales) (%)	Number of years firm in sample (%)
Autodesk Inc.	73	727.7	152.9	21.0	13.4	1.8	5
Incyte Genomics Inc.	73	158.7	146.0	92.0	1.4	0.9	5
Immunex Corp.	28	563.8	145.5	25.8	1.9	0.3	5
Intuit Inc.	73	783.3	145.1	18.5	40.6	5.2	4
Pmc–Sierra Inc.	36	326.6	144.8	44.3	0.0	0.0	4
Converse Technology Inc.	36	768.4	143.0	18.6	0.0	0.0	4
Veritas Software Co.	73	725.6	136.5	18.8	0.0	0.0	5
Mentor Graphics Corp.	73	529.3	124.9	23.6	0.0	0.0	5
Dassault Systemes S A -Adr.	73	478.3	114.3	23.9	0.0	0.0	4
Gilead Sciences Inc.	28	134.2	112.9	84.1	3.3	2.5	5
Rational Software Corp.	73	451.0	104.1	23.1	9.0	2.0	5
Axys Pharmaceuticals Inc.	28	36.8	94.5	256.7	0.0	0.0	3
Icos Corp.	28	93.6	94.2	100.6	0.0	0.0	4
Corixa Corp.	28	34.3	81.9	238.9	0.0	0.0	3
Vitesse Semiconductor Corp.	36	277.5	76.3	27.5	0.0	0.0	5
Avant Corp.	73	287.0	76.1	26.5	3.7	1.3	5
Midway Games Inc.	73	313.1	75.7	24.2	25.9	8.3	4
Biovail Corp.	28	233.3	75.4	32.3	1.5	0.6	5
Realnetworks Inc.	73	165.1	75.3	45.6	4.0	2.4	3
Cephalon Inc.	28	104.3	72.9	69.9	0.0	0.0	4
Sonicblue Inc.	35	306.9	72.2	23.5	0.0	0.0	4
Lernout & Hauspie Speech Pd	73	218.4	71.9	32.9	0.0	0.0	3
C-Cube Microsystems Inc.	36	340.4	70.5	20.7	0.0	0.0	4
Vertex Pharmaceuticals Inc.	28	71.0	69.3	97.5	0.4	0.5	5
Checkfree Corp.	73	242.7	68.9	28.4	1.6	0.7	4
Lattice Semiconductor Corp.	36	316.6	68.8	21.7	0.0	0.0	5
Averages		**1,139.1**	**264.8**	**43.0**	**7.3**	**1.0**	**4**

TABLE 6.3 Top 50 Corporate Leaders in R&D Intensity (Annual Averages, 1997–2000)

Company name	Two-digit SIC code	Sales ($ million)	R&D spending ($ million)	R&D intensity (R&D/sales) (%)	Advertising spending ($ million)	Advertising intensity (AD/sales) (%)	Number of years firm in sample
Supergen Inc.	28	6.6	29.9	454.6	0.5	8.1	4
Emisphere Technologies Inc.	28	7.2	22.6	315.4	0.0	0.0	3
Entremed Inc.	28	5.0	15.4	308.6	0.0	0.0	3
Axys Pharmaceuticals Inc.	28	36.8	94.5	256.7	0.0	0.0	3
Guilford Pharmaceutical Inc.	28	18.2	45.2	248.9	0.0	0.0	4
Ilex Oncology Inc.	28	21.1	51.9	246.1	0.0	0.0	4
Microvision Inc.	87	8.6	20.8	242.5	0.0	0.0	3
Corixa Corp.	28	34.3	81.9	238.9	0.0	0.0	3
Abgenix Inc.	28	24.3	58.0	238.4	0.0	0.0	3
Curagen Corp.	87	19.8	44.2	223.2	0.0	0.0	3
Neurogen Corp.	28	14.0	30.7	218.6	0.0	0.0	3
Cantab Pharmaceut Plc -Adr	28	9.6	21.0	217.6	0.0	0.0	3
Nanogen Inc.	87	10.2	20.6	202.3	0.0	0.0	3
Aradigm Corp.	38	20.9	41.5	198.9	0.0	0.0	4
Geltex Pharmaceuticals Inc.	28	19.3	38.3	198.5	0.0	0.0	3
Human Genome Sciences Inc.	28	26.6	51.3	192.8	0.0	0.0	3
Vical Inc.	28	8.7	16.0	184.1	0.0	0.0	5
Alliance Pharmaceutical Cp	28	27.3	49.3	180.9	0.0	0.0	3
Inhale Therapeutic Systems	28	32.8	59.2	180.8	0.0	0.0	4
Alexion Pharmaceuticals Inc.	28	12.3	21.3	173.9	0.0	0.0	4
Millennium Pharmactcls Inc.	28	170.0	290.5	170.9	0.0	0.0	5
Atrix Labs Inc.	28	9.5	16.2	169.4	0.0	0.0	3
Texas Biotechnology Corp.	28	9.1	15.1	165.3	0.0	0.0	5
Ballard Power Systems Inc.	36	20.9	34.2	163.8	0.0	0.0	4
Osi Pharmaceuticals Inc.	28	21.2	32.5	153.5	0.0	0.0	3

(continues)

137

TABLE 6.3 *(continued)*

Company name	Two-digit SIC code	Sales ($ million)	R&D spending ($ million)	R&D intensity (R&D/sales) (%)	Advertising spending ($ million)	Advertising intensity (AD/sales) (%)	Number of years firm in sample
Cell Genesys Inc.	28	27.8	42.0	151.3	0.0	0.0	4
Alkermes Inc.	28	31.2	46.5	149.3	0.0	0.0	5
Lynx Therapeutics Inc.	28	10.8	16.1	149.0	0.0	0.0	3
Genelabs Technologies Inc.	28	9.2	13.2	143.3	0.0	0.0	3
Regeneron Pharmaceut.	28	36.2	51.5	142.3	0.0	0.0	5
Genset Sa -Adr	28	26.0	36.8	141.8	0.0	0.0	4
Hyseq Inc.	28	15.5	21.1	135.8	0.0	0.0	3
Protein Design Labs Inc.	28	33.1	40.6	122.5	0.0	0.0	4
American Superconductor Cp	36	11.7	13.7	116.3	0.0	0.0	3
Neurocrine Biosciences Inc.	28	23.0	26.2	114.2	0.0	0.0	5
Cytogen Corp.	28	11.1	11.8	106.1	0.0	0.0	3
Icos Corp.	28	93.6	94.2	100.6	0.0	0.0	4
Vertex Pharmaceuticals Inc.	28	71.0	69.3	97.5	0.4	0.5	5
Genome Theraptcs	28	25.7	24.4	95.0	0.0	0.0	4
Incyte Genomics Inc.	73	158.7	146.0	92.0	1.4	0.9	5
Progenics Pharmaceutical Inc.	28	12.5	11.3	90.8	0.0	0.0	3
Myriad Genetics Inc.	28	28.9	26.0	89.8	0.0	0.0	4
Parkervision Inc.	36	11.9	10.5	88.2	0.0	0.0	3
Gilead Sciences Inc.	28	134.2	112.9	84.1	3.3	2.5	5
Vi Technologies Inc.	28	35.2	25.9	73.6	0.0	0.0	3
Scios Inc.	51	55.0	39.7	72.2	0.2	0.4	4
Cephalon Inc.	28	104.3	72.9	69.9	0.0	0.0	4
Cor Therapeutics Inc.	28	61.2	42.5	69.4	10.1	16.5	3
Isis Pharmaceuticals Inc.	28	41.0	27.3	66.5	0.0	0.0	3
Mgi Pharma Inc.	28	24.9	16.3	65.5	2.8	11.2	4
Averages		**33.8**	**44.8**	**163.4**	**0.4**	**0.8**	**4**

the extraordinary amount of R&D spending during the sample period typical of very small biotech companies. The 50 corporate leaders in terms of R&D intensity spend, on average, a proportion of sales on R&D that is roughly four times greater than the proportion of sales devoted to R&D by the top 50 corporate R&D spending leaders. The fact that extraordinary levels of R&D intensity are typical of relatively small high-tech companies suggests the importance of economies of scale or other large-firm advantages when it comes to R&D spending. Notice that the top 50 corporate leaders in terms of R&D intensity spend an average of $44.8 million per year on R&D, or less than twice the $27.5 million *Compustat* average shown in Table 6.1. This again suggests the importance of economies of scale or other large-firm advantages in R&D. As before, it is once again interesting to note the relatively modest levels of advertising typical of R&D intensity leaders. The 0.8% of sales devoted to advertising by top R&D intensity firms is again consistent with the 0.9% *Compustat* average and reinforces the suggestion that advertising and R&D are distinct forms of product differentiation.

Based on spending patterns, it is clear that R&D tends to be relatively concentrated among large firms. By itself, the fact that a relative handful of firms is responsible for a substantial portion of privately financed R&D suggests important size advantages (economies of scale) or economies of scope in R&D. This evidence provides support for the hypothesis that R&D spending is likely to be generally more effective for relatively larger firms. At a minimum, R&D spending patterns suggest the wisdom of contemplating the potential for firms size effects when considering the market-value influences of intangible capital tied to R&D spending.

V. MEASURING R&D CAPITAL USING TOBIN'S q RATIO

Starting with Lindenberg and Ross (1981), Hirschey (1982, 1985), and Jose, Nichols, and Stevens (1986), a research tradition has grown up in financial economics that uses stock market data to explore the economic sources of sustainable future cash flows. Stock-price data for individual firms offer useful insight concerning the overall consensus estimate of the net present value of future cash flows, where the value of future cash flows is discounted using an appropriate risk-adjusted discount rate. On the other hand, accounting expenditure data provide information on the resources used by firms. A comparison between stock market data and accounting information offers the opportunity to examine the economic performance implications of assorted types of expenditures, including R&D expenditures.

This study develops evidence on the comparison between stock market data and R&D expenditures to examine the extent to which R&D expenditures have the potential to generate long-lived economic benefits. This approach compares a *stock* measure, the market value of the firm, with the *flow* of R&D expenditures. On a theoretical basis, it would seem more appropriate to compare market values with the stocks of intangible capital tied to R&D. However, Hirschey and Weygandt (1985) show that if economic amortization of the exponential decay type can be assumed, along with constant percentage rates of growth in R&D expenditures, then the magnitude of intangible capital equals annual expenditures on R&D multiplied by a constant. Given these assumptions, the *stock* of intangible R&D capital is strictly proportional to the *flow* of R&D expenditures, and the net income and stock-price effects of R&D expenditures can be taken as indicative of intangible capital influences.

The basic idea of using the difference between the market value of the firm and accounting book values as an indicator of the presence of valuable intangible assets stems from the pioneering insights of Nobel laureate James Tobin, who introduced the so-called q ratio. Now referred to as Tobin's q, it is measured by the ratio of the market value of the firm divided by the replacement cost of tangible assets (see Brainard and Tobin, 1968). Tobin's intent was to examine the macroeconomic relationship between q and aggregate investment expenditures. At the margin, Tobin argued that if $q > 1$, firms would have a strong incentive to invest because the value of new capital investment would exceed its cost. If all such investment opportunities were fully exploited over time, the marginal value of q would trend toward unity ($q \rightarrow 1$) over time. Tobin contended that when marginal $q > 1$ throughout the macroeconomy, strong incentives exist for a boom in corporate investment. Conversely, if marginal $q < 1$, firms have little incentive to invest because the value of new capital investment falls below its cost. When marginal $q < 1$ throughout the macroeconomy, scant incentives exist for corporate investment, and a downturn in corporate investment and the overall economy might be projected. With relatively scarce new investment in plant and equipment, the profitability of assets in place can be expected to rise, and again the marginal value of q would trend toward unity ($q \rightarrow 1$) over time.

The use of Tobin's q to measure the presence of valuable intangible assets follows a similar logic. For a competitive firm in a stable industry with no special capabilities and no barriers to entry or exit, one would expect q to be close to one ($q \cong 1$). In a perfectly competitive industry, any momentary propensity for $q > 1$ due to an unanticipated rise in demand or decrease in costs would be quickly erased by entry or established firm growth. In a perfectly competitive industry, any momentary propensity for $q < 1$ due to an unanticipated fall in demand or increase in costs would be quickly erased by exit or contraction among established firms. In the absence of barriers to entry and exit, the marginal value of q would trend toward unity ($q \rightarrow 1$) over time in perfectly competitive industries. Similarly, a firm which is regulated so as to earn no monopoly rents would also have a q close to one. Only in the case of firms with monopoly power protected by significant barriers to entry or exit, or firms with superior profit-making capabilities, will Tobin's q ratio rise above one and stay there. In the limit, the theoretical maximum Tobin's q ratio is observed in the case of pure monopoly. If $q > 1$ on a persistent basis, one can argue that the firm is in possession of some hard-to-duplicate asset that typically escapes measurement using conventional accounting criteria. To the extent that such values are derived from ongoing expenditures that are not directly tied to physical assets, it becomes possible to argue that firms displaying $q > 1$ on a persistent basis are in possession of valuable intangible assets.

The use of Tobin's q ratio as a useful empirical indicator of valuable intangible assets tied to R&D expenditures holds significant practical appeal, despite certain obvious limitations. At any point in time, firms in various highly competitive markets can display $q > 1$ or $q < 1$ because of disequilibrium conditions caused by unanticipated rapid changes in revenues and cost conditions. In other instances, $q > 1$ if measurement errors cause accounting estimates of the economic value of tangible assets to be significantly understated. Similarly, $q > 1$ if valuable intangible assets derived from advertising, R&D, worker training, and other such expenditures with the potential for long-lived benefits are systematically excluded from consideration by accounting methodology. On the other hand, $q < 1$ if errors in accrual accounting methodology or other measurement errors cause accounting estimates of the value of intangible and/or tangible assets to be significantly overstated. The theoretical argument that $q \to 1$ over time only holds when the economic values of both tangible and intangible assets are precisely measured. If $q > 1$ on a persistent basis, and Tobin's q is closely tied to the level of R&D spending, one might argue successfully for the presence of intangible R&D capital. Intangible R&D capital can be derived from the value obtained from patents and other protections offered to firms making significant new discoveries and innovations. Alternatively, significant R&D capital can result from the nonpatented advantages gained from effective basic research and applied development. In economic terminology, superior rewards earned from exceptional productive capability or superior effort are called Ricardian rents after the early British economist David Ricardo. Monopoly rents are usually regarded as unjust compensation for the antisocial exercise of market power through high prices. Richardian rents are conventionally regarded as fair compensation for superior productive capability that results in higher revenues or lower production costs. To the extent that the firm possesses factors which increase revenues or lower costs relative to the marginal firm, it will persistently display $q > 1$. To the extent that productive R&D investments allow the firm to increase revenues and/or lower costs, and thereby persistently display $q > 1$, the firm can be said to possess significant unmeasured intangible R&D capital.

VI. THE SAMPLE

This study focuses on pooled cross-section samples of *Compustat* firms over the five-year period from 1997 through 2001, inclusive. On an overall basis, 13,144 firm-year observations are included, or an average of roughly 2600 firms per year. The overall sample is composed of 7860 (59.8%) nonmanufacturing firm-year observations (SIC < 20 or SIC ≥ 40) and 5284 (40.2%) manufacturing firm-year observations ($20 \leq SIC < 40$). As shown in Table 6.1, R&D intensity tends to be much higher among manufacturing versus nonmanufacturing firms. As a result, it seems worthwhile to consider the possibility of stock-price effect differences for R&D conducted by nonmanufacturing versus manufacturing firms.

Firm-level rather than industry-level data are analyzed to ensure an exact match between R&D and market-value figures. This approach allows for a detailed consideration of the role played by firm size and industry conditions and has the advantage of avoiding industry classification errors for widely diversified firms. Such an analysis seems worthwhile in light of findings reported by Hirschey (2002a), who finds evidence of meaningful size-based differences in the effectiveness of R&D spending according to firm size. The potential for size-based differences in the stock-price effects of R&D lies at the heart of the notion of economies of scale or other large-firm advantages in R&D.

By analyzing a simple two-part breakdown for manufacturing versus non-manufacturing firms, it becomes possible to learn the extent to which expenditures on R&D have broad rather than narrow implications for the value of the firm. By considering the market-value implications of a three-part sample partition according to firm size (measured by market capitalization), the extent to which firm size plays a role in determining the market-value effects of R&D can also be learned. By considering the influences of institutional stock ownership on the stock-price effects tied to R&D expenditures, it becomes possible to gain further evidence on the corporate governance implications of institutional stock ownership and learn how institutional ownership might affect managerial efficiency with respect to R&D investment decisions. Industry effects can be broadly indicated using intercept dummy variable interactions for two-digit SIC industry group classifications. Such two-digit SIC dummy variables isolate firm size effects on the market-value influence of R&D from other industry-specific considerations.

Following Chung and Pruitt (1994), a simple approximation of Tobin's q is estimated, where q is approximated by the sum of the market value of common stock plus the book values of preferred stock and total liabilities, all divided by the book value of tangible assets. Using *Compustat* data, this simple approximation to Tobin's q is measured by the sum of the market value of common [shares outstanding (annual data item #25) times price (#24)] plus the book value of total assets (#6) minus common equity (#60), all divided by the book value of total assets (#6). This simple approximation to Tobin's q provides an appealing, widely available market-based view of investor expectations concerning the firm's future profit potential. However, like any empirical estimate of q, this simple approximation to Tobin's q is subject to error in that accounting book values measure imperfectly the economic value of tangible assets. In addition to obvious exposure to accounting measurement error, the empirical estimate of q may be subject to accounting bias as well. As Schwert (1981) argues, q measures are likely to reflect, at least in part, the effects of accounting policy decisions. If firms capitalize nonproductive assets so as to smooth or hide monopoly profits, q will be correspondingly biased downward.

Use of Chung and Pruitt's (1994) simple approximation to Tobin's q can be justified on the basis that it is the best widely available market-based indicator of investor expectations concerning the firm's future profit potential. While it is commonly presumed that accounting replacement costs provide a measure of tangible assets that is superior to traditional book value data, the empirical evidence argues otherwise. Watts and Zimmerman (1980) argue from a market-based perspective that accounting replacement cost numbers are irrelevant for security pricing purposes. It follows that replacement cost adjustments to book value data have the potential to obscure, rather than make more precise, the level and determinants of the capitalized value of the firm (see Landsman and Magliolo, 1988). Therefore, this study focuses on the market-value implications of R&D in a manner that minimizes the potential for accounting error or bias.

The focus of this study is on the role played by R&D as an influential source of intangible capital and a significant determinant of Tobin's q. To isolate such influences, the effects of other factors that might influence the current market value of the firm must be constrained, including current profitability, growth, risk, and advertising intensity. Current profitability is measured by the firm's net profit margin, or net income (#172) divided by sales (#12). Positive stock-price effects of net profit margins can be anticipated because historical profit margins are often the best available indicator of a firm's ability to generate superior rates of return during future periods. As documented by Hirschey (1985), stock-price effects of realized rates of return include the influences of both superior efficiency and/or market power.[5] Because effective R&D investments can be expected to enhance both current and future profitability, the *marginal* effect of R&D intensity on Tobin's q becomes a very conservative estimate of the total short-term plus long-term value of R&D investments when such impacts are considered in conjunction with the stock-price effects of current net profit margins.

In their seminal analysis, Miller and Modigliani (1961) argued that growth has a positive effect on market values if future investments are expected to earn above-normal rates of return and if growth is an important determinant of these returns. Growth is measured by the least-squares estimate of the 3-year compound annual rate of growth in sales for each firm (#12). While growth affects the magnitude of anticipated excess returns, a stock-price influence may also be associated with the degree of return stability. Stock-price influences of risk are estimated here using financial leverage measured by total assets (#6) minus common equity (#60), all divided by total assets (#6). With an increase in risk, the market value of expected returns is anticipated to fall.

[5]For a perfectly competitive market in equilibrium, P = MC and constant cost conditions prevail, MC = AC. This means that net profit margins will be at a minimum for perfectly competitive industries in equilibrium, where net profit margin is defined as MGN = (P − AC)/P. The more a firm's pricing departs from the competitive norm, the higher will be realized profit margins. As such, net profit margins can be employed as useful, albeit imperfect, indicators of the stock-price effects of monopoly profits. Similarly, net profit margins include any above-normal profits due to superior product development or productive efficiency (sometimes referred to as Ricardian rents after British economist David Ricardo).

Following Chauvin and Hirschey (1993), the stock-price effects of R&D are considered after controlling for the possibility of similar influences tied to advertising expenditures (#45). Because it is relatively rare to find firms and industries that employ both methods in tandem, there is little reason to fear a commingling of such influences. In all cases, both R&D and advertising are normalized by sales (#12) to eliminate size-related influences.

Variable means and standard deviations are shown in Table 6.4. Data are shown for the overall sample and for simple three-part breakdowns according to firm size and institutional stock ownership. Cut-off points for each size class are calculated on an annual basis. Small firms were defined as those companies with market capitalizations below $369.3 million (1997), $358.8 million (1998), $361.7 million (1999), $405.8 million (2000), and $405.3 million (2001). Large firm size cut-off points were $1470.8 million (1997), $1433.9 million (1998), $1444.6 million (1999), $1808.6 million (2000), and $1623.4 million (2001). By definition, the medium firm size class falls between these size cut-off points during each period. This approach yields a roughly three-part size breakdown for the pooled cross-section samples of manufacturing and nonmanufacturing firms.

Institutional ownership is measured by the percent of total shares outstanding that is owned by institutions and is available from *Compustat* for the current quarter and for the three previous quarters. Cut-off points for institutional ownership are based on percentiles of institutional ownership averaged over the four calendar quarters ending June 2002. Low institutional ownership signifies less than 31.5% ownership by institutions, medium institutional ownership falls between 31.5 and 52.3%, and high institutional ownership exceeds 52.3% of the total number of shares outstanding.

From Table 6.4, some systematic difference in firm characteristics are obvious when the overall sample is partitioned according to firm size and institutional stock ownership. In the manufacturing sector, profit margins tend to be higher for large as opposed to small and middle market cap firms. Large manufacturers also have somewhat higher levels of risk, but display relatively lower growth rates. It is interesting to note that while advertising intensity is fairly uniform across firm size classes, R&D intensity appears to be inversely related to firm size. As suggested earlier, an inverse relationship between firm size and R&D intensity is consistent with the notion of economies of scale or other large-firm advantages in R&D. Within each size class, interesting differences in firm characteristics can be noted for firms with low versus high institutional stock ownership. Generally speaking, institutional stock ownership appears higher among firms with higher profit rates and lower risk. There is no systematic relationship evident between institutional stock ownership and growth, advertising intensity, or R&D intensity. While higher institutional stock ownership may not suggest greater R&D spending within this sample, it remains to be seen whether higher institutional stock ownership is associated with greater R&D effectiveness.

TABLE 6.4 Variable Means and Standard Deviations[a]

Subsample	Tobin's q	Profit margin	Growth	Risk	Advertising intensity	R&D intensity	Market cap	Institutional ownership	Sample size
A. Manufacturing sector (20 ≤ SIC < 40)									
Small market cap									
Low institutional ownership	2.462 (2.296)	−0.262 (0.990)	0.264 (0.459)	0.440 (0.221)	0.007 (0.025)	0.263 (0.729)	192.5 (77.3)	0.159 (0.098)	662
Medium institutional ownership	2.046 (1.569)	−0.118 (0.702)	0.183 (0.318)	0.412 (0.213)	0.008 (0.026)	0.175 (0.542)	197.1 (74.6)	0.427 (0.061)	539
High institutional ownership	1.843 (1.343)	−0.015 (0.280)	0.174 (0.322)	0.411 (0.212)	0.004 (0.013)	0.091 (0.237)	224.0 (79.9)	0.648 (0.111)	525
Manufacturing small market cap	2.144 (1.845)	−0.142 (0.751)	0.211 (0.382)	0.422 (0.216)	0.007 (0.023)	0.184 (0.563)	203.5 (78.5)	0.392 (0.223)	1,726
Middle market cap									
Low institutional ownership	2.415 (2.600)	−0.095 (0.765)	0.167 (0.335)	0.486 (0.223)	0.009 (0.026)	0.149 (0.645)	725.7 (311.6)	0.157 (0.107)	427
Medium institutional ownership	2.414 (2.165)	−0.033 (0.433)	0.199 (0.304)	0.465 (0.215)	0.006 (0.021)	0.138 (0.448)	770.7 (326.3)	0.433 (0.058)	502
High institutional ownership	2.340 (1.723)	−0.032 (0.505)	0.187 (0.304)	0.463 (0.216)	0.005 (0.017)	0.138 (0.472)	763.0 (310.9)	0.628 (0.091)	765
Manufacturing middle market cap	2.381 (2.105)	−0.048 (0.564)	0.186 (0.312)	0.470 (0.218)	0.007 (0.021)	0.141 (0.515)	755.9 (316.1)	0.452 (0.209)	1,694
Large market cap									
Low institutional ownership	2.524 (2.347)	0.045 (0.222)	0.103 (0.213)	0.566 (0.187)	0.011 (0.028)	0.066 (0.211)	22,758.6 (37,178.3)	0.097 (0.104)	600
Medium institutional ownership	3.496 (2.888)	0.062 (0.207)	0.171 (0.253)	0.518 (0.206)	0.015 (0.033)	0.084 (0.220)	24,173.5 (45,682.9)	0.441 (0.055)	649
High institutional ownership	2.895 (2.445)	0.052 (0.270)	0.154 (0.250)	0.551 (0.195)	0.009 (0.025)	0.081 (0.234)	7,244.7 (9,272.1)	0.602 (0.058)	615
Manufacturing large market cap	2.985 (2.609)	0.053 (0.234)	0.144 (0.241)	0.544 (0.197)	0.012 (0.021)	0.077 (0.222)	18,132.7 (35,459.5)	0.384 (0.221)	1,864
All manufacturing firms	2.516 (2.249)	−0.043 (0.559)	0.179 (0.316)	0.481 (0.216)	0.008 (0.025)	0.132 (0.456)	6,705.3 (22,686.4)	0.408 (0.220)	5,284

(continues)

TABLE 6.4 (continued)

Subsample	Tobin's q	Profit margin	Growth	Risk	Advertising intensity	R&D intensity	Market cap	Institutional ownership	Sample size
B. Nonmanufacturing sector (SIC < 20, or SIC ≥ 40)									
Small market cap									
Low institutional ownership	1.621	−0.035	0.266	0.670	0.005	0.037	195.5	0.142	1,349
	(1.475)	(0.787)	(0.447)	(0.250)	(0.022)	(0.198)	(76.3)	(0.093)	
Medium institutional ownership	1.510	0.027	0.253	0.598	0.004	0.019	210.0	0.413	678
	(1.054)	(0.387)	(0.364)	(0.246)	(0.018)	(0.066)	(77.5)	(0.062)	
High institutional ownership	1.698	0.031	0.324	0.520	0.009	0.026	229.2	0.661	455
	(1.016)	(0.183)	(0.489)	(0.219)	(0.024)	(0.075)	(77.2)	(0.096)	
Nonmanufacturing small market cap	1.603	−0.006	0.273	0.623	0.006	0.030	205.7	0.311	2,482
	(1.295)	(0.620)	(0.435)	(0.250)	(0.021)	(0.154)	(77.8)	(0.220)	
Middle market cap									
Low institutional ownership	1.739	0.080	0.282	0.648	0.006	0.015	722.9	0.162	939
	(1.463)	(0.242)	(0.475)	(0.234)	(0.024)	(0.104)	(317.5)	(0.100)	
Medium institutional ownership	1.910	0.059	0.266	0.608	0.004	0.024	800.7	0.421	877
	(1.589)	(0.343)	(0.420)	(0.226)	(0.015)	(0.138)	(327.4)	(0.060)	
High institutional ownership	2.107	0.072	0.309	0.544	0.007	0.024	781.3	0.657	864
	(1.541)	(0.132)	(0.325)	(0.212)	(0.018)	(0.084)	(323.3)	(0.099)	
Nonmanufacturing middle market cap	1.914	0.071	0.286	0.601	0.006	0.021	767.2	0.406	2,680
	(1.537)	(0.254)	(0.413)	(0.228)	(0.019)	(0.111)	(324.2)	(0.222)	
Large market cap									
Low institutional ownership	1.946	0.066	0.200	0.683	0.003	0.007	15,449.5	0.117	832
	(1.822)	(0.564)	(0.359)	(0.209)	(0.013)	(0.035)	(32,246.7)	(0.111)	
Medium institutional ownership	2.249	0.079	0.267	0.662	0.006	0.013	15,855.8	0.426	994
	(2.135)	(0.213)	(0.461)	(0.220)	(0.015)	(0.075)	(36,656.7)	(0.057)	
High institutional ownership	2.325	0.067	0.272	0.609	0.006	0.019	7,604.6	0.631	872
	(1.992)	(0.483)	(0.316)	(0.199)	(0.017)	(0.065)	(14,681.6)	(0.195)	
Nonmanufacturing large market cap	2.180	0.071	0.248	0.651	0.005	0.013	13,063.7	0.397	2,698
	(2.002)	(0.436)	(0.389)	(0.212)	(0.015)	(0.062)	(29,983.5)	(0.244)	
All nonmanufacturing firms	1.907	0.047	0.269	0.625	0.005	0.021	4,810.7	0.373	7,860
	(1.663)	(0.458)	(0.412)	(0.231)	(0.019)	(0.114)	(18,552.9)	(0.233)	
C. All firms	2.152	0.011	0.233	0.567	0.007	0.066	5,572.4	0.387	13,144
	(1.943)	(0.503)	(0.379)	(0.236)	(0.021)	(0.307)	(20,336.3)	(0.228)	

[a]Standard deviations are in parentheses.

VII. EFFECTS OF R&D ON TOBIN'S Q

After allowing for potentially important simultaneous influences among relations describing market values and other important elements of market structure, Connolly and Hirschey (1990) found no significant endogenous influences. Therefore, the effects of net profit margin, growth, risk, advertising, and R&D on Tobins's q can be estimated through the straightforward application of ordinary least squares (OLS). A simple linear model is estimated for pooled cross-section samples from the 1997–2001 period for both manufacturing and nonmanufacturing *Compustat* firms. In each regression, two-digit SIC code intercept dummy variables are employed to control for industry-related differences in the market value of the firm. These two-digit SIC code intercept dummy variables are supplemented with annual dummy variables to control for transitory influences related to overall stock market conditions.

Table 6.5 offers broad-based evidence of long-lived benefits to R&D by showing persistently positive and statistically significant influences of R&D intensity on the market value of the firm across broad samples of firms taken from both the manufacturing and the nonmanufacturing sectors.[6] Across all 13,144 *Compustat* firm-year observations, positive and statistically significant effects on Tobin's q are noted for profit margins, growth, advertising intensity, and R&D intensity. The predictably negative limiting influence of risk is also noted. In the case of R&D intensity, beneficial effects on both short-run and long-run profitability are undoubtably present. This means that at least some of the beneficial effects of R&D intensity on Tobin's q are reflected in the statistically significant positive effects noted for profit margins. Thus, the statistically significant and positive coefficient estimate for the R&D intensity variable undoubtably underestimates the marginal economic impact of R&D on the market value of the firm. Clearly, R&D intensity emerges as an important determining factor for Tobin's q in the overall sample.

Despite some obvious differences in explanatory power between the manufacturing and nonmanufacturing sectors, it is clear from Table 6.5 that this very simple model describes a meaningful share of the firm-by-firm variation in Tobin's q. In the manufacturing sector, roughly one-quarter of the variation in Tobin's q can be attributed to variation in profit margins, growth, risk, advertising intensity, and R&D intensity. In the nonmanufacturing sector, roughly one-third of the variation in market values can be similarly attributed. Given the relative consistency of stock-price effects due to advertising and R&D in the manufacturing and nonmanufacturing sectors, it appears safe to argue that both types of expenditures give rise to valuable intangible capital. From a statistical perspective, and while both advertising and R&D generally appear to constitute alternative forms of profitable investment intangible assets, somewhat more consistent

---

[6]Using an F-test, statistically significant differences in model fit are evident for the manufacturing and nonmanufacturing sectors ($F = 2.28$).

TABLE 6.5 Firm Size and Valuation Effects of R&D, 1997–2001

Firm size class	Intercept	Profit margin	Growth	Risk	Advertising intensity	R&D intensity	R^2	F	Sample size
A. *Manufacturing sector (20 ≤ SIC < 40)*									
Small market cap	2.296 (7.51)[a]	−0.398 (−3.72)[a]	0.840 (7.97)[a]	−1.532 (−7.70)[a]	0.538 (0.30)	0.172 (1.12)	26.99%	22.40[a]	1,726
Middle market cap	2.631 (7.08)[a]	0.499 (2.50)[b]	1.235 (8.34)[a]	−2.595 (−11.23)[a]	1.800 (0.79)	1.202 (5.24)[a]	28.16%	23.31[a]	1,694
Large market cap	2.881 (5.79)[a]	3.291 (9.94)[a]	2.267 (10.43)[a]	−3.260 (−10.96)[a]	6.318 (3.40)[a]	4.274 (11.38)[a]	37.54%	39.38[a]	1,864
All manufacturing firms	2.399 (10.18)[a]	0.668 (6.50)[a]	1.290 (14.38)[a]	−2.123 (−14.99)[a]	5.365 (4.61)[a]	1.330 (9.95)[a]	23.80%	58.61[a]	5,284
B. *Nonmanufacturing sectors (SIC < 20, or SIC ≥ 40)*									
Small market cap	2.557 (17.39)[a]	0.008 (0.17)	0.124 (2.22)[b]	−1.476 (−10.29)[a]	1.346 (1.16)	0.702 (3.64)[a]	24.76%	13.75[a]	2,482
Middle market cap	3.404 (21.04)[a]	0.332 (3.26)[a]	0.094 (1.58)[c]	−2.540 (−17.02)[a]	1.037 (0.79)	1.889 (8.02)[a]	41.09%	31.51[a]	2,680
Large market cap	3.650 (17.51)[a]	0.467 (6.59)[a]	0.608 (7.44)[a]	−2.990 (−15.10)[a]	−1.048 (−0.49)	3.773 (6.77)[a]	44.00%	35.75[a]	2,698
All nonmanufacturing firms	3.002 (28.99)[a]	0.291 (7.64)[a]	0.289 (7.10)[a]	−2.135 (−21.71)[a]	0.544 (0.61)	1.411 (8.79)[a]	32.03%	63.381[a]	7,860
C. *All firms*	2.934 (31.04)[a]	0.397 (9.90)[a]	0.578 (14.34)[a]	−2.209 (−26.62)[a]	3.013 (4.18)[a]	1.150 (16.42)[a]	28.21%	65.81[a]	13,144

Note: SIC industry group and annual dummy (binary) variables are estimated but supressed for simplicity.
[a]Indicates statistical significance at the 0.01 level (one-tail test).
[b]Indicates statistical significance at the 0.05 level (one-tail test).
[c]Indicates statistical significance at the 0.10 level (one-tail test).

and more uniformly positive stock-price effects are noted in the case of R&D intensity. In the nonmanufacturing sector, the weakly positive effect of advertising intensity on Tobin's q is not statistically significant using conventional criteria. In terms of consistency and statistical significance, R&D emerges more so than advertising as a positive long-term influence on Tobin's q. In contrast with some popular assumptions that stock market investors are myopic in their focus on short-run performance, these findings suggest that investors evaluate the advertising and R&D efforts of firms with an appropriately long-term perspective.

As described in Table 6.1, R&D intensity tends to be much higher in manufacturing industries. Across manufacturing, R&D intensity averages 13.0%, or more than 6 times greater than the 2.1% R&D intensity common among nonmanufacturing firms. Across all 5284 manufacturing firm-year observations, and among 7860 nonmanufacturing firm-year observations, positive and statistically significant effects on Tobin's q are noted for profit margins, growth, advertising intensity, and R&D intensity, as is the predictably negative limiting influence of risk. Once again, it is important to recognize that statistically significant and positive coefficient estimates for R&D intensity among manufacturing and nonmanufacturing firms undoubtably underestimates the marginal economic impact of R&D on Tobin's q because at least some of the positive influence tied to profit margins can be attributed to profitable R&D investments. Clearly, R&D emerges as an important determining factor for Tobin's q in the overall sample and among both manufacturing and nonmanufacturing firms. As such, the empirical results reported in Table 6.5 offer strong evidence in support of the hypothesis that R&D is an important source of a type of intangible asset with predictably positive effects on future cash flows.

VIII. FIRM SIZE EFFECTS

High-tech investors generally expect a firm's life cycle to follow a predictable pattern of rapid growth, maturation, and decline. According to this view, a relatively large portion of the market value of smaller firms is determined by growth opportunities, whereas the value of large firms is more closely related to cash flows derived from assets in place. Important size-based differences in the stock-price effects of cash flow and growth opportunities would be consistent with this view.

Size effects have been detected in the stock-price effects of risk factors. Using a multifactor pricing model, Davis, Fama, and French (2002), among others, offer evidence that the higher average returns earned by small-cap stocks can be justified by their idiosyncratic risks. Their results suggest that the commonly reported "abnormal" returns to small-cap stocks arise from the failure of traditional valuation approaches to reflect the multidimensional risk attributes of small-cap stocks. Size effects may also influence the market valuation of less commonly recognized fundamental factors such as R&D and advertising expenditures. Recent studies suggest that small firms (spending less than $2 million on

R&D) appear more efficient than their larger competitors in that they are able to generate a relatively larger number of patents per dollar of R&D expenditure (see Griliches, 1990). This is a controversial conclusion, however, given differences in propensities to patent between small and large firms. The success of many small high-tech firms may depend on patents, and they can be expected to pursue patent opportunities vigorously. Few large, well-established firms depend upon continuing patenting activity. Similarly, a size-based comparison of the market-value effects of advertising expenditures may offer interesting evidence on the importance of size to market valuation. Economists have long argued that economies of scale derived from the advantages of promotion in large geographic markets and the large-scale purchase of media services create significant advantages for large firms.

Over the 1975–90 period, Hirschey and Spencer (1992) found that the market-value effects of fundamental factors are surprisingly consistent over an extended period of widely varying interest rates and economic conditions. They also found that the influences of fundamental factors appear to be affected by firm size. More specifically, statistically significant stock-price effects of profitability are notable during each period and within each firm size class, but it is most important for relatively large firms; growth has a uniformly positive market-value influence on small, medium, and large firms; R&D has a dramatic positive effect on the market values of firms in all size classes. These findings suggest the potential for interesting differences in the *effectiveness* of R&D expenditures according to firm size. If R&D effectiveness is influenced by firm size considerations, the potential exists for the market-value impact of R&D to differ according to firm size. To the extent that economies of scale or other size advantages in R&D are present, the market-value effect of a dollar in R&D expenditures will be greater for larger as opposed to smaller firms. Conversely, to the extent that diseconomies of scale or other size disadvantages in R&D are present, the market-value effect of a dollar of R&D expenditures would be moderated for relatively larger firms.

Table 6.5 illustrates the influence of firm size on the market-value effects of R&D intensity using a simple three-part breakdown of each sample according to stock market capitalization into "small," "medium," and "large" capitalization firms. From Table 6.5, it is clear that the stock-price effects of various fundamental causes of Tobin's q vary according to firm size class. As suggested by Hirschey and Spencer (1992), profit margins are important within each sample of manufacturing and nonmanufacturing firms and for the overall sample, but its positive impact on Tobin's q is most consistently important for relatively large firms. While growth has a uniformly positive market-value influence on small, medium, and large firms within each sample, this positive influence appears to increase with firm size. In the case of advertising, almost all of the significant positive impact on Tobin's q appears to originate among large manufacturers. Little, if any, positive effect of advertising on Tobin's q is detected among small- to medium-size manufacturers and among nonmanufacturers.

Of primary interest to this study is the relative impact of R&D on Tobin's q across firm size classes. After controlling for other important valuation effects, evidence reported in Table 6.5 suggests that the stock-price effects of R&D intensity do indeed depend upon firm size considerations. Consistent with Hirschey (2003a), the effect of R&D intensity on market values at the start of the new millennium (1997–2001) appears positively related to firm size. In the manufacturing sector, using a t-test of the difference in coefficient estimates, the superiority of medium-size firm R&D over small-size firm R&D is statistically significant ($t = 3.73$), as is the superiority of large-size firm over medium-size firm R&D ($t = 7.20$). Similarly, in the nonmanufacturing sector, the superiority of medium-size firm R&D over small-size firm R&D is statistically significant ($t = 3.90$), as is the superiority of large-size firm over medium-size firm R&D ($t = 3.11$). These findings suggest that size advantages are relevant in determining the stock-price effects of R&D intensity. Especially when the R&D-intensive manufacturing sector is considered, large firm advantages in R&D are unmistakable. These findings are consistent with the broad cross-sectional results reported for a similar valuation model by Chauvin and Hirschey (1993) and with the previously discussed R&D event study results reported by Chan, Martin, and Kensinger (1990) and Doukas and Switzer (1992). Just as the market's response to R&D announcements is more favorable in the case of larger spending increases reported by large firms, the market capitalization of R&D seems to generally increase with firm size.

IX. INSTITUTIONAL OWNERSHIP AND R&D EFFECTIVENESS

Prior research has suggested that high institutional stock ownership might lead to more effective R&D spending if institutional investors tend to be especially savvy in their assessment and monitoring of corporate investment opportunities. In support of that hypothesis, Jiambalvo, Rajgopal, and Venkatachalam (2002) found that institutional stockholders appear to be especially adept at deciphering the hard-to-fathom future cash flow implications of R&D investments and thereby tend to favor investments in R&D intensive firms. As described earlier, Szewczyk, Tsetsekos, and Zantout (1996) examined the role of investment opportunities and free cash flow in explaining R&D-induced abnormal returns. They found a significant positive relation between R&D-induced abnormal returns and institutional ownership and suggested that institutional stock ownership may be important in affecting the *effectiveness* of R&D spending.

Table 6.6 offers perspective on the importance of institutional stock ownership for R&D effectiveness in the manufacturing sector. Estimation results are shown for the same basic valuation model described earlier when the manufacturing subsample is subdivided according to both firm size and institutional stock ownership. As before, a simple three-part size breakdown into small, medium, and large firms according to stock market capitalization is considered. As shown

TABLE 6.6 Institutional Ownership and R&D Effectiveness for Manufacturing Firms, 1997–2001

Institutional ownership level	Intercept	Profit margin	Growth	Risk	Advertising intensity	R&D intensity	R^2	F	Sample size
A. Small market cap									
Low institutional ownership	2.522 (4.09)[a]	−0.482 (−2.51)[a]	0.621 (3.47)[a]	−1.943 (−4.79)[a]	0.389 (0.12)	−0.005 (−0.02)	26.63%	8.20[a]	662
Medium institutional ownership	1.677 (3.36)[a]	−0.320 (−2.34)[a]	0.923 (4.83)[a]	−1.801 (−5.83)[a]	1.554 (0.68)	0.151 (0.79)	33.17%	9.04[a]	539
High institutional ownership	2.420 (6.08)[a]	0.210 (0.58)	1.001 (5.92)[a]	−1.069 (−3.75)[a]	−2.639 (−0.53)	1.165 (2.54)[a]	29.63%	7.46[a]	525
B. Middle market cap									
Low institutional ownership	4.581 (3.75)[a]	0.070 (0.15)	0.763 (2.11)[b]	−3.233 (−5.76)[a]	0.400 (0.08)	0.999 (1.73)[b]	27.27%	5.33[a]	427
Medium institutional ownership	2.573 (4.03)[a]	0.151 (0.34)	2.186 (7.39)[a]	−2.817 (−6.17)[a]	−3.800 (−0.71)	0.543 (1.18)	33.44%	8.49[a]	502
High institutional ownership	2.156 (5.04)[a]	0.963 (3.80)[a]	1.093 (5.76)[a]	−2.271 (−7.98)[a]	4.025 (1.21)	1.556 (5.60)[a]	33.06%	12.98[a]	765
C. Large market cap									
Low institutional ownership	1.241 (3.08)[a]	3.724 (6.06)[a]	2.312 (5.71)[a]	−1.490 (−2.77)[a]	−0.486 (−0.14)	5.308 (7.62)[a]	32.31%	10.11[a]	600
Medium institutional ownership	3.279 (2.83)[a]	4.053 (5.95)[a]	2.686 (6.78)[a]	−3.550 (−6.33)[a]	12.280 (4.13)[a]	4.565 (6.57)[a]	42.73%	16.52[a]	649
High institutional ownership	3.969 (6.16)[a]	1.978 (4.12)[a]	1.503 (4.37)[a]	−4.369 (−8.77)[a]	1.461 (0.37)	3.200 (5.51)[a]	41.77%	15.01[a]	615
D. All manufacturing firms									
Low institutional ownership	2.957 (5.48)[a]	0.104 (0.60)	0.074 (4.91)[a]	−2.264 (−8.42)[a]	1.048 (0.50)	0.808 (3.42)[a]	21.80%	16.53[a]	1689
Medium institutional ownership	2.112 (4.55)[a]	0.669 (3.69)[a]	2.055 (11.25)[a]	−2.461 (−9.00)[a]	8.123 (4.22)[a]	0.965 (4.23)[a]	27.38%	22.37[a]	1690
High institutional ownership	2.035 (6.90)[a]	1.871 (9.16)[a]	1.336 (9.80)[a]	−1.633 (−8.10)[a]	5.687 (2.59)[a]	2.569 (10.88)[a]	29.89%	27.34[a]	1905

Note: SIC industry group and annual dummy (binary) variables are estimated but supressed for simplicity.
[a]Indicates statistical significance at the 0.01 level (one-tail test).
[b]Indicates statistical significance at the 0.05 level (one-tail test).

in Table 6.6, and as suggested by Hirschey (2002b), the generally positive effects of R&D intensity on Tobin's q tend to rise with increasing institutional stock ownership in each firm size class in both the manufacturing and nonmanufacturing sector. Across all manufacturing firms, both the size of R&D coefficient estimates and their statistical significance appear to be positively affected by increasing institutional stock ownership. Rising R&D coefficient estimates and growing statistical significance according to institutional stock ownership tend to be repeated within each size class of manufacturing firms.

As shown in Table 6.7, the generally positive effects of R&D intensity on Tobin's q also tend to rise with increasing institutional stock ownership in the nonmanufacturing sectors. Across all nonmanufacturing firms, both the size of R&D coefficient estimates and their statistical significance appear to be positively affected by increasing institutional stock ownership. As in the case of manufacturing firms, this pattern of rising R&D coefficient estimates and growing statistical significance according to institutional stock ownership tends to be repeated within each size class of nonmanufacturing firms.

Taken as a whole, these findings offer support for the hypothesis that increasing institutional stock ownership tends to be associated with rising R&D effectiveness in both the R&D-intensive manufacturing sector and the less R&D-intensive nonmanufacturing sector. Like Szewczyk, Tsetsekos, and Zantout (1996), who found a significant positive relation between R&D-induced abnormal returns and institutional ownership, findings reported here suggest that higher stock prices are associated with the R&D activity of firms with high institutional stock ownership. These findings are consistent with the hypothesis that institutional investors play an important monitoring function that helps insure effective R&D investment decisions. This is an important result because it suggests that institutional stock ownership may constitute a significant positive influence on the effectiveness of R&D spending. This is an important issue, and one that merits further consideration in future research.

X. CONCLUSION

Positive effects of R&D intensity on the Tobin's q ratio, a popular cross-sectional measure of the market value of the firm, are illustrated in this chapter for broadly representative samples of *Compustat* firms. After controlling for the predictably positive stock-price effects of profit margins, growth, and advertising intensity and the limiting effects of risk, R&D emerges as a key determinant of the market value of the firm. Broadly positive effects of R&D intensity on Tobin's q are evident throughout both manufacturing and nonmanufacturing sectors. As such, R&D emerges as a consistently attractive form of investment in valuable intangible assets that have differing degrees of importance in different economic sectors.

Findings reported here support prior suggestions concerning differences in the *effectiveness* of R&D expenditures according to firm size. Consistent with

TABLE 6.7 Institutional Ownership and R&D Effectiveness for Nonmanufacturing Firms, 1997–2001

Institutional ownership level	Intercept	Profit margin	Growth	Risk	Advertising intensity	R&D intensity	R^2	F	Sample size
A. Small market cap									
Low institutional ownership	2.648 $(11.53)^a$	−0.010 $(−0.18)$	0.169 $(1.97)^b$	−1.675 $(−7.21)^a$	3.098 $(1.80)^b$	0.420 $(1.76)^b$	27.13%	8.28^a	1349
Medium institutional ownership	2.543 $(10.72)^a$	0.246 $(2.42)^a$	0.082 (0.80)	−1.415 $(−6.14)^a$	−3.361 $(−1.62)^c$	4.066 $(5.74)^a$	36.19%	6.05^a	678
High institutional ownership	2.042 $(5.19)^a$	0.646 $(2.65)^a$	0.017 (0.19)	−0.805 $(−3.25)^a$	−3.402 $(−1.68)^b$	1.512 $(2.22)^b$	39.78%	4.51^a	455
B. Middle market cap									
Low institutional ownership	2.713 $(9.55)^a$	0.144 (0.74)	0.037 (0.41)	−1.851 $(−6.72)^a$	3.385 $(1.71)^b$	3.298 $(7.45)^c$	37.82%	9.23^a	939
Medium institutional ownership	3.904 $(12.84)^a$	0.527 $(4.02)^a$	0.233 $(2.13)^b$	−3.054 $(−10.42)^a$	8.213 $(2.66)^a$	0.661 $(2.04)^b$	48.77%	13.43^a	877
High institutional ownership	3.394 $(8.29)^a$	1.214 $(2.85)^a$	−0.065 $(−0.48)$	−2.612 $(−9.77)^a$	−6.779 $(−2.63)^a$	4.066 $(5.97)^a$	45.19%	11.45^a	864
C. Large market cap									
Low institutional ownership	0.487 $(3.02)^a$	0.382 $(3.83)^a$	0.208 (1.27)	−1.681 $(−4.52)^a$	3.446 (0.75)	11.453 $(6.57)^a$	40.28%	8.99^a	832
Medium institutional ownership	4.098 $(11.54)^a$	1.724 $(6.65)^a$	0.726 $(6.20)^a$	−3.726 $(−10.91)^a$	−10.849 $(−2.71)^a$	1.749 $(2.32)^b$	52.98%	18.17^a	994
High institutional ownership	3.673 $(7.63)^a$	0.368 $(3.36)^a$	0.729 $(4.06)^a$	−3.109 $(−8.81)^a$	−1.044 $(−0.31)$	6.934 $(6.96)^a$	49.59%	13.79^a	872
D. All nonmanufacturing firms									
Low institutional ownership	2.594 $(15.98)^a$	0.148 (3.11)	0.181 $(3.01)^a$	−1.693 $(−10.49)^a$	2.001 $(1.54)^c$	1.099 $(5.28)^a$	27.64%	20.16^a	3120
Medium institutional ownership	3.273 $(16.87)^a$	0.697 $(7.24)^a$	0.501 $(7.07)^a$	−2.495 $(−13.45)^a$	2.130 (1.10)	0.976 $(3.11)^a$	36.75%	24.94^a	2549
High institutional ownership	3.103 $(11.42)^a$	0.352 $(3.81)^a$	0.144 $(1.68)^b$	−2.206 $(−12.22)^a$	−3.793 $(−2.26)^b$	4.042 $(8.48)^a$	36.47%	21.10^a	2191

Note: SIC industry group and annual dummy (binary) variables are estimated but supressed for simplicity.
[a]Indicates statistical significance at the 0.01 level (one-tail test).
[b]Indicates statistical significance at the 0.05 level (one-tail test).
[c]Indicates statistical significance at the 0.10 level (one-tail test).

some prior evidence, size advantages appear to influence the generally positive effects of R&D intensity on Tobin's q. For both manufacturing and nonmanufacturing firms, the market-value effect of a dollar in R&D spending tends to be greater for relatively larger firms. In a new finding, consistent differences in the market-value effects of R&D intensity are noted across all firm size classes according to the amount of firm stock held by institutional investors. In each size class, the generally positive influence of R&D intensity on Tobin's q increases with the level of institutional stock ownership. This result lends support to the hypothesis that institutional investors have both the resources and the financial incentives to effectively monitor management's R&D investment decisions. More than just favoring investments in R&D-intensive firms, institutional investors may play a monitoring role that actually increases R&D effectiveness.

XI. REFERENCES

Baysinger, B. D., Kosnik, R. D., and Turk, T. A. (1991). Effects of Board and Ownership Structure on Corporate R&D Strategy. *Academy of Management Journal* 34, 205–214.

Brainard, W. and Tobin, J. (1968). Pitfalls in Financial Model Building. *American Economic Review* 58, 99–122.

Bushee, B. J. (1998). The Influence of Institutional Investors on Myopic R&D Investment Behavior. *Accounting Review* 73, 305–333.

Chan, S. and Ho, K. W. (1997). Market Response to Product-Strategy and Capital-Expenditure Announcements in Singapore: Investment Opportunities and Free Cash Flow. *Financial Management* 26, 82–88.

Chan, S. H., Martin, J. D., and Kensinger, J. W. (1990). Corporate Research and Development Expenditures and Share Value. *Journal of Financial Economics* 26, 255–276.

Chan, L. K. C., Lakonishok, J., and Sougiannis, T. (2001). The Stock Market Valuation of Research and Development Expenditures. *Journal of Finance* 56, 2431–2456.

Chauvin, K. W. and Hirschey, M. (1993). Advertising, R&D Expenditures and the Market Value of the Firm. *Financial Management* 22, 128–140.

Chung, K. H. and Pruitt, S. W. (1994). A Simple Approximation of Tobin's q. *Financial Management* 23, 70–74.

Connolly, R. A. and Hirschey, M. (1990). Firm Size and R&D Effectiveness: A Value-Based Test. *Economics Letters* 27, 277–281.

David, P., Hitt, M. A., and Insead, J. G. (2001). The Influence of Activism by Institutional Investors on R&D. *Academy of Management Journal* 44, 144–157.

Davis, J. L., Fama, E. F., and French, K. R. (2002). Characteristics, Covariances, and Average Returns: 1929 to 1997. *Journal of Finance* 55, 389–406.

Doukas, J. and Switzer, L. N. (1992). The Stock Market's View of R&D Spending and Market Concentration. *Journal of Economics and Business* 44, 95–114.

El-Gazzar, S. M. (1998). Predisclosure Information and Institutional Ownership: A Cross-Sectional Examination of Market Revaluations During Earnings Announcement Periods. *Accounting Review* 73, 119–129.

Eng, L. L. and Shackell, M. (2001). The Implications of Long-Term Performance Plans and Institutional Ownership for Firms' Research and Development Investments. *Journal of Accounting, Auditing & Finance* 16, 117–139.

Graves, S. B. (1988). Institutional Ownership and Corporate R&D in the Computer Industry. *Academy of Management Journal* 31, 417–428.

Griliches, Z. (1990). Patent Statistics as Economic Indicators: A Survey. *Journal of Economic Literature* 28, 1661–1707.

Hansen, G. S. and Hill, C. W. L. (1991). Are Institutional Investors Myopic? A Time-Series Study of Four Technology-Driven Industries. *Strategic Management Journal* 12, 1–16.

Hirschey, M. (1982). Intangible Capital Aspects of Advertising and R&D Expenditures. *Journal of Industrial Economics* 30, 375–390.

Hirschey, M. (1985). Market Structure and Market Value. *Journal of Business* 58, 89–98.

Hirschey, M. (2003a). Firm Size and the Effect of R&D on Tobin's *q*. University of Kansas Working Paper.

Hirschey, M. (2003b). Institutional Ownership and R&D Effectiveness. University of Kansas Working Paper.

Hirschey, M. (2003c). *Managerial Economics, Tenth Edition.* Mason, OH: South-Western Thompson Learning, Inc. Chap. 16.

Hirschey, M. and Spencer, R. S. (1992). Size Effects in the Market Capitalization of Fundamental Factors. *Financial Analysts Journal* 48, 91–95.

Hirschey, M. and Weygandt, J. J. (1985). Amortization Policy for Advertising and Research and Development Expenditures. *Journal of Accounting Research* 23, 326–335.

Huchzermeier, A. and Loch, C. H. (2001). Project Management under Risk: Using the Real Options Approach to Evaluate Flexibility in R&D. *Management Science* 47, 85–101.

Jensen, M. C. and Meckling, W. H. (1976). Theory of the Firm: Managerial Behavior, Agency Costs and Ownership Structure. *Journal of Financial Economics* 3, 305–360.

Jiambalvo, J., Rajgopal, S., and Venkatachalam, M. (2002). Institutional Ownership and the Extent to Which Stock Prices Reflect Future Earnings. *Contemporary Accounting Research* 19, 117–145.

Jose, M. L., Nichols, L. M., and Stevens, J. L. (1986). Contributions of Diversification, Promotion, and R&D to the Value of Multiproduct Firms: A Tobin's *q* Approach. *Financial Management* 15, 33–42.

Landsman, W., and Magliolo, J. (1988). Cross-Sectional Capital Market Research and Model Specification. *Accounting Review* 63, 586–604.

Lev, B. and Sougiannis, T. (1999). Penetrating the Book-to-Market Black Box: The R&D Effect. *Journal of Business Finance & Accounting* 26, 419–449.

Lindenberg, E. B. and Ross, S. A. (1981). Tobin's *q* Ratio and Industrial Organization. *Journal of Business* 54, 1–32.

McConnell, J. J. and Muscarella, C. J. (1985). Corporate Capital Expenditure Decisions and the Market Value of the Firm. *Journal of Financial Economics* 14, 399–422.

Miller, M. and Modigliani, F. (1961). Dividend Policy, Growth and the Value of Shares. *Journal of Business* 34, 411–433.

Morck, R., Shleifer, A., and Vishny, R. W. (1988). Management Ownership and Market Valuation: An Empirical Analysis. *Journal of Financial Economics* 20, 293–315.

Ryan, H. E., Jr. and Wiggins, R. A., III. (2002). The Interactions Between R&D Investment Decisions and Compensation Policy. *Financial Management* 31, 5–29.

Schwert, G. W. (1981). Using Financial Data to Measure Effects of Regulation. *Journal of Law and Economics* 24, 121–158.

Szewczyk, S. H., Tsetsekos, G. P., and Zantout, Z. (1996). The Valuation of Corporate R&D Expenditures: Evidence from Investment Opportunities and Free Cash Flow. *Financial Management* 25, 105–110.

Toivanen, O., Stoneman, P., and Bosworth, D. (2002). Innovation and the Market Value of UK Firms, 1989–1995. *Oxford Bulletin of Economics & Statistics* 64, 39–61.

Watts, R. L., and Zimmerman, J. L. (1980). On the Irrelevance of Replacement Cost Disclosures for Security Prices. *Journal of Accounting and Economics* 2, 95–106.

7

VALUATION EFFECTS OF PATENT QUALITY

During recent years, price–earnings (P/E) and price–book (P/B) ratios have reached historic highs, especially in the case of technology stocks. On the one hand, historic P/E and P/B ratios may suggest an excessive amount of optimism on the part of tech stock investors (see Hirschey, 1998, 2001). On the other hand, an increasing divergence between stock prices and fundamental factors, such as earnings and book values, may imply a decline in the usefulness of traditional accounting information for security valuation. This may be especially true in the case of technology stocks. For new companies in emerging technologies, accounting profits, book values, and even sales can be small or nonexistent. How can investors reasonably assess the future prospects of such companies?

An interesting possibility is suggested by Amir and Lev (1996), who report on the market-value effects of nonfinancial information in the wireless communications industry. Amir and Lev (1996) found that financial information, such as earnings, book values, and cash flows, is largely irrelevant in the valuation of cellular phone companies. On the other hand, nonfinancial indicators, such as population size (a growth proxy) and market penetration (an operating performance measure), are highly relevant in the valuation of cellular stocks. Interestingly, only when combined with nonfinancial information do traditional financial accounting data make a marginal contribution to cellular stock valuation. This suggests the complementary nature of financial and nonfinancial data for cellular stocks. This chapter delves further into the notion that firm-specific nonfinancial information can be fruitfully employed by investors in innovative, fast-changing, science-based companies. Nonfinancial data may be particularly relevant in the valuation of technology stocks where the productivity of investments in intangible assets (such as patents) is a vital determinant of long-term success. Against this backdrop, it becomes relevant to ask: Can scientific data that measure the quantity and quality of inventive output be helpful in the valuation of technology stocks?

I. USEFULNESS OF NONFINANCIAL INFORMATION

Valuation effects of corporate research and development (R&D) expenditures have long been used to provide useful, albeit indirect, evidence on the economic consequences of the firm's inventive and innovative activity. For example, Hirschey and Weygandt (1985) were among the first to use market-value data to establish the importance of R&D as an important source of intangible capital. Hirschey and Spencer (1992) also show that R&D expenditures have consistently large and positive influences on the market value of all size classes and document that the strength of this relationship is inversely related to firm size. Like current cash flow information, data on R&D spending appears to help investors form appropriate expectations concerning the magnitude and variability of future cash flows. This chapter details results reported by Hirschey, Richardson, and Scholz (2001) on the economic consequences of invention and innovation as measured by the valuation effects of patenting activity.

Accounting information gives a useful perspective on the economic value of the firm that is historical, logical, and consistent. In contrast, stock market valuations reflect a forward-looking viewpoint on the value of the firm's future cash flows. Differences between the historical accounting perspective and the stock market's forward-looking perspective are to be expected. The practical value of accounting numbers is enhanced to the extent that such data can be profitably used by investors as indicators of corporate health in their ongoing assessment of the firm's economic prospects. Unfortunately, Brown, Lo, and Lys (1999) document a long-term decline in the relevance of financial statement information as an important determinant of the market value of the firm. Controlling for size effects, they find that there has been a dramatic decline in the value relevance of financial statement information during the post-World War II period. This and related findings have fed a growing concern among both academics and practitioners that corporate financial statements have lost a significant portion of their relevance for investors (Francis and Schipper, 1999). This concern has given rise to a number of research and accounting policy initiatives with the common goal to improve the practical relevance of financial reporting. Not only is value relevance a significant practical matter in the United States, growing concern over the harmonization of global accounting standards has focused attention of the volatility of accounting income and cash flow numbers and market values (Pownall and Schipper, 1999).

In a now common method, empirical market-based research seeks evidence on the value relevance of accounting and other operating data through analyses of the relation between such information and the value of the firm (Easton, 1999). For example, Ashiq and Lee-Seok (2000) take a global perspective and study country-specific factors related to financial reporting and the value relevance of accounting data. Using 1986–95 data from manufacturing firms from 16 countries, Ali and Hwang (2000) explore relations between value relevance and accounting data using several country-specific factors suggested in prior research. Value relevance is specified primarily in terms of the explanatory power of traditional accounting variables for security returns relative to explanatory power for comparable U.S. firms. Unfortunately, like many such studies, this academic research has had only limited practical implications because serious doubt yet remains concerning the needs for comprehensiveness, transparency, and full disclosure in accounting financial statements.

Accounting for R&D is an important area in which significant doubt exists concerning the appropriateness of the present level of mandated disclosure on accounting financial statements. Long-standing concerns with reliability and objectivity have caused Generally Accepted Accounting Principles (GAAP) to mandate the full expense-as-incurred treatment of R&D expenditures in financial statements. This is despite extensive research in accounting and financial economics that demonstrates consistently positive effects of R&D expenditures on the market value of the firm. Chauvin and Hirschey (1993), for example, document consistently positive valuation effects of R&D expenditures for a broad sample of firms. Similarly, Lev and Sougiannis (1996) estimate R&D capital for a large sample of public companies and find that such estimates are value relevant to investors. Similarly positive influences of R&D expenditure announcements on stock market returns, so-called "returns models," have also been reported by Chan, Martin, and Kensinger (1990) and Sundaram, John and John (1996), among others. In light of this large and growing body of research, it seems fair to conclude that the value relevance of R&D expenditures has been amply demonstrated. In terms of both economic importance and statistical significance, R&D expenditures clearly have positive effects on the market value of the firm.

II. QUESTIONS ABOUT LONG-TERM BENEFITS OF R&D

What now needs to be confronted are worries about the reliability and objectivity of market-value-based estimates of long-term benefits created by R&D expenditures. To help in this regard, this chapter contemplates the value relevance of nonfinancial patent information for high-tech companies. Accounting earnings and book value information are highly relevant for security valuation in the high-tech sector, and nonfinancial indicators of inventive output can be used to sharpen perceptions of long-term benefits derived from R&D expenditures. Within this framework, R&D expenditures can be viewed as material "input" in the invention and innovation process, and the value relevance of R&D input depends upon its effectiveness in generating useful inventive and innovative "output."

This work also hopes to provide a useful extension to earlier research on the economic importance of patent statistics. Griliches (1990) documented a stream of research in economics that points to statistically significant effects of patent count information on the market value of the firm. For example, Griliches (1986), Pakes (1985), Cockburn and Griliches (1988), and Connolly and Hirschey (1988) found large, positive, statistically significant effects of patent statistics on firm market values that are robust to a variety of model specifications. Based on prior research, it seems fair to conclude that the number of patents represents economically meaningful information about the scope, effectiveness, and future profit potential of the firm's R&D. This work extends patents research by showing how the value relevance of patent activity is related to the "scientific merit" of patent information. In a recent paper, Narin, Hamilton, and Olivastro (1997) identified the growing dependence over time of patented technology on scientific papers. This evidence suggests the possibility of using citations-based indicators of scientific merit as indicators of patent quality. The aim is to extend historical evidence on the link between the market value of the firm and the number of patents by showing the value relevance of patent "quality." Specifically, investigated are valuation effects tied to how often a company's patents are cited, how close a company's patents are to the current scientific research base, and the median age of patents cited in a company's new patents. In so doing, research on the complementary importance of financial and nonfinancial information is advanced.

The importance of nonfinancial information to investors is widely recognized. For example, the American Institute of Certified Public Accountants (AICPA) Special Committee on Financial Reporting encouraged companies to increase disclosure of such information. Committee examples of useful data specifically include "comparisons of patents obtained per year" (AICPA, 1994, Chap. 5). However, the nonfinancial data investigated are somewhat different from that envisioned by the AICPA committee because they are not obtained from firm disclosures. Instead, the data is provided by an independent third-party unfiltered by the firms' competitive considerations.

This study also extends a line of research that investigates the relationship between financial information and complementary third-party nonfinancial data. These studies include Amir and Lev (1996), who report that financial information (earnings, book values, and cash flows) is largely irrelevant in security valuation for cellular phone companies. Nonfinancial indicators, such as population size (a growth proxy) and market penetration (an operating performance measure), are highly value relevant. However, when combined with nonfinancial information, financial accounting data make a marginal contribution to the overall explanation of stock prices. Similarly, in an interesting study, Barth and McNichols (1994) found that environmental cleanup liability estimates based on Superfund site data have incremental explanatory power over the assets and liabilities (including environmental liabilities) recorded in companies' financial statements.

With respect to findings, the relation between R&D expenditures and equity values tends to be more consistent in the more successful R&D firms, where success is communicated in terms of patent quality information. Alternative accounting policy perspectives can be inferred from these results. A reasonable interpretation of the results is that companies should provide nonfinancial patent data as a supplement to their existing R&D disclosures. On the other hand, it might not be necessary to mandate additional disclosures of patent quality information so long as independent sources of such data remain widely available to investors.

III. PATENT STATISTICS

One of the most useful measures of the pace of inventive activity is the number of patents granted to a specific firm over a given time period, say 1 year. The widespread use of patent statistics stems from the fact that long-available patent data are derived from an objective and slow-changing standard. Under present law, the term of a U.S. patent is 20 years from the filing date of the patent application or, if reference is made to an earlier application, from the filing date of that earlier application. A wide body of economic research documents the strong relationship between patent numbers and R&D expenditures and implies that patents are a good indicator of differences in inventive activity across firms (see Griliches, 1990). Unfortunately, while patent statistics remain a unique and valuable resource for studies of the process of technical change, problems are encountered when patents are used as a proxy for the pace of inventive output at the firm level (Hirschey and Richardson, 2001).

While all patents must meet objective criteria in terms of novelty and utility, not all patents have the same technical scope nor do they have the same economic significance. Patent scope depends on how inventions are linked to one another and the extent to which rapid advances require a diversity of technical and non-technical inputs. Whether or not a given patent has broad or narrow scope determines the ability of competitors to produce substitutes without fear of infringement suits and helps define the amount of "monopoly power" enjoyed by the patent holder. Patents readily identifiable with end products tend to be more valuable than the average patent. Many low-value patents cover intermediate processes that, in themselves, do not lead directly to marketable products. Therefore, despite research that documents the generally robust positive effects of patent statistics on the market value of the firm, not all patents are created equal in the eyes of investors. In addition, important differences exist among firms in terms of their propensity to patent. There is no one-to-one relationship between R&D expenditures and patenting activity (see Griliches, Nordhaus, and Scherer, 1989).

In the early-1990s, Kortum (1993) noted that the patent–R&D ratio in the United States had declined steadily for over 30 years. At that time, some suggested that an exhaustion of technological opportunities had reduced the productivity of corporate R&D. Others argued that expanding world markets had raised the value of patents and that growing competition in the research sector had resulted in greater R&D expenditures per patent. Like Griliches (1990), Kortum (1993) simply found that rising costs of dealing with the patent system led researchers to patent fewer of their inventions. While industry data once supported the inference of a decline in the corporate propensity to patent, more recent data suggest the opposite. During the 1990s, there was an unprecedented surge in corporate patenting in the United States. Using both international and domestic data on patent applications and awards, Kortum and Lerner (1999) showed that the recent jump in corporate patenting reflects an increase in innovation spurred by improvements in the strategic management of corporate R&D expenditures.

The use of patent statistics in economic research has been impeded by the fact that patents vary in their economic importance or value. Hence, simple patent counts are less than fully informative about the economic value of innovative output. Trajtenberg (1990) addressed this problem by examining the usefulness of patent indicators in the context of a particular innovation, Computed Tomography scanners, one of the most important advances in medical technology of recent times. As in prior studies, Trajtenberg (1990) found that simple patent counts are highly correlated with contemporaneous research and development expenditures. Interestingly, Trajtenberg (1990) also found a close association between citation-based patent indexes and independent measures of the social value of innovations in that field. Moreover, the value weighting scheme appears to be nonlinear in the number of citations, implying that the informational content of citations rises at the margin.

IV. PATENT CITATIONS

Albert *et al.* (1991) sought early validation of citation counts as indicators of important industrial patents and found a strong association between citation counts for highly cited U.S. patents and knowledgeable peer opinion as to the patent's technical importance. A total of 20 researchers and research managers at Eastman Kodak Research Laboratories, all of who are working in the area of silver halide technology, were asked to rate the technical impact and importance of each patent in overlapping sets of Eastman Kodak silver halide patents. A total of 77 patents were selected for rating. These patents ranged from those receiving zero citations to highly cited patents, or those patents which were cited 10 or more times on the front pages of subsequent U.S. patents issued through 1988. Among infrequently cited patents, there were no statistically significant differences between peer and citation ratings. In contrast, highly cited patents were rated far more important by the evaluators. As in the case of Trajtenberg's (1990) findings, the importance of cited patents appeared to increase more than proportionately with the number of citations. In an effort to tie patent citations data to evidence of the economic merit of individual patents, Thomas (1999) analyzed the relationship between the technological impact of U.S. patents, as measured by patent citations, and the renewal decisions made by patent owners. A significant positive relationship is discovered across a number of time periods. The link between citations and renewals remains highly significant even after controlling for differences between internal and external citations and differences in technology and patent ownership. In a related study, Harhoff *et al.* (1999) use a survey to obtain private economic value estimates for 964 inventions made in the United States and Germany and on which German patent renewal fees were paid to full-term expiration in 1995. These authors find that patents renewed to full-term are much more heavily cited than patents allowed to expire prematurely. The higher an invention's economic value estimate, the more the patent was subsequently cited.

In a recent study, Deng, Lev, and Narin (1999) tie current patent citation data to the firm's subsequent P/B ratios and stock market returns. From P/B ratio regressions, Deng, Lev, and Narin (1999) conclude that the number of patents approved and patent citation data are strongly related to investor growth expectations in the chemicals, drugs, and electronics industries. A somewhat weaker association between patent citation data and subsequent stock returns is reported. Hall, Jaffe, and Trajtenberg (2000) report that firm market values are correlated with the portion of eventual citations that cannot be predicted based upon past citations. In other words, stock prices are correlated with future citations that cannot be predicted on the basis of current patent data. Hall, Jaffe, and Trajtenberg (2000) conclude that the market "already knows" the information contained in future patent citations.

This chapter builds upon this line of research by investigating the importance of patent quality information for the market value of the firm. Specifically investigated is the extent to which the stock-price effects of patent quality data are influenced by time-period, firm-specific, and industry-specific influences. In so doing, understanding is expanded concerning the importance of patent quality information for investors as studied by Deng, Lev, and Narin (1999) and Hall, Jaffe, and Trajtenberg (2000). Industry-related effects may be especially important, given Cockburn and Griliches (1988) finding of an interaction between industry-level measures of the effectiveness of patents and the market's valuation of a firm's past R&D and patenting performance (see Hirschey, Richardson, and Scholz, 2001).

V. SCIENTIFIC MERIT OF PATENTS

When a typical U.S. patent is issued, it has five or six prior U.S. patents cited on its front page that limit the claims of the patent being issued. If a patent is heavily cited in later patents, it is an indication that the earlier patent represented an important scientific advance. The "Citations Index" (CI) is the number of citations generated in the current year by patents granted to the company during the most recent 5-year period, relative to the average number of citations for firms in a given International Patent Classification (IPC) four-digit subclass and year.[1] Thus, CI measures how often a company's patent is cited in subsequent patent applications relative to the typical pace of patent citations for a given industry and year. CI = 1 represents average citation frequency and CI = 2 means that a company's patents are twice as likely as average to be cited in subsequent patent applications. CI is a synchronous indicator reflecting 5 years of patent activity. When a company's recent patents drop in impact, a decline in CI is noted during the current year. The CI is also helpful in that it involves a comparison among companies operating in the same general industry, at the same time, and with the same technology. This is important because patent citation frequency tends to vary widely from one industry and technology to another. CIs vary by technology. For example, CIs are high in semiconductors, biotechnology, and pharmaceuticals and low in glass, clay and cement, and textiles.

Another measure of inventive output quality, called "Non-Patent References" (NPR), is predicated upon how closely a company's patents in the present year are to the scientific research base in the area. NPR is a simple count of the number of references in a patent application to a wide variety of nonpatent publications, including scientific papers and articles, brochures, books, standards, documents, patent disclosure bulletins, and so on. On average, about one-half of all nonpatent references are references to scientific articles. Of course, this varies by industry. Much more than one-half of biotechnology nonpatent references are scientific in nature. Much less than one-half of nonpatent references are scientific in nature for mechanical technologies, such as automotive and aerospace. Science-based technologies such as chemistry, drugs, and medicine have much higher NPRs than do mechanical technologies.

A third measure of patent quality is the "Technology Cycle Time" (TCT) indicator. TCT is the median age, computed in years, of the prior art references to earlier U.S. or European patents. For example, if a 1990 patent cited three patents, one from 1986, one from 1987, and one from 1988, the TCT would be 3 years. For the firm as a whole, TCT represents the amount of time that has elapsed between current patents and the previous generation of patents. TCT is essentially a measure of cycle time between the current technology and a prior state of knowledge, measured from grant date to grant date. Emerging technologies have short cycle times, 4 years or less, whereas more mature technologies can display TCTs that averages 15 or more years.

An emerging body of scientific research shows how patent citations relate to the scientific merit or "scientific quality" of inventive output. For example, Narin,

---

[1]In the calculation of CI, citations generated in the current year by patents granted to the company during the most recent five-year period are considered because this is the most comprehensive citations data available.

Hamilton, and Olivastro (1997) show the growing linkage between U.S. technology and public science by illustrating the increasing dependence over time of patented technology on scientific papers. This paper considers the potential economic relevance of CI, NPR, and TCT indicators of patent quality. CI and NPR are technology impact indicators because they reflect the extent to which a firm's patenting activity forms the basis for subsequent science. They are economic indicators to the extent that patents with high technological importance also have significant economic importance and consistently positive effects on the market value of the firm. The expected economic life of a firm's patents is a positive function of TCT to the extent that the slow pace of historically slow-moving technology is a useful indicator of the speed of future invention and innovation. Positive stock-price effects of TCT represent a useful indication of the value tied to patent "durability." Conversely, negative stock-price effects may be associated with TCT to the extent that "older" technology is highly subject to competitive inroads.

VI. DATA

Patent statistics and patent citation information for this study were obtained from Tech-Line® Company Patent Profiles, a technology indicators database marketed by CHI Research, Inc. (http://www.chiresearch.com/). Tech-Line® contains technological profiles on organizations actively patenting in the United States, where each organization is responsible for at least 10 patents per year. By definition, this database focuses upon high-tech companies with active patent histories reflecting significant R&D, invention, and innovative activity. Companies included in the analysis represent a sample from 26 major industry groups arrayed across the 30 technology areas defined by the IPC system. Industry groups with the heaviest representation include chemicals (55 companies), computer equipment (44), electronics (39), instrument and optical (32), and automotive (19). The sample is taken from the 1989–95 period, and contains all Tech-Line® companies for which complete data could be obtained. A total of 1694 firm-year observations for public high-tech U.S. companies are included. For comparison purposes, the stock-price effects of U.S. patenting activity for a sample of public high-tech Japanese companies are also considered. A total of 1350 firm-year observations for public high-tech Japanese companies are included. These samples are sufficiently broad to permit a consideration of stock-price effects after controlling for the influence of industry, time period, and country of origin considerations.

Table 7.1 shows the quantity and scientific quality of U.S. patents granted over the 1989–95 period for 10 top Japanese and U.S. high-tech companies. Firm averages are reported to net out the effects of predictable year-to-year variation in each of these statistics. Notice that Japanese companies account for 6 out of 10 firms found on the list of those awarded the greatest number of U.S. patents. It may be somewhat surprising to find automakers Mitsubishi and General Motors

TABLE 7.1   Total Patents and Scientific-Based Indicators of Patent Quality for the Top 10 Leading High-Tech Japanese and U.S. Firms, 1989–95

Total Patents (PAT)		Citations Index (CI)	
MITSUBISHI (Japan)	10,141	ACTEL CORP (U.S.)	5.35
MATSUSHITA (Japan)	9,800	QUALCOMM INC (U.S.)	4.78
HITACHI (Japan)	7,969	ALTERA CORP (U.S.)	3.91
TOSHIBA (Japan)	7,716	BOSTON SCIENTIFIC CORP (U.S.)	3.57
CANON (Japan)	7,049	SYMBOL TECHNOLOGIES (U.S.)	3.45
GENERAL ELECTRIC CO (U.S.)	6,576	BARD (C.R.) INC (U.S.)	3.01
INTL BUSINESS MACHINES (U.S.)	6,532	XILINX INC (U.S.)	2.81
GENERAL MOTORS CORP (U.S.)	5,740	NORAND CORP (U.S.)	2.80
EASTMAN KODAK CO (U.S.)	5,637	CORDIS CORP (U.S.)	2.72
FUJI PHOTO (Japan)	4,848	REEBOK INTL LTD (U.S.)	2.70
Japanese sample average	**88.14**	**Japanese sample average**	**0.91**
U.S. sample average	**82.56**	**U.S. sample average**	**1.14**

Non-Patent References (NPR)		Technology Cycle Time (TCT)	
GENENTECH INC (U.S.)	24.56	HOSIDEN ELECTRONICS (Japan)	4.02
IMMUNEX CORP (U.S.)	15.37	UNISIA JECS (Japan)	4.30
CETUS CORP (U.S.)	12.87	IMMUNEX CORP (U.S.)	4.39
GENETICS INSTITUTE INC (U.S.)	11.55	ALTERA CORP (U.S.)	4.40
CHUGAI PHARMACEUTICAL (Japan)	10.08	SUN MICROSYSTEMS INC (U.S.)	4.59
CHIRON CORP (U.S.)	9.79	FUJI HEAVY INDUSTRIES (Japan)	4.63
PIONEER HI-BRED INTL (U.S.)	7.35	GENETICS INSTITUTE INC (U.S.)	4.71
UNION CAMP CORP (U.S.)	6.26	INTEL CORP (U.S.)	4.86
SEARLE (G.D.) & CO (U.S.)	5.07	MAZDA MOTORS (Japan)	4.87
WEYERHAEUSER CO (U.S.)	5.05	TEAC CORP (Japan)	4.89
Japanese sample average	**0.45**	**Japanese sample average**	**7.85**
U.S. sample average	**1.07**	**U.S. sample average**	**10.02**

Note: Total Patents (PAT) = Total U.S. patents granted over a recent (1989–95) five-year period. Citations Index (CI) = Number of citations generated by a company's most recent five years of patents, divided by the expected number of citations for similar high-tech companies. CI = 2 means that a given company's patents are twice as likely as average to be cited in subsequent patent applications. Non-Patent References (NPR) = Average number of "other references cited" on the front page of the patent, including academic journal articles and papers presented at scientific meetings. Technology Cycle Time (TCT) = Median age (in years) of earlier U.S. patents referenced on the front page of a U.S. patent.

Corp. (GM) among those with the most prolific patenting programs, but these are huge corporations in terms of sales, profits, and R&D spending. Effective competition in the automobile manufacturing industry requires ongoing invention and innovation. In addition, Mitsubishi and GM are broadly diversified companies with important operations in traditional high-tech areas such as telecommunications and electronics. Other firms that appear on the list of high patent frequency corporations can be described as leading producers of electronic and electric products for a wide variety of consumer, business, and industrial uses. The production of photographic equipment, copier products, personal computers, and computer mainframes (servers) all require intensive and continual new product development. The fact that Japanese companies are prominent on the list of firms granted the most U.S. patents is consistent with Narin's (1995) observation that Japanese companies tend to be very rapid in their pace of improvement on patented technology.

Notice from Table 7.1 that U.S. companies dominate lists of firms granted U.S. patents with the highest scientific merit, when merit is measured in terms of CI and NPR. This means that U.S. companies dominate lists of firms noted for gaining patents that are widely cited in subsequent patent applications and in academic journal articles and papers presented at scientific meetings. Several of the companies noted for gaining patents that are widely cited in subsequent patent applications (CI) are involved with traditional high-tech areas such as the design, manufacture and marketing of electronic components and semiconductors (Actel and Altera), digital wireless communications products (Qualcomm), medical devices (Boston Scientific, Bard, and Cordis), and optical character recognition (Symbol Technologies). A notable exception to this rule is provided by Reebok International Ltd., a global company engaged primarily in the design and marketing of sports and fitness products, including footwear and apparel.

Biotechnology firms dominate the list of companies noted for producing patents that are actively cited in academic journal articles and in papers presented at scientific meetings (NPR). While most of the biotech firms that rank high in terms of NPR are engaged in the production of pharmaceutical products for human consumption, the biotech operations of some large forestry and paper product manufacturers, such as Union Camp and Weyerhaeuser, are noteworthy.

And finally, despite Narin's (1995) suggestion that Japanese companies tend to be most rapid in their citation of new technology, there is no clear distinction over this time frame in the TCT of top high-tech U.S. and Japanese companies. While the average TCT is shorter at 7.85 years in our sample of Japanese high-tech firms, versus 10.02 years for U.S. companies, there is a 50/50 representation of Japanese and U.S. firms on the list of top companies according to TCT. Apparently, the speed with which a company is developing new technology is fairly dependent upon firm-specific and industry-specific factors that do not lend themselves to broad characterization on a national basis. Notice that many of the leading-edge firms that appear on the TCT list are involved with rapidly evolving high-tech industries such as semiconductor equipment (Altera and Intel) and electronic products (Hosiden, Sun, and Teac).

Therefore, while Japanese high-tech companies dominate the list of firms awarded the greatest number of U.S. patents over the 1989–95 period, U.S. companies dominate lists of firms granted U.S. patents with the highest scientific merit. Despite the fact that Japanese companies tend to be rapid in their citation of new technology, there is no clear distinction over this time frame between top Japanese and U.S. companies in terms of the speed with which they appear to be developing new technology.

TABLE 7.2 Sample Descriptive Statistics

		Market cap ($millions)	Number of patents (patents)	Citations index (CI)	Non-patent references (NPR)	Technology cycle time (TCT) (years)	Sample size
a. U.S. firm size (market cap)							
Small (market cap < $1,118.90 million)	Mean	549.14	23.68	1.22	0.95	9.96	564
	Std. Dev.	299.17	23.73	0.87	2.30	3.95	
Medium ($1,118.90 million < market cap < $3,754.10 million)	Mean	2,147.31	45.88	1.14	1.00	10.50	564
	Std. Dev.	725.32	43.76	0.85	2.43	3.48	
Large (market cap > $3,754.10 million)	Mean	16,428.10	177.81	1.07	1.27	9.59	566
	Std. Dev.	17,664.64	213.81	0.47	2.71	2.76	
b. U.S. growth opportunities (P/E ratio)							
Low (P/E ratio < 12.10)	Mean	3,586.41	77.19	1.12	1.09	10.06	560
	Std. Dev.	7,050.15	140.69	0.71	2.64	3.80	
Moderate (12.11 < P/E ratio < 18.99)	Mean	8,307.54	98.75	1.08	0.82	10.09	568
	Std. Dev.	15,229.26	161.76	0.65	1.18	3.28	
High (P/E ratio > 18.99)	Mean	7,229.74	71.64	1.23	1.30	9.90	566
	Std. Dev.	13,095.68	125.78	0.88	3.18	3.25	
Overall sample: United States	Mean	6,386.72	82.56	1.14	1.07	10.02	1,694
	Std. Dev.	12,465.53	143.93	0.76	2.49	3.45	
c. Japanese firm size (market cap)							
Small (market cap < $1,564.11 million)	Mean	795.76	26.26	0.91	0.29	7.80	450
	Std. Dev.	425.48	35.39	0.44	0.57	2.93	
Medium ($1,564.11 million < market cap < $4,510.79 million)	Mean	2,750.46	46.90	0.86	1.54	7.89	449
	Std. Dev.	799.81	54.33	0.33	1.56	2.71	
Large (market cap > $4,510.79 million)	Mean	13,965.89	190.93	0.95	0.49	7.85	451
	Std. Dev.	18,817.45	288.72	0.38	0.55	2.65	
d. Japanese growth opportunities (P/E ratio)							
Low (P/E ratio < 37.10)	Mean	5,881.17	91.51	0.91	0.52	7.82	450
	Std. Dev.	8,443.09	189.12	0.38	1.44	2.72	
Moderate (37.10 < P/E ratio < 61.75)	Mean	5,934.67	103.66	0.92	0.39	7.80	449
	Std. Dev.	10,648.84	216.28	0.38	0.64	2.73	
High (P/E ratio > 61.75)	Mean	5,721.67	69.31	0.89	0.45	7.92	451
	Std. Dev.	16,492.83	144.23	0.40	0.73	2.85	
Overall sample: Japan	Mean	5,845.68	88.14	0.91	0.45	7.85	1,350
	Std. Dev.	12,334.19	185.96	0.39	1.00	2.77	

In the empirical analysis, stock market and operating data are obtained from *Compustat*. The market value of equity is the market price of common stock (*Compustat* variable A#24) times the number of shares outstanding (A#25) as of December 31 for each year. Size effects are normalized by deflating size-related variables (market value and the number of patents) by the book value of total asset (A#6).

Table 7.2 shows sample descriptive statistics quantity and scientific quality of inventive output from Tech-Line®. Japanese companies are more prolific than their U.S. counterparts in the number of U.S. patents granted. Among firms that received 10 or more U.S. patents per year over the 1989–95 period, the typical Japanese high-tech firm was issued 88.14 patents compared to 82.56 patents for similar U.S. firms. However, many U.S. patents issued to Japanese firms appear to be of relatively lower quality and economic value. Japanese companies had an average CI of 0.91, meaning that Japanese patents receive only 91% of the typical number of citations in subsequent patent applications. U.S. patents issued to domestic firms receive 114% of the typical number of such citations. U.S. patents issued to Japanese companies are also characterized by relatively lower NPR. Japanese firms have only 45% of the typical number of "other references cited" on the front page of each patent, compared with 107% for U.S. firms. Finally, the TCT indicator value of 7.85 years for Japanese firms, defined as the median age of earlier U.S. patents referenced on the front page of a U.S. patent, is below the 10.02-year average for U.S. firms. This means that U.S. patenting activity by Japanese firms is most prolific in emerging technologies where innovation is rapid.

In estimation, it will be interesting to note the extent to which the stock market perceives any size-based differences in the effectiveness of patent activity. Similarly, it will be interesting to note the extent that patent quality appears more important for Japanese and U.S. firms with differing growth opportunities.

VII. METHODOLOGY

A simple predictive equation for stock-price changes is considered where:

$$P_{i,t+1} = \Phi \left(P_{i,t}, \ Patents_{i,t}, \ Patent \ Quality_{i,t} \ (CI_{i,t}, SL_{i,t}, TCT_{i,t}), \right. \qquad (7.1)$$

and $P_{i,t+1}$ is the next-year stock price, and $P_{i,t}$ is the present-year stock price. In this relation, notice that the stock-price effects of ordinary physical assets and other such influences are reflected in $P_{i,t}$. Following Hall, Jaffe, and Trajtenberg (2000) and a long tradition of research on the economic implications of patenting activity, a simple linear specification of this model is estimated.

The focus of interest is on how investors might use scientific indicators of patent quality as useful evidence concerning the future economic worth of the firm's patent activity. Under the main hypothesis, indicators of the scientific merit of patent output are expected to have a nonzero influence. In measuring the stock-price effects of patent quality, a panel, or longitudinal, data set for the 1989–95 period is analyzed. As is usually true in economics, the cross-section of units analyzed is much larger than the relatively brief number of time periods considered. Such a wide but short panel data set is more oriented toward cross-section analysis. Time effects are viewed as "transitions" or discrete changes of state. They are modeled as specific to the period in which they occur and are not carried across periods within a cross-sectional unit (or firm). The primary focus is on heterogeneity across firms, which are the units of the analysis.[2] The fundamental advantage of such a panel data set over a simple cross-section of data is that it allows greater flexibility in modeling differences in stock-price effects across firms.

In estimation it seems prudent to allow for the possibility that stock-price influences are specific to firms within individual industries. This method is responsive to Cockburn and Griliches' (1988) suggestion that the effectiveness of patents as a mechanism for appropriating the returns from R&D is not constant, but differs according to industry conditions. The fixed effects approach involves the use of industry-specific constant terms in the regression model. This technique is sometimes referred to as a least-squares dummy variable (LSDV) model, although the "least squares" part of the name refers to the means used to estimate the model and not to the model itself (see Greene, 2000, p. 560). The implicit assumption is that differences across industries can be captured by differences in the constant term. In principle, it is also possible to allow slope coefficients to vary across industries. However, given the large number of industries included, this method would involve a prohibitive cost in terms of lost degrees of freedom, especially in the case of subsamples arrayed according to firm size and growth opportunities. Also considered is the possibility of time-period-specific influences on stock prices. The matrix algebra and theoretical development of two-way industry and period effects in panel data models are quite complex. However, Baltagi (1995) shows that the practical application is relatively simple. Almost any application involving a second fixed effect can be handled by adding an additional set of dummy variables. Empirical results are provided for stock-price equations with fixed industry effects and fixed time-period effects, and with fixed industry and period effects. For comparison, ordinary least squares (OLS) results without any allowance for fixed effects are also estimated.

VIII. STOCK-PRICE EFFECTS OF PATENT QUALITY: U.S. COMPANIES

Table 7.3 contains the results for stock-price equations estimated with fixed industry effects, fixed time-period effects, and fixed industry and time period effects. For comparison, OLS results without any fixed industry and period effects

---

[2]Baltagi (1995) offers a book-length survey on the econometrics of panel data and includes an extensive bibliography.

TABLE 7.3 U.S. Company Stock-Price Equations with Industry and Period Effects, 1989–1995 (n = 1694)

	OLS model (no fixed effects)	Fixed industry effects	Fixed period effects	Fixed industry and period effects
Independent variables				
Intercept	−0.2290	−0.2240	0.0395	0.0380
	(−0.24)	(−2.03)^a	(0.36)	(0.32)
Market value (P_t)	1.1410	1.1250	1.1500	1.1350
	(60.92)^b	(56.90)^b	(62.60)^b	(58.47)^b
Number of Patents (patents)	3.7040	3.7480	3.6740	3.7140
	(22.18)^b	(22.20)^b	(22.48)^b	(22.49)^b
Citations Index (CI)	0.1820	0.1810	0.1700	0.1680
	(5.76)^b	(5.54)^b	(5.51)^b	(5.24)^b
Non-Patent References (NPR)	0.0102	0.0129	0.0089	0.0119
	(1.13)	(1.33)^c	(1.02)	(1.26)
Technology Cycle Time (TCT)	−0.0018	−0.0041	−0.0017	−0.0039
	(−0.26)	(−0.55)	(−0.25)	(−0.52)
Fixed effects (F-stat.)		0.09	14.61^b	3.60^b
Corrected R^2	77.7%	77.7%	78.7%	78.8%
F-stat. (entire model)	1182.10	198.11^b	571.36^a	175.60^b

Note: Dependent variable is market value for the next period (P_{t+1}).

All size-related variables are deflated using assets (t-statistics in parentheses).

^{a}Indicates significance at the 5% level (one-tailed test).

^{b}Indicates significance at the 1% level (one-tail test).

^{c}Indicates significance at the 10% level (one-tailed test).

are also given. An underlying linear functional form is hypothesized. Implicit in this estimation is the idea that the marginal influence of each independent variable is independent from the level of each independent variable. The approach is consistent with the hypothesis that the market quickly assesses the economic importance of the firm's patenting activity as reported by Hall, Griliches, and Hausman (1986).[3]

As shown in Table 7.3, after controlling for patent quality, the number of U.S. patents granted during a year has a consistently positive influence on U.S. stock prices. For the overall sample, it is reasonable to infer that the number of patents granted is a useful, albeit ambiguous, indicator of the economic worth created by the firm's inventive and innovative activity. This result is consistent with prior

[3]Durbin-Watson test statistics suggest no autocorrelation among the least squares residuals for models reported on Tables 7.3 and 7.4. However, because the Durbin-Watson test can be biased toward a finding of no autocorrelation in the presence of a lagged dependent variable, Durbin's (1970) Lagrange multiplier test was also considered as an alternative to the standard procedure. In each case, it was not possible to reject the null hypothesis of no autocorrelation (results available on request).

research and suggests that patenting activity gives rise to a type of intangible capital with important future benefits (see Hirschey, Richardson, and Scholz, 2001).

Of most direct interest to this study, Table 7.3 offers interesting evidence that patent quality statistics give investors a useful indicator of the economic merit of the firm's inventive activity. Notice that CI, which measures how often company patents are cited in subsequent patent applications relative to the typical pace of patent citations in an industry (and year), has consistently positive and statistically significant effects on stock prices in the overall sample. Moreover, positive stock-price effects of CI do not appear attenuated when significant industry and time-period effects are controlled. NPR, which measures the average number of "other references cited" on the front page of a patent, has similarly positive and statistically significant influences on stock prices. As in the case of CI, positive and statistically significant stock-price effects tied to NPR suggest that such information is incorporated by investors in their ongoing assessment of the firm's inventive and innovative activity. Like Hall, Jaffe, and Trajtenberg's (2000), the positive link between stock prices and CI and NPR data implies that these data give investors a productive means for assessing the economic merit of the firm's patent activity. The third measure of patent quality, the TCT measure of cycle time between current patents and the prior state of knowledge, has no discernable marginal influence on stock prices. While the economic life of a firm's patents is a positive function of TCT, investors may have sufficient information to correctly assess the future profitability of patent activity when the number of patents, CI, and NPR are considered.

Finally, Table 7.3 illustrates the importance of fixed period effects, but does not suggest any discernable influence tied to fixed industry effects. However, care must be exercised in interpreting this finding. By definition, the sample of patent-intensive firms considered in this analysis is dominated by firms originating from a narrow range of high-tech industries. When only patent-intensive firms from a narrow range of industries are eligible for consideration, it is natural to expect that typically important industry effects will be attenuated. As a result, in Tables 7.4 and 7.5, a more detailed consideration of the stock-price effects of patent quality will be made allowing for time-period effects only. However, it is important to keep in mind that the results reported here are only descriptive for a sample of companies from a relatively narrow selection of high-tech industries.

IX. U.S. COMPANIES: EFFECTS OF SIZE AND GROWTH OPPORTUNITIES

While Table 7.3 documents that the CI and NPR scientific measures of patent quality can be viewed as economically meaningful indicators of future profits tied to patent activity by U.S. companies, it is not clear the extent to which such influences might vary by firm size and growth opportunities. As is common in the field of finance, firm size is measured by the market capitalization of common equity.

TABLE 7.4 U.S. Company Subsample Stock-Price Equations with Fixed Period Effects, 1989–1995

	Intercept	Stock price for current period (P_t)	Number of patents (patents)	Citations index (CI)	Non-patent references (NPR)	Technology cycle time (TCT)	Corrected R^2	F-stat. (model)
a. Firm size (market cap)								
Small (market cap < $1,119.06 million)	-0.1060	1.093	3.8230	0.1680	-0.0508	0.0099	77.2%	174.72[a]
	(-0.62)	(20.63)[a]	(19.43)[a]	(3.38)[a]	(-2.69)[a]	(0.89)		
Medium ($1,119.06 million < market cap < $3,754.10 million)	-0.0352	1.048	9.0980	0.2220	-0.0212	-0.0080	64.4%	93.68[a]
	(-0.19)	(22.66)[a]	(4.65)[a]	(4.33)[a]	(-1.36)[b]	(-0.66)		
Large (market cap > $3,754.10 million)	0.5550	1.21	-2.1470	-0.0921	-0.0266	-0.0368	86.9%	340.44[a]
	(2.55)[a]	(53.17)[a]	(-1.42)[b]	(-1.13)	(-2.12)[c]	(-2.60)[a]		
b. Growth opportunities (P/E ratio)								
Low (P/E ratio < 12.10)	-0.3410	0.98	4.1050	0.1780	-0.0355	-0.0199	83.8%	264.02[a]
	(-2.26)[c]	(26.47)[a]	(25.56)[a]	(3.51)[a]	(-2.67)[a]	(-2.02)[c]		
Moderate (12.11 < P/E ratio < 18.99)	0.1950	1.1180	2.3950	0.1230	0.0261	-0.0124	79.3%	198.27[a]
	(1.55)[b]	(41.40)[a]	(2.61)[a]	(3.00)[a]	(1.26)	(-1.56)[b]		
High (P/E ratio > 18.99)	-0.1260	1.1950	1.9210	0.1850	-0.0015	-0.0033	74.2%	148.70[a]
	(-0.52)	(34.74)[a]	(1.25)	(2.98)[a]	(-0.10)	(-1.97)[c]		

Note: Dependent variable is market value for the current period (P_t).
All size-related variables are deflated using assets (t-statistics in parentheses).
[a]Indicates significance at the 1% level (one-tail test).
[b]Indicates significance at the 10% level (one-tailed test).
[c]Indicates significance at the 5% level (one-tailed test).

TABLE 7.5 Japanese Company Subsample Stock-Price Equations with Fixed Period Effects, 1989–1995 ($n = 1350$)

	Intercept	Stock price for current period (P_t)	Number of patents (patents)	Citations index (CI)	Non-patent references (NPR)	Technology cycle time (TCT)	Corrected R^2	F-stat. (model)
a. Firm size (market cap)								
Small (market cap < $1,564.11 million)	-0.0006 (-0.01)	0.7990 (25.09)[a]	-0.0002 (-1.63)[b]	-0.0430 (1.83)[c]	-0.0185 (-1.04)	-0.0017 (-0.49)	67.5%	52.89[a]
Medium ($1,564.11 million < market cap < $4,510.79 million)	0.0831 (1.02)	0.9750 (34.04)[a]	-0.0005 (-0.79)	-0.0252 (0.54)	-0.0087 (-0.99)	-0.0087 (-1.65)[c]	75.9%	75.13[a]
Large (market cap > $4,510.79 million)	0.0809 (0.96)	0.8550 (37.08)[a]	0.0017 (2.50)[a]	-0.0464 (-1.13)	0.0054 (0.22)	0.0079 (1.41)[b]	80.4%	97.93[a]
b. Growth opportunities (P/E ratio)								
Low (P/E ratio < 37.10)	-0.0439 (0.62)	1.0210 (38.38)[a]	-0.0034 (-1.52)[b]	0.0113 (0.35)	-0.0027 (-0.34)	-0.0033 (-0.77)	80.5%	98.37[a]
Moderate (37.10 < P/E ratio < 61.75)	0.0604 (0.77)	0.9230 (37.25)[a]	-0.0003 (-1.21)	0.0372 (1.02)	-0.0062 (-0.30)	-0.0014 (-0.27)	77.6%	82.85[a]
High (P/E ratio > 61.75)	0.0116 (0.19)	0.7820 (29.06)[a]	-0.0001 (-0.24)	0.0370 (1.15)	0.0368 (2.28)[c]	-0.0002 (-0.06)	73.5%	66.55[a]
All Japanese companies	0.0522 (1.37)[b]	0.9150 (63.69)[a]	-0.0002 (-1.50)[b]	0.0102 (0.53)	0.0009 (0.12)	-0.0021 (-0.78)	76.7%	445.06[a]

Note: Dependent variable is market value for the next period (P_{t+1}).
All size-related variables are deflated using assets (t-statistics in parentheses).
[a] Indicates significance at the 1% level (one-tail test).
[b] Indicates significance at the 10% level (one-tailed test).
[c] Indicates significance at the 5% level (one-tailed test).

Growth opportunities are measured by P/E ratios, where higher P/E ratios reflect investor optimism for rapid future growth and low P/E ratios reflect relatively lower growth expectations. Table 7.4 shows model estimation results after the U.S. sample has been partitioned according to market capitalization and firm P/E ratios (also see Hirschey and Richardson, 2003).

When the overall sample has been partitioned according to market capitalization, important size-based differences in the stock-price effects of the number of patents and patent quality information are readily apparent. In the case of small high-tech firms, positive stock-price effects are tied to both the number of patents and the CI indicator of patent quality. Patent quality as captured by the CI indicator may constitute especially useful information in the case of small high-tech firms that often have little in the way of reliable historical financial information. Interestingly, a small and inexplicably negative stock-price effect of the NPR indicator of patent quality is suggested in the case of the smallest U.S. high-tech companies. At the margin, the average number of other references cited on the front page of the patent, including academic journal articles and papers presented at scientific meetings, appears to moderate the large positive stock-price effects of the number of patents and relative citation frequency among the smallest high-tech companies. In the case of the smallest high-tech companies from the United States, once the number of patents and relative citation frequency are controlled, no discernable influence is noted for the TCT indicator of patent quality. Apparently, the median age (in years) of earlier U.S. patents referenced on the front page of a U.S. patent is irrelevant to investors' evaluation of inventive and innovative output among small-size high-tech companies.

In the medium cap size class, investors again appear to form appropriate expectations regarding the economic value of the firms' inventive and innovative output on the basis of the number of patents granted during the year and the CI indicator of patent quality. Also in the medium-size class, a small and inexplicably negative influence on stock prices is noted for the NPR indicator of patent quality. For medium-size firms, as in the case of smaller high-tech companies, once the number of patents and relative citation frequency are controlled, no discernable influence is noted for the TCT indicator of patent quality. Apparently, the median age (in years) of earlier U.S. patents referenced on the front page of a U.S. patent is irrelevant to investors' evaluation of inventive and innovative output among medium-size high-tech companies.

In the large cap size class, it is interesting to recognize how the number of patents and patent quality information have little discernable influence on stock prices. No positive and statistically significant stock-price effects of the number of patents and patent quality are registered, as had been true in the smaller market cap size classes. In fact, inexplicably small negative but statistically significant influences of the NPR patent quality indicator are observed. In the case of TCT, a negative coefficient estimate suggests that limiting stock-price effects are associated with large-size high-tech companies displaying relatively old (as opposed to new) technology. Findings for the large-cap universe suggest that patent quality information is especially helpful for investors seeking to infer the importance of innovative and inventive activity among small- and medium-size companies.

In a similar vein, important differences in the stock-price effects of patent quality information are apparent when the overall sample has been partitioned according to growth opportunities as reflected in firm P/E ratios. The number of patents emerges as a useful indicator of inventive and innovative output among both low and medium P/E high-tech companies. In the case of low- and medium P/E high-tech companies, an increase in the number of patents has a predictably positive influence on stock prices. Across all P/E categories, small positive and statistically significant stock-price effects are noted for the CI indicator of patent quality. Apparently, high-tech investors commonly regard relative citation frequency as a consistently useful indicator of patent quality. It is only in the case of firms with low P/E ratios that patent quality as captured by NPR has any discernable marginal influence on stock prices. For low P/E ratio firms, very small but statistically significant negative stock-price effects are tied to the NPR indicator of patent quality. Across all P/E categories, and once patent quality as captured by the number of patents, CI, and NPR is controlled, a persistently negative stock-price influence is associated with TCT. This means that after one has controlled for patent quality, negative stock-price effects are associated with high-tech companies displaying relatively old (as opposed to new) technology.

These findings add useful perspective to recent research by documenting the economic importance of scientific indicators of patent quality and by showing how the relevance of such information is affected by firm size and the firm's growth opportunities. Based upon these results, patent quality information not only appears to be important in a scientific sense, it may also be helpful to stock market investors seeking to assess the profit-making potential of the firm's inventive and innovative activity.

X. PATENT QUALITY IN JAPAN VERSUS THE UNITED STATES

On a global basis, Narin (1995) documents that Japanese companies tend to be most rapid in their citation of new technology in the patent process. In electronics, autos, pharmaceuticals, and other industries, Japanese companies have an average age of only 7 years for cited patents, quicker by 3–4 years than that typical of U.S. and European companies. Narin (1995) interprets this finding to mean that Japanese companies tend to be very rapid in their pace of improvement on patented technology. Therefore, TCT may be a useful indicator of the speed with which a company is developing new technology. Bierly and Chakrabarti (1996) study factors that influence TCT for 21 pharmaceutical firms over the 1977–91 period. Faster TCT is positively correlated to measures of the knowledge base level of firms, the breadth of firms' knowledge bases, size, and age; it is negatively correlated to advertising expenditures and the percent of U.S. firm sales to total sales. Perhaps Bierly and Chakrabarti's (1996) most notable finding is that TCT is significantly faster for firms that predominantly generate new knowledge internally and slower for firms that rely more on external sources of new knowledge.

Finally, previous research suggests the possibility of economic ramifications tied to nation-by-nation differences in the scientific merit of U.S. patenting activity, such as that discussed by Narin (1995). If Japanese companies tend to be most rapid in their citation of new technology in the patent process, implications for the value of U.S. patents by Japanese firms may be relevant. An especially rapid pace of scientific advance may, for example, reduce the economic life and value of individual patents. Indeed, national differences in the economic value of patents is suggested by Schankerman (1998), who provides evidence on the value of patent rights in France for various nationalities of ownership. Schankerman (1998) reports that the value of patents varies not only with patent propensity, but also with the nationality of the patenting firm. This is a potentially important and yet largely unexplored issue (see Hirschey and Richardson, 2001).

It is perhaps unsurprising that the number of patents granted by the U.S. Patent and Trademark Office (PTO) has grown sharply during the post-World War II period. The number of U.S. invention, design, and plant patents issued by the PTO grew from 22,293 in 1947 to 77,910 in 1972 to 122,977 in 1997. What is perhaps surprising is the rapid rate of growth in U.S. patenting activity by non-U.S. firms. In 1947, for example, foreign entities were responsible for only 7.3% or 1617 of the patents issued by the PTO. During 1972, 23,815 or 30.6% of the total number of U.S. patents were issued to non-U.S. residents. By 1997, 53,683 or fully 43.7% of the total number of U.S. patents were granted to foreign entities. As measured by patenting activity during 1997, the top five foreign countries of origin for U.S. patents were Japan (with 24,314 patents granted), Germany (7180), France (3121), Canada (2803), and Taiwan (2490).[4] To this point, whether or not the value of U.S. patenting activity varies according to the nationality of the patenting firm is unknown.

Patent statistics and patent citation information from Tech-Line® contains technological profiles on over 1000 organizations actively patenting in the United States, where each domestic or foreign organization is responsible for at least 10 patents per year. These data on U.S. patenting activity have the potential to provide interesting insight concerning the market-value effects of inventive output for Japanese firms. In this analysis, complete data could be obtained for a sample of 558 firm-year observations for public high-tech Japanese companies. This is a subsample from somewhat broader bodies of data studied by Hirschey and Richardson (2001) and Hirschey, Richardson, and Scholz (2001). Hirschey and Richardson (2001) point out that Japanese high-tech companies dominate in terms of being among those firms awarded the greatest number of U.S. patents. This finding is consistent with Narin's (1995) observation that Japanese companies

---

[4] *1997 Patent and trademark Office Annual Report*, U.S. Department of Commerce, availale at: http://www1.uspto.gov/web/offices/com/annual/1997.

tend to be very rapid in their pace of improvement on patented technology. At the same time, U.S. companies dominate in terms of being granted U.S. patents with the highest scientific merit, when merit is measured in terms of CI and NPR. This means that U.S. companies dominate lists of firms noted for gaining patents that are widely cited in subsequent patent applications and in academic journal articles and papers presented at scientific meetings. Interestingly, and despite Narin's (1995) suggestion that Japanese companies tend to be most rapid in their citation of new technology, Hirschey and Richardson (2001) report that there is no clear difference during the late-1990s between the TCT of top high-tech U.S. and Japanese companies. Apparently, the speed with which a company is developing new technology is fairly dependent upon firm-specific factors that do not lend themselves to broad characterization on a national basis.

XI. VALUATION EFFECTS OF PATENT QUALITY FOR JAPANESE COMPANIES

The valuation effects of patent quality were analyzed according to firm size class and growth opportunities for a representative sample of 1350 Japanese firm-year observations.[5] As described in Table 7.2, this sample of high-tech Japanese companies includes firms that tend to be somewhat smaller than the high-tech U.S. firms covered in the Tech-Line® database. When size is measured by market capitalization, the average Japanese company in the database has a market capitalization of only $5.8 billion versus the U.S. average of $6.4 billion. Notice, however, that the Japanese firms included in the Tech-Line® database tend to have much higher average P/E ratios than their U.S. counterparts. For example, moderate P/E ratios for Japanese companies in the sample range between 37.10 and 61.75, whereas moderate P/E ratios for high-tech U.S. companies ranged between 12.11 and 18.99 during the 1989–95 sample period. Cross-section regression results evaluated using a pooled time series and cross-section (POOLED) sample of Japanese companies are shown in Table 7.5.[6]

As suggested by Griliches (1990), among others, Table 7.3 show consistently positive effects of the number of U.S. patents on the current market value of U.S. firms. With a patents coefficient estimates of 3.6740–3.7480, the estimated marginal value per patent is roughly $3.67–3.75 million for U.S. firms. These finding support the notion that the current stock prices of high-tech U.S. firms reflect the future earnings capacity of intangible assets such as patents and that the patent process provides certification of inventive output that has predictably positive effects on long-term profitability. Conversely, as shown in Table 7.5, the market values of high-tech Japanese companies show no favorable

---

[5]For brevity, coefficient estimates for annual dummy variables are suppressed. Full results are available on request.

[6]In the analysis of Japanese companies, size normalization is accomplished by dividing each size-related variable (market value and the number of patents) by total assets (or by multiplying by A^{-1}).

influence tied to a simple count of the number of U.S. patents except in the case of the very largest high-tech Japanese companies. This finding should *not* be interpreted to mean that U.S. patenting activity is not profitable for Japanese companies. The fact that Japanese companies are so active in U.S. patenting activity argues otherwise. Instead, the failure of a simple count of U.S. patent statistics to favorably influence the market values of Japanese high-tech companies merely suggests that patent count data offer an insufficient basis for gauging the value of Japanese patenting activity in the United States. This interpretation is consistent with Narin's (1995) finding that Japanese companies tend to be very speedy in their pace of improvement on patented technology. This would have the predictable result of reducing the economic life and relative economic value of individual U.S. patents granted to Japanese companies. Alternatively, widely diversified and market-savvy U.S. firms may simply be better positioned than their Japanese counterparts to fully exploit the economic advantages conferred by U.S. patents.

In a similar vein, estimation results reported in Table 7.5 suggest little in the way of consistent effects for U.S. patent quality indicators on the stock prices of Japanese companies. These results contrast somewhat with those reported by Hirschey and Richardson (2001) who found that the scientific merit of patenting activity had a favorable influence on the values of both Japanese and U.S. firms. These findings argue in favor of the idea that while high-tech investors regard these data as useful indicators of the economic value of inventive output, the possibility of country-specific influences on the effectiveness of R&D appears to exist.

XII. CONCLUSION

Tech stock investors often face the problem of making sensible judgments about future earnings prospects for high-tech companies with only limited earnings, revenue, or book value information. This is especially true for high-tech companies with R&D programs that yield hard-to-evaluate patent output. This chapter builds upon recent research to suggest the potential for scientific measures of patent quality as useful indicators of the future earnings potential for high-tech firms.

In spite of all the difficulties, patent statistics have long been relied upon as a unique resource for the analysis of technical change. Now, sophisticated measures of patent quality can be derived from knowledge about the use of individual patents as "building blocks" in the development of subsequent science. This study is motivated by the idea that market-value data provide a useful test of the economic importance of patent numbers and these new scientific indicators of patent quality. From the firm's practical perspective, scientific measures of patent quality have the potential to offer managers useful guidance concerning the quantity and quality of inventive output and the effectiveness of the firm's investment in R&D. Within this context, it also becomes interesting to evaluate the relative quality of U.S. patenting activity by Japanese and U.S. firms as a means for gaining insight concerning the growing importance of global competitiveness in the high-technology sector. Empirical results reported here demonstrate robust positive marginal influences of the number of U.S. patents on the market values of U.S. firms, but no discernable influence in the case of Japanese companies. These findings support the assertion that patent numbers are useful but limited economic indicators of the pace of scientific advance. What is perhaps most interesting about findings reported here is that scientific measures of patent quality appear to offer useful economic insight concerning the quality of U.S. patenting activity by domestic entities. In the case of U.S. firms, patents with higher scientific merit translate into positive and generally significant effects on market values. From the perspective of individual high-tech firms, indicators of patent quality appear to have the potential to offer interesting insight concerning the effectiveness of the firm's R&D investment strategy. From the overall perspective of the high-tech sector, indicators of patent quality also appear to have the potential to offer interesting insight concerning global competitiveness in R&D. Therefore, from at least two important perspectives, the new measures of the scientific merit of patent activity studied here may have real practical relevance.

XIII. REFERENCES

Ali, A. and Hwang, L. (2000). Country-Specific Factors Related to Financial Reporting and the Value Relevance of Accounting Data. *Journal of Accounting Research* 38, 1–21.

American Institute of Certified Public Accountants (AICPA) Special Committee on Financial Reporting (1994). Improved Business Reporting—a Customer Focus. New York: AICPA, 58–64.

Albert, M. B., Avery, D., Narin, F., and Mcallister, P. (1991). Direct Validation of Citation Counts as Indicators of Industrially Important Patents. *Research Policy* 20, 251–259.

Amir, E. and Lev, B. (1996). Value-Relevance of Nonfinancial Information: The Wireless Communications Industry. *Journal of Accounting & Economics* 22, 3–30.

Ashiq, A., and Hwang, L. (2000). Country-Specific Factors Related to Financial Reporting and the Value Relevance of Accounting Data. *Journal of Accounting Research* 38, 1–21.

Baltagi, B. (1995). *Econometric Analysis of Panel Data*. New York: John Wiley and Sons.

Barth, M. and McNichols, M. F. (1994). Estimation and Market Valuation of Environmental Liabilities Relating to Superfund Sites. *Journal of Accounting Research* 32, 177–209.

Bierly, P. and Chakrabarti, A. (1996). Determinants of Technology Cycle Time in the U. S. Pharmaceutical Industry. *R & D Management* 26, 115–126.

Brown, S., Lo, K., and Lys, T. (1999). Use of R² in Accounting Research: Measuring Changes in Value Relevance over the Last Four Decades. *Journal of Accounting & Economics* 28, 83–115.

Chan, S. H., Martin, J., and Kensinger, J. (1990). Corporate Research and Development Expenditures and Share Value. *Journal of Financial Economics* 26, 255–276.

Chauvin, K. W. and Hirschey, M. (1993). Advertising, R&D Expenditures and the Market Value of the Firm. *Financial Management* 22, 128–140.

Cockburn, I. and Griliches, Z. (1988). Industry Effects and Appropriability Measures in the Stock Market's Valuation of R&D and Patents. *American Economic Review* 78, 419–423.

Connolly, R. A. and Hirschey, M. (1988). Market Value and Patents: A Bayesian Approach. *Economics Letters* 27, 83–87.

Deng, Z., Lev, B., and Narin, F. (1999). Science and Technology as Predictors of Stock Performance. *Financial Analysts Journal* 55, 20–32.

Durbin, J. (1970). Testing for Serial Correlation in Least Squares Regression When Some of the Regressors Are Lagged Dependent Variables. *Econometrica* 38, 410–421.

Easton, P. D. (1999). Security Returns and the Value Relevance of Accounting Data. *Accounting Horizons* 13, 399–412.

Francis, J. and Schipper, K. (1999). Have Financial Statements Lost Their Relevance? *Journal of Accounting Research* 37, 319–352.

Greene, W. H. (2000). *Econometric Analysis, Fourth Edition.* Upper Saddle River, NJ: Prentice-Hall.

Griliches, Z. (1986). Productivity, R&D, and Basic Research at the Firm Level in the 1970's. *American Economic Review* 76, 141–154.

Griliches, Z. (1990). Patent Statistics as Economic Indicators: A Survey. *Journal of Economic Literature* 28, 1661–1707.

Griliches, Z., Nordhaus, W. D., and Scherer, F. M. (1989). Patents: Recent Trends and Puzzles Comments and Discussion. *Brookings Papers on Economic Activity* 128, 291–330.

Hall, B. H., Jaffe, A. B., and Trajtenberg, M. (2000). Market Value and Patent Citations: A First Look. National Bureau of Economic Research (NBER) Working Paper No. W7741.

Hall, B. H., Griliches, Z., and Hausman, J. A. (1986). Patents and R and D: Is There a Lag?, *International Economic Review* 27, 265–283.

Harhoff, D., Narin, F., Scherer, F. M., and Vopel, K. (1999). Citation Frequency and the Value of Patented Inventions. *Review of Economics & Statistics* 81, 511–515.

Hirschey, M. (1998). How Much Is a Tulip Worth? *Financial Analysts Journal* 54, 11–17.

Hirschey, M. (2001). Cisco and the Kids. *Financial Analysts Journal* 57, 48–59.

Hirschey, M. and Richardson, V. J. (2001). Valuation Effects of Patent Quality: A Comparison for Japanese and U.S. Firms. *Pacific Basin Finance Journal* 9, 65–72.

Hirschey, M., Richardson, V. J., and Scholz, S. (2001). Value Relevance of Nonfinancial Information: The Case of Patent Data. *Review of Quantitative Finance & Accounting* 17, 223–235.

Hirschey, M. and Spencer, R. S. (1992). Size Effects in the Market Capitalization of Fundamental Factors. *Financial Analysts Journal* 48, 91–95.

Hirschey, M. and Weygandt, J. J. (1985). Amortization Policy for Advertising and Research and Development. *Journal of Accounting Research* 23, 326–335.

Kortum, S. (1993). Equilibrium R&D and the Patent-R&D Ratio: U.S. Evidence. *American Economic Review* 83, 450–457.

Kortum, S. and Lerner, J. (1999). What Is Behind the Recent Surge in Patenting? *Research Policy* 28, 1–22.

Lev, B. and Sougiannis, T. (1996). The Capitalization, Amortization, and Value-relevance of R&D. *Journal of Accounting & Economics* 21, 107–138.

Narin, F. (1995). Patents as Indicators for the Evaluation of Industrial Research Output. *Scientometrics* 34, 489–496.

Narin, F., Hamilton, K. S., and Olivastro, D. (1997). The Increasing Linkage Between U.S. Technology and Public Science. *Research Policy* 26, 317–330.

Pakes, A. (1985). Patents, R&D and the Stock Market Rate of Return. *Journal of Political Economy* 93, 390–409.

Pownall, G. and Schipper, K. (1999). Implications of Accounting Research for the SEC's Consideration of International Accounting Standards for U.S. Securities Offerings. *Accounting Horizons* 13, 259–280.

Schankerman, M. (1998). How Valuable Is Patent Protection? Estimates by Technology Field. *Rand Journal of Economics* 29, 77–107.

Sundaram, A. K., John, T. A., and John, K. (1996). An Empirical Analysis of Strategic Competition and Firm Values: The Case of R&D Competition 40, 459–486.

Thomas, P. (1999). The Effect of Technological Impact upon Patent Renewal Decisions. *Technology Analysis & Strategic Management* 1, 181–197.

Trajtenberg, M. (1990). A Penny for Your Quotes: Patent Citations and the Value of Innovations. *Rand Journal of Economics* 21, 172–187.

8

GOODWILL WRITE-OFF
DECISIONS: DO THEY MATTER?

Many tech stocks possess enormous market capitalizations reflective of their significant future earnings power. At the same time, many of these tech stock giants
control relatively little in the way of tangible plant and equipment. Many such
firms count hard-to-measure goodwill assets among their most prized posses-
sions. Tech stock giants Microsoft Corp., Intel Corp., and Cisco Systems, Inc. all
feature balance sheets where goodwill assets play a prominent role.

For example, in mid-2002, accounting goodwill accounted for more than
$4.3 billion or 9.9% of Microsoft's total assets. At that time, goodwill amounted
to $1.4 billion or 2.1% of Intel's total assets, and more than $3.6 billion or 9.4%
of total assets for Cisco. In addition, each of these three tech giants counted hundreds of millions of dollars in hard-to-measure intangible assets on their balance
sheets. These figures are important for a number of reasons. First, they document
the fact that goodwill and other intangible assets are a prime consideration when
assessing the balance sheets of leading tech stocks. Second, the absolute and relative importance of goodwill and intangible assets for leading tech stocks suggests that investors need to be aware of the size and health of such assets. Third,
because new accounting rules end regular amortization of goodwill and mandate
annual tests for goodwill impairment and loss recognition when appropriate, tech

stock investors need to be aware of the potential for stock market effects tied to goodwill write-off decisions.

This chapter reports that goodwill write-off announcements typically reduce the stock prices of announcing firms. What makes goodwill write-off announcements especially noteworthy is that additional negative price effects are typically seen during the postannouncement period. These findings suggest that investors initially underreact to goodwill write-off announcements, and they need to be aware of the potential for further losses in the postannouncement period.

I. GOODWILL

From an economic perspective, balance-sheet accounting goodwill data represent useful financial information if it helps investors form appropriate perceptions concerning intangible dimensions of firm value. Recent studies suggest that this is indeed the case. For example, Chauvin and Hirschey (1994) use a simple three-part recursive system of simultaneous relations to identify consistently positive market-value influences of accounting goodwill numbers in the manufacturing sector. Chauvin and Hirschey (1994) infer that accounting goodwill data offer a useful perspective on the hard-to-measure ongoing concern (reputational) value component of the economic value of the firm. In a related paper, McCarthy and Schneider (1995) support Chauvin and Hirschey's (1994) contention that the market regards accounting goodwill numbers as a useful indicator of goodwill assets. This view is corroborated by Jennings et al. (1996), who offer strong evidence that investors value purchased goodwill as an economic resource and weak evidence that purchased goodwill is declining in value.

Henning, Lewis, and Shaw (2000) add perspective to these findings by showing that investors attach different valuation weights to various components of accounting goodwill numbers. For a sample of acquisitions between 1990 and 1994, Henning, Lewis, and Shaw (2000) found differential valuation effects for (1) going-concern goodwill, measured as the difference between the fair value of recognized assets and the preacquisition value of the target; (2) synergy goodwill, or the combined cumulative abnormal returns earned by the target and the acquirer in the event window centered on the acquisition announcement; and (3) residual goodwill, or the excess of purchased goodwill over going concern goodwill plus synergy goodwill. Using a cross-sectional "balance sheet model" similar to Chauvin and Hirschey (1994), Henning, Lewis, and Shaw (2000) found significantly positive valuation effects of both going-concern goodwill and synergy goodwill, but negative market-value effects of residual goodwill. The going-concern component of goodwill appears to be valued similarly to other assets, while the synergy component of goodwill receives a higher weight by the market. This latter result suggests that acquirers pay less than the full economic value of targets and thereby share in the benefits of acquisitions. Negative market-value effects of residual goodwill suggests that historical treatments of accounting goodwill include asset values that are effectively written off by investors during the year of acquisition.

Following Hirschey and Richardson (2002), this chapter tests the information content of accounting goodwill numbers using an event-study methodology that avoids potential pitfalls of the balance sheet models tested by Chauvin and Hirschey (1994), among others. As noted by Chauvin and Hirschey (1994), important positive influences of advertising and research and development (R&D) on goodwill are apparent, as are beneficial spillover effects of identifiable intangible assets. A reservoir of customer goodwill enjoyed by large firms with significant tangible assets is also apparent. While Chauvin and Hirschey (1994) find robust support for the hypothesis that the positive valuation effects of goodwill are above and beyond the now familiar favorable market-value effects of advertising, R&D, and tangible assets, modeling problems complicate the precise identification of each respective positive market-value influence.

In the event-study framework adopted here, the market-value effects of goodwill write-off decisions are studied. Goodwill write-off announcements can be precisely identified, so any resulting market-value influence can be taken as evidence that investors regard such accounting information as useful. If goodwill write-off announcements represent meaningful information concerning the loss of economic goodwill, significant negative stock-price effects can be anticipated. By precisely identifying the timing of goodwill write-off announcements, the problem of confounding the stock-price effects of goodwill numbers with similar influences due to advertising, R&D, or tangible assets is eliminated. Negative stock-price effects tied to goodwill write-off announcements represent an important confirmation of the economic relevance of goodwill accounting numbers because such announcements typically have no direct cash flow implications. More than "mere" accounting pronouncements, negative stock-price effects tied to goodwill write-off announcements suggest the economic relevance of historical accounting goodwill numbers. Such effects also suggest the relevance of new accounting standards that mandate the timely write-off of impaired goodwill assets.

II. NEW GOODWILL ACCOUNTING STANDARDS

Until recently, goodwill accounting in the United States was governed by rules contained in the American Institute of Certified Public Accountants, *Accounting Principles Board (APB) Opinion No. 16, Business Combinations* (Issued 1970). Under *APB Opinion No. 16*, goodwill was defined as "the excess of the cost of the acquired company over the sum of the amounts assigned to identifiable assets acquired less liabilities assumed (para. 87)." Generally speaking, any excess of fair market value over the book value of the acquired firm's recognized net assets was recorded as goodwill. The amount paid for goodwill in a purchase combination was amortized over a period not to exceed 40 years. To avoid the resulting drag on reported earnings, the vast majority of companies sought to account for their combinations on a pooling of interest basis in which purchased goodwill was not recorded and amortized (see Hirschey and Richardson, 2002).

Under *APB Opinion No. 16*, goodwill accounting policy in the United States was starkly different from global standards and was thought by many to be out of step with economic reality. For example, Reither (1998) asked a group of participants in the 1996 American Accounting Association/Financial Accounting Standards Board (AAA/FASB) Financial Reporting Issues Conference to consider the entire body of accounting standards and to identify winners and losers. *APB Opinion No. 16* was voted the second worst accounting standard, next to *Accounting for Leases, FASB Statement No. 13*. Respondents gave five major reasons for rating *APB Opinion No. 16* as among the worst of all accounting standards. Concerns included the following: (1) the choice of a pooling-of-interests or purchase method treatment for a business combination is arbitrary; (2) under the standard, the form of a business combination can become more important than its substance; (3) similar business combinations are accounted for differently; (4) the standard raises the cost of business combinations as companies strive to meet pooling-of-interest requirements while avoiding Securities and Exchange Commission (SEC) enforcement actions; and (5) the U.S. standard is inconsistent with global accounting standards. In most countries, pooling-of-interests methods are exceedingly rare.

While practical problems involved with identifying and measuring goodwill make setting a clear and appropriate accounting standard difficult, users of financial statement information complained that it was difficult to compare financial results for entities that used different methods of merger accounting. Users of financial statements also indicated a need for more specific information about the value of intangible assets because intangibles have become a significant proportion of the value motivating many business combinations. Corporate management also voiced concern that differences between the pooling and purchase methods of accounting affected competition in the mergers and acquisitions markets.

After a prolonged period of study and comment, the accounting profession recently adopted historic new goodwill accounting standards. For fiscal years that end subsequent to December 15, 2001, *Financial Accounting Standards Board (FASB) Statement No. 141, Business Combinations* (Issued June 2001), supersedes *APB Opinion No. 16*. *FASB Statement No. 141* requires that all business combinations be accounted for by the purchase method.[1] In addition, *FASB Statement No. 141* requires disclosure of the primary reasons for a business combination and an allocation of the purchase price among the assets acquired. When the amounts of goodwill and intangible assets acquired are significant, disclosure must be made of the amount allocated among goodwill and each major intangible

---

[1]*FASB Statement No. 141* applies to all business combinations initiated after June 30, 2001, and all business combinations accounted for using the purchase method for which the date of acquisition is July 1, 2001, or later. This statement does not apply, however, to combinations of two or more not-for-profit organizations, the acquisition of a for-profit business entity by a not-for-profit organization, and combinations of two or more mutual enterprises.

asset class. The related *FASB Statement No. 142, Goodwill and Other Intangible Assets* (Issued June 2001), specifically governs financial reporting for acquired goodwill and other acquired intangible assets and supersedes the American Institute of Certified Public Accountants, *APB Opinion No. 17, Intangible Assets* (Issued 1970). Under the obsolete *APB Opinion 17*, goodwill and other intangible items were wasting assets with a finite life. The values assigned to goodwill and other intangible assets were amortized over an arbitrary period of time not to exceed 40 years. *FASB Statement No. 142* does away with the presumption that acquired goodwill and other acquired intangible assets have finite lives and eliminates mandatory amortization.[2] Acquired intangible assets that have finite lives will continue to be amortized over their useful lives, but without the constraint of any arbitrary ceiling.

In particular, *FASB Statement No. 142* mandates (1) annual tests for goodwill and intangible asset impairment, (2) write-offs of goodwill and intangible asset impairment losses, and (3) improved disclosure about goodwill and intangible asset values and expenses. In the first mandate, goodwill will be tested for impairment at least annually using a two-step process that begins with an estimation of the fair value of a reporting unit. The first step is a screen for potential impairment, and the second step measures the amount of impairment, if any. In the second mandate, if the carrying amount of acquired goodwill or acquired intangible assets exceeds fair value estimates, an impairment loss must be recognized against net income in an amount equal to that excess. After goodwill or intangible asset impairment losses are recognized, subsequent reversals of impairment losses are prohibited. In the third mandate, information about changes in the carrying amount of goodwill and other intangible asset categories must be disclosed on an annual basis, along with estimates of intangible asset amortization expenses for the next five years.

Under *FASB Statement No. 142*, tests for goodwill and intangible asset impairment and the write-off of impaired assets promise to become routine corporate events. This makes it timely to consider whether goodwill write-off decisions represent mere accounting transactions or, instead, signify economic events with important implications for the ongoing value of the firm.

III. GOODWILL WRITE-OFF DECISIONS

Accounting write-off decisions are material, infrequent charges against earnings for asset revaluations or provisions for future costs. Goodwill write-off decisions, like many asset write-offs, are bookkeeping adjustments that do not typically coincide with changes in tangible assets or cash flows. The information value of goodwill

---

[2]Costs of internally developing, maintaining, or restoring intangible assets (including goodwill) that are not specifically identifiable, that have indeterminate lives, or that are inherent in a continuing business and related to an entity as a whole continue to be recognized as an expense when incurred.

write-off decisions lies in the role they play as a *signal* of important changes in the value of the company's intangible assets and important changes to come in the company's future earning potential (see Hirschey and Richardson, 2002).

Goodwill write-off decisions may have similarities to the bank loan-loss reserve additions studied by Docking, Hirschey, and Jones (1997), among others. Loan-loss reserve (LLR) announcements are simple bookkeeping adjustments that do not typically coincide with changes in the value of bank loan portfolios nor with bank loan write-off decisions. The information value of loan-loss decisions rests in the role they play as a *signal* of important changes in the value of the bank's loan portfolio and important changes to come in bank loan write-off decisions, earnings, and dividend payments. Docking, Hirschey, and Jones (1997) report that "simple" bank announcements of additions to LLRs result in negative event-period returns, and such influences are markedly more negative in the case of regional versus money-center banks. Apparently, investors view such LLR announcements as foreshadowing more bad news. It is interesting to note, however, that bank LLR announcements rarely have such simple negative effects. Most LLR announcements are made at the same time that other important operating information is disclosed. The generally negative stock-price effects of simple LLR additions are nullified when such announcements are accompanied by favorable earnings announcements. Investors appear to regard LLR announcements accompanied by earnings decreases, losses, or dividend reductions or omissions as much more threatening, resulting in negative event-period returns that are consistent with those reported for broader samples of industrial firms reporting unfavorable earnings or dividend information. As a result, the negative stock-price effects associated with LLR announcements can be largely attributed to the expected influence of bank earnings or dividends. Absent new earnings or dividend information, investors appear to react to simple LLR announcements in a manner that is consistent with an expectation of future adverse effects on bank earnings and dividends.

As Bartov, Lindahl, and Ricks (1998) point out, write-offs are important corporate events due to the large dollar amounts involved and their significant ramifications for firm performance and value. What makes the assessment of write-off decisions difficult is the fact that they tend to be infrequent and ambiguous in the information that they convey. Write-offs can represent good news when management rids the company of relatively unprofitable operations in order to refocus on its "core competence." Write-offs can represent bad news when reductions in asset values foreshadow even deeper troubles yet to come.

This chapter seeks to offer information germane to the goodwill accounting standards setting process by providing evidence regarding stock-price behavior tied to company goodwill write-off announcements. From an accounting perspective, valuation effects associated with company goodwill write-off decisions have the potential to offer new evidence on the extent to which accounting goodwill numbers capture the value of intangible factors with asset-like characteristics. From an economic perspective, negative valuation effects tied to accounting goodwill write-off decisions provide evidence that such accounting adjustments reflect the loss of important intangible assets (see Hirschey and Richardson, 2002).

IV. SAMPLE

This study of goodwill write-off decisions focuses on discretionary announcements taken by companies during the 1992–96 five-year period. This time frame allows consideration of event-period returns that are unaffected by discussions surrounding recent accounting changes and consideration of stock market returns during long-window preannouncement and postannouncement periods. Event dates for goodwill write-off announcements are identified from *The Wall Street Journal Index* online (*WSJI*). The *WSJI* is an attractive source for event-day (0) information because it offers a precise indication of when the stock market first received relevant news regarding the firm's write-off decision. Searches were conducted using the key words "goodwill" and "write-off" or "charge." To be included in the sample, the common stock of each firm must be listed on either the New York Stock Exchange (NYSE), the American Stock Exchange (AMEX), or the Nasdaq and included on the *Center for Research for Security Prices* (CRSP) daily stock returns file for six months prior to the goodwill write-off announcement. Firms also need to be continuously listed over the estimation and event periods to be included.

This sample selection method resulted in a total sample of $n = 80$ goodwill write-off announcements broadly distributed across 32 different Standard Industrial Classification (SIC) code two-digit industry groups. It is interesting to note that while goodwill write-off announcements occur in a number of settings, they appear most common in manufacturing ($20 \leq SIC < 40$) where 43 of 80 sample goodwill write-off announcements are found. This is especially true in the Industrial and Commercial Machinery industry group ($SIC = 35$) where 10 sample firms made goodwill write-off announcements over the 1992–96 period.

A typical example of the $n = 27$ simple goodwill write-off announcements covered in this study was provided by Voice Control Systems, Inc. on January 3, 1995:

BUSINESS BRIEF—VOICE CONTROL SYSTEMS INC.: CHARGE FOR FOURTH QUARTER OF $2.7 MILLION IS EXPECTED—Voice Control Systems Inc., Dallas, expects to take a special charge of about $2.7 million, or around $0.84 a share, for the fourth quarter.

The company, which makes speech-recognition hardware and software, said the charge provides for the write-off of goodwill capitalized as a result of the August merger of VCS Industries Inc. into Scott Instruments Corp. Scott Instruments changed its name to Voice Control Systems in that merger.

Voice Control Systems, which made the announcement after the close of the market Friday, said that including the charge, it expects to post a loss in the fourth quarter. For the 9 months ended September 30, the company reported a loss of $4 million on revenue of $4.2 million.

In most instances, 53 out of 80 cases studied here, companies tie goodwill write-off announcements to the simultaneous release of partially offsetting favorable earnings information, exacerbating unfavorable earnings information, or miscellaneous other information that might be regarded by investors as either favorable or unfavorable. A typical example of the $n = 13$ companies making goodwill write-off decision announcements at the same time positive operating earnings are released was given by the Greiner Engineering, Inc. on November 3, 1995:

> BUSINESS BRIEF—GREINER ENGINEERING INC.: THIRD-QUARTER LOSS POSTED ON $5.4 MILLION IN CHARGES—Greiner Engineering Inc., Irving, Texas, reported a third-quarter loss of $4.3 million after it took charges of $5.4 million. The company said its fourth-quarter results also will be affected. The company reported year-earlier net income of $776,000, or $0.16 a share. Revenue rose 4.1 per cent to $39.7 million from $38.2 million a year earlier. Greiner said it took a $3.1 million charge to cover the costs of cutting operations and reducing the goodwill on residential-land-development operations in California. The company said it will take a fourth-quarter charge to cover the cost of staff cuts in California. Greiner also took a $2.3 million hit from a valuation adjustment of a tollway-managing partnership with Dallas-based Perot Group.

In some situations, goodwill write-off announcements are linked to the simultaneous release of negative operating earnings information. A typical example of $n = 21$ companies making goodwill write-off decision announcements at the same time losses are reported was given by Sulcus Computer Corp. on April 18, 1995:

> BUSINESS BRIEF—SULCUS COMPUTER CORP.: COMPANY'S LOSS FOR 1994 WIDENED TO $11.7 MILLION—Sulcus Computer Corp., Greensburg, Pa., said its 1994 loss widened to $11.7 million, or 84 cents a share, from $3.1 million, or $0.22 a share, from a year earlier. The computer-systems developer said the 1994 figure included $3.7 million in unusual charges, including a $1.8 million write-off of software development costs and a $1.3 million write-off of goodwill related to the company's Asian units.

Sulcus said its revenue fell about 12% to $43.1 million from $49.3 million.

Finally, goodwill write-off announcements are sometimes accompanied by operating information that cannot be precisely tied to earnings performance. A common example of $n = 19$ companies making goodwill write-off decision announcements at the same time other important operating information is released was given by Tredegar Industries, Inc. on August 29, 1994:

> BUSINESS BRIEF—TREDEGAR INDUSTRIES INC.: PLANT TO BE CLOSED; CHARGE AND WRITE-OFF ARE PLANNED—Tredegar Industries Inc., Richmond, Va., said it plans to lease a facility in Graham, N.C., to produce injection-molded packaging components, and close a similar facility in Alsip, Ill., which has 128 employees. Tredegar said it will record a charge of $1.3 million, or $0.12 a share, for the planned plant closing, and a goodwill write-off of $3.1 million, or $0.29 a share, due to disappointing performance in certain lines of the molded-products unit. Both charges will be taken in the third quarter.

Tredegar manufactures plastics and metal products.

In sum, complete data could be obtained on a sample of $n = 80$ accounting goodwill write-off announcements composed of $n = 27$ simple goodwill write-off announcements, $n = 13$ companies making goodwill write-off decision announcements at the same time positive operating earnings are released, $n = 21$ companies making goodwill write-off decision announcements at the same time losses are reported, and $n = 19$ companies making goodwill write-off decision announcements at the same time other important favorable or unfavorable operating information is released. The overall sample of $n = 80$ goodwill write-off announcements is broadly distributed across 32 different SIC code two-digit industry groups (see Table 8.1).

TABLE 8.1 Goodwill Write-off Sample Breakout by Industry (SIC Code)

Two-digit SIC code	SIC code description	Number
20	Food and Kindred Products	5
22	Textile Mill Products	4
23	Apparel	3
27	Printing, Publishing and Allied Industries	2
28	Chemicals and Allied Products	3
30	Rubber and Misc. Plastic Products	2
31	Leather and Leather Products	1
34	Fabricated Metal Products	1
35	Industrial and Commercial Machinery	10
36	Electronic and Other Electrical Equipment	3
37	Transportation Equipment	4
38	Measuring, Analyzing and Controlling Instruments	5
42	Motor Freight Transportation and Warehousing	1
48	Communications	1
49	Electric, Gas and Sanitary Services	3
50	Wholesale Trade - Durable Goods	1
52	Building Materials, Hardware, Garden Supply and Mobile Home Dealers	1
54	Food Stores	1
57	Home Furniture, Furnishings, and Equipment Stores	1
58	Eating and Drinking Establishments	3
59	Miscellaneous Retail	1
60	Depository Institutions	4
61	Nondepository Credit Institutions	1
62	Security and Commodity Brokers, Dealers, Exchanges and Services	1
63	Insurance Carriers	4
64	Insurance Agents, Brokers and Service	1
65	Real Estate	1
73	Business Services	6
76	Miscellaneous Repair Services	1
78	Motion Pictures	1
80	Health Services	2
87	Engineering, Accounting, Research, Management and Related Services	2
Total sample		**80**

Consistent with findings reported by Docking, Hirschey, and Jones (1997) in their study of LLR announcements, most goodwill write-off disclosures are "messy" announcements. In most instances, goodwill write-off announcements are made at the same time that other significant positive or negative earnings information is released. 'Simple' goodwill announcements unaccompanied by other important corporate announcements are in the minority. In the present study, $n = 53$, or 66.3% of the goodwill write-off announcements studied, are accompanied by the contemporaneous disclosure of other important operating information.

Information effects on the stock prices of announcing firms are reported for the $(-1,0)$ event period for all $n = 80$ firms and for each subsample. From an accounting perspective, negative and statistically significant stock-price effects tied to goodwill write-off decisions give evidence of a loss of future profit-generating capability.

V. ESTIMATION METHOD

To test for robustness, three alternative estimates of abnormal stock returns surrounding company goodwill announcements in *The Wall Street Journal* are considered. First, it is assumed that security returns follow a single factor market model:

$$R_{jt} = \alpha_j + \beta_j R_{mt} + \varepsilon_{jt}, \tag{8.1}$$

where R_{jt} is the rate of return on the common stock of the jth firm on day t; R_{mt} is the market rate of return using the equally-weighted CRSP index on day t; ε_{jt} is a random variable with an expected value of zero, uncorrelated with R_{mt} and $R_{kt,k \neq j}$, not autocorrelated, and homoscedastic; α_j is an intercept; and β_j is a slope parameter that measures the sensitivity of R_{jt} to the market index. The ordinary least squares (OLS) market model is employed to estimate the prediction error, PE, (or abnormal return) for the common stock of firm j on day t, such that

$$PE_{jt} = R_{jt} - \left(\alpha_j + \beta_j R_{mt} \right). \tag{8.2a}$$

Prediction errors are also estimated using two alternative methods. In a second approach, prediction errors are estimated using market-adjusted returns computed by subtracting the observed return on the market index for day t, R_{mt}, from the rate of return of the common stock of the jth firm on day t. Prediction errors estimated using market-adjusted returns are

$$PE_{jt} = R_{jt} - R_{mt}. \tag{8.2b}$$

And third, prediction errors are estimated using comparison period mean-adjusted returns. Prediction errors using comparison period mean-adjusted returns are computed by subtracting the arithmetic mean return of the common stock of the jth firm computed over the estimation period, $\overline{R}_j$ from its return on day t:

$$PE_{jt} = R_{jt} - \overline{R}_j. \tag{8.2c}$$

In all instances, a 255-day estimation period is used that begins 300 trading days before the event date, $t = -300$, and ends 45 trading days before the event date, $t = -45$. The event date, $t = 0$, is typically assumed to be *The Wall Street Journal* announcement date, but may be the prior day if an earlier announcement is specifically noted in *The Wall Street Journal*.

Daily prediction errors are averaged over the sample of n firms to yield average prediction errors, APE, (or average abnormal returns):

$$APE_t = \frac{\sum_{j=1}^{n} PE_{jt}}{n}. \tag{8.3}$$

Cumulative average prediction errors, CAPE, (or cumulative average abnormal returns) are then calculated over an event interval period of 2 days $(-1,0)$:

$$CAPE_{T_1,T_2} = \frac{\sum_{j=1}^{n} \sum_{t=T_1}^{T_2} PE_{jt}}{n}. \tag{8.4}$$

Following Haw, Pastena, and Lilien (1990), among others, a t-test is applied to examine the hypothesis that the $CAPE_{T_1 T_2}$ are not significantly different from zero. Under the null hypothesis, each PE_{jt} has mean zero and constant variance $\sigma_{E_{jt}}^2$. The maximum likelihood estimate of the variance is

$$S_{PE_{jt}}^2 = S_{PE_j}^2 \left[1 + \frac{1}{D_j} + \frac{(R_{mt} - \overline{R}_m)^2}{\sum_{k=1}^{D_j} (R_{mk} - \overline{R}_m)^2} \right], \tag{8.5}$$

where

$$S_{PE_j}^2 = \frac{\sum_{k=1}^{D_j} PE_{jk}^2}{D_j - 2}, \tag{8.6}$$

R_{mt} is the observed return on the market index on day t, $\overline{R}_{mt}$ is the mean market return over the estimation period, and D_j is the number of nonmissing trading day returns used to estimate the parameters for firm j.

Define the standardized prediction error as

$$SPE_{jt} = \frac{PE_{jt}}{S_{PE_{jt}}}. \tag{8.7}$$

Under the null hypothesis, each SPE_{jt} follows the student's t distribution with $D_j - 2$ degrees of freedom. Summing the SPE_{jt} across the sample, gives

$$TSPE_t = \sum_{j=1}^{n} SPE_{jt}. \tag{8.8}$$

The expected value of $TSPE_t$ is zero. The variance of $TSPE_t$ is

$$Q_t = \sum_{j=1}^{n} \frac{D_j - 2}{D_j - 4}. \tag{8.9}$$

The test statistic for the null hypothesis that $CAPE_{T_1,T_2} = 0$ is

$$Z_{T_1,T_2} = \frac{1}{\sqrt{n}} \sum_{j=1}^{n} Z_{T_1,T_2}^{j}, \tag{8.10}$$

where

$$Z_{T_1,T_2}^{j} = \frac{1}{\sqrt{Q_{T_1,T_2}^{j}}} \sum_{t=T_1}^{T_2} SPE_{jt}, \tag{8.11}$$

and

$$Q_{T_1,T_2}^{j} = (T_2 - T_1 + 1)\frac{D_j - 2}{D_j - 4}. \tag{8.12}$$

Under cross-sectional independence of the Z_{T_1,T_2}^{j} and other conditions (see Patell, 1976), Z_{T_1,T_2} follows the standard normal distribution under the null hypothesis.

VI. ANNOUNCEMENT PERIOD EFFECTS

Figure 8.1 and Table 8.2 depict cumulative average prediction errors (CAPEs) (or cumulative abnormal returns, CARs) during the announcement period for all sample companies making goodwill write-off announcements during the five-year 1992–96 period. Estimation results for the equally weighted market-model approach are contrasted with those from alternate mean-adjusted and market-adjusted returns methods. Estimation results for the stock market reaction to goodwill write-off announcements by subgroups of goodwill announcement

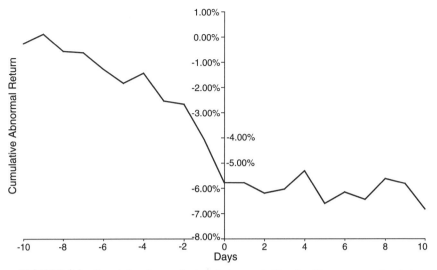

FIGURE 8.1   Cumulative abnormal return during goodwill write-off announcement period.

types and industry groups are also given. In all cases, CAPEs are reported for the two-day $(-1,0)$ event period.[3]

From Table 8.2, it is clear that event-period CAPEs are generally negative and statistically significant at the 1% level for the overall sample of $n = 80$ goodwill write-off announcements. On average, goodwill write-off announcements lead to uniformly large and statistically significant own stock-price reactions (event-period returns) of -2.94% ($t = -4.75$) using the market-model approach, -3.31% ($t = -5.22$) using the mean-adjusted approach, and -3.52% ($t = -5.63$) using the market-adjusted approach. These findings are consistent with the hypothesis that company goodwill write-off announcements signal a meaningful deterioration in the firm's future profit-making potential. In a regression-based test (results available on request), no strong relationship between goodwill write-off size and abnormal returns emerged. These results suggest that investors regard the fact of a goodwill write-off, and not necessarily its size, as important from a valuation perspective.

Following Docking, Hirschey, and Jones (1997) study of significant negative contagion effects for bank LLR announcements, it is worth considering the possibility of contagious stock-price reactions stemming from corporate goodwill write-off announcements. However, there is no evidence of contagious stock-price reactions for competing firms. Therefore, it seems reasonable to conclude that goodwill write-offs are essentially a firm-specific event.

[3]Each of these methods assumes time series independence in the stock-price reaction tied to goodwill write-off announcements. Following Beatty, Chamberlain, and Magliolo (1996), a test was conducted to see if later announcements were as "important" as earlier announcements, but there was no statistically significant difference related to time of announcement (results available on request).

TABLE 8.2   Cumulative Average Prediction Errors (CAPEs) Over the (−1,0) Event Period for Firms Announcing Goodwill Write-off Decisions, 1992–1996 (n = 80)

Goodwill write-off subsample		Market model adjusted CAPE	Mean adjusted CAPE	Market adjusted CAPE
Panel A: Goodwill write-offs by type of announcement				
'Simple' goodwill write-off	CAPE	−2.23%	−2.48%	−2.83%
announcement (n = 27)	t-statistic	(−2.31)[b]	(−2.51)[a]	(−2.93)[a]
Goodwill write-off w/contemporaneous	CAPE	−3.30%	−3.73%	−3.86%
announcement (n = 53)	t-statistic	(−4.48)[a]	(−4.90)[a]	(−5.17)[a]
Positive earnings (n = 13)	CAPE	1.82%	1.76%	1.57%
	t-statistic	(1.69)[b]	(1.61)[c]	(1.46)[c]
Negative earnings (n = 21)	CAPE	−6.86%	−7.45%	−7.69%
	t-statistic	(−4.63)[a]	(−4.82)[a]	(−5.07)[a]
Miscellaneous (n = 19)	CAPE	−2.91%	−3.43%	−3.42%
	t-statistic	(−2.91)[a]	(−3.35)[a]	(−3.42)[a]
Panel B: Goodwill write-offs by industry group				
Manufacturing firms (n = 43)	CAPE	−3.32%	−3.43%	−3.77%
	t-statistic	(−4.36)[a]	(−4.33)[a]	(−4.87)[a]
Industrial and commercial	CAPE	−6.03%	−6.60%	−6.72%
machinery firms (SIC 35) (n = 10)	t-statistic	(−2.71)[a]	(−2.89)[a]	(−2.99)[a]
Nonindustrial and commercial	CAPE	−2.50%	−2.47%	−2.88%
machinery mfg firms (n = 33)	t-statistic	(−4.05)[a]	(−3.90)[a]	(−4.63)[a]
Nonmanufacturing firms (n = 37)	CAPE	−2.52%	−3.21%	−3.25%
	t-statistic	(−2.70)[a]	(−3.42)[a]	(−3.49)[a]
Total sample (n = 80)	CAPE	−2.94%	−3.31%	−3.52%
	t-statistic	(−4.75)[a]	(−5.22)[a]	(−5.63)[a]

Note: Market-model, mean-adjusted, and market-adjusted cumulative abnormal returns (CAPEs) and t-statistics are shown for the (−1,0) event-period window by type of goodwill write-off announcements in panel A and by industry group in panel B. The analysis suggests a 2–3% adverse stock-price reaction to goodwill write-off announcements irrespective of contemporaneous announcements or industry grouping.
[a]Statistically significant at the 0.01 level (one-tailed test).
[b]Statistically significant at the 0.05 level (one-tailed test).
[c]Statistically significant at the 0.10 level (one-tailed test).

VII. ANNOUNCEMENT EFFECTS AND CONTEMPORANEOUS ANNOUNCEMENTS

Firms typically make other important corporate announcements at the time goodwill write-offs are made. Thus, it becomes interesting to learn the extent to which the typically negative stock-price effect associated with goodwill write-offs is affected by the nature of contemporaneous announcements. To do so, it becomes interesting to consider the valuation effects of goodwill write-offs for samples of firms with various types of confounding announcements.

In Table 8.2, event-period CAPEs are generally negative and statistically significant at the 1% level for the $n = 27$ sample of simple goodwill write-off announcements. Simple goodwill write-off announcements lead to a relatively large and statistically significant stock-price reaction (event-period return) of -2.23% ($t = -2.31$) using the market-model approach, -2.48% ($t = -2.51$) using the mean-adjusted approach, and -2.83% ($t = -2.93$) using the market-adjusted approach. On average, the stock-price reaction to simple goodwill write-off announcements is somewhat smaller than the effect when such announcements are accompanied by the contemporaneous disclosure of other important information.

For $n = 53$ goodwill write-offs tied to the announcement of other important information, large and statistically significant stock-price reactions are noted using the market-model approach (-3.30%, $t = -4.48$), the mean-adjusted approach (-3.73%, $t = -4.90$), and the market-adjusted approach (-3.86%, $t = -5.17$). Table 8.2 shows that while $n = 13$ companies making goodwill write-off announcements also report positive earnings, many more report operating losses ($n = 21$) or other information ($n = 19$) regarded as negative by investors, such as the sale of a division, corporate restructuring, plant closures, etc. For $n = 13$ goodwill write-off announcements by companies with positive operating earnings, the stock-price reaction appears immaterial using the market-model approach (1.82%, $t = 1.69$), the mean-adjusted approach (1.76%, $t = 1.61$), and the market-adjusted approach (1.57%, $t = 1.46$). For $n = 21$ goodwill write-offs announced by firms with operating losses, large and statistically significant stock-price reactions are noted using the market-model approach (-6.86%, $t = -4.63$), the mean-adjusted approach (-7.45%, $t = -4.82$), and the market-adjusted approach (-7.69%, $t = -5.07$). For $n = 19$ goodwill write-offs tied to the announcement of other miscellaneous corporate restructuring information, material and statistically significant stock-price reactions are noted using the market-model approach (-2.91%, $t = -2.91$), the mean-adjusted approach (-3.43%, $t = -3.35$), and the market-adjusted approach (-3.42%, $t = -3.42$).

These results are also important because they confirm the stock market importance of goodwill write-off decisions, despite the fact that such announcements are often messy in the sense of being accompanied by contemporaneous disclosures. Like findings reported by Docking, Hirschey, and Jones (1997), these results suggest that investors interpret important corporate announcements, such as goodwill write-off decisions, within the context of other company information.

VIII. ANNOUNCEMENT EFFECTS BY INDUSTRY GROUP

Table 8.1 shows that the majority of announcements concerning goodwill write-off decisions are made by manufacturing companies, with a significant representation of firms from the Industrial and Commercial Machinery industry group (SIC = 35). It therefore seems worth asking if the valuation effects described previously are broadly descriptive of all such goodwill write-off announcements or more narrowly relevant for certain manufacturing firms.

For $n = 43$ goodwill write-off announcements by manufacturing firms ($20 \leq$ SIC < 40), Table 8.2 shows material negative stock-price reactions tied to goodwill write-offs using the market-model approach (-3.32%, $t = -4.36$), the mean-adjusted approach (-3.43%, $t = -4.33$), and the market-adjusted approach (-3.77%, $t = -4.87$). For $n = 10$ goodwill write-off announcements by firms in the Industrial and Commercial Machinery industry group (SIC $= 35$), large negative stock-price reactions tied to goodwill write-offs are evident using the market-model approach (-6.03%, $t = -2.71$), the mean-adjusted approach (-6.60%, $t = -2.89$), and the market-adjusted approach (-6.72%, $t = -2.99$). For $n = 33$ goodwill write-offs announced by manufacturing firms that are *not* in SIC $= 35$, negative and statistically significant stock-price reactions are also noted using the market-model approach (-2.50%, $t = -4.05$), the mean-adjusted approach (-2.47%, $t = -3.90$), and the market-adjusted approach (-2.88%, $t = -4.63$). And finally, for $n = 37$ goodwill write-off announcements by nonmanufacturing firms, negative and statistically significant stock-price reactions are again noted using the market-model approach (-2.52%, $t = -2.70$), the mean-adjusted approach (-3.21%, $t = -3.42$), and the market-adjusted approach (-3.25%, $t = -3.49$).

Based on these results, it seems fair to conclude that negative valuation effects of goodwill write-off announcements are relevant for firms across a broad cross-section of U.S. industry. In the eyes of investors, goodwill write-offs generally suggest the loss of intangible factors with asset-like characteristics.

IX. PREANNOUNCEMENT AND POSTANNOUNCEMENT PERIOD EFFECTS

Our finding that goodwill write-off decisions lead to -2.94 to -3.52% adverse stock-price reactions during the announcement period is compatible with Bartov, Lindahl, and Ricks' (1998) discovery of -2.14% announcement period returns for tangible asset write-down announcements. Because the typical tangible asset write-down announcement represented about 20% of the value of announcing firms, Bartov, Lindahl, and Ricks (1998) contend that their relatively modest announcement effects are anomalous. As a result, they suggest that the market either anticipates or underreacts to write-off announcements. In this study, the mean goodwill write-off is $148.2 million and represents 16.3% of the market value of announcing firms. Long-window effects during the goodwill write-off preannouncement and postannouncement periods have the potential to offer an intriguing comparison with evidence concerning tangible asset write-downs.

Figure 8.2 and Table 8.3 show long-window stock-price behavior tied to goodwill announcements during the preannouncement and postannouncement periods. In the 1-year ($-250,-10$) period that immediately precedes goodwill

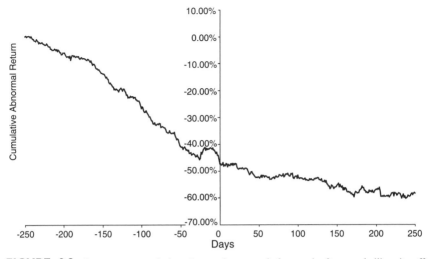

FIGURE 8.2 Long-term cumulative abnormal returns before and after goodwill write-off announcement period.

write-off announcements, the market-adjusted cumulative average abnormal return is a large and statistically significant -41.77% ($t = -7.04$) for the overall sample. Negative and statistically significant preannouncement period effects are also noted for simple goodwill write-off announcements (-47.55%, $t = -4.89$) and for such announcements accompanied by other important information (-38.81%, $t = -5.62$). Large negative and statistically significant preannouncement period effects are also typical for both manufacturing (-39.71%, $t = -4.98$) and nonmanufacturing firms (-44.02%, $t = -4.97$). Negative abnormal returns during the preannouncement period document that goodwill write-off announcements come after a prolonged period of market underperformance. As such, goodwill write-off announcements may be interpreted as management's official recognition that a recently severe downturn in the company's stock portends a permanent rather than transitory decline in the value of firm assets. Negative preannouncements effects also suggest that investors partially anticipate goodwill write-off decisions.

Table 8.3 also shows that goodwill write-off announcing firms experience large negative abnormal returns during the 1-year (day = 10, 250) postannouncement period. The average negative postannouncement period effect of -11.02% ($t = -1.86$) is statistically significant over the entire sample of $n = 80$ firms. Despite some variability across various subsamples, there is statistically significant evidence of a link between the magnitude of negative announcement effects and negative postannouncement drift.

After controlling for the relative size of intangible assets (intangibles/market capitalization) and firm size (market capitalization), a regression analysis of

TABLE 8.3 Cumulative Average Prediction Errors (Capes) Over Three Windows (−250, −10), (−1,0) and (+10, +250) Event Period for Firms Announcing Goodwill Write-off Decisions, 1992–1996 (n = 80)

Goodwill write-off subsample		CAPE year −1 (−250, −10)	CAPE announcement period (−1, 0)	CAPE year +1 (+10, +250)
Panel A: Goodwill write-offs by type of announcement				
'Simple' goodwill write-off	CAPE	−47.55%	−2.83%	−14.55%
announcement (n = 27)	t-statistic	(−4.89)^a	(−2.93)^a	(−1.50)^c
Goodwill write-off w/	CAPE	−38.81%	−3.86%	−8.98%
contemporaneous	t-statistic	(−5.62)^a	(−5.17)^a	(−1.30)^c
announcement (n = 53)				
Positive earnings (n = 13)	CAPE	−14.22%	1.57%	−5.21%
	t-statistic	(−1.27)	(1.46)^c	(−0.47)
Negative earnings (n = 21)	CAPE	−55.10%	−7.69%	−18.97%
	t-statistic	(−3.57)^a	(−5.07)^a	(−1.23)
Miscellaneous (n = 19)	CAPE	−39.40%	−3.42%	−0.96%
	t-statistic	(−3.90)^a	(−3.42)^a	(−0.09)
Panel B: Goodwill write-offs by industry group				
Manufacturing firms (n = 43)	CAPE	−39.71%	−3.77%	−11.89%
	t-statistic	(−4.98)^a	(−4.87)^a	(−1.49)^c
Industrial and commercial	CAPE	−39.42%	−6.72%	−6.82%
machinery firms (SIC 35)	t-statistic	(−1.71)^b	(−2.99)^a	(−0.30)
(n = 10)				
Nonindustrial and commercial	CAPE	−39.81%	−2.88%	−12.93%
machinery mfg firms (n = 33)	t-statistic	(−5.92)^a	(−4.63)^a	(−1.92)^b
Nonmanufacturing firms (n = 37)	CAPE	−44.02%	−3.25%	−10.19%
	t-statistic	(−4.97)^a	(−3.49)^a	(−1.15)
Total sample (n = 80)	CAPE	−41.77%	−3.52%	−11.02%
	t-statistic	(−7.04)^a	(−5.63)^a	(−1.86)^b

Note: Market-adjusted cumulative abnormal returns (CAPEs) and t-statistics are shown for the year preceding (−250, −10), announcement period (−1,0) and the year following (+10, +250) the goodwill write-off announcement event-period windows by type of goodwill write-off announcements in panel A and by industry group in panel B.
^{a}Statistically significant at the 0.01 level (one-tailed test).
^{b}Statistically significant at the 0.05 level (one-tailed test).
^{c}Statistically significant at the 0.10 level (one-tailed test).

postannouncement period buy-and-hold returns on announcement period returns shows (t-statistics in parentheses):[4]

$$Return_{(10, 250)} = -0.169 + 1.557\ Return_{(-1, 0)} -0.218\ Intangibles/Market\ cap + 2.228\text{--}06\ Market\ cap$$
$$(-2.72)\quad (3.11)\qquad\qquad (-2.17)\qquad\qquad\qquad (0.29)$$

$R^2 = 20.5\%$, $F = 5.594$

[4]Intangible assets include goodwill, patents, and other intangible items and are measured using *Compustat* Annual Item #33. Market capitalization is computed by multiplying common shares outstanding (Compustat # 24) and share price at fiscal year end (Compustat #199). Our regression analysis

These results show that, on average, negative returns during the one-year (10,250) postannouncement period are more than one and one-half times as large as the negative announcement period returns (–1,0). This negative postannouncement drift is somewhat larger for firms with a relatively high percentage of market capitalization accounted for by intangible assets.[5] There is no evidence that the amount of negative postannouncement period drift depends upon firm size, when firm size is measured by market capitalization.

Thus, it appears that not all of the negative valuation effects tied to goodwill write-off announcements are realized by the end of the announcement period. Some investor underreaction to goodwill write-off announcements is apparent.[6] Moreover, the size of negative valuation effects in the postannouncement period is tied to the size of negative announcement period effects. Firms with large negative stock-price reactions to goodwill write-off announcements tend to have somewhat larger negative postannouncement period effects. Investors need to be aware of the potential for value-reducing goodwill write-off announcements and that such announcements portend further losses in the postannouncement period.

X. CONCLUSION

Until recently, goodwill accounting was based on the premise that goodwill and other intangible items were wasting assets with a finite life. The values assigned to goodwill and other intangible assets were amortized over an arbitrary period of time not to exceed 40 years. A new accounting pronouncement, *FASB Statement No. 142*, does away with the presumption that acquired goodwill and other acquired intangible assets have finite lives and eliminates mandatory amortization. Acquired intangible assets that have finite lives will continue to be amortized over their useful lives, but without the constraint of any arbitrary ceiling.

Under these new accounting standards, goodwill will be tested for impairment at least annually using a two-step process that begins with an estimation of the fair value of a reporting unit. The first step is a screen for potential impairment, and the second step measures the amount of impairment, if any. If the carrying amount of acquired goodwill or acquired intangible assets exceeds fair value estimates, an impairment loss must be recognized against net income in an amount equal to that excess. *FASB Statement No. 142* improves financial reporting

---

is based on a subsample of 69 firms for which complete *Compustat* information could be obtained. In this case, buy-and-hold returns show the returns earned by an investor who purchased and held the goodwill write-off portfolio over the postannouncement period (10,250). In other studies, buy-and-hold returns have been examined to provide evidence of overreaction in the initial public offering (IPO) market (e.g., see Loughran and Ritter, 1996).

[5]It is now well known that both advertising and R&D give rise to "intangible assets" with favorable effects on long-term profitability and the market value of the firm (see Hirschey Weygandt, 1985).

[6]For more detailed information about the underreaction hypothesis, see Hirschey and Richardson (in press). Hirschey (2003) gives a detailed introduction to behavioral finance.

by helping users of financial statements better understand corporate investments in goodwill and other intangible assets and their subsequent performance. Adoption of *FASB Statement No. 142* is relevant for investors because this statement promises to make goodwill write-off decisions routine corporate events based upon a quantitative approach.

This chapter reports evidence discovered by Hirschey and Richardson (2002) about investor reactions tied to company goodwill write-off announcements. Goodwill write-off decisions have the potential to offer evidence on how investors process potentially important information about the firm's profit-making potential. Stock-price effects associated with goodwill write-off decisions have the potential to offer new evidence on the extent to which accounting goodwill numbers capture the economic value of intangible factors with asset-like characteristics. Statistically significant negative abnormal returns tied to goodwill write-off announcements are obvious. Announcement effects are typically negative and material, on the order of −2.94 to −3.52% of the company's stock price. Importantly for investors, average negative postannouncement period effects of roughly −11.02% suggest that a significant portion of the negative valuation effects tied to goodwill write-off announcements are realized *after* the announcement period. Determining the cause of such negative postannouncement period effects is beyond the scope of this chapter. A lack of investor focus, or insufficient appreciation for the importance of goodwill write-offs as indicators of a further deterioration in the earning power of the firm, may be to blame. In any event, the evidence presented here suggests that investors must be wary of negative valuation effects tied to goodwill write-off decisions and the potential for continued underperformance in the postannouncement period. Information effects narrowly tied to goodwill write-off announcements are typically negative and material, on the order of 2–3% of the company's stock price. In the one-year preannouncement period, negative information effects on the order of −40% are also noted. Postannouncement period information effects of roughly −11% suggest that much, but perhaps not all, of the negative information (valuation) effects tied to goodwill write-off announcements are realized by the end of the announcement period. Negative stock-price effects tied to goodwill write-off decisions indicate that accounting goodwill numbers capture a significant aspect of the intangible dimension of firm value and suggest that accounting theory and practice is adept at identifying when such intangible assets are impaired.

This chapter extends prior research through further consideration of the information content of accounting goodwill numbers. Limited prior research suggests that despite the obvious shortcomings of historical (purchase) accounting goodwill numbers, these data are economically meaningful in that they are systematically reflected in the market value of the firm. These results are consistent with the notion that stock market investors regard goodwill numbers as favorable indicators of the firm's future profit-making potential. In this way, prior studies support the hypothesis that firms derive significant "future economic benefits" from goodwill, a key criteria necessary for asset recognition. However, a possible limitation of prior results is that cross-sectional valuation effects of accounting goodwill numbers have the potential to reflect, at least in part, similarly positive valuation effects of advertising and R&D expenditures, among other such influences. It is now well known that both advertising and R&D give rise to "intangible assets" with favorable effects on long-term profitability and the market-value of the firm (see Hirschey Weygandt, 1985).

This study reports on a simple test of the economic relevance of accounting goodwill numbers within an event-study framework that is not apt to be influenced by the valuation effects of advertising, R&D, or other intangible assets. Specifically, information effects tied to company goodwill write-off announcements are proposed and tested as an interesting basis upon which to judge the economic relevance of accounting goodwill numbers. Goodwill write-off decisions, like asset write-offs, are bookkeeping adjustments that do not typically coincide with any changes in tangible assets or cash flows. However, from an economic standpoint, goodwill write-off decisions are meaningful to the extent that they provide information regarding important future changes in company earnings.

While one must always be cautious when drawing public policy implications, results reported here suggest that accounting goodwill numbers do, in fact, embody aspects necessary for asset recognition on the financial statements of business enterprises. Like balance sheet models that show positive valuation effects of accounting goodwill numbers, negative stock-price effects tied to goodwill write-off decisions indicate that these data capture a significant aspect of the intangible dimension of firm value. Negative and statistically significant stock-price reactions tied to goodwill write-off decisions also suggests that accounting theory and practice is adept at identifying when such intangible assets are impaired.

From the perspective of tech stock investors, goodwill write-off announcements are not only important value-reducing events during the announcement period, they are associated with a further fundamental deterioration in the market value of the firm during the subsequent year-long period. It is apparent that investors underreact to the economic importance of goodwill write-off announcements. Negative valuation effects during the preannouncement period indicate that investors partially anticipate goodwill write-off decisions. Negative valuation effects during the postannouncement period suggest investor underreaction to goodwill write-off announcements and the need for investors to be wary of continued underperformance by goodwill write-off announcing firms.

XI. REFERENCES

American Institute of Certified Public Accountants. (1970). *Accounting Principles Board (APB) Opinion No. 16, Business Combinations*, New York.
American Institute of Certified Public Accountants. (1970). *Accounting Principles Board (APB) Opinion No. 17, Intangible Assets*, New York.

Beatty, A., Chamberlain, S., and Magliolo, J. (1996). An Empirical Analysis of the Economic Implications of Fair Value Accounting for Investment Securities. *Journal of Accounting and Economics* 22, 43–77.

Bartov, E., Lindahl, F. W., and Ricks, W. E. (1998). Stock Price Behavior Around Announcements of Write-Offs. *Review of Accounting Studies* 3, 327–346.

Chauvin, K. W. and Hirschey, M. (1994). Goodwill, Profitability, and Market-value of the Firm. *Journal of Accounting & Public Policy* 13, 159–180.

Docking, D. S., Hirschey, M., and Jones, E. (1997). Information and Contagion Effects of Bank Loan-Loss Reserve Announcements. *Journal of Financial Economics* 43, 219–239.

Financial Accounting Standards Board. (2001). *Statement No. 141, Business Combinations.* Financial Accounting Foundation, Norwalk, CT.

Financial Accounting Standards Board. (2001). *Statement No. 142, Goodwill and Other Intangible Assets.* Financial Accounting Foundation, Norwalk, CT.

Francis, J., Hanna, J. D., and Vincent, L. (1996). Causes and Effects of Discretionary Asset Write-Offs. *Journal of Accounting Research* 34, 117–134.

Haw, I., Pastena, V. S., and Lilien, S. B. (1990). Market Manifestation of Nonpublic Information Prior to Mergers: The Effect of Capital Structure. *Accounting Review* 65, 432–451.

Henning, S. L., Lewis, B. L., and Shaw, W. S. (2000). Valuation of the Components of Purchased Goodwill. *Journal of Accounting Research* 38, 375–386.

Hirschey, M. (2003). Extreme Return Reversal in the Stock Market. *Journal of Portfolio Management* 29, 1–13.

Hirschey, M. and Richardson, V. J. (in press). Investor Underreaction to Goodwill Write-Offs. *Financial Analysts Journal* 59.

Hirschey, M. and Richardson, V. J. (2002). Information Content of Accounting Goodwill Numbers. *Journal of Accounting & Public Policy* 21, 173–191.

Hirschey, M. and Weygandt, J. J. (1985). Amortization Policy for Advertising and Research and Development. *Journal of Accounting Research* 23, 326–335.

Jennings, R., Robinson, J., Thompson, R. B., and Duvall, L. (1996). The Relation Between Accounting Goodwill Numbers and Equity Values. *Journal of Business Finance & Accounting* 23, 513–533.

Loughran, T. and Ritter, J. R. (1996). Long-Term Market Overreaction: The Effect of Low-Priced Stocks. *Journal of Finance* 51, 1959–1970.

McCarthy, M. G. and Schneider, D. K. (1995). Market Perception of Goodwill: Some Empirical Evidence. *Accounting & Business Research* 26, 69–81.

Patell, J. M. (1976). Corporate Forecasts of Earnings Per Share and Stock Price Behavior: Empirical Tests. *Journal of Accounting Research* 14, 246–274.

Reither, C. L. (1998). What Are the Best and Worst Accounting Standards? *Accounting Horizons* 12, 283–292.

9

SHARK REPELLENTS AND RESEARCH AND DEVELOPMENT: DOES MANAGEMENT HAVE A LONG-RUN PERSPECTIVE?

One of the most difficult challenges faced by tech stock investors is the need to ensure that management maintains an appropriate long-term perspective. In a well-functioning high-tech environment, management pursues those investment projects that promise stockholders the largest payoff when dollars are measured in risk-adjusted net present-value terms. At times, the most meritorious high-tech investment projects involve chancy research and development (R&D) investments that take months, if not years, to bring to fruition. R&D is, at best, a risky bet that can be lost if management abandons basic research projects with significant long-term potential in favor of development projects that promise only modest but near-term benefits. If management lessens its focus on worthy R&D projects because of a myopic concern with near-term results, shareholder results and economic performance both suffer.

To provide interesting perspective concerning the effects of important management decisions on R&D, this chapter reports evidence discovered by Hirschey and Jones (1995) concerning firm performance and financial policy decisions in the periods prior to and following corporate adoptions of antitakeover charter amendments, often called shark repellents. Firm performance is examined in terms of the accounting cash flow margin on sales, cash flow return on assets, and total asset turnover and in terms of the market-based total return to shareholders.

Financial policy is evaluated using the ratio of capital spending to the market value of assets, R&D expenditures relative to the market value of assets, the dividend payout ratio, and leverage as measured by the debt-equity ratio.

Estimation results indicate that shark repellent-adopting firms generally have long-term performance that exceeds industry norms during both pre- and post-adoption periods. Similarly, shark repellent-adopting firms are generally characterized by financial policies that are compatible with the long-term interests of shareholders during both pre- and postadoption periods. These findings are inconsistent with the notion that shark repellents are adopted to enhance the job security of inefficient or otherwise self-interested management at the expense of shareholders. Instead, these findings are compatible with the hypothesis that shark repellents are adopted by above-average firms that pursue unusually long-term or risky investment projects and, as suggested by Stein (1988), can be consistent with the long-run interests of shareholders.

I. SHARK REPELLENTS

Stock market evidence is mixed concerning the economic consequences of corporate charter amendments that invoke antitakeover restrictions, commonly called shark repellents.[1] These equivocal results stem from the fact that studies by Brickley, Coles, and Terry (1994), Malatesta and Walking (1988), and Ryngaert (1988), among others, find that the adoption of shark repellents conveys at least two different pieces of information to the marketplace.

Shark repellent adoption may be construed as unfavorable evidence that company management is inclined to oppose takeover bids. This explains early documented evidence of a negative stock market reaction to shark repellents over certain samples and time periods (e.g., Jarrell and Poulsen, 1987). On the other hand, shark repellent adoption is favorable evidence that company management has reason to believe that a takeover offer is either likely or imminent. Despite the fact that shark repellents are designed to discourage takeover interest, stock market evidence indicates that the probability of receiving a takeover offer is high for shark repellent-adopting firms and that this higher probability of takeover is sometimes reflected in a positive overall stock-price reaction (Linn and McConnell, 1983; McWilliams 1990).

Given the conflicting nature of potential information effects, it is perhaps unsurprising that Brickley, Coles, and Terry (1994) and Ryngaert (1988), among others, report that the average cumulative abnormal return associated with shark repellent adoption is only slightly negative and statistically insignificant.

[1]Corporate bylaws have been rewritten in at least 41 states to limit or otherwise control corporate takeovers. Almost all such laws involve more than a single antitakeover mechanism, such as regulations on nonstockholder/nonmonetary considerations, limits on business combination/freeze-out provisions, fair price requirements, poison-pill prohibitions, anti-greenmail stipulations, compensation restrictions, and so on. See *Mergers & Acquisitions* 29 (September/October 1994), 52–53.

Thus, even though shark repellent adoption has the clear potential to discourage takeover bids and entrench inefficient management (see Pound, 1987), conflicting stock market evidence implies the need to examine more closely the economic characteristics of shark repellent-adopting firms. For example, Brickley, Coles, and Terry (1994) discovered that the stock market reaction to shark repellent announcements was positive for firms with a majority of outside directors, and negative otherwise. Brickley, Coles, and Terry (1994) concluded that at least some shark repellent adoptions can be beneficial and that outside directors serve shareholder interests.

Evidence concerning the economic motivation for shark repellent adoptions can be gained by considering the long-term performance and financial policy characteristics of shark repellent-adopting firms in the pre-adoption period. According to the *management-entrenchment hypothesis*, shark repellents are adopted to enhance the job security of inefficient or otherwise self-interested management at the expense of shareholders (see Mahoney and Mahoney, 1993). If the management-entrenchment hypothesis holds, inferior long-term performance and financial policy decisions would be observed for shark repellent-adopting firms in the pre-adoption period. An alternative *shareholder-interest hypothesis* posits that shark repellents are adopted by above-average firms that pursue unusually long-term or risky investment projects. If shareholders are imperfectly informed, temporarily low earnings may cause a company to become temporarily undervalued in the stock market, thereby increasing the probability of a takeover at an unfavorable price (see Stein, 1988). The extent of such a problem depends on a variety of factors, including the attitudes and beliefs of shareholders, the degree to which corporate raiders have inside information, and the degree to which managers are concerned with keeping control of their firms. If the shareholder-interest hypothesis holds, superior long-term performance and financial policy decisions should be observed for shark repellent-adopting firms in the pre-adoption period. The shareholder-interest hypothesis would also explain why Pound (1989) finds that countersolicitations against management antitakeover proposals are relatively rare.

This chapter also reports evidence on the economic implications of shark repellent adoptions by considering the long-term performance and financial policy decisions of shark repellent-adopting firms in the postadoption period. According to the management-entrenchment hypothesis, shark repellents exacerbate, rather than mitigate, any shareholder or managerial myopia concerning the value of unusually long-term or risky investments. In support of the management-entrenchment hypothesis, and contrary to Stein's (1988) prediction, Meulbroek et al. (1990) found a decrease in the percentage of sales revenue devoted to R&D following the implementation of antitakeover amendments. A reduction in relative R&D spending is consistent with the notion that shark repellents entrench inefficient management and is compatible with stock market evidence that defensive measures have the potential to harm target shareholders. If the management-entrenchment hypothesis holds, inferior long-term performance and financial policy decisions should continue to be observed for shark repellent-adopting firms in the postadoption period (see Hirschey and Jones, 1995).

If the alternative shareholder-interest hypothesis is relevant, one might expect a continuation of superior long-term performance and financial policy decisions for shark repellent-adopting firms during the postadoption period. For example, in contrast with Meulbroek et al. (1990), Pugh, Page, and Jahera (1992) found a significant increase in capital spending relative to sales, capital spending relative to assets, R&D relative to sales, and R&D relative to assets in the posta-doption period. In all instances, changes in financial policy are evaluated in terms of changes in each respective investment ratio over the two-year period sur-rounding the shark repellent adoption period. Pugh, Page, and Jahera (1992) also look at industry-adjusted ratios and conclude that managers are able to adopt a more effective long-term investment strategy in the postadoption period. More recently, Bhagat and Jefferis (1994) found that the performance of firms that pay greenmail is no worse than the performance of similar-size firms that operate in the same industry, either prior to or following the share repurchase decision.

Finally, it is worth noting that the managerial-entrenchment hypothesis presumes that shark repellents are adopted as an effective means for takeover prevention and not as a negotiating ploy in the normal give-and-take between bidders and targets (see Harris, 1990; Hirschey, 1986). While Pound (1987) reports that the probability of takeover does, in fact, decrease following shark repellent adoptions, McWilliams (1990) suggests that firms with low managerial ownership use shark repellents to increase their bargaining power. Since Linn and McConnell (1983) and McWilliams (1990) found positive and statistically sig-nificant poison-pill announcement effects, the favorable share-price influence tied to an increase in managerial bargaining power can sometimes more than offset any negative share-price influence resulting from the decreased probability of takeover.

II. DATA

Jarrell and Poulsen (1987) study a sample of $n = 649$ firms adopting shark repel-lents over the 1979–85 period as obtained from Drexel Burnham Lambert, Kidder Peabody, and the Security and Exchange Commission (SEC) Office of Tender Offers. In Appendix A of their article, Jarrell and Poulsen (1987) list their sample of shark repellent-adopting firms, the proxy signing date, inside ownership, insti-tutional ownership, and amendment type. To estimate the market model for their event study, they require at least 50 trading days in a 150-day estimation period. Using the *Investment Statistical Listing* (ISL) tapes from Interactive Data Services, Inc., they are able to obtain sufficient data to estimate market-model regressions for 551 out of 649 firms.

Given the availability of reliable data over meaningful pre- and postadoption periods, the Jarrell and Poulsen (1987) sample constitutes an attractive basis for this examination of the long-term performance and financial policy implications of shark repellent adoptions. Therefore, this study follows Hirschey and Jones (1995) in adopting the Jarrell and Poulsen (1987) sample for analysis. To ensure comparability with previous and subsequent research, this study relies upon widely available *Compustat* data in the calculation of firm performance and financial policy decision variables. This results in some modest information loss, since only 505 of Jarrell and Poulsen's (1987) 551 firms have sufficient data available on *Compustat*. Nevertheless, with 91.6% coverage of the Jarrell and Poulsen (1987) sample, the $n = 505$ sample studied here is sufficiently broad to offer interesting evidence on the long-term implications of shark repellent adoptions.

III. LONG-TERM PERFORMANCE AND FINANCIAL POLICIES

To provide broad-based evidence on the economic implications of shark repellent adoptions, it is worth considering alternative indicators of firm performance and financial policy decisions in the period surrounding shark repellent adoption decisions. As in Healy, Palepu, and Ruback (1992), firm performance is evaluated using a variety of accounting ratios, including the cash flow margin on sales (cash flow/sales), cash flow return on assets (cash flow/assets), and the total asset turnover (sales/assets) ratio. The cash flow margin on sales and the cash flow return on assets measure the firm's profit-making performance. Higher ratios are consistent with superior performance and are a favorable indication of the firm's future growth prospects. These cash flow-based measures of firm performance may be superior to more traditional accounting measures, such as the return on shareholders' equity, because they "look through" the effects of differing assumptions regarding depreciation and other noncash expenses. In addition to being relatively unaffected by accrual accounting conventions, these cash flow-based measures of firm performance are invariant to capital structure decisions. Total asset turnover reflects the firm's wise use of assets in terms of its ability to generate a high level of sales. The higher the total asset turnover ratio, the more efficient the firm is in its use of assets.

Beyond such accounting-based measures of firm performance, it is interesting to consider a market-based indicator of firm performance in the pre- and postadoption periods. The total return to shareholders, including both capital gains and dividends, is a useful indicator of long-term performance in the pre- and postadoption periods. As such, it has the potential to shed meaningful light on the economic motivation for and implications of shark repellent adoptions.

The relationship between shark repellent adoptions and the firm's investment policy, dividend policy, and capital structure decisions is also evaluated using a variety of measures. Managerial myopia and the management-entrenchment hypothesis is most relevant to the extent that shark repellent-adopting firms can be characterized by relatively low levels of capital spending and R&D investment in the pre- and postadoption periods. The shareholder-interest hypothesis is most relevant to the extent that shark repellent-adopting firms can be characterized by relatively high levels of capital spending and R&D investment. The potential relevance of dividend policy and capital structure decisions is suggested by Jensen's (1986) free cash flow hypothesis, which recognizes high dividend payout ratios and high debt-to-equity (leverage) ratios as effective means for controlling the agency costs of free cash flow. If the self-interested management of shark repellent-adopting firms is typically insulated from market discipline, a significant amount of slack should be observed in these commonly employed corporate control mechanisms. Thus, the managerial-entrenchment hypothesis would predict relatively low dividend payout ratios and low leverage for shark repellent-adopting firms during the pre- and postadoption periods. Conversely, if shark repellents are adopted by firms with managers who are highly motivated to maximize shareholder value, high dividend payout ratios and high leverage should be typical. It follows that effective constraints on the agency costs of free cash flow during the pre- and postadoption periods are consistent with the competing shareholder-interest hypothesis. By considering the link between shark repellent adoptions, investment policy, dividend policy, and leverage during the pre- and postadoption periods, it becomes possible to arrive at some discriminating evidence concerning the predictive capability of the management-entrenchment and shareholder-interest hypotheses.

IV. MEASURES OF LONG-TERM PERFORMANCE AND FINANCIAL POLICIES

The cash flow margin on sales reflects the ability of the firm to generate a profit contribution on each dollar of sales revenue. Following Healy, Palepu, and Ruback (1992), the cash flow margin on sales ($CFMS_t$) employed in this study is

$$CFMS_t = \frac{CF_t}{SALES_t}, \tag{9.1}$$

where CF_t is cash flow defined as net income plus depreciation.[2] This cash flow-based measure of profitability is used rather than a more traditional approach in order to minimize the influences of accrual accounting conventions and firm-by-firm differences in accounting policy choice decisions. Whereas a high cash flow margin indicates a commensurately high rate of operating efficiency, a low cash flow margin on sales can reflect the fact that expenses are out of control. Of course, the cash flow margin on sales is related to the effectiveness of the firm's operating policies and to the vigor of industry competition.

---

[2]From *Compustat*, INC_DEP (*Compustat* item #13) is used for income before depreciation, and DEPREC (*Compustat* item #14) is used for depreciation.

The cash flow return on assets demonstrates how effective the firm is in employing its assets. Not only does the cash flow return on assets indicate whether or not the firm is able to generate profits on assets already in place, it also offers a suggestion of the firm's future growth prospects. Following Healy, Palepu, and Ruback (1992), the cash flow return on assets ($CFMV_t$) is defined as

$$CFMV_t = \frac{CF_t}{MV_{t-1}}. \tag{9.2}$$

Again, to minimize measurement problems, market values rather than accounting book values of assets in place at the end of the prior year are employed.

Total asset turnover reflects the firm's ability to generate sales relative to the firm's asset base. Higher ratios indicate a relatively efficient use of assets when the total asset turnover (TAT_t) ratio is defined as

$$TAT_t = \frac{SALES_t}{MV_{t-1}}, \tag{9.3}$$

and MV_{t-1} is market value defined as total liabilities, plus the book value of preferred, plus the market value of common equity for the year prior to the shark repellent adoption period. The market value of common equity is calculated as the common stock price at the beginning of the year times the number of shares outstanding.[3] Like in Healy, Palepu, and Ruback (1992), the market value of the firm is used rather than the more traditional book value of assets in the calculation of the total asset turnover ratio. This approach is designed to minimize the effects of differences in accounting policy choice decisions among firms.

In addition to these accounting-based measures of firm performance in the pre- and postadoption periods, it is worth considering performance measures more directly tied to shareholder returns. A simple market-based performance measure is the total stock price plus dividend return (TR_t) defined as

$$TR_t = \frac{P_t - P_{t-1} + D_t}{P_{t-1}}, \tag{9.4}$$

where P_t is the closing price for year t, P_{t-1} is the prior-year closing price, and D_t is the dividend paid in year t. TR_t is an attractive measure of the total (capital gains plus dividend) return earned by long-term shareholders.

---

[3]From *Compustat*, LIABTOT (*Compustat* item #181) is used for total liabilities, and PS_CVAL (*Compustat* item #130) is used for the book value of preferred stock. AD_CLOSE (same as closing price, CLOS_PR, *Compustat* item #24, after adjusting for stock splits and dividends) is used for the closing stock price at the end of the year, and ADJ_TRAD (same as common shares traded, CS_TRADE, *Compustat* item #28, after adjusting for stock splits an dividends) is used for the number of shares outstanding.

If firms that adopt shark repellents are typical of underperforming targets in the market for corporate control, accounting and market-based performance measures will be inferior to that of industry rivals during the pre-adoption period. If managerial efficiency changes following shark repellent adoptions, relative firm performance will change significantly during the postadoption period.

V. NONPARAMETRIC TESTS OF RELATIVE PERFORMANCE

When using either cash flow-based or market-based measures of firm performance, or a variety of indicators of the firm's financial policy, it is important to recognize the importance of industry-related considerations. Accounting performance, market-based performance, and measures of financial policy are all sensitive to the structure of production, the vigor of industry competition, regulatory climate, and so on. As a result, it is appropriate to measure changes in firm performance and financial policy in the pre- and postadoption periods from within the context of industry norms.

Following Healy, Palepu, and Ruback (1992), firm performance and financial policy information are collected from *Compustat* for each sample observation and for major competitors drawn from each sample observation's two-digit Standard Industrial Classification (SIC) code industry. Firm performance and financial policy ratios are then computed for each sample observation and for each sample observation's main competitors. Industry norms are then defined in terms of the median firm performance and financial policy ratios identified for each sample observation's main competitors. Industry median rather than industry average ratios are employed as descriptive of industry norms because the distribution of firm performance and financial policy ratios is unknown. Use of industry medians rather than industry averages also reduces the potential for bias due to the excessive influence of extreme outliers.

To test for differences in firm performance and financial policy decisions for shark repellent-adopting firms, each relevant ratio is compared to the median ratio of the firm's two-digit SIC industry. Industry-adjusted firm performance and financial policy are measured by each sample observation's ratio minus the relevant industry median ratio (IAR_{it}):

$$IAR_{it} = R_{it} - IR_{it}, \tag{9.5}$$

where IAR_{it} is the industry-adjusted firm performance or financial policy ratio for firm i during period t, R_{it} is the relevant firm ratio, and IR_{it} is the relevant median industry ratio. In these calculations, it is important to keep in mind that each sample observation is excluded from the determination of industry norms.

Median firm performance and financial policy ratios, and median industry-adjusted ratios, are computed for all sample observations for each of the 5 years prior to the poison-pill-adoption period and for each of the 5 years in the postadoption period. Again, medians are employed rather than sample averages to minimize the influence of extreme observations. Median firm performance and financial policy ratios are defined for each sample period t:

$$Median\ R_t = Median\,(R_{it},\dots,R_{nt}), \qquad (9.6)$$

where n is the number of sample observations.

Median industry-adjusted firm performance and financial policy ratios are defined for each sample t:

$$Median\ IAR_t = Median\,(IAR_{it},\dots,IAR_{nt}). \qquad (9.7)$$

Since the sample distribution is unknown, a nonparametric test statistic is an attractive method for evaluating these industry-adjusted ratios. As in Healy, Palepu, and Ruback (1992), a Wilcoxon signed rank test is employed to test whether or not the median industry-adjusted performance and financial policy ratios are statistically different from zero. In this technique, sample observations are sorted from smallest to largest industry-adjusted ratios. Each observation is then assigned a rank, r_i, with the smallest ratio being assigned a rank of 1, the second smallest a rank of 2, and so on. If the value of the industry-adjusted ratio is less than zero, it is given a sign indicator, z_i, of zero. If the value of the industry-adjusted ratio is greater than zero, then z_i equals one. The test statistic, w, is

$$w = \sum z_i r_i. \qquad (9.8)$$

To test the statistical significance of w_i, the null hypothesis is that the industry-adjusted ratio in question is not significantly different from zero. In this hypothesis test, r^+ is the number of industry-adjusted ratios greater than zero over the entire sample of poison-pill-adopting firms, r^- is the number of industry-adjusted ratios less than zero, and r is the smaller of these two numbers. The null hypothesis can be rejected at the $\alpha = 5\%$ level if r is greater than $w_{0.975}$ or less than $w_{0.025}$, where w represents the tails of the Wilcoxon and values for w can be found in a table of the critical values for the Wilcoxon signed rank test (see Pfaffenberger and Patterson, 1987).

The 5-year median firm performance and financial policy ratios are calculated for years $t = -5$ to $t = -1$, and for years $t = +1$ to $t = +5$. Then, the median for each ratio over each time frame is calculated. For example, the median ratio for each firm for the $t = -5$ to $t = -1$ is calculated as

$$Median\ R_i = Median\,(R_{i,-5},\dots,R_{i,-1}). \qquad (9.9)$$

Median ratios for all poison-pill-adopting firms over the $t = -5$ to $t = -1$ period are

$$Median\ R_{t=-5\ to\ -1} = Median\,[(Median\ R_1),\dots,(Median\ R_n)]. \qquad (9.10)$$

Identical statistics are also derived over the $t = +1$ to $t = +5$ period.

The median industry-adjusted ratio is found for each firm for years $t = -1$ to $t = -5$ by first finding the industry-adjusted ratio for each year and each firm as seen in Eq. (9.7).Then, the industry-adjusted median for years $t = -1$ to $t = -5$ for each firm is found as

$$Median\ IAR_i = Median\ [(Median\ IAR_{i,-5}),\ldots,(Median\ IAR_{i,-1})]. \quad (9.11)$$

The industry-adjusted median performance and financial policy ratios across all firms are found as

$$Median\ IAR_{t=-5\ to\ -1} = Median\ [(Median\ IAR_{1,}),\ldots,(Median\ IAR_n)]. \quad (9.12)$$

As before, identical statistics are also derived over the $t = +1$ to $t = +5$ period.

As described previously, a Wilcoxon signed rank test is conducted to test whether or not the industry-adjusted 5-year medians are significantly different from zero.

VI. NONPARAMETRIC RESULTS FOR INDUSTRY-ADJUSTED PERFORMANCE

Tables 9.1 and 9.2 show that industry-adjusted firm performance measures are generally superior in the pre- and postadoption periods for shark repellent-adopting firms. Industry-adjusted firm performance is superior and statistically significant for shark repellent-adopting firms in the preadoption period for all four measures of relative firm performance. In three of four instances, industry-adjusted firm performance is also superior and statistically significant for shark repellent-adopting firms in the postadoption period.

In Table 9.1, the cash flow margin on sales for adopting firms is uniformly better than that earned by competitors in both the pre- and postadoption periods. In fact, adopting firms have a greater cash flow margin on sales than their industry counterparts in each subperiod analyzed. In the 5 years prior to shark repellent adoption, the median cash flow margin on sales for adopting firms is 15.39%. Moreover, adopting firms display a median cash flow margin on sales that is 1.89% greater than the median performance of industry competitors. In the 5-year postadoption period, the median cash flow margin on sales for adopting firms is roughly the same at 15.53% and displays a similar performance margin of 2.21% over industry competitors. In both periods, roughly three-fifths of shark repellent-adopting firms generate cash flow margin on sales performance that is superior to industry competitors.

Table 9.1 also shows that the median cash flow return on assets earned by adopting firms is 27.72% in the pre-adoption period and 19.42% in the postadoption period. As in the case of the cash flow margin on sales, the cash flow return on assets for adopting firms is uniformly better than that earned by competitors in the pre- and postadoption periods. The pre-adoption period

TABLE 9.1 Cash Flows are Relatively High for Shark Repellent-Adopting Firms

Year	Cash flow margin on sales (CFMS)				Cash flow return on assets (CFMV)			
	Median (%)	Industry-adjusted median (%)[b]	Percent positive (%)[b]	n	Median (%)	Industry-adjusted median (%)[b]	Percent positive (%)[b]	n
-5	16.14	1.70	63.7	438	34.76	2.84	59.0	405
-4	15.27	1.84	63.0	449	30.76	2.87	60.9	417
-3	15.17	1.98	64.4	458	27.95	3.89	61.4	435
-2	15.04	2.14	63.6	464	25.97	3.34	62.8	449
-1	15.20	2.09	62.2	468	25.06	3.08	63.2	457
-5 to -5	15.39	1.89	64.8	469	27.72	2.68	63.6	459
1	15.43	2.39	62.2	445	21.51	1.90	59.8	443
2	15.35	1.63	59.5	425	20.59	1.58	58.7	424
3	15.61	1.78	61.5	405	18.51	1.38	57.6	403
4	16.06	2.72	62.7	381	18.94	1.96	59.5	375
5	15.61	2.54	65.5	371	19.40	2.46	60.9	363
1 to 5	15.53	2.21	62.6	447	19.42	1.73	60.1	446

$$IACFMS_{post} = 0.029 + 0.289 IACFMS_{pre}$$
$$(5.09)^b \quad (35.97)^b \quad n = 467$$
$$R^2 = 62.48\% \quad F = 776.01^b \quad n = 467$$

$$IACFMV_{post} = 0.027 + 0.145 IACFMV_{pre}$$
$$(5.49)^b \quad (7.13)^b \quad n = 435$$
$$R^2 = 10.48\% \quad F = 50.82^b \quad n = 435$$

Note: The industry-adjusted median cash flow margin on sales (CFMS) and cash flow return on assets (CFMV) are both relatively high for shark repellent-adopting firms in the 5-year pre- and postadoption periods. Statistically significant intercept coefficients from a simple regression of postadoption industry-adjusted medians on preadoption levels indicate statistically significant increases in both CFMS and CFMV between the pre- and postadoption periods for shark repellent-adopting firms. *IACFMS* is the industry-adjusted cash flow margin on sales. *IACFMV* is the industry-adjusted cash flow return on assets.

[a]Significant with 95% confidence ($\alpha = 5\%$).
[b]Significant with 99% confidence ($\alpha = 1\%$).

TABLE 9.2 High Total Asset Turnover and Superior Total Returns are Evident for Shark-Repellent Adopting Firms

	Total asset turnover (TAT)				Total return (TR)			
Year	Median (%)	Industry-adjusted median (%)[b]	Percent positive (%)[b]	n	Median (%)	Industry-adjusted median (%)[b]	Percent positive (%)[b]	n
−5	214.86	−0.35	49.5	434	18.25	0.50[b]	50.6	441
−4	205.32	1.45[b]	53.1	448	20.29	5.16[b]	57.2[b]	451
−3	186.75	0.92[a]	52.8	466	13.84	1.76[b]	52.9	467
−2	170.88	0.98[b]	51.2	484	18.06	4.61[b]	57.9[b]	487
−1	152.68	1.54[b]	52.9	493	21.19	7.75[b]	60.6[b]	498
−5 to −1	180.70	0.26[a]	51.3	495	19.13	4.35[b]	61.9[b]	499
1	129.94	−0.10	50.0	474	10.03	4.86[b]	55.4[a]	478
2	121.46	−1.32	47.3	455	11.90	4.52[a]	57.6[b]	460
3	105.17	−0.81	47.8	431	7.95	4.59[b]	55.9[a]	433
4	105.71	−0.25	49.3	404	11.05	6.15[b]	60.9[b]	414
5	105.56	−1.19	47.7	390	9.33	4.97[b]	59.9[b]	387
1 to 5	115.22	0.15	50.5	477	11.26	5.75[b]	64.6[b]	480

$$IATAT_{post} = -0.001 + 0.593 IATAT_{pre}$$
$$(-0.02) \quad (27.86)^b$$
$$R^2 = 74.49\% \quad F = 1293.76^b \quad n = 444$$

$$IATR_{post} = 0.062 - 0.011 IATR_{pre}$$
$$(6.21)^b \quad (-0.43)$$
$$R^2 = 0.04\% \quad F = 0.18 \quad n = 472$$

Note: Relatively high industry-adjusted median total asset turnover (TAT) is characteristic of shark repellent-adopting firms during the 5-year preadoption period; TAT is typical of industry norms in the postadoption period. Superior total returns (TR) to shareholders (dividends plus capital gains) are evident for shark repellent-adopting firms in both the 5-year pre- and postadoption periods. The intercept coefficient from a simple regression of postadoption industry-adjusted medians on preadoption levels indicate a statistically significant favorable increase in TR between the pre- and postadoption periods. *t*-statistics are in parentheses. IATAT is the industry-adjusted total asset turnover. IATR is the industry-adjusted total return to shareholders.

[a]Significant with 95% confidence (α = 5%).
[b]Significant with 99% confidence (α = 1%).

industry-adjusted median cash flow return on assets is 2.68% higher for adopting firms than for their industry counterparts; it is 1.73% higher than industry competitors during the postadoption period. Also, as in the case of the cash flow margin on sales, roughly three-fifths of shark repellent-adopting firms generate a cash flow return on assets that is superior to industry competitors.

In Table 9.2, the industry-adjusted total asset turnover ratio is higher for adopting firms in the period prior to shark repellent adoptions, but not in the postadoption period. The statistically significant industry-adjusted total asset turnover ratio of 0.26% in the pre-adoption period signifies that the median ratio of 180.70% for adopting firms is 0.26% greater than the median total asset turnover ratio for competitors. This signals a relatively wise use of assets by adopting firms in the pre-adoption period in that relatively high amounts of revenue are generated for a fixed level of capital investment. However, there may be some slight deterioration in the asset management performance of adopting firms in the postadoption period. The median total asset turnover ratio of 115.22% for adopting firms in the postadoption period is not statistically different than the median total asset turnover ratio for competitors.

Table 9.2 also shows that the median total capital gain plus dividend return earned by shareholders of adopting firms is 19.13% in the pre-adoption period and 11.26% in the postadoption period. As in the case of the cash flow-based performance measures, the total return for adopting firms is uniformly better than that earned by competitors in the pre- and postadoption periods. The pre-adoption period industry-adjusted median total return is 4.35% higher for adopting firms than for their industry counterparts; it is 5.75% higher than industry competitors during the postadoption period. As in the case of the cash flow-based performance measures, roughly three-fifths of shark repellent-adopting firms generate a total return to shareholders that is superior to industry competitors.[4]

In sum, these nonparametric results for industry-adjusted performance are broadly consistent with the shareholder-interest hypothesis and inconsistent with a management-entrenchment explanation of shark repellent adoptions. As predicted by the shareholder-interest hypothesis, firms that adopt shark repellents can be characterized as superior performers during the pre- and postadoption periods. This may be construed as some evidence that managers use the takeover protection offered by shark repellents to make investments in profitable projects

---

[4]A more comprehensive market-based measure of the total return to equity stakeholders in poison-pill-adopting firms would explicitly incorporate the effects of equity buyback decisions. After adjustment for equity buybacks, superior returns for shareholders of poison-pill-adopting firms remain evident. In the pre-adoption period, the median return to shareholders is 22.08%; in the postadoption period, the median return to shareholders is 14.20%. During both periods, the median return to shareholders of adopting firms is greater than the median return earned by industry competitors. The pre-adoption period industry-adjusted median return to shareholders is 3.97% higher for adopting firms than for their industry counterparts; it is 6.58% higher than industry competitors during the postadoption period. After adjustment for buybacks, roughly three-fifths of adopting firms display superior returns to shareholders over each of the pre- and postadoption periods.

that are unusually risky or long-term in nature. In any event, it seems fair to characterize shark repellent-adopting firms as relatively good performers when compared against industry counterparts.

VII. MEASURES OF FIRM FINANCIAL POLICY

According to the management-entrenchment hypothesis, shark repellents are adopted to enhance the job security of inefficient or otherwise self-interested management (see Mahoney and Mahoney, 1993). Any such failure to adopt optimal performance standards and financial policies is a type of agency problem that arises when slack in the managerial labor market permits managers to pursue value-reducing projects with excess or free cash flow (see Jensen, 1986). Thus, a myopic focus on short-term or low-risk projects and low rates of capital spending and R&D expenditures would be typical if the management-entrenchment hypothesis is descriptive of shark repellent-adopting firms. In a similar vein, notable managerial slack due to relatively low dividend payout ratios or low leverage in the pre- and postadoption periods would be consistent with the management-entrenchment hypothesis.

By way of contrast, the shareholder-interest hypothesis suggests that shark repellents might be adopted by above-average firms that pursue unusually long-term or risky investment projects. When shareholders are imperfectly informed, temporarily low earnings could cause a company to become temporarily undervalued in the stock market, thereby increasing the probability of a takeover at an unfavorable price (see Stein, 1988). Accordingly, the shareholder-interest hypothesis predicts relatively high rates of capital spending and R&D expenditures by shark repellent-adopting firms in the pre- and postadoption periods. Similarly, an absence of managerial slack due to relatively high dividend payout ratios or significant leverage in the pre- and postadoption periods would be consistent with the shareholder-interest hypothesis.

To examine the possibility of changes in the pace of capital expenditures in the period surrounding shark repellent adoptions, the ratio of capital spending over the market value of assets is also investigated as suggested by Healy, Palepu, and Ruback (1992). The capital spending ($CSMV_t$) ratio is defined as

$$CSMV_t = \frac{CAPITAL\ SPENDING_t}{MV_{t-1}}. \tag{9.13}$$

where $CAPITAL\ SPENDING_t$ is expenditures on fixed capital for the firm, and MV_t is the market value of the firm as defined previously.[5]

---

[5]From *Compustat*, SC_CAPSP (*Compustat* item #128) is used for capital spending.

As in Healy, Palepu, and Ruback (1992), spending on R&D relative to the market value of assets is used as a measure of the firm's rate of spending on "intangible capital" that has the potential to improve the firm's long-run profit potential. The R&D spending intensity $(R\&DMV_t)$ ratio is defined as

$$R\&DMV_t = \frac{R\&D_t}{MV_{t-1}},\qquad(9.14)$$

where $R\&D_t$ is expenditures on R&D, and MV_t is as defined beforehand.[6] Because the payoff from R&D investment is relatively long-term and risky in nature, changes in the firm's R&D financial policy have the potential to provide insight concerning any myopic behavior, or changes in myopic behavior, on the part of management. Of particular interest to this study is the extent to which managerial myopia might be induced or changed by shark repellent adoptions.

To capture the resource management practices of firms that adopt shark repellents, this study considers the possibility of changes in the dividend payout ratio during the pre- and postadoption periods. The dividend payout ratio (DPR_t) is defined as total dividends divided by net income:

$$DPR_t = \frac{D_t \cdot S_t}{NET\ INCOME_t},\qquad(9.15)$$

where D_t is the annual dividend per share, and S_t is the number of common shares outstanding.[7]

As a further indication of the influence of shark repellent adoptions on resource management practices in the pre- and postadoption periods, this study considers the possibility of changes in the firm's capital structure. Like an increase in the dividend payout ratio, an increase in leverage and required interest payments can have the effect of reducing managerial slack in the deployment of free cash flow. As in Healy, Palepu, and Ruback (1992), any change in leverage in the period surrounding shark repellent adoptions is measured using the debt-equity ratio (DER_t) defined as[8]

$$DER_t = \frac{TOTAL\ LIABILITIES_t}{COMMON\ EQUITY_t}.\qquad(9.16)$$

---

[6]From *Compustat*, RD_EXP (*Compustat* item #46) is used for R&D.

[7]From *Compustat*, ADJ_DIV (same as DIV_PS, *Compustat* item #26, after adjusting for stock splits and dividends) is used for the annual dividend paid per share, and NET_INC (*Compustat* item #172) is used for net income.

[8]From *Compustat*, STHOEQ (*Compustat* item #216) is used for common equity.

VIII. NONPARAMETRIC RESULTS FOR INDUSTRY-ADJUSTED FINANCIAL POLICY

Nonparametric results for industry-adjusted financial policy decisions are generated using the same methodology as that described for the industry-adjusted analysis of firm performance.

Simply put, Table 9.3 offers support for the shareholder-interest hypothesis that shark repellent-adopting firms invest unusually large amounts in long-term or risky investment projects in the pre-adoption period. Table 9.3 offers no support for the management-entrenchment hypothesis that shark repellent-adopting firms underinvest in plant and equipment or R&D in the pre-adoption period. In Table 9.3, the industry-adjusted ratio of capital spending to the market value of the firm is higher for adopting firms in both the pre- and postadoption periods. The statistically significant industry-adjusted capital spending to market value ratio of 1.58% in the pre-adoption period indicates that the median ratio of 11.63% for adopting firms is 1.58% greater than the median capital spending to market value ratio for competitors. This suggests marginally higher plant and equipment investment activity on the part of adopting firms in the pre-adoption period. However, there may be some modest deterioration *vis-a-vis* competitors in this margin of investment intensity in the postadoption period. The median capital spending to market value ratio of 6.61% for adopting firms in the post-adoption period is only 0.32% higher than the industry-adjusted median. Still, the modestly higher ratio of capital spending to the market value of the firm for adopting firms is statistically significant. Table 9.3 also shows that the R&D to market value ratio for adopting firms is generally higher than that of competitors in the pre-adoption period, but not during the postadoption period. In the 5 years prior to shark repellent adoption, the median R&D to market value ratio for adopting firms is 2.75%, or a modest premium of 0.02% above industry norms. In the 5-year postadoption period, the R&D to market value ratio falls slightly to 2.43%, a percentage that is roughly the same as industry competitors.

Table 9.4 reports on the dividend policy and capital structure decisions of shark repellent-adopting firms. As predicted by the shareholder-interest hypothesis, shark repellent adoptions appear to be common among firms that display relatively high payouts of dividends (have high free cash flow) and relatively high leverage. Table 9.4 reveals that the median dividend payout ratio by adopting firms is 7.47% in the pre-adoption period and 12.09% in the postadoption period. The pre-adoption period industry-adjusted median payout ratio is 3.50% higher for adopting firms than for their industry counterparts; it is 8.39% higher than industry norms during the postadoption period. In both periods, the industry-adjusted median payout ratio is statistically significant. It is also interesting to note that dividend payout ratios exceed industry norms for roughly two-thirds of shark repellent-adopting firms. Table 9.4 also shows that the median debt-to-equity ratio for adopting firms is 120.36% in the pre-adoption period and 129.98% in the postadoption period. This pre-adoption period industry-adjusted

TABLE 9. 3 Capital Spending and R&D are High for Shark-Repellent Adopting Firms

	Capital spending to market value (CSMV)				R&D to market value (R&DMV)			
Year	Median (%)	Industry-adjusted median (%)[b]	Percent positive (%)[b]	n	Median (%)	Industry-adjusted median (%)[b]	Percent positive (%)[b]	n
−5	13.31	1.21[b]	57.5[b]	381	2.61	0.06[b]	52.9[a]	221
−4	12.71	1.72[b]	62.2[b]	392	2.89	0.17[b]	52.0[a]	223
−3	11.94	1.78[b]	60.5[b]	408	3.01	0.09[b]	53.2[a]	231
−2	10.07	1.40[b]	59.7[b]	422	3.16	0.23[b]	52.8[a]	235
−1	9.39	0.79[b]	57.9[b]	430	2.86	0.00	46.8	237
−5 to −1	11.63	1.58[b]	60.5[b]	433	2.75	0.02[b]	50.6	265
1	8.03	0.41[b]	52.2	414	2.86	0.00	44.7	228
2	6.97	0.31[b]	51.7	393	2.74	0.00	41.8	213
3	5.98	−0.00	49.2	372	2.37	0.00	43.0	200
4	5.50	0.00	49.6	345	2.23	0.00	39.7	184
5	5.70	0.38[b]	53.8	333	2.43	0.00	42.5	181
1 to 5	6.61	0.32[a]	52.7	421	2.43	0.00	42.7	241

$IACSMV_{post} = 0.341 \times 10^{-3} + 0.243 IACSMV_{pre}$
(0.14)   (8.36)[b]

$R^2 = 14.63\%$ $F = 69.90^b$ $n = 409$

$IAR\&DMV_{post} = 0.003 + 0.057 IAR\&DMV_{pre}$
(1.63)   (4.12)[b]

$R^2 = 6.92\%$ $F = 16.94^b$ $n = 229$

Note: Relatively high industry-adjusted median capital spending to market value (CSMV) and median research and development to market value (R&DMV) are typical for shark repellent-adopting firms in the 5-year preadoption period. CSMV also exceeds industry norms in the postadoption period, whereas the R&DMV of shark repellent-adopting firms is typical of industry counterparts in the postadoption period. Insignificant intercept coefficients that result from a comparison of these two measures over the pre- and postadoption periods suggest no meaningful change due to shark repellent adoption. *t*-statistics are in parentheses. *IACSMV* is the industry-adjusted capital spending to market value ratio. *IAR&DMV* is the industry-adjusted R&D to market value ratio.

[a]Significant with 95% confidence ($\alpha = 5\%$).
[b]Significant with 99% confidence ($\alpha = 1\%$).

TABLE 9.4 Dividend Payout Ratios and Leverage are High for Shark-Repellent Adopting Firms

Year	Dividend payout ratio (DPR)				Debt-to-equity ratio (DER)			
	Median (%)	Industry-adjusted median (%)[b]	Percent positive (%)[b]	n	Median (%)	Industry-adjusted median (%)[b]	Percent positive (%)[b]	n
−5	6.40	2.18	64.4	449	120.21	3.53[a]	51.7	468
−4	6.72	3.07	64.5	467	122.43	4.82[b]	51.8	479
−3	7.89	3.51	63.3	485	119.85	2.92[b]	51.9	493
−2	7.95	4.22	63.8	494	119.23	7.61[b]	55.0[a]	500
−1	9.54	5.88	65.4	503	116.72	6.22[b]	52.9	505
−5 to −1	7.47	3.50	65.1	504	120.36	4.21[b]	52.5	505
1	10.02	7.12	62.9	474	128.26	12.25[b]	57.0[b]	477
2	12.15	9.09	62.3	453	129.98	13.57[b]	59.0[b]	458
3	12.44	8.35	61.5	426	135.82	14.71[b]	56.7[b]	434
4	11.02	6.72	63.1	401	142.43	12.97[b]	56.8[b]	410
5	9.87	7.16	63.1	382	144.97	16.11[b]	59.3[b]	398
1 to 5	12.09	8.39	65.0	475	129.98	14.91[b]	57.1[b]	478

$$IADPR_{post} = 0.125 + 0.445 IADPR_{pre}$$
$$(4.50)^b \quad (1.92)$$
$$R^2 = 0.78\% \quad F = 3.69 \quad n = 472$$

$$IADER_{post} = 0.276 + 0.482 IADER_{pre}$$
$$(2.59)^a \quad (6.24)^b$$
$$R^2 = 7.58\% \quad F = 38.97^a \quad n = 476$$

Note: Relatively high industry-adjusted medians for the dividend payout ratio (DPR) and median debt-to-equity (DER) are typical for shark repellent-adopting firms in both the 5-year pre- and postadoption periods. Intercept coefficients from a simple regression of postadoption industry-adjusted medians on preadoption levels indicate a statistically significant favorable increase in both measures between the pre- and postadoption periods. *t*-statistics are in parentheses. *IADPR* is the industry-adjusted dividend payout ratio (dividends over net income). *IADER* is the industry-adjusted debt-to-equity ratio.

[a]Significant with 95% confidence (α = 5%).
[b]Significant with 99% confidence (α = 1%).

median leverage ratio is 4.21% higher for adopting firms than for their industry counterparts; it is 14.91% higher than industry competitors during the postadoption period. During both periods, shark repellent-adopting firms display payout ratios that are significantly higher than those for industry counterparts.

In sum, based upon nonparametric results shown in Table 9.3, it is fair to conclude that shark repellent-adopting firms tend to display higher than typical levels of investment in plant and equipment and R&D. Based upon results shown in Table 9.4, it also is fair to deduce that shark repellent-adopting firms display relatively high dividend payout and leverage (debt-to-equity) ratios. None of these findings is consistent with the concept of management entrenchment and the use of shark repellents by managers of firms that underinvest in risky or long-term projects. The fact that shark repellent-adopting firms tend to invest heavily in long-term or risky projects, pay out relatively high amounts of free cash flow, and employ significant leverage is consistent with the shareholder-interest hypothesis.

Industry-adjusted medians reported in Tables 9.1–9.4 are interesting because they offer useful insight concerning adopting firm performance and financial policy in the pre- and postadoption periods. For a direct test of changes in firm performance and financial policy resulting from shark repellent adoptions, it is necessary to analyze changes in firm performance and financial policy decisions in the period surrounding shark repellent adoptions.

IX. REGRESSION MODEL SPECIFICATION

Following Healy, Palepu, and Ruback (1992), simple cross-sectional regressions are estimated to capture statistical differences between postadoption industry-adjusted ratios and corresponding pre-adoption ratios. These simple regression equations take the form

$$IAR_{i,post} = \alpha + \beta IAR_{i,pre} + u, \qquad (9.17)$$

where $IAR_{i,post}$ is the median industry-adjusted firm performance or financial policy ratio for the 5-year postadoption period, and $IAR_{i,pre}$ is similar median industry-adjusted ratios for the 5-year pre-adoption period as defined in equation.

In this simple regression, the estimated slope coefficient, β, captures the correlation between pre- and postadoption firm performance and financial policy decisions. More important is the size and statistical significance of α, the intercept term. The estimated intercept coefficient α is independent of pre-adoption performance and reflects significant changes in the industry-adjusted relative position of adopting versus nonadopting firms in the postadoption period. Using this approach, significant changes in relative firm performance or financial policy decisions in the postadoption period are reflected by statistically significant intercept coefficient estimates.

X. REGRESSION RESULTS FOR CHANGES IN FIRM PERFORMANCE

Tables 9.1 and 9.2 report simple regression results with the potential to shed light on the statistical significance of changes in adopting firm performance between the pre- and postadoption periods.

From Table 9.1, some modest increase in the relative cash flow margin on sales can be noted. To see this, notice the statistically significant intercept coefficient of 0.029 in the cash flow margin on sales regression equation. This means that, on average, the industry-adjusted cash flow margin on sales is 0.029% higher for adopting versus nonadopting firms in the postadoption period. Therefore, the relative position of shark repellent-adopting firms improves modestly versus industry counterparts over this time frame. Table 9.1 also shows a statistically significant intercept coefficient estimate of 0.027 in the cash flow return on assets regression. This means that the median industry-adjusted cash flow return on assets is 0.027% higher for shark repellent-adopting firms versus industry counterparts in the postadoption period.

In a similar vein, Table 9.2 indicates no change in the relative total asset turnover performance of shark repellent-adopting firms is apparent, but depicts a statistically significant intercept coefficient estimate of 0.062 in the total capital gains plus dividend return regression equation. This implies that the median industry-adjusted total return is 0.062% higher for adopting firms versus industry counterparts in the postadoption period.

Taken as a whole, this simple regression analysis of changes in industry-adjusted firm performance suggests a pattern of generally improving relative performance for shark repellent-adopting firms over the pre- and postadoption periods. As such, firm performance over the pre- and postadoption periods is inconsistent with the management-entrenchment hypothesis and instead suggests that shark repellent-adopting firms are relatively good performers that act in the interest of shareholders.

XI. REGRESSION RESULTS FOR CHANGES IN FINANCIAL POLICY DECISIONS

Tables 9.3 and 9.4 report simple regression results with the potential to shed light on the statistical significance of changes in adopting firm financial policy decisions between the pre- and postadoption periods.

In Table 9.3, statistically insignificant intercept coefficients for the capital spending and R&D expenditure regressions suggest no meaningful change in the investment policies of shark repellent-adopting firms over the pre- and postadoption periods. During both periods, adopting firms display relatively high levels of capital spending, while above-average pre-adoption period R&D intensity reverts to industry norms during the postadoption period.

Table 9.4 shows that the already high dividend payout ratios and debt-to-equity (leverage) ratios for adopting firms increase somewhat following the adoption of shark repellents. The statistically significant intercept coefficient estimate of 0.125 in the dividend payout ratio regression means that the median industry-adjusted level is 0.125% higher for adopting versus nonadopting firms in the postadoption period. The statistically significant intercept coefficient estimate of 0.276 in the debt-to-equity (leverage) ratio regression means that the median industry-adjusted level is 0.276% higher for adopting versus nonadopting firms in the postadoption period. Again, these ratio increases are noted despite the fact that pre-adoption period payout and leverage ratios exceed industry norms for shark repellent-adopting firms.

On an overall basis, steady capital spending and R&D expenditures and higher payout ratios and financial leverage appear to be typical following shark repellent adoption. As such, the financial policies for adopting firms seem quite compatible with the shareholder-interest hypothesis and inconsistent with the management-entrenchment hypothesis.

XII. CONCLUSION

Hirschey and Jones (1995) investigates firm performance and financial policy decisions in the period surrounding the adoption of antitakeover corporate charter amendments, commonly referred to as shark repellents. To provide broad-based evidence on the economic implications of shark repellent adoptions, a wide range of accounting-based cash flow measures and market-based measures of firm performance are considered. The implications of shark repellent adoptions for financial policy decisions are also evaluated using a variety of measures.

The purpose of this analysis is to test competing management-entrenchment and shareholder-interest hypotheses. The management-entrenchment hypothesis holds that shark repellents are adopted to enhance the job security of inefficient or otherwise self-interested management at the expense of shareholders (see Mahoney and Mahoney, 1993). If the management-entrenchment hypothesis holds, inferior long-term performance and financial policy decisions should be observed for shark repellent-adopting firms in pre- and postadoption periods. An alternative shareholder-interest hypothesis posits that shark repellents are adopted by above-average firms that pursue unusually long-term or risky investment projects. If shareholders are imperfectly informed, temporarily low earnings may cause a company to become temporarily undervalued in the stock market, thereby increasing the probability of a takeover at an unfavorable price (see Stein, 1988). If the shareholder-interest hypothesis holds, superior long-term performance and financial policy decisions should be observed for shark repellent-adopting firms in the pre- and postadoption periods. By considering the implications of shark repellent adoptions for long-term performance and financial policy decisions, it becomes possible to arrive at some discriminating evidence concerning the predictive capability of competing management-entrenchment and shareholder-interest explanations of shark repellent adoptions.

Nonparametric results suggest uniformly superior long-term performance for shark repellent-adopting firms in the pre-adoption period. This finding undermines the notion that shark repellents are adopted by the self-interested management of poorly performing firms. In the postadoption period, the cash flow margin on sales, the cash flow margin on assets, and the total return to shareholders remain above industry medians, while total asset turnover is consistent with industry norms. In terms of long-term performance, there is no evidence that the long-term performance of poison-pill-adopting firms falls below industry medians during the postadoption period.

Nonparametric results also suggest consistently superior investment policy, dividend policy, and leverage decisions for shark repellent-adopting firms in the pre-adoption period. Again, this finding undermines the notion that shark repellents are adopted by the self-interested management of firms that shun unusually long-term or risky investment projects. It is fair to suggest that shark repellent-adopting firms display above-normal levels of investment in plant and equipment, dividend payout ratios, and financial leverage in the postadoption period. R&D intensity is also above industry norms in the pre-adoption period for shark repellent-adopting firms. Because R&D intensity is consistent with industry norms in the postadoption period, there is no evidence of a meaningful and systematic underinvestment in R&D activity following shark repellent adoption. None of these findings is consistent with the concept of managerial entrenchment and the use of shark repellents by managers of firms that operate in a nonvalue-maximizing manner.

A simple regression analysis of changes in industry-adjusted long-term performance and financial policy decisions over pre- and postadoption periods is consistent with nonparametric results and the shareholder-interest hypothesis. In three of four instances (cash flow margin on sales, cash flow return on assets, and total return to shareholders), the relative improvement in long-term performance for shark repellent-adopting firms is statistically significant. No change in relative total asset turnover is noted in the postadoption period. In two of four instances (dividend payout ratio and leverage), the relative change in financial policy for shark repellent-adopting firms is also statistically significant. Importantly for high-tech investors, no meaningful change in capital spending or R&D expenditures is apparent.

Taken as a whole, these findings suggest that shark repellents are adopted by firms with long-term performance that is generally above industry norms during both pre- and postadoption periods. When significant change is noted, long-term performance improves during the postadoption period. Because shark repellent-adopting firms also commonly adopt financial policies that are compatible with shareholder interests, it is fair to suggest that there is no necessary conflict between shark repellent adoptions and shareholder interests.

XIII. REFERENCES

Bhagat, S. and Jefferis, R. H., Jr. (1994). The Causes and Consequences of Takeover Defense: Evidence From Greenmail. *Journal of Corporate Finance* 1, 201–231.

Brickley, J. A., Coles, J. L., and Terry, R. L. (1994). Outside Directors and the Adoption of Poison Pills. *Journal of Financial Economics* 35, 371–390.

Harris, E. G. (1990). Antitakeover Measures, Golden Parachutes, and Target Firm Shareholder Welfare. *Rand Journal of Economics* 21, 614–625.

Healy, P. M., Palepu, K. G., and Ruback, R. S. (1992). Does Corporate Performance Improve After Mergers? *Journal of Financial Economics* 31, 135–175.

Hirschey, M. (1986). Mergers, Buyouts and Fakeouts. *American Economic Review* 76, 317–322.

Hirschey, M. and Jones, E. (1995). Long-Term Performance and Financial Policies of Shark Repellent-Adopting Firms. In Hirschey, M. and Marr, M. W. (eds.), *Advances in Financial Economics*, 1. Greenwich, CN: JAI Press, 155–181.

Jarrell, G. A. and Poulsen, A. B. (1987). Shark Repellents and Stock Prices: The Effects of Antitakeover Amendments Since 1980. *Journal of Financial Economics* 19, 127–168.

Jensen, M. C. (1986). Agency Costs of Free Cash Flow, Corporate Finance, and Takeovers. *American Economic Review* 76, 323–329.

Jensen, M. C. and Ruback, R. S. (1983). The Market for Corporate Control: The Scientific Evidence. *Journal of Financial Economics* 11, 5–50.

Linn, S. C. and McConnell, J. J. (1983). An Empirical Investigation of the Impact of 'Antitakeover' Amendments on Common Stock Prices. *Journal of Financial Economics* 11, 361–399.

Mahoney, J. M. and Mahoney, J. T. (1993). An Empirical Investigation of the Effect of Corporate Charter Antitakeover Amendments on Stockholder Wealth. *Strategic Management Journal* 14, 17–31.

Malatesta, P. H. and Walking, R. A. (1988). Poison Pill Securities: Stockholder Wealth, Profitability and Ownership Structure. *Journal of Financial Economics* 20, 347–376.

McWilliams, V. B. (1990). Managerial Share Ownership and the Stock Price Effects of Antitakeover Amendment Proposals. *Journal of Finance* 45, 1627–1640.

Meulbroek, L. K., Mitchell, M. L., Mulherin, J. H., Netter, J. M., and Poulsen, A. B. (1990). Shark Repellents and Managerial Myopia: An Empirical Test. *Journal of Political Economy* 98, 1108–1117.

Pfaffenberger, R. C. and Patterson, J. H. (1987). *Statistical Methods*. New York: Irwin, pp. 1019–1020, 1176.

Pound, J. (1987). The Effects of Antitakeover Amendments on Takeover Activity: Some Direct Evidence. *Journal of Law and Economics* 30, 353–367.

Pound, J. (1989). Shareholder Activism and Share Values: The Causes and Consequences of Countersolicitations Against Management Antitakeover Proposals. *Journal of Law and Economics* 32, 357–379.

Pugh, W. N., Page, D. E., and Jahera, J. S., Jr. (1992). Antitakeover Charter Amendments: Effects on Corporate Decisions. *Journal of Financial Research* 15, 57–67.

Ryngaert, M. (1988). The Effect of Poison Pill Securities on Shareholder Wealth. *Journal of Financial Economics* 20, 377–417.

Stein, J. C. (1988). Takeover Threats and Managerial Myopia. *Journal of Political Economy* 96, 61–80.

10

CORPORATE GOVERNANCE AND THE LEGAL ENVIRONMENT

During recent years, investors and the general public have been stunned by spectacular examples of corporate wrongdoing at Enron Corp., Tyco International, and WorldCom Group, to name just a few examples of gregarious management malfeasance. In each case, fraudulent transactions had the effect of enriching management at the expense of stockholders, employees, and the general public. More than just a glitch in the system, these examples of criminal behavior by the top management of leading corporations reflect a breakdown in what is called the corporate governance system. The corporate governance system is a network of controls that help corporations effectively manage, administer, and direct economic resources. Some of these corporate governance systems operate within the firm's corporate structure. Examples of internal corporate governance mechanisms include the centralized versus decentralized design of the organization, or the ownership structure of the firm. Some other corporate governance systems operate outside the firm's corporate structure. Good examples of external corporate governance mechanisms are provided by the entire system of federal and state laws, rules, and regulations that govern corporate behavior.

This chapter describes key factors that play a prominent role in the effective administration and governance of corporations, in general, and tech stocks, in particular. Boards of directors, large institutional investors, and the legal/regulatory system all help to ensure that research and development (R&D) and other corporate resources are effectively administered on behalf of stockholders. The role of the legal/regulatory system is of particular interest given the recent rise to importance of state and federal enforcement actions in the wake of recent high-profile breakdowns in the effectiveness of traditional corporate control mechanisms.

I. ROLE PLAYED BY BOARDS OF DIRECTORS

A large and growing corporate governance literature builds upon the work of Jensen and Meckling (1976), who contemplate the role of corporate control mechanisms as means for helping ameliorate the potential divergence of interests between managers and stockholders.[1] Jensen and Meckling (1976) describe how a variety of monitoring mechanisms inside and outside the firm work together to establish an optimal set of restrictions on firm activity and why firms themselves often suggest such restrictions.

The most important and closely monitored corporate governance mechanism is the company board of directors. The board of directors is a group of people legally charged with the responsibility for governing a corporation. In a for-profit corporation, it is generally accepted that the board of directors is responsible to stockholders. Some adopt the broader perspective that the board is responsible to "corporate stakeholders," that is, to everyone who is interested and/or can be affected by the corporation. Corporate stakeholders include stockholders, customers, employees, the community at large, and so on. In a nonprofit corporation, the board generally reports to stakeholders, particularly the local communities in which the nonprofit serves. Boards of directors provide continuity for the organization by maintaining a legal existence. A primary responsibility is to select, appoint, and review the performance of a chief executive officer responsible for day-to-day decision making and administration of the organization.

Table 10.1 shows five important attributes of effective corporate boards of directors and corresponding limitations of ineffectual corporate boards.

The National Center for Nonprofit Boards, in their booklet *Ten Basic Responsibilities of Nonprofit Boards*, itemize 10 responsibilities for nonprofit boards.

- Determine the organization's mission and purpose
- Select the executive
- Support the executive and review his or her performance
- Ensure effective organizational planning
- Ensure adequate resources
- Manage resources effectively
- Determine and monitor the organization's programs and services
- Enhance the organization's public image

---

[1]For a detailed analysis of organization structure and corporate governance, see Hirschey (2003).

TABLE 10.1 **Attributes of Effective and Ineffectual Boards of Directors**

Attribute	Effective board	Ineffectual board
Integrity	Board members must take pains to ensure that words and actions are in the best long-term interests of large and small shareholders.	Board decisions and management compensation plans are sometimes structured to favor entrenched management at the expense of stockholders.
Competence	Training and business experience of board members must be up to the task of providing value-added oversight to managerial decisions.	Board members with little or no relevant training or business experience are too often encountered. Celebrities are great at cocktail parties, but make poor board members.
Independence	Through words and deeds, it must be clear that the board of directors effectively represents shareholder interests in its oversight of managerial decisions.	Cronies of top management, or cozy consulting arrangements between companies and board members, can compromise, if not undermine, board member independence.
Accountability	Clear lines of authority and responsibility must be drawn. Both the board and top management must be held accountable for corporate performance.	Some boards are too large by design. When the board of directors has more than a dozen members, it can quickly become impossible to wield effective decision-making power.
Transparency	Actions must be carefully and completely disclosed in timely shareholder reports and SEC filings.	Too many boards of directors allow management to hide subpar corporate performance through misleading corporate communications or endless restructuring.

- Serve as a court of appeal
- Assess its own performance

Though intended as a guide to nonprofit institutions, these responsibilities often apply to the boards of directors for profit-seeking corporations as well.

A. Do Company Boards of Directors Make Good Corporate Watchdogs?

Do company boards of directors make good corporate watchdogs? Perhaps the best way to answer this question is to look at some evidence.

Hiring the right chief executive officer (CEO) is widely viewed as a board of director's most difficult task. However, firing a deficient CEO can be even more important because board negligence can leave a company permanently impaired. Dismissing an underperforming CEO is tough because it constitutes an implicit concession that the board failed to hire an executive that was up to the task. Indeed, researchers have found that turnover among directors after the dismissal of a CEO is higher than after a normal CEO succession. Still, faced with rapidly deteriorating corporate performance, boards sometime have no alternative but to seek new leadership.

For example, in July 2000, database software maker Informix Corp. fired CEO Jean-Yves Dexmier, replacing him with board member Peter Gyenes. The change came little more than a week after Informix surprised investors with weaker-than-expected second quarter operating results. A spokeswoman for the Informix board simply reported that the board had met and decided that "a change was in order." Dexmier had only held the job for little more than a year; Gyenes was CEO at Ardent Software Inc., which Informix had bought out earlier. Rick Thoman, who presided over an unsuccessful restructuring at Xerox Corp., was ousted as CEO in May 2000. After a rocky tenure of only 13 months, Thoman was sacked following earnings disappointments and a sharp fall in the company's stock price. Although the Xerox board is to be applauded for moving quickly to stem a growing management crisis, replacing the CEO is seldom easy and never cheap. Thoman received an annual retirement benefit of $800,000, another $375,000 as a prorated 2000 bonus, and $200,000 in lieu of continued life-insurance benefits.

In a poorly concealed and drawn termination process, Lucent Technologies fired CEO Rich McGinn during late October 2000. After three consecutive quarters of earnings warnings, the board of directors decided that it would be best to find a CEO with "a different set of skills." Although Lucent shareholders were justifiably pleased with McGinn's removal, they were gratified to learn that Lucent's management and business model remain sound. At the time of McGinn's ouster, leading analysts pointed out that Lucent did not have three bad quarters. Rather, it kept having the same bad quarter over and over. The company had simply refused to take its medicine and flush its financial system of bad debts and questionable accounting practices. So long as reported profits and revenues were growing, there was little pressure to reform. However, Lucent's practice of giving generous credit terms to shaky customers was bound to create problems during a downturn in the economy, and it did. McGinn's termination stemmed from the fact that he failed to effectively manage the company's financial resources and product cycle. Worse yet, presented with an erroneous corporate strategy, McGinn failed to quickly and decisively make it right. Faced with similar problems, the heads of Oracle, Corning, and Nortel did the right thing and survived a sharp industry downturn. McGinn did not and got canned.

In many other instances, shareholder-led boardroom revolts have led to dramatically improved performance for trimmed down and refocused corporate giants. After such stunning success in improving management strategy and operating performance, stockholders and stockholder groups have finally gotten the attention they deserve from refocused and energized corporate boards of directors. As shown in Table 10.2, some of the best corporate boards have clearly gotten the message; some of the worst corporate boards still have much to learn.

II. CORPORATE GOVERNANCE MECHANISMS INSIDE THE FIRM

Corporate control mechanisms inside the firm are useful means for helping ameliorate the potential divergence of interests between managers and stockholders. Organization design, including the degree of vertical integration and the horizontal scope of the corporation, is an example of an essential corporate governance mechanism inside the firm. When inputs can be reliably obtained from suppliers operating in perfectly competitive markets, it is seldom attractive to produce such components in-house. Simple market procurement tends to work better. Similarly, when important economies of scale in production are operative, it is preferable to obtain inputs from large specialized suppliers. A high degree of vertical integration only makes sense when input production is within the firm's core competency and supply is erratic or suppliers charge excessive markups. In such instances, vertical integration can result in better coordination of the production process and thereby protect the firm's tangible and intangible investments.

Vertical integration is sometimes seen as a useful means for deterring competitor entry into a company's primary market. Years ago, IBM made a huge strategic error in licensing Intel Corp. to manufacture key components for the personal computer (PC). Intel started out as simply a microprocessor manufacturer supplying the "brains" to manufacturers of PCs and other "smart" electronics. Today, Intel dominates that business with a market share approaching 90% and enjoys sky-high margins and an enviable rate of return on investment. To spur future growth, Intel is now branching out into the production of other PC components such as modems, networking equipment, and so on. Soon, the famous trademark "Intel Inside" may have to be replaced with "Intel Inside *and* Outside." Meanwhile, IBM earns only anemic returns in the PC business. All manufacturers would do well to contemplate IBM's experience with Intel before licensing to others the production of key components.

Another useful means for controlling the flow of corporate resources is provided by internal markets established among divisions to better balance the supply and demand conditions for divisional goods and services. So, too, is incentive compensation perhaps the most obvious corporate governance mechanism inside the firm. In many circumstances, the proper design and implementation of a appropriate incentive pay plan is the most fundamental determinant of whether or not corporate resources will be administered effectively and equitably. Like any effective corporate governance mechanism inside the firm, such arrangements must further the objective of minimizing transaction costs by effectively joining decision authority with the system of performance evaluation and rewards.

TABLE 10.2   Ten of the Best and Ten of the Worst Boards of Directors

10 top boards of directors		10 worst boards of directors	
Company	Details	Company	Details
Campbell Soup	Board ties pay with performance for top management and the board itself.	Archer Daniels Midland	Company has the dubious distinction of consistently failing to heed shareholder interests; nepotism and cronyism run rampant here.
Cisco Systems	A small and nimble board represents shareholder interests effectively in a rapidly changing industry.	Bank of America	Big mergers have created a board that is too big and too unwieldy to effectively look after shareholder interests.
General Electric Co.	Board reads like a business hall of fame; both inside and outside directors hold millions of dollars in GE stock.	Cendant	Board has been too willing to trust management expertise; lack of oversight led to huge merger snafu.
Home Depot	Board members are required to get out and "kick the tires" as they visit the stores.	Dillards Department Stores	Dillard family rules the roost and has stood idly by while the fox ravaged the chicken coop.
IBM	Blue chip board gets high marks for independence and accountability.	Enron Corp.	Board looked the other way while management self-dealing led to largest U.S. bankruptcy.
Intel	A business-savvy and independent board boosts shareholder interests.	Fruit of the Loom	Board stood by while the company slid from prominence to bankruptcy.
Johnson & Johnson	Board members are widely recognized for business expertise; company sets the standard for board independence and accountability.	General Motors	The board has sat idly by while management focuses on financial engineering rather than on designing high-quality cars that customers like to drive.
Lucent Technologies	Strong board has dealt decisively with industry turmoil; nobody here is afraid of making tough decisions.	Tyco International	Board looked the other way while CEO plundered the company.
Merck	Outsiders dominate this action-oriented board.	The Walt Disney Co.	Board reads like a who's who of Hollywood celebrities; too bad so few have the business expertise to ensure shareholder-motivated decision making.
Texas Instruments	Industry smarts, mandated TI shareholding, and independence make for a shareholder-motivated board.	WorldCom	Inside dealing, too cozy relationships with investment bankers, and accounting fraud led to spectacular collapse.

III. FRANCHISE AGREEMENTS

A wide variety of monitoring mechanisms outside the firm work together with mechanisms inside the firm to establish an optimal set of restrictions on firm activity. Interestingly, firms themselves often suggest such restrictions. Commercial bank loan covenants, financial audits by independent auditors, and performance scrutiny by independent security analysts are all common examples of outside monitoring mechanisms agreed to by firms.

Franchise agreements are a prime example of voluntary contractual arrangements outside the firm that can be viewed as corporate governance mechanisms. Franchise agreements give local companies the limited right to offer goods or services developed or advertised on a national basis. Franchise agreements are especially popular in instances where personalized customer service is crucial to success and when the performance of local managers is hard to measure over short periods of time.

For example, McDonald's Corp. operates an extensive franchise system of fast-food restaurants throughout the world. Local franchise owners make a credible commitment to the company by paying for the construction of local restaurants and undergoing extensive training at "Hamburger University," as McDonald's likes to call its Oak Brook, IL, training facility. In turn, McDonald's makes a credible commitment by awarding local franchisees exclusive rights to market McDonald's food in a given trade area. In this way, McDonald's can be assured that local outlets will be run effectively, and local franchisees have the assurance that McDonald's will continue its aggressive advertising and franchise development programs. Both parties hold viable threats over the other. The valuable right to sell McDonald's food products can be taken away from local franchisees if food quality or store cleanliness falters. Local managers could choose to withhold their support for corporate marketing and pricing policies if they deem that insufficient support has been provided for local markets.

In addition to the fast-food business, franchise agreements are common in the automotive repair business. In automotive repair, performance is hard to measure because shoddy repair service shows up only over long periods of time. The quality assurance offered to repair service customers improves when local managers of auto service outlets have an owner's incentive to stand behind work quality. Similarly, franchise agreements give local managers and owners incentive to develop the economic potential of local markets. Like the local customers of gas and service stations, car buyers benefit from a network of new car dealers who promote and stand behind the quality of products produced by Ford, DaimlerChrysler, General motors, and other major automobile manufacturers. Without an owner's incentive to build and maintain customer loyalty, the new car business would suffer from many of the same image problems that have dogged the used-car business for decades.

IV. STRATEGIC ALLIANCES

Strategic alliances are formal operating agreements between independent companies that also can be viewed as corporate governance mechanisms. These combinations are increasingly used to improve foreign marketing. Cereal Partners Worldwide, a strategic alliance between General Mills, Inc. and Nestlè, is used to market breakfast cereal products. Snack Food Ventures Europe, a partnership between General Mills and Pepsico, markets snack foods in Belgium, France, Holland, Spain, Portugal, and Greece. Another proposed alliance between British Airways and American Airlines was abandoned after serious antitrust concerns were raised in Britain and the United States because such an arrangement has the potential to allow the companies to squeeze out competition and dominate the lucrative U.S.–London business and tourist travel market.

Cisco Systems, Inc. is one of the most aggressive proponents of corporate strategic alliances. At Cisco, strategic alliances are designed to help deliver a customer-centric, total solutions approach to solving problems. Cisco and its partners have found strategic alliances to be an effective means for exploiting business opportunities and creating sustainable competitive advantages for its customers. For example, IBM Global Services and Cisco Systems have a strategic alliance to drive development of the global Internet economy by combining their mutual strengths in the rapid deployment of networking applications and joint creation and delivery of end-to-end e-business solutions. The IBM–Cisco strategic alliance is helping businesses successfully migrate to an Internet infrastructure, thereby enabling higher levels of customer satisfaction. In another alliance, Hewlett-Packard and Cisco are collaborating to deliver end-to-end, network-enabled solutions that will allow new and joint customers to optimize and reduce the complexity of their networks.

Strategic alliances also arise when participating companies enjoy complementary capabilities. For example, Oracle Corp. develops, manufactures, and distributes computer software that helps corporations manage and grow their businesses. Oracle software products can be categorized into two broad areas: systems software and Internet business applications software. Systems software is used to deploy applications on the Internet and corporate intranets. It includes database management software that allows users to create, retrieve, and modify the various types of data stored in a computer system. Internet business applications software allows users to access information or use applications through a simple Internet browser. In a collaborative alliance, Oracle and Cisco, a networking equipment supplier, have agreed to develop network-enhanced database technology and enterprise applications. Oracle and Cisco plan to deliver flexible and secure solutions to maximize customer advantage and satisfaction.

Another longtime proponent of strategic alliances is TRW Inc., a global manufacturing and services company focused on supplying advanced technology. The Cleveland, OH-based company uses strategic alliances to acquire technology, create synergy, extend its own manufacturing capabilities, enter new markets, and build existing customer relationships. TRW strategic alliances produce automotive occupant safety systems, chassis systems, electronics, and engine components for spacecraft and space communications, defense systems, telecommunications products, information technology, public safety systems, and other complex integrated systems.

V. OWNERSHIP STRUCTURE AS A CORPORATE GOVERNANCE MECHANISM

Investors have long placed great emphasis on the firm's debt versus equity financing decision. More recently, interest has shifted to the corporate governance implications of the ownership structure of the firm, or the complex array of divergent claims on the value of the firm.

The capital structure of the firm has been traditionally described in terms of the share of total financing obtained from equity investors versus lenders (debt). Today, interest has shifted from capital structure to ownership structure, as measured along a number of important dimensions, including inside equity, institutional equity, widely dispersed outside equity, bank debt, and widely dispersed outside debt. Among these, the percentage of inside equity financing receives the most attention. Inside equity is the share of stock closely held by the firm's CEO, other corporate insiders including top managers, and members of the board of directors. Employees are another important source of inside equity financing, perhaps as part of an employee stock ownership plan (ESOP). The balance of equity financing is obtained from large, single-party, outside shareholders; mutual funds; insurance companies; pension funds; and the general public.

When the share of insider holdings is "large," a similarly substantial self-interest in the ongoing performance of the firm can be presumed. Managers with a significant ownership interest have an obvious incentive to run the firm in a value-maximizing manner. Similarly, when ownership is concentrated among a small group of large and vocal institutional shareholders, called institutional equity, managers often have strong incentives to maximize corporate performance. On the other hand, when the amount of closely held stock held is "small," and equity ownership is instead dispersed among a large number of small individual investors, that top management can sometimes become insulated from the threat of stockholder sanctions following poor operating performance.

To get some direct insight on ownership structure among large firms, Table 10.3 shows insider and institutional stock ownership for a sample of large firms included in the Standard & Poor's (S&P) 500 index. These companies have an average market capitalization of $23.3 billion. The CEO, other members of top management, and members of the board of directors together own an average 5.9% of the corporations they lead. Because insiders at the largest U.S. corporations typically own only a small percentage of the companies they lead, the median amount of inside ownership in the S&P 500 is only 2.8%. In addition to inside ownership, institutions own an average 62.7% of these companies.

TABLE 10.3 Insider and Institutional Stock Ownership among S&P 500 Firms

Company name	Industry	Market capitalization ($ millions)	Insider holdings (%)	Institutional holdings (%)	Insider plus institutional (%)
A. High market capitalization companies					
General Electric	Electrical equipment	285,550	0.5	50.9	51.4
Microsoft Corp.	Computer software & services	261,057	17.3	49.3	66.6
Wal-Mart Stores	Retail store	232,810	38.9	35.3	74.2
Exxon Mobil Corp.	Petroleum (integrated)	228,522	0.5	49.6	50.1
Pfizer Inc.	Drug	199,802	0.5	60.5	61.0
Johnson & Johnson	Medical supplies	162,121	0.2	62.1	62.3
Amer. International Group	Financial services	157,580	7.0	59.6	66.6
Citigroup Inc.	Financial services	155,077	0.5	62.1	62.6
Coca-Cola	Beverage (soft drink)	125,392	8.1	56.2	64.3
International Business Mach.	Computer & peripherals	124,922	0.5	52.0	52.5
Averages		**193,283**	**7.4**	**53.7**	**61.1**
B. High inside ownership companies					
eBay Inc.	Internet	15,656	73.0	47.6	120.6
Brown-Forman 'B'	Beverage (alcoholic)	4,747	62.0	71.6	133.6
Freeport-McMoRan C&G	Metals & mining (div.)	2,063	46.8	67.7	114.5
Carnival Corp.	Recreation	14,078	40.0	48.5	88.5

Wal-Mart Stores	Retail store	232,810	38.9	35.3	74.2
Franklin Resources	Financial services	9,097	35.0	41.6	76.6
Broadcom Corp. 'A'	Telecom. equipment	4,329	35.0	42.2	77.2
AutoZone Inc.	Retail (special lines)	7,492	31.9	86.9	118.8
Cintas Corp.	Industrial services	7,382	30.2	57.8	88.0
Nordstrom Inc.	Retail store	2,688	29.7	49.1	78.8
Averages		**30,034**	**42.3**	**54.8**	**97.1**
C. High institutional ownership companies					
Lockheed Martin	Aerospace/defense	29,123	1.0	98.1	99.1
BJ Services	Oilfield services/equip.	4,344	1.5	96.6	98.1
Big Lots Inc.	Retail store	1,969	1.9	96.4	98.3
Toys 'R' Us	Retail (special lines)	2,825	3.2	93.4	96.6
Ambac Fin'l Group	Financial services	5,907	3.3	93.4	96.7
ACE Limited	Insurance (prop/casualty)	7,091	3.2	93.1	96.3
Health Mgmt. Assoc.	Medical services	4,500	7.4	92.3	99.7
MGIC Investment	Financial services	6,199	1.1	92.4	93.5
Aetna Inc.	Medical services	6,155	1.8	92.3	94.1
SLM Corporation	Financial services	14,341	0.5	91.7	92.2
Averages		**8,245**	**2.5**	**94.0**	**96.5**
Averages for S&P 500 companies		**16,568**	**2.8**	**68.7**	**72.4**
Medians for S&P 500 companies		**7,003**	**5.5**	**67.2**	**70.9**

Data source: The Value Line Investment Survey for Windows, October 2002.

239

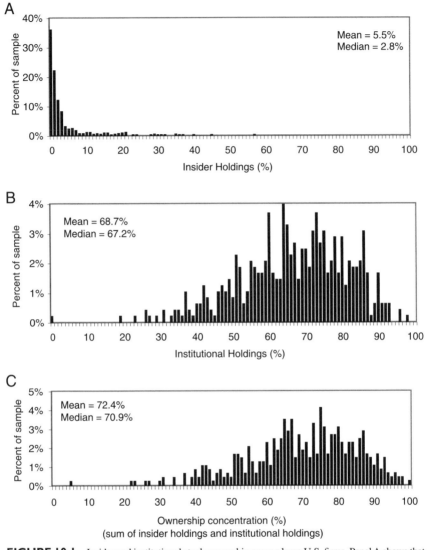

FIGURE 10.1   Insider and institutional stock ownership among large U.S. firms. Panel A shows that the percentage of insider holdings, or common stock held by persons or associated with the company, is strongly skewed toward zero. In panel B, the percentage of institutional holdings is seen as somewhat more evenly distributed than insider holdings, although moderate skewness toward zero is again evident. When the percentage of insider holdings shares and institutional holdings are added together, as in panel C, the distribution of ownership concentration becomes nearly normal. This suggests a substitute-type relationship between each source of ownership concentration.

The median amount of institutional ownership among such firms is 63.4%. Inasmuch as insider holdings tend to be relatively large when institutional holdings are relatively small, and vice versa, the percentage of closely held shares, or insider plus institutional holdings, has a mean of 66.2% and a median of 67.3%. This implies that 32.7% of a typical S&P 500 company's common stock is widely dispersed among the general public.

Notice how the share of insider and institutional share ownership tends to vary according to firm size, even among corporate behemoths. Among true corporate giants such as GE, Exxon, Citigroup, and Pfizer, for example, insiders own little stock in their employer when insider ownership is measured on a percentage basis. For them, insider ownership is much smaller than institutional ownership. Still, insider holdings of roughly 1% at GE, for example, represent an equity commitment of $4.4 billion—more than enough to provide top management with strong incentives to operate efficiently. Thus, even though the percentage of common stock held by insiders is relatively low among corporate giants, the dollar values involved can be more than sufficient to provide necessary incentives for value maximization.

Figure 10.1, panel A depicts the percentage of insider and institutional holdings for the S&P 500. As illustrated in Fig. 10.1, panel A, insider holdings are clearly skewed toward zero. The percentage of institutional holdings is more uniformly distributed.

VI. IS OWNERSHIP STRUCTURE ENDOGENOUS?

Data described in Table 10.3 and in Fig. 10.1 reflect the well-established trend toward replacement of small atomistic shareholders by large institutional investors. Because this trend toward institutional share ownership is relatively recent in the United States, the economic advantages it entails may be relatively unappreciated.

Clearly, the probability that outside investors will discover evidence of managerial inefficiency or malfeasance is increased when institutional ownership is substantial. Many institutional investors are forced to liquidate their holdings in the event of dividend omissions or bankruptcy filings. As a result, institutional investors are especially sensitive to such possibilities. Fiduciary responsibility also forces many institutional investors to tender their shares in the event of an above-market tender offer or takeover bid. At the same time, when institutional share ownership is high, the costs of proxy solicitations are reduced. Thus, managers of firms with high institutional ownership are relatively more susceptible to unfriendly takeover bids. Fiduciary responsibility and the dynamics of ownership concentration have the potential to make institutional stockholders especially effective in the managerial monitoring process.

Insider and institutional stock ownership represent alternative forms of ownership concentration that combine to form an effective method for monitoring managerial decisions. Remember, a relatively high concentration of insider *plus* institutional ownership is descriptive of the modern corporation.

Four general forces affecting corporate ownership structure have been identified, including

- Amenity potential
- Regulatory potential
- Quality control potential
- Ownership control potential

Amenity potential is derived from the ability to influence the type of goods produced. Such benefits can be derived from ownership of mass media and professional sports teams, for example, and explain why such endeavors tend to be tightly controlled by top management. On the other hand, the diffuse ownership structure of regulated utilities can be explained by extensive rate-of-return regulation, or regulatory potential, that limits the capacity of managers to influence firm performance. In the case of firms that produce easily identifiable products subject to economies of scale in production, a relatively diffuse ownership structure can be consistent with shareholder wealth maximization. In the case of firms that produce goods and services with the potential for high quality variation, or quality control potential, a more concentrated ownership structure may be required to give shareholders the amount of control necessary to mollify other suppliers and customers. Finally, the ownership control potential of the firm is the wealth gain achievable through more effective monitoring of managerial performance. For example, heavy advertisers or high-tech firms that depend on hard-to-monitor advertising or R&D activity for their success may require more concentrated ownership structure than would be true of low-tech firms that produce easily monitored goods and services. When the quality of output is hard to measure and production involves inputs with little collateral value, a high degree of ownership concentration gives outside investors, suppliers, and customers the confidence necessary for quality assurance.

In short, ownership structure appears to vary systematically across firm size classes and among industries in ways that are consistent with value maximization. It thus appears relevant to argue that observed differences in corporate ownership structure are an important reflection of underlying economic forces.

VII. FEDERAL LAW ENFORCEMENT ACTIONS AS TOOLS FOR CORPORATE GOVERNANCE

Commercial bank loan covenants, financial audits by independent auditors, and performance scrutiny by independent security analysts are all common examples of outside monitoring mechanisms agreed to by firms. Other outside monitoring mechanisms can be mandatory. Such compulsory mechanisms include the wide variety of federal, state, and local laws and regulations that govern corporate behavior. As Fama and Jensen (1983) and Hirschey and Jones (2001) point out, the potential exploitation of stockholders, bondholders, and other residual claimants by opportunistic decision agents is often reflected in arguments leading to the establishment of broad regulatory initiatives, such as those stemming from establishment of the SEC.

Calculated or inadvertent violations of federal laws have the potential to impose significant costs on shareholders and other residual claimants. The pursuit of illegal short-term strategies can represent a form of self-dealing by managers who seek to reap short-term personal gain while escaping detection. Actual or suspected violations of federal laws have the potential to result in significant costs measured in terms of investigation expenditures, litigation expenses, fines and seizures, and lost reputational capital for the firm—all of which can measurably reduce future cash flows and current market values. Within this context, federal laws can be seen as part of the institutional framework that contributes to the range of control mechanisms that originate inside and outside the firm to comprise an effective system of corporate governance. Because short-term hit and run managers may possess incentives to cut legal and ethical corners, the design and administration of federal laws can be seen as a means of outside monitoring designed to ensure a coincidence of managerial incentives, stockholder interests, and broader social objectives.

Given the high-profile nature of recent federal law enforcement initiatives, it is worth considering the impact of federal law enforcement actions as important elements in the institutional framework of corporate governance. From this context, it becomes interesting to consider the stock market reaction to the law enforcement activities of three federal agencies: the Department of Justice (DOJ), the Federal Trade Commission (FTC), and the SEC. Evidence of stock market wealth effects is presented for a variety of enforcement activities, including informal investigations, formal investigations, lawsuits, and settlements. Evidence of this nature is of interest because it documents the extent to which announcements regarding the enforcement activity of the executive branch and federal agencies represent a source of important new information for capital markets. Such evidence is also important because it demonstrates the role of actual or threatened legal action in corporate governance and as a tool for competition policy in dynamic markets.

Economic effects of federal law enforcement actions on the value of the firm can be expected to differ across firms according to the relative importance of intangible factors in firm valuation. If one thinks of firm value as derived from assets in place and growth opportunities stemming from R&D, advertising, and other such expenditures, high-tech firms may be especially susceptible to federal law enforcement actions when adverse reputational and growth-option consequences are large.

VIII. ADMINISTRATION OF FEDERAL LAWS AND REGULATIONS

Federal and state statutes govern a broad range of corporate activities, including, for example, the registration, offering, and sale of securities. The design and administration of these statutes play a key role in determining the institutional framework and competitive environment of securities markets. In terms of administration, formidable roles are played by three federal bodies: the DOJ, FTC, and SEC.

Chief purposes of the DOJ, an executive department headed by the attorney general, are to enforce federal laws, to furnish legal counsel in federal cases, and to construe the laws under which other departments act. The FTC is an independent agency created by Congress in 1914 and given broad powers to promote free and fair competition in interstate commerce through the prevention of trade restraints such as price fixing, false advertising, boycotts, illegal combinations of competitors, and other unfair methods of competition. The FTC is responsible for much of the substantive regulation in the legal environment of business, including antitrust where duties are shared with the DOJ.

Major federal acts administered by the SEC include the Securities Act of 1933, the Securities Exchange Act of 1934, the Public Utility Holding Act of 1935, the Trust Indenture Act of 1939, the Investment Adviser's Act of 1940, and the Investment Company Act of 1940. The Securities Act of 1933 provides for the registration of securities which are to be sold to the public and for complete information as to the issuer and the stock offering. The Securities Exchange Act of 1934 created the SEC, an independent administrative agency with five commissioners, and governs the operation of stock exchanges and over-the-counter trading and the publication of information concerning stocks listed on these exchanges. The SEC has broad rule-making authority. Formal rules carry the force of law; informal communications clarify and interpret current enforcement strategies and viewpoints (see Butler, 1987).

In practice, DOJ, FTC and SEC staff investigations are often informal at first and terminated if insufficient evidence exists to charge the target of the investigation with a violation of federal laws. Alternatively, staff investigations may be terminated if investigation targets agree to stop engaging in the allegedly unfair or deceptive practice. Many, if not most, informal investigations can be settled with limited fanfare. For example, if the FTC determines that there is adequate basis for bringing a formal complaint, defendants can settle their dispute by agreeing to the terms of a consent decree. Consent decrees often contain the terms of the settlement, including redress for injured consumers, payment of penalties, and prohibition of certain practices. If the defendant and the FTC cannot agree on a settlement, then the matter goes to trial before an administrative law judge who may dismiss the complaint or issue a cease and desist order. In some instances, the FTC may file a lawsuit in federal district court, perhaps with the support of the DOJ and/or SEC, to seek an injunction against some disapproved of practice while it is being challenged in FTC proceedings (see Butler, 1987).

IX. VALUATION EFFECTS OF ENFORCEMENT ACTIONS

In a fully informed stock market, news regarding the enforcement of federal laws against publicly traded firms would have no effect on target firm stock prices. A "rational expectation's hypothesis" predicts that investors would be unaffected by announcements concerning the enforcement actions of federal agencies because current stock prices accurately reflect discounted future cash flows based upon all relevant information. An absence of announcement effects tied to federal law enforcement actions would suggest that the market is fully aware of illegal activity, the probability of getting caught, and the potential sanctions tied to detection and conviction. Future cash flows lost following federal law enforcement actions can include the costs of sacrificing illegal advantages over competitors, investigation expenditures, litigation expenses, and lost reputational capital. An absence of abnormal returns tied to federal law enforcement actions does not mean that there is no cost to being caught; it simply implies that the market correctly anticipates the magnitude and probability of such costs. Here it is important to recognize that the term "caught" does not necessarily imply guilt as well. Under the rational expectation's hypothesis, market participants also know the probability of innocent firms being investigated or sued.

Positive abnormal returns associated with public announcements regarding the enforcement actions of federal agencies could lead to different conclusions regarding market efficiency and enforcement efficacy. Positive abnormal returns could suggest that news regarding the enforcement process represents favorable new information for investors. Positive abnormal returns could simply represent "good news" for target firms in that enforcement sanctions are more narrow than generally expected. Alternatively, prior to public announcements surrounding enforcement activity, government agencies might possess information that is relevant to the estimation of future cash flows for target firms. While such good information is not reflected in the pre-enforcement activity announcement price, prices adjust favorably in the post-announcement period.

Negative abnormal returns tied to announcements concerning federal law enforcement actions would also suggest that news regarding the enforcement process represents a source of new information for investors. That is, prior to *The Wall Street Journal* announcements, federal agencies have damaging information that is relevant to a target firm's future cash flows, but is not reflected in its pre-enforcement announcement price. Why such news is "bad" is unclear. Announcements in *The Wall Street Journal* regarding enforcement activities might reveal information about illegal behavior not previously known by the market. On the other hand, "guilty" firms whom the market did not believe would be caught may now be the recognized target of costly enforcement sanctions. Alternatively, "innocent" firms who have not engaged in any illegal behavior are now subject to enforcement activities. In both instances, the direct and indirect costs tied to federal law enforcement actions could be expected to lead to a negative stock market response during the announcement period.

X. PREVIOUS STUDIES

A few prior studies have been conducted to test limited aspects of the stock market reaction to enforcement activity of the executive branch and federal agencies. However, none of these studies are as comprehensive as the one reported on here, nor do they address the role of federal regulatory agencies in monitoring managerial behavior (see Hirschey and Jones, 2001).

For example, in an early study, Garbade, Silber, and White (1982) investigated the possibility of abnormal returns for a sample of 34 firms resulting from antitrust lawsuits filed by the FTC or DOJ. Garbade, Silber, and White (1982) also conducted a cross-sectional analysis comparing the magnitude of abnormal returns with the fraction of the firm's sales revenue originating under the area of attack, the financial position of the firm, and a dummy variable for pre- or postdating of a landmark case in the acceptance of treble damages for antitrust violations. Garbade, Silber, and White (1982) found a statistically significant drop of -5.87% (t-statistic $= -7.71$) in the value of the stock of these companies within four trading days (0,+3) after the filing of a DOJ or FTC suit. After day (4), Garbade, Silber, and White (1982) found no mean abnormal returns less than zero. In terms of cross-sectional results, Garbade, Silber, and White (1982) found that the magnitude of the share-price response tied to DOJ and FTC lawsuit announcements is related to variables that indicate the likely effects of such suits on future earnings.

Feroz, Park, and Pastena (1991) consider the stock market response to the disclosure of accounting violations and subsequent SEC enforcement actions. These authors focus on stock-price effects associated with news of the alleged reporting violation, associated SEC investigation, and resulting settlement. They also offer a cross-sectional analysis of the relationship between the magnitude of abnormal returns and the income effect of the disputed accounting convention, the type of accounting ledger item in question, and the possibility that such a reporting error is fraud related. Feroz, Park, and Pastena (1991) found that reports of disclosure violations had a statistically significant average two-day $(-1,0)$ abnormal return of -12.9% (t-statistic $= -3.75$) for 58 firms.[2] Even for a subsample of 20 firms that had previously disclosed the effect of some disputed accounting on earnings, the subsequent announcement of an SEC investigation led to a statistically significant two-day abnormal return of -6.0% (t-statistic $= -2.38$). This means that the market reacts negatively to announcements of an SEC investigation, even when there is prior specific knowledge of the accounting errors

---

[2]For 54 of the 58 firms in the Feroz, Park, and Pastena (1991) sample, day (0) is the announcement date in *The Wall Street Journal*, or in a publication followed in the *Funk and Scott's Index*. In the other four instances, day (0) is the registrant's press release disclosure date.

involved. Such incremental effects of SEC investigation announcements on share-holder wealth may stem from the negative publicity generated and the possibility of third-party lawsuits. At a minimum, Feroz, Park, and Pastena (1991) argue that the ability of SEC investigation announcements to affect the share prices of target firms suggests that the agency possesses a potent sanction that gives managers a market-based incentive to avoid investigation. Interestingly, Feroz, Park, and Pastena (1991) report no significant abnormal returns tied to the announcement of settlements of SEC investigations. Apparently, the market discounts such favorable news well in advance of the formal announcement.

And finally, other recent studies of interest include Bittlingmayer (1993) and Bhagat, Brickley, and Coles (1994). Bittlingmayer argues that increased govern-ment antitrust enforcement is related to declines in the broad market indexes. Moreover, Bittlingmayer provides evidence of abnormally negative monthly returns for the common stock of 11 firms sued by the federal government between January 1904 and July 1914. For these 11 firms, negative abnormal returns of −3.47% (*t*-statistic = −11.47) exist over the 2-year period surrounding the month in which such lawsuits are filed. Bittlingmayer argues that the existence of negative abnormal returns prior to filing dates can be explained by the fact that government antitrust filings are anticipated over a period of several months, on average, and are typically preceded by costly investigations. Bhagat, Brickley, and Coles (1994) conducted an analysis of the stock market reaction to interfirm litigation. Event study results show that the combined wealth effect for matched pairs of plaintiffs and defendants is a negative and statistically significant −1.04% (*z*-statistic = −3.56). Defendants see a significant drop in their stock price of −0.92% (*z*-statistic = −4.18); the effects on plaintiff stock prices are a more muted and statistically insignificant −0.18% (*z*-statistic = −0.48). Importantly, plaintiffs do not gain by the same amount as defendants lose. Bhagat, Brickley, and Coles (1994) concluded that bargaining among firm claimants sometimes leads to inefficient outcomes because of the costs of increased financial distress imposed on defendants. The Bhagat, Brickley, and Coles (1994) study is of inter-est here because it represents the most comprehensive study of the wealth effects of private litigation. Their study creates a structure for thinking about how the cost and benefits of private litigation are distributed. The intent of this study is to create a similar foundation for the analysis of litigation tied to the enforcement actions of public agencies.

XI. DATA

Following Hirschey and Jones (2001), this study of enforcement actions against firms is restricted to those taken by the DOJ, FTC, and SEC during the 1992–95 4-year period. Event dates for enforcement action announcements are identified from *The Wall Street Journal Index* online (*WSJI*). The *WSJI* is an attractive source for event-date information because it offers a precise indication of when the stock market first received relevant news regarding specific law enforcement actions. It is extremely difficult to identify when the market receives details regarding investigations, suit filings, and settlements when they are reported in original sources such as SEC filings or official court documents. Following Feroz, Park, and Pastena (1991), we typically identify event day (0) as the announcement date in *The Wall Street Journal*. In 23 of 163 instances, *The Wall Street Journal* announcement specifically indicated that a company press release had been made on the prior day. In these 23 cases, the company's press release disclosure date was identified as event day (0).

Searches were conducted using the key words "department of justice" *or* "SEC" *or* "FTC" *and* "investigation" *or* "suit" *or* "criminal." To be included in the sample, the common stock of each firm against which enforcement action was taken must be listed on either the New York Stock Exchange (NYSE), the American Stock Exchange (AMEX), or the Nasdaq and included on the *Center for Research for Security Prices* (CRSP) daily stock returns file for six months prior to the enforcement action announcement. Firms also need to be continuously listed over the estimation and event periods to be included. This method of sample selection permits the collection of a broad and public base of evidence concerning the stock-price reaction associated with the enforcement of federal laws by the DOJ, FTC, and SEC.

A typical example of an informal investigation announcement is provided in the case of securities dealer Merrill Lynch & Co., where

> Sources say that the SEC and the securities regulators of Florida, Virginia and New Mexico are looking into the sales practices of Merrill Lynch & Co in the 1980s with regard to partnerships.... (*The Wall Street Journal*, January 27, 1994, C1)

Sometimes, announcements of federal law enforcement actions involve a number of companies. A formal investigation announcement involving Goodyear Tire & Rubber Co., among others, is a common illustration

> The Justice Department said on August 23, 1995 that it is investigating potential price-fixing among American tire makers. Several tire companies, including Goodyear Tire & Rubber Co, Bridgestone/Firestone Inc., Michelin North America, Dunlop Tire Corp. and Cooper Tire & Rubber Co, admitted that they had submitted documents in response to a Justice Department subpoena.... (*The Wall Street Journal*, August 24, 1995, A3)

A standard suit filing announcement involving two companies, here software makers Microsoft Corp. and Intuit Inc., is

> The Justice Department filed an antitrust suit to block Microsoft Corp.'s $2.1 billion acquisition of Intuit Inc., arguing that the acquisition would decrease competition and innovation in the market for personal-finance software.... (*The Wall Street Journal*, April 28, 1995, A3)

And finally, an ordinary settlement announcement, this in the case of the insurer Presidential Life Corp., is

> As part of a settlement with the SEC, Presidential Life Corp., principally an issuer of annuity contracts through its Presidential Life Insurance Co. unit, will restate its financial

results for several years to reflect a markdown of some junk securities in its portfolio....
(*The Wall Street Journal*, March 2, 1993, B4)

Complete data could be obtained on a sample of $n = 13$ informal investigations, $n = 97$ formal investigations, $n = 28$ lawsuit filings, and $n = 24$ settlements. Information effects are measured and reported for all these $n = 162$ law enforcement actions.[3]

XII. ESTIMATION METHOD

The event-study methodology of James (1987) is used to obtain estimates of abnormal stock returns surrounding announcements in *The Wall Street Journal* concerning various enforcement actions taken by the DOJ, FTC, and SEC. The ordinary least squares (OLS) market model is employed to calculate the abnormal return or prediction error for the common stock of firm j on day t, such that

$$PE_{jt} = R_{jt} - (\alpha + \beta_j R_{int}), \qquad (10.1)$$

where R_{jt} = rate of return on the common stock of the jth firm on day t, R_{mt} = rate of return of the CRSP value-weighted market index over period t, α_j = OLS estimate of the intercept, and β_j = OLS estimate of the slope parameter that measures the sensitivity of R_{jt} to the market index.

A 180-day estimation period is used that begins 225 trading days before the event date, $t = -225$, and ends 46 trading days before the event date, $t = -46$. The event date, $t = 0$, is typically assumed to be *The Wall Street Journal* announcement date, but may be the prior day if an earlier announcement on that day is specifically noted in *The Wall Street Journal* article. Daily prediction errors are averaged over the sample of n firms yielding the average prediction errors (average abnormal returns):

$$APE_t = \frac{\sum_{j=1}^{n} PE_{jt}}{n}. \qquad (10.2)$$

$$CAPE_{T_1 T_2} = \frac{\sum_{j=1}^{n} \sum_{t=T_1}^{T_2} PE_{jt}}{n}. \qquad (10.3)$$

[3]A few additional miscellaneous announcements of enforcement activities of the DOJ, FTC, and SEC were also noted, including nine Civil Investigative Demands (CIDs), four simultaneous announcements of a suit being filed and settled, three Wells Submissions, five administrative actions, three convictions and/or guilty pleas, and eight announcements of investigations being ended. A detailed analysis revealed no statistically significant valuation effects of each of these types of announcements. Estimation results are available on request.

Cumulative average prediction errors (CAPEs) (cumulative average abnormal returns) are calculated over event-interval periods (T_1,T_2) of 2 days [(−1,0) and (0,+1)], 3 days [(−1,+1) and (0,+2)], and 4 days [(−1,+2) and (0,+3)]. A t-test is applied to examine the hypothesis that the $CAPE_{T_1 T_2}$ are not significantly different from zero. Under the null hypothesis, each PE_{jt} has a mean zero and constant variance equal to the portfolio variance of the APE_t. The estimated standard deviation of the APE_t is

$$S_{APE} = \sqrt{\frac{\sum_{t=-225}^{-46}(APE_t - \overline{APE})^2}{D_j - 2}}.$$ (10.4)

APE is the mean of the average prediction errors, where this mean is defined as

$$\overline{APE} = \frac{\sum_{t=-225}^{-46} APE_t}{D_j},$$ (10.5)

and D_j equals the number of nonmissing trading days in the estimation period. The portfolio test-statistic for the average error on any day is

$$t = \frac{APE_t}{S_{APE}}.$$ (10.6)

Assuming time-series independence, the test-statistic for each $CAPE_{T_1 T_2}$ is

$$t = \frac{CAPE_t}{S_{APE}\sqrt{T_2 - T_1 + 1}}.$$ (10.7)

Since the test-statistic standard deviation is calculated using the time series of portfolio returns, the potential problem of cross-sectional correlation among individual security returns is avoided.

Because there are only a small number of observations for certain event types, median CAPEs and nonparametric statistics for each announcement type are also reported. Following Corrado (1989), a z-statistic is developed to test whether median CAPEs are different from zero. Using the daily prediction errors for firm j in both the 180-day estimation period (day $t = -225$ to $t = -46$) and the 5-day event period (day $t = -1$ to $t = +3$), a rank from 1 to 185 is assigned to each daily prediction error. Accordingly, the rank for firm j's prediction error on day t, K_{jt}, is given by

$$K_{jt} = rank(PE_{jt}).$$ (10.8)

If PE_{ji} is greater than or equal to PE_{ji}, then K_{ji} is greater than or equal to K_{ji}. The smallest prediction error for firm j will have rank $K_{ji} = 1$. The next smallest prediction error for firm j will have rank $K_{ji} = 2$, and so on; the largest prediction error will have rank $K_{ji} = 185$.

The median rank for each firm j is given by

$$\overline{K} = \frac{185+1}{2} = 93. \tag{10.9}$$

The average rank across all firms at time t is

$$\overline{K}_t = \frac{1}{n} \sum_{j=1}^{n} K_{jt}. \tag{10.10}$$

The average rank across all firms for the event window T_1 to T_2 is

$$\overline{K_{T_1,T_2}} = \frac{1}{T_2 - T_1 + 1} \sum_{t=T_1}^{T_2} \overline{K}_t. \tag{10.11}$$

The rank z-statistic for the event window T_1 to T_2 is

$$z = (T_2 - T_1 + 1)^{1/2} \left\{ \frac{\overline{K_{T_1,T_2}} - 93}{\left[\frac{1}{185} \sum_{t=1}^{185} (\overline{K}_t - 93)^2 \right]^{1/2}} \right\}. \tag{10.12}$$

XIII. ANNOUNCEMENT EFFECTS BY TYPE OF ENFORCEMENT ACTIVITY

Table 10.4 summarizes market-model CAPEs for all firms subject to federal law enforcement announcements in *The Wall Street Journal* during the 4-year 1992–95 period. CAPEs are categorized based upon the nature of enforcement activity by the DOJ, FTC, and SEC, including informal investigations, formal investigations, lawsuits filed, and settlements. Of primary interest is the wealth effect realized over the $(-1,0)$ event period. However, to test for the robustness of $(-1,0)$ results, CAPEs are reported for five additional event-period windows, including $(-1,+1)$, $(-1,+2)$, $(0,+1)$, $(0,+2)$, and $(0,+3)$.[4]

On average, informal investigations have statistically significant negative wealth effects over the $(-1,0)$ event window of -5.96% ($t = -4.96$). Negative wealth effects appear to be fairly robust for informal investigations in that statistically significant results, not shown in Table 10.4, are also found over the $(-1,+1)$ and $(-1,+2)$ event periods. Nonparametric results provide corroborating evidence in that statistically significant negative wealth effects of -0.77% (z-statistic = -1.41) are noted over the $(-1,+2)$ event period. Paradoxically, nonparametric results suggest weak but statistically significant positive wealth effects of informal

---

[4]Parametric results for CAPEs were also estimated using the market model and an equally weighted index, the market-adjusted return model and a value-weighted index, the market-adjusted return model and an equally weighted index, the standardized abnormal return market model and an equally weighted index, and the standardized abnormal return market model and a value-weighted index. These estimation results are substantially the same and available on request.

TABLE 10.4 Cumulative Average Prediction Errors (CAPEs) for Enforcement Acitivities of the DOJ, FTC, and SEC

	Event-period window	CAPEs (%)	t-statistic	Event-period window	Median CAPEs (%)	z-statistic
A. Informal investigations ($n = 13$)						
	(−1,0)	−5.96	−4.96[a]	(−1,0)	−0.02	−0.30
	(−1,+1)	−4.47	−3.04[a]	(−1,+1)	0.00	−0.30
	(−1,+2)	−4.25	−2.50[a]	(−1,+2)	−0.01	−1.41[b]
	(0,+1)	−0.74	−0.62	(0,+1)	0.00	1.37[b]
	(0,+2)	−0.52	−0.36	(0,+2)	0.00	−0.30
	(0,+3)	0.31	0.19	(0,+3)	0.01	1.37[b]
B. Formal investigations ($n = 97$)						
	(−1,0)	−2.34	−5.94[a]	(−1,0)	−0.01	−3.13[a]
	(−1,+1)	−2.06	−4.28[a]	(−1,+1)	−0.02	−3.13[a]
	(−1,+2)	−2.24	−4.01[a]	(−1,+2)	−0.02	−2.93[a]
	(0,+1)	−1.99	−5.04[a]	(0,+1)	−0.01	−2.93[a]
	(0,+2)	−2.16	−4.47[a]	(0,+2)	−0.02	−2.12[c]
	(0,+3)	−2.19	−3.93[a]	(0,+3)	−0.01	−2.32[c]
C. Suits filed ($n = 28$)						
	(−1,0)	−1.19	−1.58[b]	(−1,0)	−0.01	−0.53
	(−1,+1)	−1.43	−1.55[b]	(−1,+1)	−0.01	−1.67[c]
	(−1,+2)	−1.01	−0.95	(−1,+2)	−0.01	−0.91
	(0,+1)	−1.41	−1.88[c]	(0,+1)	−0.01	−2.42[a]
	(0,+2)	−0.99	−1.07	(0,+2)	−0.01	−0.91
	(0,+3)	−0.85	−0.80	(0,+3)	−0.01	0.22
D. Settlements ($n = 24$)						
	(−1,0)	1.56	1.14	(−1,0)	0.00	−0.29
	(−1,+1)	1.63	0.97	(−1,+1)	0.01	1.77[c]
	(−1,+2)	1.10	0.57	(−1,+2)	0.00	0.54
	(0,+1)	−0.23	−0.17	(0,+1)	0.00	0.95
	(0,+2)	−0.76	−0.45	(0,+2)	−0.01	−0.70
	(0,+3)	−1.03	−0.53	(0,+3)	−0.01	−1.11

Note: Market-model cumulative average prediction errors (CAPEs), t-statistics, and z-statistics are shown for a variety of event-period windows for each type of enforcement activity. Parametric and nonparametric statistics are shown, as are the size and statistical significance of mean (average) and median differences in announcement effects for various enforcement activities. The statistical significance of mean differences are evaluated using a t-test; median differences are evaluated using a z-test.
[a]Significant at the 1% level (one-tail test).
[b]Significant at the 10% level (one-tail test).
[c]Significant at the 5% level (one-tail test).

investigations of 0.20% (z-statistic = 1.37) over the (0,+1) event period and 1.05% (z-statistic = 1.37) over the (0,+3) event period.

Formal investigations have statistically significant average wealth effects of −2.34% ($t = −5.94$) over the (−1,0) event window. Nonparametric results for wealth effects tied to formal investigation announcements are similarly significant at −1.17% (z-statistic = −3.13) over the (−1,0) event window. Using both parametric and nonparametric methods, announcements of formal investigations exhibit negative wealth effects that are robust; significant negative wealth impacts are tied to formal investigation announcements for all six event-period windows.

Sample firms also realize smaller but still statistically significant average wealth effects of -1.19% ($t = -1.58$) on the announcement of a federal lawsuit filing over the $(-1,0)$ event period. Similarly significant average wealth effects of -1.43% ($t = -1.55$) are noted over the $(-1,+1)$ event period and -1.41% ($t = -1.88$) are noted over the $(0,+1)$ event period. The robustness of such effects is demonstrated by statistically significant nonparametric wealth influences. Nonparametric results for wealth effects tied to suit filing announcements are similarly significant at -0.98% (z-statistic $= -1.67$) over the $(-1,+1)$ event window and -1.11% (z-statistic $= -2.42$) over the $(0,+1)$ event window.

And finally, using parametric and nonparametric methods, there is scant evidence that firms who announce settlement agreements with the DOJ, FTC, or SEC realize statistically significant wealth effects. The lone exception to this rule is found in median wealth effects of 0.74% ($z = 1.77$) over the $(-1,+1)$ event period.

What results reported in Table 10.4 tell about the efficacy of federal law enforcement actions is ambiguous. In the case of informal investigations, formal investigations, and lawsuits, negative abnormal returns suggest that the market regards such information as "bad news" for target firms. However, why such news is bad is unclear. There are at least three broad explanations for a negative response. First, announcements in *The Wall Street Journal* regarding enforcement activities might simply reveal information about illegal behavior not previously known by the market. Such information is bad because it represents news that the target cash flows will now be lower than expected. Second, firms whom the market did not believe would be caught are now the target of enforcement activity. That is, these results do not rule out the possibility that the market does have knowledge of illegal activities. Rather, these results may only indicate that the market is unable to precisely predict the probability of getting caught. And third, as suggested by Feroz, Park, and Pastena (1991), effects of federal law enforcement actions on shareholder wealth may stem from the negative publicity generated and the possibility of third-party lawsuits.

Results reported in Table 10.4 also suggest that reports in *The Wall Street Journal* of a settlement agreement may represent good news concerning settlement negotiations not previously known to the market. Target firm cash flows may now be higher and more consistent than previously anticipated because the investigatory process was shorter than expected. Alternatively, following such announcements the market may be better informed regarding the (limited) scope of illegal activity by the target firm. Positive stock-price effects could also result if investors conclude that target firms are able to shield some aspect of their illegal advantage from enforcement agencies. Finally, positive abnormal returns could result if the market overestimates the probability or size of damage awards, fines, or other monetary penalties.[5]

---

[5]An exploratory cross-sectional regression analysis was also conducted to learn if any consistent relationship was present between event-period CAPEs and the ownership structure of the firm, various firm size measures, or indicators of firm performance and leverage. No such substantive linkages were discovered.

XIV. ANNOUNCEMENT EFFECTS BY VIOLATION CATEGORY

Table 10.5 summarizes market-model CAPE information by the actual or suspected violation category to provide additional perspective on $(-1,0)$ event-period wealth effects tied to the enforcement activities of the DOJ, FTC, and SEC. Again, to test for robustness, both parametric and nonparametric results are reported.

Informal investigations delve into a wide variety of actual or suspected violations. The most common among these are three suspected accounting reporting violations and three inside trading investigations. Based upon statistically significant parametric results, both of these common types of informal investigations give rise to meaningfully negative average wealth effects over the $(-1,0)$ event window. In the case of suspected accounting reporting violations, event-period average wealth effects of a whopping -18.07% $(t = -6.39)$ are noted. Event-period average wealth effects of -9.25% $(t = -2.31)$ are also large and statistically significant in the case of suspected inside trading activity. Less common informal investigation announcements tied to franchising practices and violations of consent decrees also appear to engender statistically significant negative wealth effects, according to parametric findings. However, with the exception of suspected accounting reporting violations, where statistically significant event-period median wealth effects of -19.40% $(z = -1.76)$ are noted, informal investigations do not generate median valuation effects that are statistically significant using nonparametric methods. Taken as a whole, these findings imply that the negative wealth effects tied to informal investigations are both somewhat smaller and less robust than the negative wealth effects associated with announcements concerning the launch of formal investigations. The lone exception to this rule may be informal investigations into suspected accounting reporting violations, where both parametric and nonparametric results suggest consistently large and statistically significant negative wealth effects.

As seen in Table 10.4, consistently large negative and statistically significant negative wealth effects are associated with announcements concerning the launch of formal investigations by the DOJ, FTC, and SEC. As shown in Table 10.5, the most common types of formal investigations surround suspected accounting reporting violations (12), general restraints of trade (14), inside trading (25), mergers and acquisitions (6), and price fixing (20). Of these five violation categories, accounting reporting violations, mergers and acquisitions, and price fixing result in negative and statistically significant average wealth effects over the $(-1,0)$ event window. In the case of accounting reporting violations, average wealth effects are -10.33% $(t = -5.72)$, and for mergers and acquisitions, average wealth effects are -2.05% $(t = -2.31)$. For price fixing, statistically significant average wealth effects of -1.26% $(t = -1.86)$ are noted. Formal investigation announcements tied to alleged inside trading result in a positive and statistically significant wealth effect of 2.84% $(t = 3.24)$. This anomalous result contrasts with a negative and statistically significant median reaction to investigations of inside trading of -1.12% $(z = -1.79)$. The 14 announcements of formal investigations initiated

TABLE 10.5 Cumulative Average Prediction Errors (CAPEs) by Actual or Suspected Violation Category

Violation category	Sample size	CAPEs (%)	t-statistic	Median CAPEs (%)	z-statistic
A. Informal investigations ($n = 13$)					
Accounting reporting violations	3	−18.07	−6.39[a]	−19.40	−1.76[b]
Franchising practices	1	−6.30	−1.51[c]	−6.30	−1.24
Fraudulent sales practices	1	3.66	2.03[b]	3.66	1.02
Illegal foreign business practice	1	1.25	0.68	1.25	1.02
Illegal trading	1	1.64	0.68	1.64	1.00
Illegal use of company funds	1	0.58	0.24	0.58	0.90
Insider trading	3	−9.25	−2.31[b]	−14.09	−0.41
Mergers and acquisitions	1	−1.77	−0.57	−1.77	−1.01
Violation of consent decree	1	5.44	1.76[b]	5.44	0.98
B. Formal investigations ($n = 97$)					
Accounting reporting violations	12	−10.33	−5.72[a]	−5.30	−2.61[a]
Attempting to monopolize	1	−0.97	−0.52	−0.97	−0.95
Bid rigging	1	−2.09	−1.05	−2.09	−0.90
Boycotts	3	1.21	0.79	1.76	0.64
Civil rights violations	1	−2.53	−1.25	−2.53	−1.01
Failure to report risk	1	−3.02	−1.81[b]	−3.02	−1.00
Fraudulent sales practices	2	−3.93	−2.65[a]	−3.93	−1.38[c]
General restraints of trade	14	0.04	0.06	0.82	0.74
Illegal foreign business practice	1	1.49	0.62	1.49	0.99
Illegal trading	4	−28.47	−8.53[a]	−26.71	−1.89[b]
Illegal use of company funds	2	−2.16	−0.37	−2.16	0.07
Insider trading	25	2.84	3.24[a]	−1.12	−1.79[b]
Mergers and acquisitions	6	−2.05	−2.31[b]	−2.14	−1.49[c]
Price fixing	20	−1.26	−1.86[b]	−1.03	−1.08
Questions regarding research results	2	−5.03	−1.75[b]	−5.03	−1.35[c]
Territorial divisions	1	1.02	0.45	1.02	1.13
Tying	1	0.95	0.43	0.95	1.01
C. Suits filed ($n = 28$)					
Environmental violations	1	−4.57	−1.32[c]	−4.57	−0.81
Failure to report risk	1	0.15	0.09	0.15	1.00
False advertising	2	6.23	1.49[c]	6.23	1.24
Filing false claims with government	1	−6.04	−0.72	−6.04	−0.58
Fraudulent sales practices	1	−5.34	−1.86[b]	−5.34	−0.97
Illegal trading	1	−3.30	−1.12	−3.30	−1.03
Insider trading	1	0.84	0.20	0.84	1.03
Mergers and acquisitions	9	−1.20	−1.09	0.61	0.40
Noncompliance with government production standards	1	−2.97	−2.84[a]	−2.97	−0.90

(continues)

TABLE 10.5 (*continued*)

Violation category	Sample size	CAPEs (%)	*t*-statistic	Median CAPEs	*z*-statistic
Obstructing justice	1	−2.76	−1.34[c]	−2.76	−1.14
Overcharging on government contracts	2	3.34	3.10[a]	3.34	0.07
Price fixing	6	−1.98	−1.34[c]	−1.96	−0.68
Questions regarding research results	1	−5.92	−1.50[c]	−5.92	−0.89
D. Settlements (*n* = 24)					
Accounting reporting violations	7	4.95	1.86[b]	1.35	0.78
Aiding fraudulent companies	1	5.13	1.24	5.13	1.12
Fraudulent sales practices	1	−2.22	−0.87	−2.22	−1.02
General restraints of trade	2	−1.15	−0.63	−1.15	−1.36[c]
Illegal foreign business practice	1	−2.15	−1.66[b]	−2.15	−0.95
Illegal trading	3	7.10	1.34[c]	1.80	0.91
Mergers and acquisitions	1	0.77	0.39	0.77	1.05
Overcharging on government contracts	5	−1.71	−1.74[b]	−1.10	−0.29
Poor certificate destruction	1	−0.49	−0.15	−0.49	−0.91
Unknown	1	−5.52	−0.91	−5.52	−0.91
Wire and mail fraud	1	−3.15	−0.23	−3.15	−0.72

Note: Market-model cumulative average prediction errors (CAPEs), *t*-statistics, and *z*-statistics are shown for the (−1,0) event-period window for each type of actual or suspected violation category. Parametric and nonparametric statistics are shown, as are the size and statistical significance of mean (average) and median differences in announcement effects for various enforcement activities. The statistical significance of mean differences are evaluated using a *t*-test over the 180-day estimation period; median differences are evaluated using a *z*-test.
[a]Significant at the 1% level (one-tail test).
[b]Significant at the 5% level (one-tail test).
[c]Significant at the 10% level (one-tail test).

to look into accusations of general restraints of trade result in no significant wealth effects. Several less common formal investigations, including failure to report risk, fraudulent sales practices, illegal trading, and questions regarding research results, have statistically significant negative wealth effects. With the exception of the nonparametric results for inside trading, nonparametric statistics for formal investigation announcements are consistent with and corroborate parametric results.

Table 10.4 illustrates that average wealth effects associated with announcements concerning the filing of lawsuits are generally negative, but only weakly significant on a statistical basis. From Table 10.5, it seems clear that such negative influences stem from lawsuit announcements concerning alleged environmental violations (−4.57%, *t* = −1.32), fraudulent sales practices (−5.34%, *t* = −1.86), non-compliance with government production standards (−2.97%, *t* = −2.84), obstruction of justice (−2.76%, *t* = −1.34), price fixing (-1.98%, $t = -1.34$), and questions regarding research results (-5.92%, $t = -1.50$). Among these, lawsuit announcements concerning alleged price fixing tend to be most common. However, it is worth noting that when lawsuit filing announcements are sorted by violation category, none of the nonparametric test results show statistically significant median wealth effects. This suggests that the generally negative wealth effects tied to lawsuit filing announcements tend to be both smaller and less consistent than similar impacts of informal investigation and formal investigation announcements.

And finally, with respect to settlement announcements, Table 10.5 shows that average wealth effects are positive and statistically significant for settlements involving accounting reporting violations (4.95%, $t = 1.86$) and illegal trading (7.10%, $t = 1.34$). Conversely, average wealth effects are negative and statistically significant for settlements involving illegal foreign business practices (-2.15%, $t = -1.66$) and overcharging on government contracts (-1.71%, $t = 1.74$). The suggestion of a diverse market-value effect of settlement announcements is reinforced by the fact that median influences are negative and statistically significant only in the case of general restraint of trade settlements (-1.15%, $z = -1.36$). This diversity is a reasonable reflection of the fact that some settlement announcements can involve surprisingly large or punitive damages. Thus, it seems reasonable to conclude that the effect of settlement announcements on the value of the firm can be quite variable on a case-by-case basis.

XV. ANNOUNCEMENT EFFECTS BY INDUSTRIAL CLASSIFICATION

Table 10.6 summarizes market-model CAPE information for the $(-1,0)$ event period when such data are arrayed according to the industrial classification of the actual or suspected violator. Our purpose here is to learn if wealth effects tied to the enforcement activities of the DOJ, FTC, and SEC vary systematically from one competitive environment to another, even though market structure can only be captured imperfectly at the very broad two-digit Standard Industrial Classification (SIC) industry sector level of aggregation. Chauvin and Hirschey (1993), for example, show that the market value of the firm is dependent, at least in part, upon intangible factors such as the magnitude of advertising and R&D activity. It seems plausible that the valuation effects of enforcement activities of the DOJ, FTC, and SEC might be especially severe for companies that operate in a market environment where reputational capital, perhaps due to advertising, R&D, or other such factors, is especially important. Again, to test for robustness, both parametric and nonparametric results are reported.

Table 10.6 shows that negative and statistically significant average wealth effects related to informal investigations are most common for firms that make industrial and commercial machinery and computer equipment (-6.69%, $t = -3.32$) and manufacturers of electronic and other electrical equipment (-18.87%, $t = -1.90$).

TABLE 10.6 Cumulative Average Prediction Errors (CAPEs) by Industrial Classification of the Actual or Suspected Violator

SIC code	Industry description	Sample size	CAPEs (%)	t-statistic	Median CAPEs (%)	z-statistic
A. Informal investigations ($n = 13$)						
20	Food and kindred products	1	0.58	0.24	0.58	0.90
35	Industrial and commercial machinery and computer equipment	4	−6.69	−3.32[a]	−6.42	−0.02
36	Electronic and other electrical equipment	1	−18.87	−1.90[b]	−18.87	−0.76
48	Communications	1	−4.99	−1.15	−4.99	−0.93
53	General merchandise stores	1	−1.77	−0.57	−1.77	−1.01
59	Miscellaneous retail	1	−29.83	−6.11[a]	−29.83	−1.08
62	Security and commodity brokers, dealers, exchanges, and services	2	2.65	1.82[b]	2.65	1.43[c]
73	Business services	2	−0.55	−0.19	−0.55	−0.15
B. Formal investigations ($n = 97$)						
2	Agricultural production— livestock and animal specialties	1	−2.14	−0.34	−2.14	−0.82
16	Heavy construction— nonbuilding contractors	1	4.94	2.36[a]	4.94	1.00
20	Food and kindred products	5	−2.61	−2.05[b]	−2.18	−1.22
21	Tobacco products	3	−1.04	−0.74	−1.38	−0.47
22	Textile mill products	1	−5.17	−1.25	−5.17	−1.06
25	Furniture and fixtures	1	−6.71	−3.21[a]	−6.71	−1.00
27	Printing, publishing, and allied industries	5	−0.59	−0.47	−0.58	−2.07 [b]
28	Chemicals and allied products	6	−1.93	−2.17[b]	−1.82	−1.51[c]
30	Rubber and miscellaneous plastic products	2	−2.58	−1.46[c]	−2.58	−1.41[c]
32	Stone, clay, glass, and concrete products	3	−1.64	−0.88	−2.18	−0.49
33	Primary metal industries	4	0.49	0.27	0.83	1.12
35	Industrial and commercial machinery and computer equipment	6	−4.32	−2.32[b]	−2.32	−0.53
36	Electronic and other electrical equipment	12	−3.73	−3.68[a]	−1.03	−0.92
37	Transportation equipment	7	−0.77	−0.51	−0.61	−0.29
38	Measuring, analyzing, and controlling instruments; photographic, medical and optical goods; watches and clocks	4	−10.25	−4.24[a]	−4.62	−1.87[b]
39	Miscellaneous manufacturing industries	1	−10.52	−3.31[a]	−10.52	−0.98

(*continues*)

TABLE 10.6 (*continued*)

SIC code	Industry description	Sample size	CAPEs (%)	t-statistic	Median CAPEs (%)	z-statistic
41	Local and suburban transit and interurban highway passenger transportation	1	−6.19	−0.84	−6.19	−1.06
45	Transportation by air	2	2.22	1.27	2.22	1.44[c]
48	Communications	5	−3.92	−1.21	−2.89	−0.20
49	Electric, gas, and sanitary services	1	−4.71	−0.70	−4.71	−0.67
51	Wholesale trade—nondurable goods	1	−73.10	−10.07[a]	−73.10	−0.96
53	General merchandise stores	1	−2.41	−1.08	−2.41	−1.06
59	Miscellaneous retail	1	1.02	0.45	1.02	1.13
60	Depository institutions	2	−1.95	−1.60[c]	−1.96	−1.36[c]
62	Security and commodity brokers, dealers, exchanges, and services	2	−0.16	−0.11	−0.16	0.09
67	Holding and other investment offices services	8	−0.85	−0.77	−0.36	−0.48
73	Business services	8	9.62	5.94[a]	−0.56	−0.56
80	Health services	2	−12.65	−2.36[a]	−12.65	−1.32[c]
95	Environmental services	1	7.45	2.93[a]	7.45	1.03
C. Suits filed (n = 28)						
10	Metal mining	1	−0.64	−0.24	−0.64	−1.01
21	Tobacco products	1	2.94	1.09	2.94	1.05
22	Textile mill products	1	−4.57	−1.32[c]	−4.57	−0.81
25	Furniture and fixtures	1	−2.76	−1.34[c]	−2.76	−1.14
31	Leather and leather products	1	7.18	0.86	7.18	0.73
34	Fabricated metal products (nontransportation, nonmachinery)	1	0.61	0.36	0.61	0.94
35	Industrial and commercial machinery and computer equipment	3	−3.84	−2.27[b]	−4.86	−0.58
36	Electronic and other electrical equipment	3	−0.73	−0.52	−2.97	−0.41
37	Transportation equipment	1	−0.01	−0.01	−0.01	−0.99
38	Measuring, analyzing, and controlling instruments; photographic, medical and optical goods; watches and clocks	2	3.06	1.26	3.06	1.47[c]
45	Transportation by air	6	−1.98	−1.34[c]	−1.96	−0.68
50	Wholesale trade—durable goods	1	−6.04	−0.72	−6.04	−0.58
60	Depository institutions	1	0.15	0.09	0.15	1.00
62	Security and commodity brokers, dealers, exchanges, and services	1	−3.30	−1.12	−3.30	−1.03

(*continues*)

TABLE 10.6 (*continued*)

SIC code	Industry description	Sample size	CAPEs (%)	t-statistic	Median CAPEs (%)	z-statistic
67	Holding and other investment offices services	1	−5.34	−1.86[b]	−5.34	−0.97
73	Business services	3	−0.73	−0.28	1.36	0.71
D. Settlements (*n* = 24)						
27	Printing, publishing, and allied industries	2	2.80	0.62	2.80	0.08
28	Chemicals and allied products	2	1.06	0.47	1.06	1.64
35	Industrial and commercial machinery and computer equipment	1	−0.17	−0.05	−0.17	−0.97
36	Electronic and other electrical equipment	4	−3.81	−2.27[b]	−3.84	−0.90
37	Transportation equipment	1	−1.10	−0.52	−1.10	−0.98
38	Measuring, analyzing, and controlling instruments; photographic, medical and optical goods; watches and clocks	3	14.26	2.02[b]	21.85	1.09
51	Wholesale trade— nondurable goods	1	−0.02	−0.01	−0.02	−0.67
63	Insurance carriers	2	1.17	0.33	1.17	0.08
67	Holding and other investment offices services	5	0.42	0.33	−0.49	−0.35
73	Business services	2	0.03	0.03	0.03	0.14
80	Health services	1	−1.03	−0.07	−1.03	−0.81

Note: Market-model cumulative average prediction errors (CAPEs), *t*-statistics, and *z*-statistics are shown for the (−1,0) event-period window according to the two-digit Standard Industrial Classification (SIC) code of the actual or suspected violator. Parametric statistics and nonparametric statistics are shown, as are the size and statistical significance of mean (average) and median differences in announcement effects for various enforcement activities. The statistical significance of mean differences are evaluated using a *t*-test over the 180-day estimation period; median differences are evaluated using a *z*-test.

[a]Significant at the 1% level (one-tail test).
[b]Significant at the 5% level (one-tail test).
[c]Significant at the 10% level (one-tail test).

Companies that operate in these industries operate within some of the most R&D-intensive sectors of the economy (see Chauvin and Hirschey, 1993). It stands to reason that the launch of informal investigations would have the potential for severe adverse effects on the reputational capital of such firms. An informal investigation announcement concerning a single miscellaneous retail establishment also had a negative and statistically significant wealth effect of a whopping −29.83% (*t* = −6.11). In this instance, the launch of an informal investigation might be expected to engender the risk of a significant loss in reputational capital stemming from advertising expenditures. In a somewhat puzzling manner, positive and statistically significant average wealth effects are tied to informal investigation announcements concerning two security and commodity brokers (2.65%, $t = 1.82$). Using nonparametric methods, the median wealth effect of 2.65% ($z = 1.43$) is also significant. At least in these two instances, investors may have been relieved that more serious enforcement activity, such as a formal investigation, was not announced.

Table 10.6 also shows that consistently negative average wealth effects associated with formal investigation announcements are most common for firms operating in food and kindred products (-2.61%, $t = -2.05$), chemicals and allied products (-1.93%, $t = -2.17$), rubber (-2.58%, $t = -1.46$), industrial and commercial machinery and computer equipment (-4.32%, $t = -2.32$), electronic and other electrical equipment (-3.73%, $t = -3.68$), and measuring instruments (-10.25%, $t = -4.24$). These generally adverse average wealth effects tied to formal investigation announcements tend to be corroborated by nonparametric results concerning median effects. Interestingly, with the exception of food and kindred products, where advertising is very important, each of the other industries mentioned above is highly R&D intensive. This lends support to arguments that negative wealth effects tied to the launch of formal investigations by the DOJ, FTC, or SEC are most severe for firms that stand to lose significant amounts of reputational capital derived from intangible assets such as advertising and R&D.

And finally, Table 10.6 also shows the industrial affiliations of companies with typically negative average wealth effects associated with lawsuit filing announcements and the mixed average wealth effects generated by settlement announcements. Consistently negative average wealth effects associated with lawsuit filing announcements are most common for firms operating in industrial and commercial machinery and computer equipment (-3.84%, $t = -2.27$) and air transportation (-1.98%, $t = -1.34$). Settlement announcements commonly result in negative average wealth effects for firms that produce electronic and other electrical equipment (-3.81%, $t = -2.27$), but positive average wealth effects for firms that produce measuring instruments (14.26%, $t = 2.02$). However, all such effects appear to be less consistent than wealth effects tied to both informal and formal investigation announcements in that they do not tend to be corroborated by nonparametric results concerning median effects. Thus, one must be somewhat more cautious in arguing that negative wealth effects associated with lawsuit and/or settlement announcements by the DOJ, FTC, or SEC are most severe for firms that stand to lose significant amounts of reputational capital.

XVI. CONCLUSION

Corporate governance is the system of controls that helps the corporation effectively manage, administer, and direct economic resources. Outside the high-tech sector, franchise agreements are a prime example of voluntary contractual arrangements outside the firm that can be viewed as corporate governance mechanisms. Among tech stocks, strategic alliances are formal operating agreements between independent companies that also can be viewed as corporate governance mechanisms. In both cases, ownership structure, or the array of divergent claims on the value of the firm, can be thought of as an important internal corporate governance mechanism. Inside equity is the share of stock closely held by the firm's managers, directors, and employees. When ownership is concentrated among insiders or a small group of large and vocal institutional shareholders, called institutional equity, managers often have strong incentives to maximize corporate performance. The ownership structure of corporations appears to be sensitive to economic influences such as amenity potential, or the ability to influence the type of products produced. Such benefits explain why mass media and professional sports teams tend to be tightly controlled by top management. Diffuse ownership structures are common for utilities because their regulatory potential limits the capacity of managers to influence firm performance. In the case of high-tech firms that produce goods and services with the potential for high quality variation, or quality control potential, a more concentrated ownership structure may be required to give shareholders the amount of control necessary to mollify other suppliers and customers.

Given the recent interest in a series of high-profile cases of corporate malfeasance, this chapter pays special attention to the role of actual or suspected violations of federal laws that have the potential to result in significant costs measured in terms of investigation expenditures, litigation expenses, fines and seizures, and lost reputational capital for the firm—all of which can measurably reduce future cash flows and current market values. Within this context, federal laws can be seen as part of the institutional framework that contributes to the range of control mechanisms that originate inside and outside the firm to comprise an effective system of corporate governance. Because short-term hit and run managers may possess incentives to cut legal and ethical corners, the design and administration of federal laws can be seen as a means of outside monitoring designed to ensure a coincidence of managerial incentives, stockholder interests, and broader social objectives. The economic importance of such monitoring is suggested by evidence concerning the stock market reaction to public announcements concerning enforcement activities of the DOJ, FTC, and SEC, including informal investigations, formal investigations, lawsuits, and settlement agreements. Negative abnormal returns are consistently observed over event periods in which news of DOJ, FTC, and SEC investigations (both informal and formal) or lawsuits appear in *The Wall Street Journal*. Evidence on the average wealth effects tied to settlement announcements is mixed, with both negative and positive abnormal returns evident on a case-by-case basis. Negative abnormal returns are observed for news regarding settlements involving illegal foreign business practices and overcharging on government contracts; positive abnormal returns are noted for settlements of accounting reporting violations and illegal trading activity. Both types of results suggest that prior to *The Wall Street Journal* announcement date, these government bodies maintain information that is relevant to the determination of future cash flows for target firms. Because such announcements consistently result in statistically significant stock-price effects, they can be regarded as important in the formation of investor expectations concerning future cash flows.

Findings reported here have direct relevance for competitive policy in dynamic high-tech markets and for the corporate governance literature. Our findings lend empirical support to arguments that negative wealth effects tied to the launch of enforcement activity by the DOJ, FTC, or SEC are most severe for high-tech firms that stand to lose significant amounts of reputational capital. Moreover, analysis of the competitive environment of affected firms suggests that such reputational capital is derived from intangible assets such as advertising and R&D. Federal law enforcement activities of the DOJ, FTC, and SEC may thus be seen as part of what Jensen and Meckling (1976) describe as monitoring mechanisms inside and outside the firm that work together to establish an optimal set of restrictions on firm activity, including the investment in and management of intangible assets. With this context, public announcements regarding federal law enforcement actions represent a flexible tool that can be used to facilitate competition policy in dynamic high-tech markets.

XVII. REFERENCES

Bhagat, S., Brickley, J. A., and Coles, J. L. (1994). The Costs of Inefficient Bargaining and Financial Distress. *Journal of Financial Economics* 35, 221–247.

Butler, H. N. (1987). *Legal Environment of Business*. Cincinnati, OH: South-Western Publishing Co.

Bittlingmayer, G. (1993). The Stock Market and Early Antitrust Enforcement. *Journal of Law and Economics* 36, 1–31.

Chauvin, K. W. and Hirschey, M. (1993). Advertising, R&D Expenditures and the Market Value of the Firm. *Financial Management* 22, 128–140.

Corrado, C. J. (1989). A Nonparametric Test for Abnormal Security-Price Performance in Event Studies. *Journal of Financial Economics* 23, 385–395.

Fama, E. F. and Jensen, M. C. (1983). Separation of Ownership and Control. *Journal of Law and Economics* 26, 301–325.

Feroz, E. H., Park, K., and Pastena, V. S. (1991). The Financial and Market Effects of the SEC's Accounting and Auditing Enforcement Releases. *Journal of Accounting Research* 29, 107–142.

Garbade, K. D., Silber, W. L., and White, L. J. (1982). Market Reaction to the Filing of Antitrust Suits: An Aggregate and Cross-Sectional Analysis. *Review of Economics and Statistics* 64, 686–691.

Hirschey, M. (2003). *Managerial Economics, Tenth Edition*. Mason, OH: South-Western Thompson Learning, Inc., Ch. 16.

Hirschey, M. and Jones, E. (2001). The Role of Federal Law Enforcement Actions in Corporate Governance. In Hirschey, M., John, K., and Makhija, A. (eds.), *Advances in Financial Economics*, 6. Amsterdam, The Netherlands: Elsevier Science, pp. 117–141.

James, C. (1987). Some Evidence on the Uniqueness of Bank Loans. *Journal of Financial Economics* 19, 217–235.

Jensen, M. C. and Meckling, W. H. (1976). Theory of the Firm: Managerial Behavior, Agency Costs and Ownership Structure. *Journal of Financial Economics* 3, 305–360.

Myers, S. C. (1977). Determinants of Corporate Borrowing. *Journal of Financial Economics* 5, 147–175.

INDEX

A

AAR, *see* A *see* verage abnormal return
Abnormal return (AR), estimation, 65–66
Accounting
  data limitations in stock valuation, 158–159
  fraud, *see* Fraud
  managerial bias, 43–44
Advertising
  effects on goodwill assets, 185
  federal law enforcement action impact, 257, 261
  research and development expense correlation, 134
Agency problem
  managers versus stockholders, 39–40
  origins, 40
America Online (AOL)
  growth expectations, 94–95
  Microsoft growth comparison, 90–91, 94
  The Motley Fool ownership stake, 59
  risk assessment, 94

  Time-Warner merger and valuation, 90, 98–100
  valuation
    customer value, 97–98
    growth stock, 95–96
    private-market value, 98
    value stock, 96–97
Antitakeover charter amendments, *see* Shark repellants
AOL, *see* America Online
AR, *see* Abnormal return
Average abnormal return (AAR), estimation, 66

B

Barings Bank, downfall, 40
Board of directors
  attributes of effective and ineffectual boards, 230–231
  best and worst list of boards, 233–234
  chief executive officer termination, 231–232
  corporate stakeholder responsibilities, 230

Board of directors *(Continued)*
  responsibilities for nonprofit boards,
    230–231
Boring Portfolio, *see* The Motley Fool
Bubble, *see* Stock market bubble
Buy/sell recommendations
  The Motley Fool recommendation impact on
    stock price
    all portfolio returns, 68–71
    Celera buy recommendation, 60
    individual portfolio returns, 72–78
    methodology for study, 65–68
    overview, 52, 78–79
  print media recommendation impact on stock
    price, 53–54, 78

C

Capital spending ratio, shark repellant effects,
  218, 220–221
CAR, *see* Cumulative average abnormal return
Cash flow margin on sales, shark repellant
  effects, 210–211, 214–215
Cash flow return on assets, shark repellant
  effects, 214–215, 217
Cellular phone companies, data sources for
  valuation, 157–158
CEO, *see* Chief executive officer
Chief executive officer (CEO)
  compensation
    long-term performance enhancement,
      41–42
    overview, 42
    research and development expenditure
      effects, 129
  demographics, 41
  end-of-game problem, 42–43
  termination, 231–232
CI, *see* Citations Index
Citations Index (CI)
  patent quality analysis, 164–165
  stock price impact studies, 172, 175–176
Cold calling, three-call technique, 45
Corporate governance
  board of directors, 230–233
  federal law enforcement actions
    enforcing agencies
      Department of Justice, 243–244,
        262–263
      Federal Trade Commission, 243–244,
        262–263
      Securities and Exchange Commission,
        244, 262–263

informal investigations, 244
shareholder costs, 243
valuation effects
  advertising impact, 257, 261
  data for analysis, 247–249
  firm rankings, 250–251
  industry differences, 257–261
  ordinary least squares market
    model, 249
  overview of studies, 246–247
  positive versus negative abnormal
    returns, 245–246
  prediction errors, 249–250
  research and development impact, 257,
    260–261
  type of enforcement activity announce-
    ment effects, 251–253
  violation category announcement
    effects, 254–257
franchise agreements, 235
mechanisms within firm, 233
ownership structure, 237–242
strategic alliances, 236–237
Crash, *see* Return reversal
Cumulative average abnormal return (CAR)
  estimation, 66
  goodwill write-off announcement effect on
    stock price, 194–196
  The Motley Fool portfolios
    all portfolio returns, 68–71
    individual portfolio returns, 72–78

D

Daily returns, patterns in stock indexes, 32–35
Debt-equity ratio, shark repellant effects, 219,
  220, 222
Department of Justice (DOJ)
  federal law enforcement actions, 243–244,
    262–263
  informal investigations, 244
  valuation effects of actions
    advertising impact, 257, 261
    data for analysis, 247–249
    firm rankings, 250–251
    industry differences, 257–261
    ordinary least squares market model, 249
    overview of studies, 246–247
    positive versus negative abnormal returns,
      245–246
    prediction errors, 249–250
    research and development impact, 257,
      260–261

type of enforcement activity announcement effects, 251–253

violation category announcement effects, 254–257

Dividend payout ratio, shark repellant effects, 209–210, 219, 220, 222

Dividend Reinvestment Plan Portfolio, *see* The Motley Fool

Dividend yield

Dow Jones Industrial Average over time, 22–23

importance to shareholder income, 23

DJIA, *see* Dow Jones Industrial Average

DOJ, *see* Department of Justice

Dow Jones Industrial Average (DJIA)

correlation with other market indexes, 31–32

daily return patterns versus other indexes, 32–35

dividend yield over time, 22–23

price/book ratio over time, 21–22

price/earnings ratio over time, 21–22

E

Earnings per share (EPS)

growth rate versus price/earnings ratio, 95

Nasdaq 100 growth estimates, 9–16, 26

Efficient market hypothesis

assumptions, 30, 48–49, 101, 106–107

exceptions, 49, 101

implications, 30

random walk theory relationship, 107

EPS, *see* Earnings per share

F

Federal Trade Commission (FTC)

federal law enforcement actions, 243–244, 262–263

informal investigations, 244

valuation effects of actions

advertising impact, 257, 261

data for analysis, 247–249

firm rankings, 250–251

industry differences, 257–261

ordinary least squares market model, 249

overview of studies, 246–247

positive versus negative abnormal returns, 245–246

prediction errors, 249–250

research and development impact, 257, 260–261

type of enforcement activity announcement effects, 251–253

violation category announcement effects, 254–257

Foolish Four Portfolio, *see* The Motley Fool

Franchise agreements, industry distribution and corporate governance, 235

Fraud

cold calling, 45

corporate governance, *see* Corporate governance

federal law enforcement actions

enforcing agencies

Department of Justice, 243–244, 262–263

Federal Trade Commission, 243–244, 262–263

Securities and Exchange Commission, 244, 262–263

informal investigations, 244

shareholder costs, 243

valuation effects

advertising impact, 257, 261

data for analysis, 247–249

firm rankings, 250–251

industry differences, 257–261

ordinary least squares market model, 249

overview of studies, 246–247

positive versus negative abnormal returns, 245–246

prediction errors, 249–250

research and development impact, 257, 260–261

type of enforcement activity announcement effects, 251–253

violation category announcement effects, 254–257

federal regulation, 44–45

Internet pump-and-dump, 46–48

management examples, 229

FTC, *see* Federal Trade Commission

G

Goodwill assets

abundance in tech giants, 183

accounting standards, 185–187, 201–202

advertising effects, 185

loan-loss reserve announcement similarity with write-off announcements, 188, 195

research and development effects, 185

valuation effects, 184–185, 188

write-off announcement effect on stock price

Goodwill assets *(Continued)*
  announcement period effects, cumulative
    abnormal returns, 194–196
  assumptions in analysis, 192
  confounding contemporaneous
    announcement effects, 196–197
  industry-specific effects, 197–198
  overview, 184–185, 202–203
  postannouncement period effects, 198–202
  preannouncement period effects, 198–201
  prediction error estimation, 192–194
  prospects for research, 202–203
  sample selection and breakout by industry,
    189–192
Greed versus fear
  rationale for contrarian view in stock buying
    and selling, 123–124
  stock market bubble creation, 38

H

Holland tulip mania
  historical perspective, 81, 83, 86
  price estimation in present dollars, 84–86
  psychology of manias, 87–88
  rationale for study, 82
  tulip cultivation in Europe, 82

I

IAR, *see* Industry-adjusted ratio
Industry-adjusted ratio (IAR), shark repellant
    effects, 212–214, 223
Inside equity, ownership structure, 237–241
Institutional investors
  ownership structure, 237–241
  tech stock buying during Nasdaq surge, 20–21
The Intelligent Investor, 123–124
Internet
  advantages in information dissemination, 54
  bulletin board information quality, 46–47
  chat rooms and message boards, 57
  fraud prevention, 47
  Motley Fool recommendations, *see* The
    Motley Fool
  pump-and-dump forums, 46–48
  Web sites for investing information, 54–57
Internet stocks
  earnings and investor attitides, 51
  valuations at peak versus present price, 88–90

J

Japanese market
  Nasdaq comparison

crash similarity, 120–122
  recovery time for return reversal, 122–124
  Nikkei Index in 1990s, 120
  patent quality, 165–167, 176–178

L

LLR, *see* Loan-loss reserve
Loan-loss reserve (LLR), announcement simi-
    larity with goodwill write-off announce-
    ments, 188, 195

M

Mania
  psychology, 87–88
  tulip mania, *see* Holland tulip mania
Market capitalization
  Nasdaq 100, 9–13
  tech company changes over time, 18–19
Microsoft, America Online growth comparison,
    90–91, 94
The Motley Fool (TMF)
  America Online stake, 59
  Boring Portfolio, 64–65, 72–75
  Dividend Reinvestment Plan Portfolio, 64,
    72–75
  Foolish Four Portfolio, 64, 72–74
  historical perspective, 52, 57–58
  portfolio holdings, table, 62–63
  recommendation impact on stock price
    all portfolio returns, 68–71
    Celera buy recommendation, 60
    individual portfolio returns, 72–78
    methodology for study, 65–68
    overview, 52, 78–79
  Rule Breaker Portfolio
    principles, 58–60, 65
    returns, 72–78
    risk tolerance, 59–61
    stock components, 58, 60–61
  Rule Maker Portfolio, 61, 63–64, 72–74

N

Nasdaq 100
  allure, 17–18
  composition, 7–13
  correlation with other market indexes, 31–32
  daily return patterns versus other indexes,
    32–35
  earnings per share growth estimates, 9–16, 26
  eligibility criteria, 6
  historical perspective on overvaluation
    level, 25

institutional investors, 20–21
large-cap stocks, 15–17
Nifty 50 comparison, 1–2, 5, 8, 14–15, 26
QQQ popularity, 6
rebalancing, 6
returns in 1990s, 7–8
tech stock dominance, 16–18
valuation, 1–2, 8–14, 23–25
Nasdaq Composite Index
composition, 7
Japanese market versus Nasdaq
crash similarity, 120–122
Nikkei Index in 1990s, 120
recovery time for return reversal, 122–124
return on stockholders' equity versus Dow stocks, 25
return reversal versus Standard & Poor's 500
bear markets and subsequent returns, 112–113
distribution of rolling 12-month rates of return, 107–109
extreme cases, 112
nonoverlapping period analysis, 112
worst and best historical 12-month returns, 110–111
Newsletters
herd behavior, 53
recommendation quality, 52–53
Nifty 50
price plunge in bear market, 2
returns from 1972–1993, 2–5
tech bubble comparison, 1–2, 5, 8, 14–15, 26
valuation, 1–2
Nikkei Index, *see* Japanese market
Non-Patent References (NPR)
patent quality analysis, 164–165
stock price impact studies, 172, 175–176
NPR, *see* Non-Patent References

O

Overreaction hypothesis, return reversal of markets, 116–119
Ownership structure
factors affecting, 242
inside equity, 237–241
institutional investors, 237–241

P

Patents
citation analysis, 162–163
growth by country, 177
Japanese patent quality, 165–167, 176–178

quality measures
Citations Index, 164–165
Non-Patent References, 164–165
Technology Cycle Time, 164–165, 176–177
research and development effectiveness measure, 159–161
scientific merit, 163–166
statistics in economic research, 161–162
stock price impact studies
data sources, 165–167, 169–170
Japanese companies, 178–179
least-squares dummy variable model, 170
ordinary least squares model, 170
predictive equation for stock price changes, 169
prospects for study, 179–180
sample descriptive statistics, 168–169
U.S. companies
Citations Index analysis, 172, 175–176
firm size effects, 172, 175–176
fixed period effects, 172–174
growth opportunity effects, 175–176
Non-Patent References analysis, 172, 175–176
overview of stock price impact, 170–172
Technology Cycle Time analysis, 172, 175–176
total patents and quality indicators for high-tech Japanese and U.S. firms, 165–167
P/B, *see* Price/book ratio
PE, *see* Price/earnings ratio
Price/book ratio (P/B)
Dow Jones Industrial Average over time, 21–22
Nasdaq 100 valuation, 24–25
Price/earnings ratio (PE)
company size influences, 15
Dow Jones Industrial Average over time, 21–22
historical averages, 25
Nasdaq 100 valuation, 1–2, 8–14, 23–25
Nifty 50 valuation, 1–2
Profit, mean reversion, 104–106

Q

QQQ, *see* Nasdaq 100

R

R&D, *see* Research and development
Random walk
drift bias, 37

Random walk *(Continued)*
  efficient market hypothesis relationship, 107
  information flow, 35, 37, 39
  market bubbles, 38
  research, 37–38
  theory, 35
Rebound, *see* Return reversal
Recession, definition, 105
Regression to the mean
  Galton's experiments, 114
  percent formula, 115
  stock markets, 114–116
Research and development (R&D)
  chief executive officer compensation
    relationship to spending, 129
  corporate leaders in spending and intensity,
    134–139
  effects on goodwill assets, 185
  federal law enforcement action impact, 257,
    260–261
  Generally Acceptable Accounting Principles
    in expenditure reporting, 159
  industry group distribution of spending,
    131–134
  institutional stock ownership and expenditure
    effectiveness impact, 151–154
  levels of spending, 128–130
  intangible capital source, 126–128
  patents, *see* Patents
  shark repellant effects, 205–208, 218–221,
    223, 226
  stock price effects of expenditures
    event studies, 126–127
    firm size effects, 125–126, 147–151, 155
    investment opportunities hypothesis,
      126–127
    overview, 125, 158
    stock measure versus flow of expenditures,
      139–140
  Tobin's q measure of research and
    development capital
    Compustat data study
      approximation of q, 142–143, 147
      constraining non-research and
        development factors, 143–144
      firm size and valuation effects, 147–148
      manufacturing versus nonmanufacturing
        firms, 142, 147, 149
      sample, 141–142
      variable means and standard deviations,
        144–146
    intangible capital derivation, 141
    limitations, 141
  overview, 139–140
  theoretical maximum, 140
Return on stockholders' equity (ROE), Nasdaq
  versus Dow stocks, 25
Return reversal
  business profit mean reversion, 104–105
  Japanese market versus Nasdaq
    crash similarity, 120–122
    Nikkei Index in 1990s, 120
    recovery time for return reversal, 122–124
  overreaction hypothesis, 116–119
  overview, 103–104
  regression to the mean, 105–106, 114–116
  Standard & Poor's 500 versus Nasdaq
    bear markets and subsequent returns,
      112–113
    distribution of rolling 12-month rates of
      return, 107–109
    extreme cases, 112
    nonoverlapping period analysis, 112
    worst and best historical 12-month returns,
      110–111
Risk management, manager compensation for
  long-term performance, 40–41
ROE, *see* Return on stockholders' equity
Rule Breaker Portfolio, *see* The Motley Fool
Rule Maker Portfolio, *see* The Motley Fool

S

Salomon, Inc., employee ownership and
  manager compensation for long-term
  performance, 41
S&P 500, *see* Standard & Poor's 500
SAR, *see* Standardized abnormal return
SEC, *see* Securities and Exchange Commission
Securities and Exchange Commission (SEC)
  company filing requirements, 44
  EDGAR database, 44, 46
  federal law enforcement actions, 244,
    262–263
  fraud prevention, 46–47
  informal investigations, 244
  Internet fraud regulation, 47
  valuation effects of actions
    advertising impact, 257, 261
    data for analysis, 247–249
    firm rankings, 250–251
    industry differences, 257–261
    ordinary least squares market model, 249
    overview of studies, 246–247
    positive versus negative abnormal returns,
      245–246
    prediction errors, 249–250

research and development impact, 257, 260–261

type of enforcement activity announcement effects, 251–253

violation category announcement effects, 254–257

Shark repellants

definition, 205–206

long-term performance and financial policy effects

capital spending ratio, 218, 220–221

cash flow margin on sales, 210–211, 214–215

cash flow return on assets, 214–215, 217

data, 208–209

debt-equity ratio, 219, 220, 222

dividend payout ratio, 219, 220, 222

dividend policy, 209–210

firm performance effects

measures, 209

overview, 205, 208

leverage ratios, 210

nonparametric tests of relative performance

financial policy ratios, 213

median industry-adjusted ratio, 212–214, 223

test statistic, 213

regression model

financial policy decisions, 224–225

firm performance results, 224

specification, 223

research and development impact, 205–208, 218–221, 223, 226

total asset turnover, 211, 216–217

total stock price plus dividend return, 211–212, 216–217

management-entrenchment hypothesis, 207, 218

shareholder-interest hypothesis, 207–208, 218, 220

takeover prevention, 206–207

Standard & Poor's (S&P) 500

correlation with other market indexes, 31–32

daily return patterns versus other indexes, 32–35

return reversal versus Nasdaq

bear markets and subsequent returns, 112–113

distribution of rolling 12-month rates of return, 107–109

extreme cases, 112

nonoverlapping period analysis, 112

worst and best historical 12-month returns, 110–111

Standardized abnormal return (SAR), estimation, 67

Stock market bubble

definition, 38

greed versus fear, 38

historical examples, 38

rational bubbles, 39

theory, 38–39

Strategic alliances, examples, 236–237

T

TAT, *see* Total asset turnover

TCT, *see* Technology Cycle Time

Technical analysis, utility, 37–38

Technology Cycle Time (TCT)

patent quality analysis, 164–165, 176–177

stock price impact studies, 172, 175–176

Time-Warner, America Online merger and valuation, 90, 98–100

TMF, *see* The Motley Fool

Tobin's q

intangible capital derivation, 141

measure of research and development capital and stock price influence

Compustat data study

approximation of q, 142–143, 147

constraining non-research and development factors, 143–144

firm size and valuation effects, 147–148

manufacturing versus nonmanufacturing firms, 142, 147, 149

sample, 141–142

variable means and standard deviations, 144–146

limitations, 141

overview, 139–140

theoretical maximum, 140

Total asset turnover (TAT), shark repellant effects, 211, 216–217

Total return (TR), shark repellant effects, 211–212, 216–217

TR, *see* Total return

Tulip mania, *see* Holland tulip mania